Praise for
Sons of Wichita

"SONS OF WICHITA feels as close to the truth as anyone is likely to get for a long time to come." —*Financial Times*

"A riveting biography...fair-minded and inquisitive. Schulman offers carefully observed details that help flesh out our image of the men whose money has so dramatically remade our politics, revealing much about their motives as well as the demons that haunt them." —*Washington Post*

"A complex story of epic sibling rivalry with important political dimensions." —*Publishers Weekly*

"Compulsively readable...a bias-free book that illuminates two of the most influential figures on the American landscape while telling a remarkable, if cautionary, tale about money, power, and the bonds of brotherhood." —*Booklist*

"A straightforward, evenhanded and often riveting assessment." —*Kirkus*

"If you care about politics and the ultimately far more powerful cultural direction of these United States...this book is mandatory reading." —Nick Gillespie, *Daily Beast*

Sons of Wichita

HOW THE KOCH BROTHERS
BECAME AMERICA'S MOST POWERFUL
AND PRIVATE DYNASTY

———

Daniel Schulman

GRAND CENTRAL
PUBLISHING

NEW YORK   BOSTON

For Stacey, my partner
on this and all other journeys
and
For Mom and Dad,
who made the path possible

Grand Central Publishing
Hachette Book Group
1290 Avenue of the Americas
New York, NY 10104

www.HachetteBookGroup.com

Printed in the United States of America

LSC-C

Originally published in hardcover by Hachette Book Group.

First trade edition: May 2015

10 9 8 7 6 5 4 3

Grand Central Publishing is a division of Hachette Book Group, Inc.
The Grand Central Publishing name and logo are trademarks of Hachette Book Group, Inc.

The Hachette Speakers Bureau provides a wide range of authors for speaking events. To find out more, go to www.hachettespeakersbureau.com or call (866) 376-6591.

The publisher is not responsible for websites (or their content) that are not owned by the publisher.

LCCN: 2013050789

ISBN 978-1-4555-1872-2 (pbk.)

Contents

Prologue

Morris eased the pickup truck to the side of the road. The wide, busy thoroughfares of 1950s Wichita, Kansas, were just five miles southwest, but here on the largely undeveloped outskirts of the city, near the Koch family's 160-acre property, the landscape consisted of little more than an expanse of flat, sun-bleached fields, etched here and there by dusty rural byways. The retired Marine, rangy and middle-aged, climbed out of the truck holding two sets of scuffed leather boxing gloves.

"Okay, boys," he barked, "get outside and duke it out."

David and Bill, the teenaged Koch twins, were at each other's throats once again. Impossible to tell who or what had started it. But it seldom took much. The roots of the strife typically traced to some kind of competition—a game of hoops, a round of water polo in the family pool, a footrace. They were pathologically competitive, and David, a gifted athlete, often won. Everything seemed to come easier for him. Bill was just nineteen minutes younger than his fraternal twin, but this solidified his role as the baby of the family. With a hair-trigger temper, he threw the tantrums to match.

David was more even-keeled than Bill, but he knew how to push his brother's buttons. Once they got into it, neither backed down. Arguments between the twins, who shared a small room, their beds within pinching range of each other, transcended routine sibling rivalry.

Morris always kept their boxing gloves close at hand to keep the brothers from seriously injuring each other when their tiffs escalated into full-scale brawls, as they often did. The brothers' industrialist father had officially hired the ex-soldier to look after the grounds and livestock on the family's compound. But his responsibilities also included chauffeuring the twins and their friends to movies and school events, and refereeing the fights that broke out unpredictably on these outings.

Holding their boxing gloves, Morris summoned the feuding twins from the truck. They knew the drill. He laced up one brother, then the other. The boys, both lean and tall, squared off, and when Morris stepped clear, they traded a barrage of punches.

A few minutes later, once they'd worked it out of their systems, Morris reclaimed the gloves and the brothers piled breathlessly into the cab of the truck. He slipped back behind the wheel, started the engine, and pulled onto the road.

Another day, another battle.

Pugilism was an enduring theme in the lives of the Koch family. The patriarch, Fred Koch—a college boxer known for his fierce determination in the ring—spent the better part of his professional life warring against the dark forces of communism and the collective might of the nation's major oil companies, which tried to run him out of the refining business. As adults, Fred's four sons paired off in a brutal legal campaign against one another over the business empire he bequeathed to them, a battle with plotlines that would seem far-fetched in a daytime soap opera. "It would make 'Dallas' and 'Dynasty' look like a playpen," Bill once said.

The roles the brothers would play in the saga were established from boyhood. Fred and Mary Koch's oldest son, Frederick, a lover of theater and literature, left Wichita for boarding school in the Northeast and barely looked back. He was uninterested in the family business and a disappointment to his tough, bootstrapping father. An intensely private man who assiduously avoided the public eye, Frederick became a prolific arts patron and collector, with a passion for restoring historic properties stretching from France's Côte d'Azur to New York's Upper East Side.

Their father saw glimpses of himself in his rebellious second son, Charles, whom Fred Koch molded from an early age into his successor. After eight years in Boston studying chemical and nuclear engineering at MIT and working for a consulting firm, Charles returned to Wichita to learn the intricacies of his family's oil refining, engineering, and ranching businesses.

David and Bill followed Charles (and their father before him) to MIT and eventually they, too, joined the family business. But that's where their paths diverged. David became Charles's loyal wingman, while Bill, still nursing childhood resentments, grew at first into a gadfly and then, in his brothers' eyes, a hostile presence within the company. The public would know Bill best for his flamboyant escapades: as a collector of fine wines who embarked on a litigious crusade against counterfeit *vino*, as a playboy with a history of messy romantic entanglements, and as a yachtsman who won the America's Cup in 1992—an experience he likened, unforgettably, to the sensation of "10,000 orgasms."

Charles and David, meanwhile, built their father's Midwestern empire—with about $250 million in yearly sales and 650 employees in the late 1960s—into a corporate behemoth Fred Koch would scarcely recognize, a company with $115 billion in annual revenues, more than 100,000 employees, and a presence in 60 countries. Under Charles's leadership, Koch Industries grew into the second largest private corporation in the United States (only the Minneapolis-based agribusiness giant Cargill is bigger). Koch made its money the old-fashioned way—oil, chemicals, cattle, timber—and in its dizzying rise, Charles and David amassed fortunes estimated at $40 billion apiece, tying them for sixth place among the wealthiest men on the planet. (Bill ranks 329th on *Forbes*'s list of the world's billionaires.)

They preferred to operate quietly—to run, as David once put it, "the biggest company you've never heard of." But Koch Industries' products touch everyone's lives—from the gas in our tanks to the steak on our forks and the fertilizer that helps our crops grow, and from the drywall, windowpanes, and carpets in our homes and offices to the Brawny paper towels and Dixie cups we keep in the pantry. The company ranks among the world's largest commodities traders, operates three ranches that sprawl over 425,000 acres, and processes some 750,000 barrels of crude oil daily. A day doesn't pass when we don't encounter a Koch product, though we often probably don't know it. Koch Industries is omnipresent, but the Kochs managed to remain so under the radar that many Americans confuse the pronunciation of their surname with that of a former New York City mayor, Ed Koch, rather than pronouncing it like the soft drink, Coke.

David has lived the quintessential billionaire's life. He traded provincial Wichita for New York City, where his name is etched into the façades of some of Manhattan's most important cultural landmarks, including the Lincoln Center theater that's home to the New York City Ballet. When not in his oceanfront mansion in Southampton, his Palm Beach villa, or Aspen ski lodge, David and his family reside in a storied Park Avenue high-rise, former home to John D. Rockefeller Jr., among other heirs to vast industrial fortunes.

Charles, by contrast, remained in his hometown, a city with an unassuming, head-down, and entrepreneurial character that matched his own. He lives in a modern, boxy mansion of stone and glass on the same compound where he grew up—just the multibillionaire next door in his east Wichita neighborhood, where strip malls and chain restaurants have overtaken the once wide-open terrain.

Schooled by his conservative father in the evils of government, Charles gravitated to libertarianism, a philosophy that advocates the maximum of personal and corporate freedom and the most minimal government, if only to tend to the defense of these liberties. He grew to believe zealously in the power of markets to guide human behavior, and to loathe the government regulations and subsidies that distorted markets—and behavior itself—by trying to impose false order. Blending the ideas of the libertarian movement's intellectual forefathers, Charles devised a unique management philosophy that placed a relentless emphasis on the bottom line, where even the lowliest pipefitter was meant to envision himself as an entrepreneur. This system, which Charles called Market-Based Management, helped him to build a conglomerate that generates massive profits, but which has often found itself in regulators' crosshairs after blood was spilled or waterways were contaminated.

Charles has done more than just construct one of the world's largest industrial empires. With David, he has spent decades trying to remake the American political landscape and mainstream their libertarian views. Together, the brothers pumped hundreds of millions of dollars into this endeavor. Unlike other major political donors, they offered more than just money; a strategic vision. They funded academics, think tanks, and political organizers to coalesce public support around their causes. The Tea Party movement that rose up after the election of President Barack Obama germinated, in part, from the intellectual seeds the Kochs had planted over the years. Though the brothers downplayed any connection to this cadre of irate citizen activists, they helped to provide the key financing and organizational support that allowed the Tea Party to blossom into a formidable political force within the Republican Party—one that paralyzed Congress and eventually ignited a GOP civil war.

Politicians, as Charles sees it, are merely vessels for the ideas you fill them with—or as one of his political advisors once put it, stage actors working off a script produced by the nation's intellectual class. So while creating and financing the intellectual infrastructure to promote their ideology, he and David have backed a constellation of conservative candidates to do battle in the political arena—politicians such as Wisconsin's Scott Walker, who upon assuming the governor's office in 2011, staged a fractious showdown with the public employee unions of his state; or South Carolina's Jim DeMint, one of the ringleaders of a Republican revolt against raising the nation's debt ceiling that brought the nation to the brink of default.

Charles and David brought their political resources to bear as never before during the 2012 election, which Charles called "the mother of all wars." Yet they emerged from the crucible of the campaign having gained little more than a reputation as cartoonish robber barons, all-powerful political puppeteers who with one hand choreographed the moves of Republican politicians and with the other commanded the Tea Party army. As with all caricatures, this one bore only a faint resemblance to reality.

For all the unwanted attention the Kochs received during the 2012 campaign—including the "other Koch brothers," as the media sometimes dubbed Frederick and Bill—America came through that political battle knowing little about who they really are. Like other great dynasties, the Kochs have a mythology of their own that polishes the rough edges of history into a more pristine version of the truth. And the family's legacy (corporate, philanthropic, political, cultural) is far more expansive than most people realize—and will be felt long into the future. In their lifetimes, the four Koch brothers have become some of the most influential, powerful, celebrated, and despised members of their generation. Understanding what shaped them, what drove them, what set them upon one another, requires traveling back to a time before the battles began.

CHAPTER ONE

Sons of Wichita

Strong-jawed and broad-shouldered, with reddish hair and a pair of wire-rim glasses that gave him an air of industriousness, Fred Chase Koch cut a dashing figure galloping up and down the polo field at the Kansas City Country Club. It was a September day in 1932, and debutantes crowded the sidelines to watch the match between the local old-money boys and the visiting squad from Wichita—a town newly flush with oil wealth, where Fred was a partner in a fledgling engineering company that catered to the refining industry. One of those society belles was Mary Clementine Robinson, the twenty-four-year-old daughter of a prominent Kansas City surgeon and granddaughter of a founding faculty member at Kansas University. She was tall, graceful, and erudite, with delicate features and a wavy bob of chestnut hair. A graduate of Wellesley with a degree in French, she was a talented artist and had worked as a designer for the Kansas City apparel maker Nelly Don.

Fred had remained a bachelor into his early thirties. There had been little time for settling down. He traveled regularly to far-flung locales to oversee the construction of refinery equipment and scare up new business opportunities for his firm, the Winkler-Koch Engineering Company. Recently, his work had even taken him to the Soviet Union, where Fred's firm helped to overhaul the country's archaic oil refineries, a lucrative contract that had made him and his partner millionaires.

That Fred was riding on the same polo field as the elite of Kansas City and in the company of women like Mary Robinson, whose ancestors included some of the earliest colonial settlers, spoke to his rapid rise from hardscrabble origins.

The second son of a Dutch immigrant turned frontier newspaperman, Fred was born on September 23, 1900, in Quanah, Texas, a poor but plucky town just east of the panhandle. To a boy, unaware of the hardships of frontier life, this whistle-stop town on the Fort Worth and Denver City Railway seemed like paradise. It had streams to fish, plentiful game to hunt, and fields to roam. At the turn of the century, Indians still periodically came to town, including Quanah's stoic namesake, Comanche Chief Quanah Parker, who enjoyed visiting Fred's father, Harry, to gawk at his modern printing press.

Though a magical place for a boy, Quanah's allure diminished year by year as Fred grew into an ambitious young man. He came of age in a time of rapid technological change, and he suspected his future lay beyond his hometown, an enclave surrounded by prairie that stretched to the horizon, interrupted by occasional stands of spindly mesquite.

When Fred was born, there were fewer than eight thousand cars in the United States. They were expensive and impractical, the playthings of the rich. Yet by Fred's sophomore year at Quanah High School, there were 2 million. Thanks, in part, to Henry Ford's decision to forgo steam or electricity for gas-powered internal combustion engines in his signature automobiles, there was now a growing national thirst for gasoline, once considered a useless by-product of converting crude oil to kerosene.

Texas ranchers had once shaken their heads bitterly as they drilled down through the bone-dry soil in search of water, only for viscous oil to ooze to the surface. Now wildcatters raced to sink wells and tap the next big gusher. Among those lured in by the oil boom was Fred's uncle, Louis B. "L. B." Simmons, who had established a refinery in the oil town of Duncan, Oklahoma. The future, to Fred's way of thinking, no longer belonged to those who could make crops grow in the soil, but to the engineers and entrepreneurs who could extract wealth from what lay beneath the surface.

A gifted student with a particular aptitude for science and math, Fred left home in the fall of 1917 for the newly established Rice University in Houston. The bustling oil-rich city was a significant change of pace from Quanah, where the Koch family's home phone number had been all of a single digit—3. Fred thrived at Rice. His teachers considered him a standout student and his peers elected him president of his sophomore class. But like his father, Harry, whose wanderlust had led him from the Dutch harbor city of Workum to a dusty frontier town in Texas, Fred soon grew restless to experience the world.

He spent the summer after his sophomore year working aboard the SS *Coweta*, a Merchant Marine vessel, as it steamed to England. When he returned, he did not go back to Rice. Instead, he moved east to Boston, matriculating to the elite Massachusetts Institute of Technology. Along with his studies, he also took up boxing and briefly captained the MIT team.

Fred's engineering skills were in demand, and even before graduating, he accepted a position with Texas Company (later Texaco), where he worked as a research engineer at the company's Port Arthur refinery on the Gulf Coast. But he saw little future there: "The way up the ladder in that large organization looked very steep and difficult." So he quit, joined another oil company, then resigned from that one, too. As he struggled to drum up work as a consultant, Fred heard from an MIT friend, Carl de Ganahl, whose father was building a refinery in England and who would become a mentor to the callow engineer.

Charles Francis de Ganahl's résumé read like an adventure

novel. He was an explorer and entrepreneur who as a young man had established a sugar plantation deep in the Mexican interior after opening the country's upper Panuco River to boat navigation. Over his trail-blazing career he dabbled in everything from shipbuilding to oil, and from plane manufacturing to gold mining, with business interests that spanned three continents.

In the early 1920s, with the domestic supply of oil increasingly controlled by the major U.S. oil companies, Ganahl established a petroleum refinery and storage facility in England. The Soviet Union supplied the refinery with the bulk of its oil, transporting it by tanker from the Georgian city of Batoum on the Black Sea.

Located on the Isle of Grain, where the Thames and Medway Rivers flow into the North Sea, Ganahl's Medway Oil and Storage Company was ideally situated to provide deepwater access to oceangoing tankers. But the terrain, largely reclaimed marshland, posed an array of engineering challenges.

In 1924, Ganahl—seeking to build out Medway as a refining and distribution hub—took a chance on Fred, making him the chief engineer on the project. Fred worked alongside Ganahl's son, the company's operations manager, to design and construct a new refinery on the island. Ganahl would later call Fred "the soundest chemical engineer in the world" and say he possessed "as brilliant a pair of brain lobes as are worn by any young man of my acquaintance." The admiration was mutual. Fred considered Ganahl a mentor, if not a father figure, and the men remained close the rest of their lives.

In 1925, with the refinery project completed, Fred headed back to the United States. He planned to go straight to Texas to visit his parents, but detoured to Wichita, Kansas, at the invitation of an MIT classmate named Percival "Dobie" Keith. Keith had recently partnered with Lewis E. Winkler, a self-taught engineer and former Army sergeant, to form a new engineering firm. He wanted Fred to come to work for them.

If Fred had learned anything from Charles de Ganahl, it was that the most successful men controlled their destinies—they were owners, not employees. Fred countered Keith's offer with his own. He wouldn't work for them—but he would work with them, as a full partner in the engineering firm. Keith and Winkler agreed to his terms. For $300, Fred bought a one-third stake in the outfit.

It was hard to imagine that the confident, worldly, and fabulously rich man standing in front of Mary Robinson had, just a few years earlier, been so poor that he had lived in his office, located in Wichita's Continental Oil building on the banks of the Arkansas River. As players and spectators mingled on the manicured polo field after the match, Mary and Fred were introduced. Smitten, he pursued his courtship of her as if closing the most important business deal of his life. Fred came from a humble background, but Mary's parents approved of him. He came across as a man of substance and sound judgment. After all, Fred had quickly parlayed a $300 investment into an enviable fortune. On October 22, 1932, a month (and six dates) after Fred and Mary met, they married.

Fred and his bride were opposites. He was "a typical old country boy," as one friend put it, "except everything he touched turned to money." She was artistic and sophisticated, an extrovert who seemed most in her element buzzing around a cocktail party. "She was the epitome of a lady. Absolutely beautiful," Mary's niece, Carol Margaret Allen, recalled. "She was one of the loveliest hostesses I've ever known in my life."

Fred, by contrast, was a quiet, serious man, who did his best to avoid parties and social gatherings, abhorred chitchat and gossip, and generally eschewed superfluous things. "Fred was a strong man; he wasn't a party man. . . . When you could get him out he would gravitate to the smartest man at the party," Mary remembered. He preferred to pass the time with a book, tinkering with a new refinery design at his drafting desk, or out hunting or fishing in the solitude of nature.

For their many differences, the couple complemented each other. Fred shared his love of the outdoors with Mary, teaching his wife how to hunt and shoot. Mary schooled Fred in fine art.

If the newlyweds had little time to get acquainted during their brisk courtship, their honeymoon remedied that. Fred planned an extravagant, seven-month sojourn that spanned four continents, carrying them by air, land, and sea to some of the remotest and most exotic reaches of the world. The inspiration for the elaborate trip came from Fred's former boss, Ganahl, who had taken his wife on a similar globe-spanning journey.

The Kochs sailed from New York that November, visiting the white-sand beaches of Cuba, touring the Panama Canal, and exploring the barrios of Santiago, Chile. One day, as they prepared to board a train that would carry them across the Andes, a clerk stopped the couple and informed Mary she would have to leave her steamer trunk behind; space was limited and they had brought too much luggage. Mary was adventurous, and she had her rugged side, but she was also accustomed to a certain level of comfort.

"But this is my trousseau!" Mary pouted.

Fred attempted to soothe his new wife. "Don't worry," he said, "I'll buy you 10 trousseaus."

The offer was little consolation. When the train departed later that day without her trunk, Mary was sullen. Staring mournfully out the window, she noticed a small plane trailing closely behind them. Fred saw her following it with her eyes and leaned over, smiling: "Mary, that's the charter plane I've hired to bring over your trousseau."

After crisscrossing South America, from small jungle villages to the cosmopolitan cities of Rio de Janeiro and Buenos Aires, they traveled to Portugal and Spain, taking in the plazas of Madrid and catching a bull fight in Seville. From Gibraltar, they crossed into

Africa, browsing the open-air bazaars of Tangiers and Alexandria. Wearing pith hats and outfitted head to toe in khaki, they toured the Sudan and spent weeks on safari in Tanzania and Kenya. Fred felled a pair of leopards and later had their pelts made into a fur coat for Mary.

Loaded down with souvenirs and artifacts, the couple returned to Wichita in May 1933, settling on a rambling tract on the rural outskirts of the city. Initially, they lived in a modest, white home with black shutters, but Fred soon began construction of a grand Tudor-style mansion on the grounds.

Built of light-colored stone, the house had archways, gables, and a heavy, Gothic-looking front door that gave it the feel of an English manor. It featured a stately circular drive and espaliered shrubbery, a wading pool on a patio off the dining room, and a four-car garage. Elsewhere on the property were stables for Fred's twelve polo ponies, which Mary helped to exercise nearly every morning.

The mansion's interior mingled both of their styles, rustic and elegant—on one wall the mounted head of an antelope, on another Renoir's *Girl in Lavender Skirt*. Thomas Hart Benton's *The Music Lesson* hung above a plush burnt-orange sofa in the half-timbered living room. A downstairs game room, draped with animal skins, housed the Kochs' growing collection of hunting trophies, including a wall crammed with the heads of exotic horned creatures.

Mary had returned from their honeymoon pregnant with their first child. Before long, the Koch mansion echoed with the voices of four young boys.

Born in August 1933, Frederick Robinson Koch was named for his father, but with a twist of refinement. The patriarch was just plain old Fred. Mary gave birth to another boy in November 1935. Following a family tradition established by Fred's father, Harry, they named their second son after a business associate. "Am very greatly honored and delighted but shocked that you are so cruel to the boy," the child's namesake telegrammed, playfully, after receiving news of the birth of Charles de Ganahl Koch.

In May 1940 came the birth of fraternal twins David Hamilton Koch and William Ingraham Koch. With the arrival of four sons in seven years, Fred had given a lot of thought to forging his boys into men. He had come up in a place where sometimes all that separated prosperity from poverty was an unfortunate turn in the weather. Quanah was a town of strivers. This environment—and watching his own father's rise from penniless immigrant to successful local businessman—had fueled Fred's ambition. If he handed his boys everything, what would motivate them to make something of themselves? Fred feared that a life of privilege would little by little erode their independence, and he worried that they would rely on his successes and never bother to achieve their own. "The most glorious feeling," Fred often told his sons, "is the feeling of accomplishment."

"He wanted to make sure, because we were a wealthy family, that we didn't grow up thinking that we could go through life not doing anything," Charles once recalled. Fred's mantra, drilled repeatedly into their minds, was that he had no intention of raising "country-club bums." Complicating matters, the Koch compound sat directly across East 13th Street from the exclusive Wichita Country Club.

Fortunes were being made in Wichita. Known as "The Magic City," it had become a magnet for risk takers, entrepreneurs, and fortune seekers of all stripes. The Texas gas-lamp salesman W. C. Coleman had established a thriving business there. So had Walter Beech and Clyde Cessna, the airplane manufacturers who would help to establish the city as America's "Air Capital."

Though they grew up on an estate, Fred went out of his way to make sure his children did not feel wealthy. "Their father was quite tight with his resources," recalled Jay Chapple, an elementary and middle school friend of the Koch twins, who spent time in the family's home. "He did not shower them with toys and that kind of thing." Until well into the 1950s, Chapple said, Fred refused to buy a television. "Every family was getting a TV set that could possibly afford one, but Fred Sr. just said no."

The brothers received no allowances, though they were paid for chores they completed around the house. Still, Fred kept such a tight rein on his wallet that even cobbling together the pocket change to see a movie could be a struggle: "If we wanted to go to the movies, we'd have to go beg him for money," David told an interviewer. In the local public school, where the wealthy Koch twins began their educations alongside the sons and daughters of blue-collar workers from the Cessna and Beech factories, it was their classmates who often seemed like the rich ones, he remembered: "I felt very much of a pauper compared to any of them."

To his sons and their friends, Fred came across as a larger-than-life figure, whose gruff mien and rugged ways evoked comparisons to Western gunslingers. "He was like John Wayne," David has said. "Just like John Wayne." Fred even "kind of looked like John Wayne with glasses," recalled longtime Koch family friend Nestor Weigand. "He was a tough, tough guy." He described Fred's style as "my way or the highway."

Fred rarely displayed affection toward his sons, as if doing so might breed weakness in them. "Fred was just a very stiff, calculated businessman," said Chapple. "I don't mean this in a critical way, but his interest was not in the kids, other than the fact that he wanted them well educated." He was not the kind of dad who played catch with his boys; rather, he was the type of father, one Koch relative said, who taught his children to swim by throwing them into a pool and walking away. "The old man didn't put up with any—" Sterling Varner, who went to work for Fred Koch in the 1940s and later became president of Koch Industries, once said. "He was papa, and that was that."

Or as the Koch relative put it, "He ruled that house with an iron fist."

The Koch patriarch was determined to instill in his sons the voracious work ethic that he attributed to his own success in business. He ensured his boys' hands knew calluses, and their muscles experienced the ache of a long day of manual labor. He put them to work milking cows, bailing hay, digging ditches, mowing lawns, and whatever else he could think of. The never-ending routine of chores was especially torturous during the summer months, when other local kids from Wichita's upper crust whiled away the afternoons at the country club, the sounds of their delight literally wafting across 13th Street to the Kochs' property. "It used to be so hot there in the summertime," David remembered. "My best friend came from a wealthy family in Eastborough. He used to spend every day at the swimming pool of the country club. The wind would blow from the south and carry the noise across the street, and I'd hear him laughing, splashing in the pool, and I would be out there working and feeling sorry for myself."

Periodically during the summers, David and Bill spent a few weeks in Quanah with their cousins, where they made the most of their freedom from their father's strict household, spending their days shooting tin cans, swimming, and generally goofing off with no chores or expectations hanging over their heads. "I think Uncle Fred kept them reined in pretty good," said Carol Margaret Allen, the daughter of Fred's older brother, John Anton, who had remained in Quanah to work at the family's newspaper, the *Quanah Tribune-Chief*. "They lived out in the country. There was nothing around them much. I don't think they did a whole lot of things except stay out there and do chores. So I think when they got away, they had a little fun."

In Quanah, the twins loved visiting the local drugstore, where they could sprawl out on the floor with comic books and order chocolate milk or ice cream from the soda fountain, charging their purchases to their uncle's expense account. They found the concept of a charge account almost as thrilling as the latest *Superman* comic. Because of their rigid upbringing—and Fred's deep aversion to debt—they had no idea such a thing as credit even existed.

Fred traveled frequently on business, but when he was home, the Koch household took on an air of Victorian formality. After work, Fred often retreated to his wood-paneled library, its shelves filled with tomes on politics and economics, emerging promptly at 6:00 p.m., still in coat and tie, for dinner in the formal dining room. "He just controlled the atmosphere," Chapple recalled. "There was no horseplay at the table." Fred would occasionally use family dinners to impart advice to his sons or to lecture them on government and politics. "My father was quite a student of history, so we got a lot of history lessons at the dinner table," Charles remembered.

In the Koch brothers' early childhood, Fred's stern demeanor was not improved by the fact that he spent much of the time in great physical pain. Doctors treated a cancerous tumor on his palate with radiation and surgery, but the treatment itself left behind a quarter-sized hole in the roof of his mouth. It made it difficult for him to eat and hindered his speech. The nature of his business forced him to interact regularly with clients and potential customers. As this became increasingly difficult, he began to reflect on his career and considered retreating to a quieter, simpler life.

Fred came from ranching country, growing up around such legendary spreads as the Matador, the Swenson, and the Pitchfork. Collectively, these historic ranches sprawled across more than a million acres, expansive monuments to Texas's proud cowboy and frontier heritage. The ranching life always appealed to Fred. Ranchers were the men of status and wealth during his childhood. During a particularly bleak stretch in Quanah's history, when wheat crops failed and a local bank went under, Fred's dad had managed to tread water in the newspaper business by convincing ranchers—the only local businessmen still prospering—to advertise their cattle brands in his paper.

In 1941, Fred purchased Spring Creek Ranch in the majestic Flint Hills of eastern Kansas, where the state's otherwise flat, homogenous landscape suddenly gives way to a gently undulating terrain of shimmering bluestem tall grass, peppered with ponds and woven with veins of gurgling creeks. Fred added to its acreage over time until the ranch grew to 10,000 acres.

It was not just a business, but also a frequent spot for family getaways. On weekends, Fred enjoyed piling his clan in their wood-paneled station wagon and setting out for Spring Creek, located about 60 miles east of Wichita. The property featured a small white cottage with a screen porch. Down a slope was a pond, with a raft in the middle and a dock with a diving board, from which the Koch boys—when they weren't mucking stalls, or performing any number of other chores—leapt into the crisp water. (A few decades later, when Bill made one of his first major art purchases, he selected Claude Monet's *Field of Oats and Poppies*, because it reminded him of a favorite family picnic spot on the ranch.)

A plastic surgeon eventually cured Fred's palate condition. He maintained a foothold in the oil business, but his focus turned increasingly to ranching. He sold a refinery in Illinois and offloaded oil leases in northwestern New Mexico, channeling some of the proceeds into the December 1950 purchase of the 257,000-acre Beaverhead Ranch in southern Montana on the edge of the Continental Divide. The Beaverhead became the crown jewel of Fred's burgeoning ranching empire. In 1952, he formed the Matador Cattle Company to oversee his ranch holdings, and in early 1953, he purchased three parcels of the historic Matador Ranch, founded in 1882 and located 70 miles west of Quanah in Motley County, Texas. Fred did not just buy choice acreage known for its "fat cattle and nutritious grass," in the words of the Matador

Cattle Company's onetime president John Lincoln; he acquired approximately 105,000 acres of Texas history.

The ranches were a fixture of the Koch boys' childhood, and during the summers Fred and his sons spent at least a month at Beaverhead, driving there by a different route each time in order to take in new sights as they made the 1,300-mile journey from Wichita. Trips to the family ranches were not vacations; they were yet another opportunity for Fred to break his children of any privileged tendencies through long days of labor.

The boys drove tractors, dug fence posts and irrigation ditches, rode herd, cleaned stalls, and performed other assorted jobs. On the ranches, the multimillionaire's sons were treated no differently than lowly cowhands, and they lived alongside Fred's employees in no-frills bunkhouses. One summer Charles bunked in a log cabin nestled in Montana's Centennial Valley alongside a colorful cowboy named "Bitterroot Bob," who was known to take potshots at flies as he lay in bed at night cradling his pistol. On his way back to prep school at the end of the summer, Charles and one of Fred's employees stopped for lunch in Dillon, Montana. Charles glanced around the divey restaurant. "It sure is clean here," he said.

Charles and his younger brothers endured their summers working on the ranches—and later even came to appreciate the character-building experience of it—but the eldest Koch brother rebelled against Fred's reign. Every dictatorship has its dissident, and Frederick played this part within the Koch family's rigid power structure.

Frederick was the outlier among his rough-and-tumble, ultra-competitive brothers. While the three younger boys took after their father, he gravitated toward his mother's interests. Mary helped to nourish Frederick's artistic side, and when he grew up, mother and son would enjoy spending time together taking in plays and attending performing arts festivals. Artsy and effete, Fred was a student of literature and a lover of drama, who liked to sing and act. He wasn't athletic, displayed no interest in business, and loathed the work-camp-like environment fostered by his father, with whom he shared little in common, beyond a love of opera.

Fred bonded with his sons through manly pursuits, especially father-son hunting expeditions to far-off places, such as the Arctic and Africa. Frederick had no interest in such primeval excursions. Unlike his brothers, "Freddie didn't want to learn" to shoot, Mary recalled. He was in "another world."

The more Fred glimpsed signs of effeminacy in his son, the more he tried to toughen him up—and the more Frederick resisted. Finally, Frederick had a nervous breakdown, according to Charles, during a summer of forced labor on one of the family's ranches. ("I have never had a 'nervous breakdown,'" Frederick said. He added that after one summer of work at Spring Creek, he had subsequent summer jobs at a music store and a handful of banks in Wichita.)

"Father wanted to make all his boys into men and Freddie couldn't relate to that regime," Charles explained. "Dad didn't understand and so he was hard on Freddie. He didn't understand that Freddie wasn't a lazy kid—he was just different."

By the late 1950s, when Frederick was in his twenties, it was an open secret among the family's circle of friends in Wichita that he was gay. "We all knew Freddie was gay," said someone who spent time with the family and their friends in the 1950s and 1960s. "You know, those things—especially in an environment like Wichita—were almost whispered. It was common knowledge."

Frederick could do little to relate to his father or win his approval. "Freddie was a sophisticate and a man of the world in addition to the fact that he was gay," said Koch family friend Nestor Weigand. "It wasn't something that was easily accepted in those days." (According to Frederick, he is not gay.)

For eighth grade, Frederick's parents sent him off to boarding school at Pembroke Country Day in Kansas City. He attended high school at Hackley, an elite private school located in New York's Hudson Valley, where he was the class valedictorian. "My parents," he explained, "were concerned that I needed to attend a prep school that would raise my academic level so that I could get into an Ivy League university. My father had gone to MIT, and my mother had gone to Wellesley, and they wanted their sons to go to [an] Ivy League university. They weren't going to decide which one."

Once he left home, Frederick's lifeline to the family was largely through his mother, who remained close with her oldest son. "Freddie sort of segregated himself from the family very early on," said family friend and Wichita real estate developer George Ablah. "And I think everyone was more comfortable with that." According to Bill, "Freddie wanted no part of the family and did his own thing."

"Unlike my brothers," Frederick said, "I was interested in music, art, and literature. This did not mean I wanted 'no part of the family.' I always took an interest in the activities of my parents and my brothers."

During their childhood, mention of Frederick caused noticeable discomfort among his brothers. "They just didn't want Freddie's name brought up," said one family friend. "They knew there was something different about him. You didn't hear much about Freddie at all....It was almost like he wasn't part of the family."

In the 1960s, mention of Frederick even vanished from one of his father's bios: "He and Mrs. Koch have three sons," it read, "Charles, William, and David."

Fred's disappointment in his eldest son caused him to double-down on Charles, piling him with chores and responsibilities by the age of nine. "I think Fred Koch went through this kind of thing that I must have been too affectionate; I must have been too loving, too kind to Freddie and that's why he turned out to be so effeminate," said John Damgard, who went to high school with David and remains close with David and Charles. "When Charles came along, the old man wasn't going to make that mistake. So he was really, really tough on Charles. He taught him the work ethic; he was tougher than nails." David and Bill had it slightly easier, Damgard added. "I think Mary did a lot to protect the twins from the hard-driving father."

Fred viewed Charles early on as the heir to his business empire, and rode him especially hard. Charles grew up with the impression that he was being picked on—and he was. As an eleven-year-old boy, tearfully pleading for his parents to reconsider, Charles was shipped off to the first of several boarding schools, this one in Arizona. "Charles was thrown out into the world at an early age," said his friend Leslie Rudd, owner of Dean & DeLuca, the chain of gourmet markets, who believes this experience shaped Charles's life.

As Charles admits, there was little about his teenaged self that suggested he was destined for greatness. He was smart, but with the type of unharnessed intellect that tends to get young men into trouble. Charles acted out, got into fights, stayed out late drinking and sowing wild oats. David has called his older brother a "bad boy who turned good," and said, "Charles did some awful things as a teenager." When it came time for high school, his exasperated parents sent him to Culver Military Academy in northern Indiana, whose notable alumni include the late New York Yankees owner George Steinbrenner, actor Hal Holbrook, and Crown Prince Alexander II of Yugoslavia. Charles considered it a prison sentence. The elite military school had a reputation for taking in wild boys and spitting out upright, disciplined men. Charles soon ran afoul of the administration.

On the train ride back to Culver after spring break of his junior year, Charles got busted for drinking beer and was promptly tossed out of school. Asked later how old Fred took the news of his expulsion, the best Charles could say of his father's fury was, "I'm still alive."

David remembered: "Father put the fear of God in him. He said, 'If you don't make it, you'll be worthless. You've disappointed me.' Father was a severe taskmaster. He could do that sort of thing so effectively." Fred banished Charles to live with family in Texas, where he spent the remainder of the school year working in a grain elevator. It took some begging, but Culver ultimately reinstated Charles, with the proviso that he attend summer school.

"It was a miracle that such a successful businessperson developed from such a rebellious kid," Harry Litwin, a friend and business partner of Charles's father, once remarked.

When Charles became Fred Koch's work-in-progress, he also became a lightning rod for his brother Bill's jealousy. Being four-and-a-half years older than the twins, Charles was the alpha dog in the house, and he affected each of the twins in different ways. Bill was in some respects the most cerebral of the four Koch brothers, but he was also the most socially awkward and emotionally combustible. "[Bill] was kind of born with a temper," Bill's childhood friend, Jay Chapple, said. In his baby book, Mary had scrawled notations including "easily irritable," "angry," and "jealous."

As a young boy, Bill resorted to desperate gambits for attention. "He was perverse," Charles has said. "I remember when we were little, and the twins were drying off after a shower, and there was a little wall heater there, the kind with the grate and the little holes, and Mother said, 'Billy, don't touch that.' And so Billy put his little bottom up against it and it burned him so bad he looked like a waffle." On another occasion, when Mary warned her son to take a hog's nose ring out of his mouth, Bill proceeded to gulp it down, necessitating a trip to the hospital.

Charles viewed Bill as a walking time bomb. "He'd lash out. He was violent. He'd throw tantrums." Bill's volatile emotions made it difficult for him to concentrate in school, and his worried parents eventually sent him to a psychologist, who advised that the only way to help Bill was to remove the source of his smoldering resentment—Charles. "We had to get Charles away because of the terrible jealousy that was consuming Billy," Mary told *The New York Times*'s Leslie Wayne in a 1986 interview. So off he went to Arizona.

Bill recalled a *Lord of the Flies*–like childhood, in which his parents frequently left him and his brothers in the care of the household help "to grow up amongst ourselves," while Fred traveled the world tending to his business empire and Mary either accompanied him or was out of the house at cocktail parties or society events. When Fred was home, his emotional distance caused his sons to clamor for attention and approval. As Bill put it, "When you're one of four kids, the only currency you have is the love of your father, and we all fought for that."

Bill remembered Charles as a mischievous bully, who perched astride the family storm cellar during backyard games of King of the Hill and gleefully flung him down to the ground whenever he tried to scramble to the top. And Bill has said that his older brother took sadistic pleasure in provoking fights between him and David. Bill nevertheless idolized his older brother, though Charles made it painfully clear that he preferred David's company.

Bill and David were twins, but David and Charles were natural compatriots. David was self-confident and athletic, with a mild temperament and a contagious laugh. "Charles and David were so much alike, they were always really good friends. And Bill probably felt a little left out," said their cousin Carol Margaret Allen. "Charles always had quite a following of girls, and so did David. And Bill—I think he would have liked to have had more girls following him. He was not as gregarious and outgoing."

Bill sprouted up quickly before his body could grow accustomed to the spurt. Awkward and uncoordinated, he spent his childhood trying to keep up with his brothers and feeling constantly left out by Charles. Bill felt like the family geek. His self-esteem plummeted. "For a long time," he later reflected, "I didn't think I was worth shit."

Though the Kochs exiled Charles to boarding school, the seeds of a bitter sibling rivalry were already sown. Fred did not help the brotherly dynamic. He even encouraged the twins to fight. Home movies, in which the brothers can't be older than five or six, show Bill and David battering each other wearing puffy boxing gloves the size of each other's heads. "He wanted his boys to grow up to be men," said David's friend John Damgard. "And I think the old man would pit the twins together because they were the same age and he was teaching them techniques in boxing. And that probably started the rivalry."

Day to day, sometimes hour to hour, David and Bill were either the best of friends or the worst of enemies. The twins did everything together and shared the same tight-knit circle of friends, most of whom played together on the basketball team of Wichita's Minneha Middle School. One of the brothers' favorite pastimes was "bushwhacking." This involved first cajoling Morris, the tough but good-natured property foreman who squired them around Wichita, to drive them up and down the rural roads near the Koch compound after dark. The idea was to search for couples pulled over at secluded make-out spots. When they spotted a parked car, Morris flicked off the lights and crept up on it, as one of the brothers or their friends lit the fuse on a cherry bomb. When they were almost on top of the vehicle, Morris switched on the high beams and out the window the firecracker flew, scaring the bejesus out of their target. Cackling maniacally, the boys peeled off into the night looking for more couples to terrify.

Bill possessed a firecracker-like fuse of his own, and he and

David frequently brawled. A certain antagonism between brothers isn't uncommon, but the combativeness between the Koch twins was anything but standard. During one bout, Bill bashed his twin over the head with a polo mallet. During another altercation, witnessed by members of the twins' middle school clique, Bill brandished a butcher knife against his brother and had to be calmly talked down. David still bears a scar from the time Bill pierced him in the back with a ceremonial sword that their father brought back from one of his African adventures.

When it came time for the twins to attend prep school, they had their pick of prestigious institutions. David chose Deerfield Academy, an all-boys boarding school in northwestern Massachusetts that groomed East Coast Brahmins for the Ivy League. He credited the school, where he would go on to distinguish himself on the basketball and track teams, with transforming him "from an unsophisticated country boy into a fairly polished, well informed graduate."

Bill opted for another path. Of all the schools he could have selected, he chose the alma mater of the older brother he alternately revered and resented. Bill's choice of the Culver Military Academy alarmed Mary, who later confided to an interviewer that her son had become unhinged in his fixation on Charles.

"You've got to talk to a psychiatrist to analyze it," David would later sigh, reflecting on the Bill-Charles dynamic.

"This was not a lovey-dovey family," mused a member of the extended family. "This was a family where the father was consumed by his own ambitions. The mother was trapped by her generation and wealth and surrounded by alpha males. And the boys only had each other, but they were so busy in pursuit of their father's approval that they never noticed what they could do for each other."

"Everything," the relative added, "goes back to their childhood. Everything goes back to the love they didn't get."

CHAPTER TWO

Stalin's Oil Man

Fred's business success—both at home and abroad—came at a steep price for the Koch family patriarch and cast long shadows over his sons' formative years. The innovation that made him rich also invited an onslaught of patent infringement litigation from a company called Universal Oil Products, which was owned by a consortium of major U.S. oil companies, including the remnants of John D. Rockefeller's Standard Oil. The lawsuits drove him to look abroad for business opportunities, including to Josef Stalin's U.S.S.R.

When Fred entered the oil business, a new refining process called thermal cracking was sweeping the industry. Standard Oil of Indiana first employed this method commercially in 1913, but it didn't come into wider use until the 1920s. Prior to its discovery, refineries relied on a simple, but wasteful process for distilling crude oil into gas, fuel oil, kerosene, and other petroleum-based products.

Petroleum consists of a stew of organic compounds that separate at the right boiling point. The lighter, more volatile hydrocarbons (gasoline) vaporize at lower temperatures than the heavier, more stable ones (fuel oil). Before thermal cracking, refineries used a process called straight-run distillation, in which they heated crude oil in metal stills and, as each of the petroleum "fractions" reached their respective boiling points, siphoned off the vapor and recondensed it. Through this technique, a barrel of crude yielded perhaps 11 percent gasoline.

Refineries could double gas yields—or better—using thermal cracking. By applying the right combination of heat and pressure, the process altered the chemical makeup of petroleum, breaking it into simple molecules and "cracking" heavy hydrocarbons into lighter ones, squeezing more gasoline from each barrel of oil.

Cracked gasoline (the only kind modern consumers know) was initially unpopular with the American public, owing to its yellowish hue and pungent odor, in contrast to the clear and somewhat sweet-smelling product they were used to. But as demand soared, the commercial advantages of the cracked product became impossible to ignore. Before long, oil company chemists, freelance inventors, and amateur tinkerers of all kinds had flooded the U.S. Patent and Trademark Office with patent applications covering every conceivable aspect of the cracking process. By 1926, the government had issued more than 2,500 cracking-related patents.

In the 1920s, cracking technology was largely proprietary, either exclusive to the big oil companies that had been spun off from Standard or available at a steep per-barrel licensing fee. Fred's company, Winkler-Koch, having developed its own cracking method, had a different business model. It didn't license its process; it charged clients only for the design and installation of its cracking equipment.

Independent refineries found Winkler-Koch attractive for other reasons, too. When cracking was first introduced, its main drawback was that the process caused a thick film of carbon residue, known as coke, to form in the refining equipment. This forced refineries to shut down regularly in order to chisel the coke from the chambers of their machinery before running another batch of oil. The equipment designed by Fred and his partner, however, could crack the heaviest of hydrocarbons while producing little buildup.

In 1928, Winkler-Koch installed its cracking process at a refinery in Duncan, Oklahoma, owned by Fred's uncle, L. B. Simmons. And over the next year the orders poured in. Before long, the engineering firm had inked sixteen contracts at refineries across the Midwest, netting a tidy $520,000 profit.

Word of the Winkler-Koch process spread quickly and far. This attracted customers, but also placed Fred's company on a collision course with the more established players in the refining business.

Chicago-based Universal Oil Products, which had developed a popular cracking method and owned a trove of related patents, spent much of the 1920s suing the nation's biggest oil companies for pirating its technology. The aggressive company proved such an industry menace that a group of major oil companies ultimately banded together to buy Universal, if only to put a stop to the merciless legal campaign.

During the late 1920s, the name "Winkler-Koch" was on the lips of all the refinery owners in the Southwest, or at least it seemed that way to G. W. Miller, a Universal sales engineer who canvassed Arkansas, Kansas, Louisiana, Oklahoma, and Texas in pursuit of new licensees. Miller would recall that Fred Koch's company was "conducting a very aggressive, active campaign and sales program, and that was the chief competition during those years."

Not only was Winkler-Koch courting potential Universal Oil Products licensees, but it had poached at least one existing customer, Arkansas-based Root Refining Company. As Miller worked his territory, he gathered intelligence about his competition's activities and relayed it back to Universal's headquarters. The company soon fixed its gaze on its competitor in Wichita.

In early 1929, the oil industry buzzed with rumors that Universal was poised to strike. With the specter of a lawsuit looming, Fred and his partner took preemptive action. On February 25,

1929, they gathered their clients for an emergency meeting at the Winkler-Koch offices in Wichita.

Fred's pitch was simple: By going it alone, they stood little chance; Universal, with its army of lawyers, could bleed a smaller competitor dry with the legal fees alone. Their only chance was to band together to fight back against this latest attempt at oil industry monopoly. They needed to consider a lawsuit against one of them as a threat to all of them.

The previous week, Koch and Winkler had incorporated a new company for this purpose—the Winkler-Koch Patent Company would act as a legal defense fund for users of the Winkler-Koch cracking process. The plan initially called for each customer to chip in $5,000 for every Winkler-Koch still it operated; in exchange customers would be defended in any litigation brought by Universal Oil Products. To supplement the fund, which in the years to follow ballooned to more than a million dollars, Winkler-Koch tacked a one-cent royalty on to each barrel of oil cracked using its method.

Less than two weeks after the Wichita summit, Universal made its move, filing suit against Root Refining, its former customer, and Winkler-Koch.

Fred Koch's two-decade legal battle against Universal is now a central part of the identity of Koch Industries and of the Koch family. His sons drank it in along with their milk at the family dinner table, and as grown men they recounted the story often, as both a point of pride and a cautionary tale. It features in nearly every news account describing the clan's history and the origins of their wealth. The narrative plays out along a familiar story line—an underdog company that fought back against would-be monopolists and a tough-as-nails engineer who refused to back down in the face of great odds and held firm to his principles of fairness and justice.

The truth is more complicated.

Before going into business for themselves in 1925, Fred's partners, Lewis Winkler and Dobie Keith, worked for Universal Oil Products, and they knew the company's patented cracking process intimately. The technique was developed by Carbon Dubbs, a burly, bald-headed inventor said to possess a temperament as volatile as the element he was named for. Before leaving Universal, Winkler had been Universal's chief engineer, overseeing the construction and start-up of the Dubbs cracking units built in the Midwest. In 1921, Winkler had worked shoulder to shoulder with Carbon Dubbs in Roxana, Illinois, where Universal engineers installed the first commercial cracking unit that relied on the inventor's process at a refinery owned by a U.S. subsidiary of Royal Dutch Shell.

Dubbs, the son of an eccentric tinkerer from Pennsylvania oil country, had managed to solve the problem of carbon residue accumulating and hardening like burnt coffee in the refining machinery.

Between 1918 and 1919, working out of a remote asphalt plant near Independence, Kansas, Dubbs pioneered a method he called "clean circulation," which allowed refiners to run crude oil without interruption for weeks. The key was continuously circulating cracked oil with crude at 865 degrees Fahrenheit and 100 pounds of pressure per square inch.

The discovery revolutionized the industry, and Universal banked on the fact that oil refiners would pay handsomely to license its cracking process. What the company didn't expect was that, before it could fully capitalize on its technology, ex-employees would go head-to-head with Universal in the cracking arena.

In July 1932, when Universal's case against Winkler-Koch and Root Refining, the former Universal licensee, went to trial in Wilmington, Delaware, Lewis Winkler declined to testify. Even so, lawyers highlighted his past association with Universal and close knowledge of the cracking method that Winkler's ex-employer had accused his new firm of imitating. A letter was also introduced in the case in which a Winkler-Koch employee touted the firm's principals as "post graduates of Universal."

Fred Koch's lawyer J. Bernhard Thiess portrayed Universal as what today would be called a "patent troll." He argued that Universal was "exclusively a patent holding company" that existed solely to wage "commercial warfare" against competitors. He framed Universal's business model as a form of extortion, where "a small refiner who is threatened by a powerful patent holding company, is told that if he does not take a license he will suffer the penalty."

The case dragged on for more than a month, as Fred anxiously watched the proceedings from the gallery. At one point, Warren K. Lewis, the chair of MIT's chemical engineering department, whom Fred would have remembered from his college years, took the stand to testify—for the plaintiffs. He proclaimed the Winkler-Koch process a Dubbs knockoff. "The differences that do exist are modifications that do not affect the principle and the process as Dubbs disclosed them, in my opinion."

The verdict, nearly two years in coming, arrived on a Friday in late April 1934. Finding for Universal, the ruling cited Professor Lewis's testimony at length. The *Chemical Bulletin* called the court decision a "decisive victory" for Universal and added ominously, "It is understood that Universal now proposes to proceed vigorously against all infringers of its cracking patents."

Though Winkler-Koch's lawyers quickly appealed to the Third Circuit in Philadelphia, a three-judge panel upheld the lower court verdict in June 1935. Universal wasted no time telegramming the news to the nation's oil refiners: "We assume you will be interested to know that the Federal circuit court of appeals, Philadelphia, unanimously affirms validity of Dubbs clean circulation.... Copy of opinion will be mailed to you." The message sounded benign enough, but it was a warning: Take out a license with Universal. Or else.

On October 21, 1935, less than two weeks before the birth of Fred's second son, Charles, he received the distressing news that the U.S. Supreme Court had declined to hear the case. Subsequent events would send Fred a strong message that the U.S. legal system was deeply flawed.

Though Fred didn't know it then, he would eventually learn that the ruling that had sealed his company's fate had been bought and paid for. A few days after the Supreme Court decided against hearing the case, J. Warren Davis, a veteran judge on the Third Circuit Court of Appeals, the body that upheld the lower court's infringement verdict against Winkler-Koch, worked out a complex transaction with a Pennsylvania lawyer named Morgan Kaufman. Kaufman, who was on Universal's payroll, was an undistinguished attorney with no experience in the area of patent law, but his real value lay in his association with the judge, an ordained Baptist minister appointed to the federal bench by President Woodrow Wilson. The men agreed that Kaufman would loan $10,000 to one of the judge's distant cousins, who would then repay the loan—with 8 percent interest—to Davis. Universal had taken no chances that its competitor's legal challenge would prevail. This was Davis's payoff—delivered at the conclusion of the case—for making sure Winkler-Koch and Root Refining lost their appeal.

In March 1941, a highly publicized bribery scandal erupted when a federal grand jury indicted Davis and Kaufman, along with Hollywood producer William Fox (namesake of 20th Century Fox), who'd made two similar "loans" to the judge while his bankruptcy case was pending before the appeals court.

Fox pleaded guilty, spilling his guts on the witness stand against Davis and Kaufman. The pair escaped conviction, but the extensive federal investigation into Davis's dealings sullied his other

rulings. This opened up a legal avenue for Winkler-Koch's lawyers, who, in June 1941, requested an inquiry.

The infringement verdict was ultimately vacated. The irony
was that if Universal had not resorted to bribery, it likely would
have prevailed over Root and Winkler-Koch—and the tale of Fred
Koch's war with Big Oil would have read quite differently.

With Universal ensconced in scandal over bribery allegations,
Fred went on the legal offensive, striking back at the adversary
that had put his company through a nightmarish campaign of litigation. The oil giants who owned Universal hastily offloaded the
company to distance themselves from the controversy, but Fred
and his lawyers went after them with a vengeance. By 1952, he
managed to extract $1.5 million from his foes.

The victory was bittersweet. The lengthy battle had taken a
toll on Fred's partnership with Lewis Winkler. The businessmen
severed ties in 1944. (Dobie Keith, Fred's old MIT pal who had
brought him to Wichita, left their start-up a few months after Fred
joined for a steadier opportunity in Boston.)

Spanning the Koch brothers' childhood, their father's twenty-
three-year struggle loomed large in their impressionable minds.
The brothers grew up glimpsing the concern knitted into his brow
and feeling his anxiety, an apprehension so great it almost seemed
to occupy physical space in their household. "It was a living hell
to him," David remembered. "...It was very damaging to his business, and he had an extremely unhappy experience—just the time,
the wear and tear, the mental strain on him." Fred's legal war
especially affected Bill, Charles, and David, and the brothers each
took different lessons from it.

Based on their father's experience, Charles and David, who
initiated their share of lawsuits over the years, nevertheless came
to view litigation as a last resort, a necessary evil. According to
Charles, Fred's advice to his sons, after prevailing over Universal,
was, "Never sue. The lawyers get a third, the government gets a

third, and you get your business destroyed." Bill Koch took away a different lesson: He would grow up to see litigation as a weapon of righteous retribution. In their father's stand, the brothers saw a man of iron will and concrete principle who wouldn't be cowed or coerced, who wouldn't back down in the face of a just fight. Each of the brothers, in his own way, internalized these values. As they grew up, the brothers recognized these same traits at work in their father's crusade against the spread of communism.

The last place Fred Koch expected to be on his thirtieth birthday was deep in the Russian Caucasus in the company of a diminutive and joyless Bolshevik. But the toll that the Universal Oil Products battle took on Winkler-Koch's revenues had pushed Fred and his partner out of the United States and into the welcoming embrace of Josef Stalin's Soviet Union.

In the late 1920s, the newly formed U.S.S.R. dispatched scientists and engineers to the United States to search for cracking technology that could aid Stalin's plans for rapid industrialization. Just a few decades earlier, Czarist Russia had led the world in petroleum production. The empire's rich oil fields in the Caucasus, along the Caspian and Black Seas, made the Russians such a formidable force that Rockefeller's Standard Oil had scrambled to establish a network of overseas subsidiaries in a battle for market share.

The biggest blow to the Russian oil sector was self-inflicted. Over the course of three days in August 1905, on the heels of the first Russian Revolution, oil workers in the Absheron Peninsula of Azerbaijan rioted. They burned more than 1,400 oil derricks, sabotaged well shafts, and mangled drilling equipment. Oil production plummeted. For at least the next decade, Russia's oil industry limped forward as the U.S. oil sector took off. Then came World War I, and a wave of uprisings in 1917 that ushered in a Bolshevik government, which gradually consolidated the oil industry under state control.

Revolution and war had decimated the region's economy, and the Soviet Union's new communist leaders placed a premium on revitalizing the oil industry to turn around the U.S.S.R.'s economic prospects. The Soviets looked to the West for technology and technical expertise. Sometimes in exchange for oil concessions or royalties, American and European companies began to supply modern drilling equipment. And Western oil field workers and engineers poured into the region to professionalize the Soviet Union's drilling operations and oversee the construction of pipelines.

But even as the Soviets revamped oil production sites, modern refining technology remained elusive. The country's leaders desperately wanted to transition to thermal cracking, but the major American companies, the leaders in this field, were reluctant to provide this technology, especially to a regime with which the United States had severed diplomatic relations.

Many American companies did business with the Soviet Union during this era, but the subject of trade relations between the countries was controversial and a matter of considerable national debate. During a speech in 1931, Representative Hamilton Fish III, a New York Republican and the grandson of Ulysses Grant's secretary of state, summed up the opposition to aiding the Soviets for his congressional colleagues on the Ways and Means Committee. "It is plain to the mind of anyone living in a capitalistic country, that what is contemplated is a plan for a great world revolution," he said. "...That 5-year plan aims at just one thing—the economic ruin of every nation in the world that has not the Soviet form of government, and they contemplate eventually the establishment of the Soviet government in this country and everywhere else."

Fred Koch and his partner didn't have the luxury to worry about Soviet plans for world domination. They needed work, and Koch's summons to Russia began innocently enough. Visiting the United States in the late 1920s, Alexander Sakhanov, research director of the Soviet oil concern Grozneft, discovered Winkler-Koch. The company did not possess the best or most advanced cracking technology, Sakhanov wrote home in an April 1929 letter, but "its merit consists in extreme simplicity and, as a consequence, cheapness."

The year of Sakhanov's visit, Winkler-Koch signed contracts with Amtorg, the Soviet Union's U.S.-based trade representative, to design and construct fifteen oil cracking stills in the U.S.S.R. at refineries located in Baku, the capital of Azerbaijan; the Chechen capital of Grozny; the Russian Black Sea port town of Tuapse; Yaroslavl, located 160 miles northeast of Moscow; and other locations. The deal, worth nearly $5 million, also called for the engineers to consult on the construction of dozens more cracking units.

The Soviets were demanding customers. They requested detailed technical data and specifications, and their deal with Winkler-Koch also required the company to use its contacts to place thirty Soviet engineers at American manufacturing plants and refineries, where they could study their operations during six-month internships. This would later allow the U.S.S.R. to replicate Winkler-Koch's cracking stills using its own engineers.

On August 27, 1930, when Fred arrived in Moscow to check on the progress of his engineers, the Soviet government assigned a minder to keep tabs on him during his month-and-a-half-long journey to the refineries in Grozny, Tuapse, Batumi, and other cities where the installation of Winkler-Koch cracking units was under way.

Jerome Livschitz, who had spent twelve years living in the United States before returning to Russia to take part in the 1917 revolution, inspired fear wherever he went. Along with a near-constant sneer, the little man, with graying hair and a pinched face, wore an ill-fitting suit. What small pleasure Livschitz derived out of life seemed to come from goading Fred about the plans of the communists to infiltrate every aspect of American society. The schools, the churches, the unions, the military, the government—all were communist targets. Just you wait and see, Livschitz taunted, "we will make you rotten to the core."

One day, as they convoyed through the Georgian capital of Tblisi, the car carrying Livschitz flipped. Fred and another American engineer rushed to free him from the wreck. Dazed from the crash, the Bolshevik seemed surprised the Americans had come to his aid. "Why did you save my life?" he asked. "We are enemies. I would not have saved yours." He paused and reflected, momentarily feeling in a charitable mood. "Perhaps when the revolution comes to the U.S.A., and I return there, I will spare your lives."

Fred had traveled widely, but he had never seen conditions like the ones he witnessed in the Soviet Union. A deep gloom pervaded the country, and an undercurrent of trepidation pulsed through the populace. He "found it a land of hunger, misery, and terror." Citizens were allotted a monthly ration of food that was barely enough to subsist on. The government provided coupons redeemable for bland and ill-made clothes, and issued citizens a half-bar of soap each month for washing. Communist informants lurked everywhere. A trip to Siberia—if not a bullet in the head—awaited anyone suspected of disloyalty.

During his travels, Fred befriended a Russian family who had lived in the United States before returning to their homeland following the Bolshevik revolution. Their English-speaking children worked as translators for Winkler-Koch's American engineers. One of them, a daughter named Mary, begged Fred to carry a letter out of the country for her, in order to sneak it past the Soviet censors who monitored the mail. He agreed, but later couldn't help himself from peeking at the contents: "We are here just like slaves," Mary had written to a friend. "We cannot do anything we want but we do what they tell us to do....I cannot write it to you on paper how terrible it is here."

In late October 1930, as Fred began his journey home following a round of meetings with Soviet officials in Moscow, Livschitz saw him off at the train station. The communist's parting words chilled him: "I'll see you in the United States sooner than you think." Etched into his mind, this troubling memory visited Fred often in the years ahead, as slowly but surely he saw the plot of communist subversion unfold—just as Livschitz promised it would. To the end of his days, he was deeply haunted by what he'd seen in the Soviet Union and conflicted by the role he and his company had played in empowering the U.S.S.R.

"I was naïve enough to think in that far away day that I could help the Russian people by what I was doing," he wrote in a 1964 letter to the editor that ran in *The Washington Post*. "What I saw in Russia convinced me of the utterly evil nature of communism.... What I saw there convinced me that communism was the most evil force the world has ever seen and I must do everything in my power to fight it, which I have done since that time."

CHAPTER THREE

"The Dead Will Be the Lucky Ones"

On the morning of December 8, 1958, as a light snow fell in Indianapolis, Fred Koch strode up the walkway to the sprawling brick Tudor home at 3650 Washington Boulevard. Stepping out of the chill and shedding his coat, Fred was greeted by Marguerite Dice, the widow who had volunteered to host the meeting that would mark the birth of the John Birch Society.

Fred found a seat in Dice's spacious living room, where plush chairs and davenports had been arrayed in a semicircle. There with him were ten others, including T. Coleman Andrews, former commissioner of the Internal Revenue Service, who had resigned his post in 1955, coming out as a vocal foe of the income tax; Col. Laurence Bunker, a former aide to General Douglas MacArthur; Wisconsin industrialist William Grede; W. B. McMillan, president of the Hussman Refrigerator Company; and University of Illinois classics professor Revilo Oliver, later a hero of white supremacists for his racist and anti-Semitic jeremiads.

Robert Welch had convened the meeting. He was a former candy company executive who in the mid-1950s had quit his job to devote himself full-time to fighting communism. How could he continue peddling Sugar Babies and Junior Mints when America—the world—was in crisis?

Welch was a child prodigy who had entered college at the age of twelve. He had dabbled in politics, launching a 1950 bid for lieutenant governor in Massachusetts on a platform of repelling the creep of socialism into state and federal government. He lost the race, but his dystopic vision of a subverted, subjugated America gained traction. To disseminate his ideas, Welch founded a magazine, *One Man's Opinion* (later renamed *American Opinion*). And that was the problem: Welch was just one man. If he hoped to defeat the existential threat of communism, he would need an army.

Fred Koch, whose fervent anticommunism had brought him to Welch's notice, seemed like an ideal general. Since returning from the Soviet Union in 1930, he had watched his four sons grow up in a world where the words of his old Bolshevik minder seemed to be coming true. Fred now saw evidence of communist infiltration everywhere. Jerome Livschitz's taunt—*we will make you rotten to the core*—echoed in his ears. His time among the Soviets, and his firsthand experiences witnessing a society fully under the boot heel of government, was regular table talk for the Koch boys.

"He was constantly speaking to us children about what was wrong with government and government policy," David has said. "It's something I grew up with—a fundamental point of view that big government was bad, and imposition of government controls on our lives and economic fortunes was not good."

Fred's experiences in the Soviet Union, which in turn drove his interest in politics and economics, especially influenced Charles. "That sparked the evolution of Charles's political views," said Tony Woodlief, a former Koch Industries management consultant who knows Charles well. "You can blame it on Standard Oil."

The more Fred traveled the world, the more horrified he became at the growing influence of socialism and communism—to the point where, on the cusp of World War II, he even saw something laudable in the rise of fascism. "Although nobody agrees with me,

I am of the opinion that the only sound countries in the world are Germany, Italy, and Japan, simply because they are all working and working hard," he reported in an October 1938 letter to his mentor Charles de Ganahl, after an extensive trip that included stops in imperial Japan and ("violently socialistic") New Zealand.

The laboring people in those countries are proportionately much better off than they are any place else in the world. When you contrast the state of mind of Germany today with what it was in 1925 you begin to think that perhaps this course of idleness, feeding at the public trough, dependence on government, etc., with which we are afflicted is not permanent and can be overcome.

At the end of World War II, Fred believed that the next great clash would be fought between the forces of capitalism and collectivism, but to his frustration, few people seemed to recognize the peril. He saw it as his duty to raise the alarm. "I think these times are far more serious even than Civil War days," he confided to a friend and retired military officer. "That war was merely to decide whether we were going to be one nation or two, whereas the fight that is going on now in this country is going to decide whether we are going to be free men or slaves." (This was a bizarre comment to make, since the Civil War was fought, in large part, to eradicate slavery.)

As he became increasingly outspoken about the menace of communism, Fred returned to Moscow in 1956 (his first visit in twenty-six years), joining a delegation of ten prominent Wichita businessmen on a "friendship tour" to refute Soviet propaganda about the evils of capitalism. "We have been painted as oppressive masters of the laboring people," one of Fred's companions said at the time. "We are nothing of the sort. Although we are wealthy in terms of worldly goods, we are humanitarians in every respect."

The quixotic trip only reinforced the immutability of the ideological battle under way.

When Welch summoned Fred to Indianapolis, he did not tell the industrialist the reason for the meeting. He merely said that the topic was of the gravest importance.

"The meeting will be completely 'off the record'—you will simply be in Indianapolis, or just in the Midwest, on business," Welch wrote to the small circle of prominent men he had picked to attend the conclave. "And since there is no way I can tell you of the ideas which I hope to see thoroughly discussed there, without writing volumes, you will have to take for granted that I would not ask such busy men to give up two whole days in this way unless I thought it would be worthwhile."

When all his guests took their seats, Welch made his entrance toting a thick stack of note cards. Tall, with thinning gray hair and pursed lips, Welch looked a bit like Mr. Magoo. He shook hands with the men and, knowing there was much ground to cover, took his place rigidly behind a podium that he had borrowed from a nearby church.

"Before tomorrow is over," Welch said, "I hope to have all of you feeling that you are taking part, here and now, in the beginning of a movement of historical importance." Speaking for hours on end in his customary monotone, interrupted only by small breaks for food, Welch outlined the dizzying breadth of the communist conspiracy, reaching back to the Roman and Greek empires— civilizations that "did perish of the cancer of collectivism"—to illustrate the tragic fate that could be awaiting the West.

"This octopus is so large," Welch said, "that its tentacles now reach into all of the legislative halls, all of the union labor meetings, a majority of the religious gatherings, and most of the schools of the whole world. It has a central nervous system which can make its tentacles in the labor unions of Bolivia, in the farmers' co-operatives of Saskatchewan, in the caucuses of the Social Democrats of West Germany, and in the class rooms of Yale Law School, all retract or reach forward simultaneously. It can make all of these creeping tentacles turn either right or left, or a given percentage turn right while the others turn left, at the same time, in accordance with the intentions of a central brain in Moscow or Ust-Kamenogorsk. The human race has never before faced any such monster of power which was determined to enslave it."

To others, this might have sounded like pure lunacy. But Fred knew better. Of the men who had assembled in Indianapolis, he perhaps had the most direct experience with communism. He had seen the beast up close.

The communists had either executed or banished to Siberia many of the Soviet engineers Fred worked with in the early 1930s. Even the loyal Bolshevik Jerome Livschitz had faced a firing squad in 1936 for allegedly plotting with Stalin's nemesis, Leon Trotsky.

Fred suspected Stalin's assassins had struck even closer to home. In 1930, Winkler-Koch trained a Russian engineer by the name of Hachatouroff, who while en route back to the Soviet Union, received word that his life was in danger. He returned to Wichita, where Fred gave him a job. But a few months later, Hachatouroff was found dead after falling from a hotel window. The authorities ruled his death a suicide. When Charles was old enough to hear the gruesome tale, Fred told him about Hachatouroff and about the brutality of the Soviet regime, where a man's life was not his own and where almost any transgression was punishable with death. Fred said that he didn't buy the official explanation of the Russian engineer's demise. He believed the KGB had murdered him. "He was always convinced that they pushed him out," Charles remembered.

Only as dusk fell on that first day in Indianapolis did Welch unveil his vision. Defeating this many-tentacled monster, Welch

explained, required its own multipronged approach: the establishment of Christian Science–like reading rooms and bookstores, to
educate people on "the true history of events and developments
of the past two decades"; the organizing of front groups ("little
fronts, big fronts, temporary fronts, permanent fronts, all kinds
of fronts"); and support for conservative news outlets—Welch's
American Opinion, but also William F. Buckley's *National
Review* (then a mere three years old), the *Dan Smoot Report*, and
Human Events.

Additionally, Welch's movement would make prodigious use of
the "letter-writing weapon," causing a "continuous overwhelming
flood" of correspondence to descend on everyone from Washington lawmakers and executive agency heads to newspaper editors,
TV sponsors, and educators. Welch intended to place their weight
onto "the political scales in this country as fast and as far" as
possible.

It wasn't until the following day that Welch gave a name to
his movement: the John Birch Society. For those unfamiliar with
Birch, Welch handed out packets containing copies of the 1954
biography he had written of the young Baptist preacher and Army
captain, who was shot dead by Chinese communists in August
1945, a week-and-a-half after V-J Day. Welch considered Birch the
first martyr of the Cold War. "It is my fervent hope that the John
Birch Society will last for hundreds of years and exert an increasing influence for the temporal good and spiritual ennoblement of
mankind throughout those centuries," Welch told the men seated
in front of him.

Over the course of the two-day retreat, Welch succeeded in stirring the patriotic instincts of his guests, who had needed little convincing that the nation was on a destructive path. Before Welch
even concluded his presentation, Hussman Refrigerator Company's W. B. McMillan scratched out a check for $1,000: "Here,
Bob, we're in business." Fred Koch enthusiastically signed on, too,

later joining the John Birch Society's National Council, along with most of the other attendees.

After Indianapolis, Fred threw himself more vigorously than ever into the fight against communism. He besieged lawmakers with letters demanding they address the peril facing the nation, writing to one congressman that "inaction means in a very few years Red Chinese and Red Russian soldiers will be marching in our streets. In that event the dead will be the lucky ones." And in 1960, Fred self-published a short tract called *A Business Man Looks at Communism*, which warned of an impending communist takeover. The pamphlet was an outgrowth of a talk on communism he'd given to Wichita Rotarians, and which he was subsequently asked to reprise on local radio station KFH. So many listeners called in asking for copies that Fred decided to expand on his remarks in a 39-page booklet.

He produced a forceful, though deeply paranoid polemic intended to jar Americans from their apathy: "It is not the Communists who are destroying America," he wrote. "America is being destroyed by citizens who will not listen, are not informed, and will not think."

One likely path to a communist coup, he wrote, was the "infiltration of high offices of government and political parties until the President of the U.S. is a Communist.... Even the Vice Presidency would do, as it could be easily arranged for the President to commit suicide."

Fred saw the specter of communism lurking behind everything from American foreign aid ("the U.S.A. is following Stalin's spending prescription") to tax-free nonprofits ("using the astronomical sums of money in their control to bring on socialism"), and from college campuses ("one of the breeding grounds of recruits for the Communist Party") to churches ("ministers don't become Communists but Communists become ministers").

Even modernist painters were part of the conspiracy: "The idea is to make our civilization seem degraded, ugly, and hopeless." According to Bill Koch, Fred found Pablo Picasso particularly loathsome. "My father hated Picasso because he was a communist."

The American civil rights movement also figured into the plot. "The colored man looms large in the Communist plan to take over America," Fred wrote, noting that he'd been told that the Communist Party had influenced the welfare laws in major American cities "to make it attractive for rural Southern Negroes and Puerto Ricans to come to those cities." Later, when the communists wanted to seize control of urban centers, they "will use the colored people by getting a vicious race war started."

Fred reserved special scorn for labor unions, which endeavored to "have the worker do as little as possible for the money he receives," he wrote. "This practice alone can destroy our country." And he alleged that the "Communist-infiltrated union" whose members controlled the wire traffic in and out of the Pentagon had "probably" handed over America's secrets to the communists.

Fred initially printed 12,500 copies of his pamphlet, which he distributed to every weekly newspaper in the country, along with other interested parties. Demand was so great that by late 1961, it had entered its ninth printing. At least 2.6 million copies of *A Business Man Looks at Communism* would ultimately go into circulation.

Readers of Fred's anticommunist call to arms included FBI agents, who received numerous inquiries about the Wichita businessman. Worried Americans deluged FBI director J. Edgar Hoover with letters asking if Fred's claims about the depth of the communist infiltration were valid—and in some cases wondering if his pamphlet was part of a subversive plot of its own.

"Would you consider Fred Koch...a security risk?" asked one letter writer. "...I am astonished and appalled at the contents of this Publication."

Along with his pamphlet, Fred gave frequent speeches across the Midwest on the subject of communism. In 1960, he was the commencement speaker at Wichita State University, where he warned that the "tentacles" of socialism had crept "further and further" into the body politic, creating a national craving for government handouts that he likened to morphine addiction.

The sad fact is that once people begin to get something for nothing then they want more and more at the same price. It destroys their independence, their self-reliance, and transforms them into dependent animal creatures without their knowing it. The end result is the human race as portrayed by Orwell—a human face ground into the earth by the large boot of benevolent Big Brother.

Fred knew that many people viewed him as a red-baiting crackpot. Speaking out was uncharacteristic of him. He was a private man, who revealed little about himself, his family, and his company. But given the stakes, he did not consider silence an option. The time had come to fight. "Maybe you don't want to be controversial by getting mixed up in this anti-communist battle," he told members of Kansas's Northeast Johnson County Women's Republican Club. "But you won't be very controversial lying in a ditch with a bullet in your brain."

Driving into Wichita from the west on Highway 54 during the 1960s, you could easily tell that you were entering Bircher country. IMPEACH EARL WARREN, the billboard on the edge of town implored. The Chief Justice of the Supreme Court was an early target of the Birch Society, which in addition to ads and billboards, launched petition drives seeking the judge's ouster. Birchers reviled Warren for presiding over 1954's *Brown v. Board of Education* ruling, which paved the way for school desegregation, inflaming the South and enraging conservatives who believed the high court had violated the Constitution. ("If many of the opinions of the Warren Supreme Court had been written in the Kremlin they could not have served the Communist better," Fred wrote in *A Business Man Looks at Communism*.)

Fred had taken on a high-profile role within the society, as one of its national leaders. Family friend and fellow Wichita businessman Bob Love, the youthful president of the Love Box Company, also got involved with the movement. The pair had teamed up in the past to promote political causes. Love, who was closer in age to Fred's sons, was a founder of Kansans for the Right to Work. Together he and Fred had led the successful effort to curb the power of unions in Kansas via a 1958 constitutional amendment. Now, the pair commanded Wichita's growing Birch Society contingent, whose ranks included many of the same business leaders involved in the right-to-work battle.

Fred's chapter met frequently in the basement trophy room of the Koch family's stone mansion. "The room looks practically medieval," recalled one visitor, a doctoral student doing his dissertation on the John Birch Society. "...Its walls are crowded with stuffed heads from the disappearing wildlife of Africa and North America." During one meeting, the Ph.D. student wrote, a "speaker said that if the Communists take over, they will point to this as the place where the Americanist conspirators met."

Charles joined the Birch Society in the early 1960s, and he held occasional political discussions of his own in the basement of his family's mansion, inviting over members of the local chapter of Young Americans for Freedom to wax philosophical about the nature of government and its role in pilfering liberties from the people. Charles seemed to steer clear of the more hysterical claims being made by his father and other society luminaries, preferring to talk about big picture ideas. "He didn't take the conspiracy stuff very seriously," one participant in these discussions remembered.

But the "conspiracy stuff" gathered steam in Wichita, a Birch Society stronghold thanks to the efforts of Fred Koch and Bob Love.

The city's schools and colleges became an early target of Wichita's Birchers, who critics accused of running stealth candidates for school board positions and employing McCarthyesque tactics in the classroom. A former Wichita high school debate teacher recalled that "the Birch Society was giving the superintendent of schools and Board of Education a lot of headaches with their complaints." One source of their ire was the UNICEF collection boxes children toted around during Halloween: "The Birch Society just went nuts over it." She drew their wrath when the topic of the United Nations came up in her classroom: "I got phone calls from parents just furious because of something some debater said about the United Nations—didn't I know that the United Nations was evil and trying to take over the world and destroy our independence?"

Meanwhile, Fred had even begun to harbor doubts about the patriotic commitment of his beloved alma mater, MIT. He had donated regularly to the school, and in 1955, he served a five-year term on its board of trustees, a period when Bill, Charles, and David attended college there. But he came to believe the communist infestation had taken root at MIT, as it had elsewhere in the country.

Fred considered the university's tolerance of a Dutch mathematician named Dirk Jan Struik particularly egregious. A member of MIT's faculty since 1926, Struik was an unapologetic Marxist, who had joined the Communist Party in his native Netherlands. In 1951, Struik was hauled before the House Committee on Un-American Activities, where he pleaded the Fifth. A couple months later, Massachusetts indicted Struik for conspiring to teach and advocate the violent overthrow of the government. MIT immediately suspended him pending the outcome of the case. "They used my textbook on differential geometry, but I myself was not allowed to teach it," he reflected years later. "...I've always said that that time was half Nazi Germany, half Alice in Wonderland."

There was scant evidence to support the traitorous acts Struik was accused of, and in 1956, the charges were dropped. MIT reinstated the professor, who resumed teaching at the school during Charles's senior year. The decision infuriated Fred. The man was an admitted communist, after all, and here he was once again in a position to mold young minds, maybe even his son's. The professor's retention, Fred griped to a fellow anticommunist, "meant... that there would be an MIT Alger Hiss some day for sure."

Fred complained bitterly about Struik and wrote to MIT administrators warning of the communist influence on the campus where his sons were spending their college years. When an MIT fund-raiser visited Fred in Wichita, the industrialist told him he was "down on Tech" because the administration had done little to take a stand against Struik or other communists in its ranks.

"Fred Koch used all of his influence and all of his wallet and everything else to try to get this guy off the faculty—and he failed," said John McManus, the current president of the John Birch Society. As a young Bircher in the mid-1960s, McManus recalled meeting Fred at a society function, where the businessman was still fuming about his inability to purge Struik from MIT.

By the early 1960s, the John Birch Society had some 60,000 members, 58 full-time employees, and annual revenues of $1.6 million. It was growing rapidly—and stirring up controversy across the nation. The *Saturday Evening Post* reported that its rabble-rousing members "are said to have infiltrated Republican organizations, disrupted school boards, harassed city councils and librarians and subverted PTA's near and far."

The society's fierce letter-writing and lobbying campaigns targeted issues ranging from U.S. participation in the United Nations

("Get U.S. Out!") to water fluoridation, which members claimed was a tool of communist dominion. (In Wichita, a Birch Society–led effort repealed by referendum a city fluoridation plan.)

Birchers also bitterly opposed the Civil Rights Act of 1964 on states' rights grounds, and believed that the civil rights movement itself was a communist creation to divide and conquer America. ("It always seemed to me that when the Communists...begin to light these racial fires all over the country as they are now doing, that it would be the beginning of a decisive move on their part," Fred wrote to a fellow Birch Society council member in 1963.)

The Birchers formed the vanguard of a far-right awakening in America, and the group's extreme rhetoric, charges of treason directed at the nation's politicians, and aggressive recruiting practices, frightened not just the political Left, but the Right as well.

Such torchbearers of conservatism as the *National Review*'s William F. Buckley eyed the movement warily, seeing in the Birch Society's rise the possible implosion of the conservative movement. Through the head-spinning conspiracies of Robert Welch—who had called President Dwight D. Eisenhower a "dedicated, conscious agent of the Communist conspiracy" and claimed Soviet censorship of Boris Pasternak's Nobel Prize–winning *Doctor Zhivago* was actually an elaborate ruse so that the subversive book would be embraced by the West—the Birch Society risked branding all conservatives as cranks and kooks.

At first, Buckley and his allies took care to distance themselves from Welch without offending their fellow conservatives, who were joining the Birch Society in droves. Barry Goldwater, the charismatic Republican senator from Arizona and 1964 presidential nominee, was particularly mindful of his base of support within the society, which was populated with many deep-pocketed businessmen. He feared alienating men like Fred Koch, who had generously supported his political career: Upon the 1960 publication of *The Conscience of a Conservative*, Fred promptly ordered 2,500 copies of the polemic that propelled Goldwater to political stardom and put them in the hands of every opinion maker in Kansas. In 1961, Goldwater managed to praise the society's members without endorsing the views of the group's controversial Svengali, telling reporters he was "impressed by the type of people" in the society. "They are the kind we need in politics."

But by early 1962, as the society gained strength and numbers, it grew clear to Buckley and his allies that more drastic action was needed. By embracing Goldwater, Birchers threatened his chances of broader Republican appeal. Buckley, Goldwater, and other conservative leading lights convened that January at Palm Beach's upscale Breakers Hotel, where they spent considerable time discussing the Birch Society problem. There, Buckley volunteered for the assignment of making Robert Welch into a pariah. That February he unleashed a 5,000-word haymaker in *National Review*, titled "The Question of Robert Welch," which slammed the Birch Society leader for harming the cause of anticommunism. "How can the John Birch Society be an effective political instrument while it is led by a man whose views on current affairs are, at so many critical points...so far removed from common sense?" Buckley wrote.

Senior members of the society had already begun to chafe under Welch's autocratic leadership. (Democracy, he famously said, was "a weapon of demagoguery and a perennial fraud.") Buckley's essay caused further unrest. But Fred remained one of Welch's defenders.

"I wrote Buckley and told him that possibly if the Communists ever took over he would be a prime candidate for the firing squad and that by attacking Welch he was hastening the day considerably," he reported to the conservative journalist Elizabeth Churchill Brown.

*   *   *

Fred's hard-line conservative politics were controversial not only to the broader public, but also within his extended family, causing what one relative called a "schism" between the Kochs and the family of Mary's younger brother, William Robinson, a prominent lawyer in Wichita. While Fred organized the Birch Society in the early- and mid-1960s, Robinson chaired the Democratic Central Committee of Sedgwick County (which includes Wichita). In 1964, the year Fred enthusiastically backed Goldwater's presidential bid, Robinson attended the Democratic National Convention in Atlantic City as a delegate.

Robinson ran twice, unsuccessfully, for Congress, making a bid for the 4th district congressional seat in 1960 and challenging Bob Dole in the 1968 Senate race. "That was the death of the relationship between the Robinsons and the Kochs," the relative said. Bill Koch, however, remained close to his uncle and aunt, especially in adulthood. "They were like surrogate parents. They were the loving parents that he always wanted." Bill's uncle was fiercely loyal to his nephew. "Billy is a very compassionate guy, unlike the rest of his family," Robinson sniped in 1992.

Fred's conservatism influenced his children in different ways. Bill, for his part, never fully embraced the extreme politics of his father. He even considered following in the footsteps of his uncle, contemplating a Senate bid in Kansas as a Democrat in the late 1990s—an indignity that Fred, who had passed on by this point, was mercifully spared. Nor was the old man alive to see Bill augment his art collection with paintings by modern artists (including Picasso) who he considered communists.

David inherited his conservative views on government from Fred, but he has implied that some of his father's more conspiratorial beliefs about communism were out there. "Father was paranoid about communism, let's put it that way," David told *New York* magazine. Frederick—save for a 1980s run-in with the British bureaucracy over his plans to renovate a historic mansion in London—steered clear of politics entirely.

Of the four brothers, Charles most heartily imbibed their father's hard-line political views; part of this likely owed to his arrival back in Wichita in the early 1960s, after attending college and grad school in Boston, during the height of Fred's John Birch Society organizing. One Wichitan recalled going on a blind date with Charles in the early 1960s, where he spent much of the evening discoursing on the evils of communism and discussing *Communism on the Map*—one of a series of propagandistic films screened at Birch Society chapter meetings, in which the nations of the world are shown slowly being covered by an ooze of pink or red. His date was not impressed. "I ended up leaving early and walking home," she remembered.

Like his father, Charles occasionally speechified about the dangers of collectivism and the encroaching welfare state. "The U.S. government is trying to win votes—not to satisfy consumers," he told an audience of college students in 1965. "In this form of collectivism, the society controls everything that should be controlled by individuals."

With Koch family friend Bob Love, Charles opened a John Birch Society bookstore on Wichita's East 13th Street, down the road from his family's compound. He curated a section there on Austrian economics (a school of thought that heavily influenced libertarianism) and enjoyed introducing customers to the works of economists including Ludwig von Mises and Friedrich Hayek.

A family acquaintance recalled visiting the Koch family's home one day in the 1960s, carrying a dog-eared copy of Ernest Hemingway's *The Sun Also Rises*, the assigned reading in a college literature class. When Charles answered the door, his eyes lingered on the book's cover. After an uncomfortable pause, he finally asked the visitor to leave the Hemingway book outside, since it could not enter the house.

"Is there a problem?" the puzzled visitor asked. It wasn't like he was carrying a copy of *Tropic of Cancer*.

"Well," Charles explained, "he was a communist."

The guest entered. Hemingway remained on the stoop.

Communism may have been sweeping the world, but there was at least one threshold where, by God, it would not cross.

CHAPTER FOUR

May Day at MIT

On May 1, 1961, two weeks after the Bay of Pigs invasion, a fraternity brother at MIT's Beta Theta Pi house dug an old ROTC uniform out of his closet and fashioned an effigy of Fidel Castro. He impaled it with a bayonet, then hoisted the effigy up the flagpole at 119 Bay State Road in Boston's Kenmore Square. Large speakers were placed on the fire escape of the four-story, red-brick row house, across Storrow Drive from the Charles River, and one of the Betas barked into a microphone leading the Koch twins and their fraternity brothers in chants of "Yankee Sí, Castro No!"—their anticommunist twist on the rallying cry of the Cuban revolution.

With their fellow Betas, David and Bill, now college juniors and two days short of their twenty-first birthday, had cooked up a little counterrevolution of their own—a display of anticommunist fervor that would have made Fred Koch proud. With finals approaching, it seemed like as good an excuse as any to get loaded on keg beer and blow off some steam. Making the rounds on MIT's Cambridge campus, Bill, one classmate recalled, advertised the protest on the blackboards of his engineering classes: "Anti-Castro Rally: Free Beer at the Beta House."

Fraternities and student dormitories lined Bay State Road, and as night fell, a small but rowdy crowd of about fifty formed outside the Kochs' fraternity house. Soon, the sound of sirens was in the air and three paddy wagons screeched to a stop. But instead of subduing the crowd, the arrival of the cops attracted a new wave of onlookers. Diagonally across the street from the Beta house sat a large dormitory that housed Boston University coeds. The Betas knew it well. The mathematically minded fraternity brothers had developed a grid system for spying on the B.U. girls. On many an evening a Beta would suddenly call out a coordinate—say, 6-D— and the brothers would then scramble to train a set of Navy-issue binoculars on the sixth floor, fourth window from the right, where a coed had forgotten to draw the shades before disrobing.

The Boston University students had mostly watched the Betas' rally from their windows. But when the police arrived, they poured out of the dorm "like ants out of an ant hill," recalled Kent Groninger, a member of the fraternity. The four blocks surrounding the Beta house suddenly swarmed with hundreds of rowdy, chanting college students. During the melee, Groninger and another tipsy Beta hauled a bale of hay a half-block to the corner of Deerfield Street, then lit it on fire. "The Boston Fire Department responded—big time," chuckled Groninger. "They brought a number of trucks, the hook and ladder, the whole damn thing." The police struggled to restore order, all the while being pelted with bottles and cherry bombs. "Holy shit," Groninger said, recalling the events of fifty years ago, "it turned into a riot."

The Boston Police arrested more than thirty students, including a handful of Betas, and spent nearly two hours dispersing the crowd. No sooner had the students dissipated than a new anti-Castro protest erupted on the MIT campus across the river. A mob of two hundred students then marched up Massachusetts Avenue bound for Harvard Yard, where "the Engineers prostrated themselves before the statue of John Harvard," *The Harvard Crimson* reported. The next morning, the front page of *The Boston Globe* blared: "MIT, B.U. Riot Follows Hanging of Castro Effigy." News of the anticommunist student uprising even reached the Soviet Union, published in the Russian newspaper *Pravda*.

The incident prompted a halfhearted MIT investigation. Later, the Beta brothers proudly took credit for the melee in the school's yearbook—and singled out the Koch twins for inciting it. "The Betas enjoyed a very successful year," the fraternity reported. "But our activities were far from being on the limited side of life. Led by the brothers Koch, we staged Mayday 1961, as an expression of our conservative and anti-communist sentiments (much to the dismay of the I.F.C. [Interfraternity Conference] and Fidel Castro, who hung in effigy)."

"Great friends, wild parties, athletic triumphs, academic successes, and actually learning something useful"—that's how David later summed up his college experience in an MIT alumni questionnaire. Bill joked that his most vivid college memories were "not fit for publication."

Like Charles, who graduated with an engineering degree in 1957, a year before his younger brothers enrolled at MIT, David and Bill pledged Beta Theta Pi and took up residence in the fraternity house.

"Dave was always up for a party," recalled Groninger, who was one year behind the Koch twins. Partying was largely confined to Saturday nights, when the Betas invited dates over and dressed in coats and ties for a formal dinner. Afterward, the beer and hard liquor flowed, while Johnny Mathis and other crooners echoed through the fraternity house's spacious library. "Guys would get a little loaded, a little lewd," Groninger said, hastening to point out that their partying was mild by modern standards.

During these occasions the differences between the Koch twins seemed the most pronounced. David was gregarious, popular with women, and liked to be the center of attention; he showboated for his dates on the dance floor. Bill was more reserved. During Beta parties, he was more likely to be found off in a quiet corner deep in conversation. "Billy has a little warmer self. He's not as egotistical as Dave. A little softer of a guy, humble," said Groninger, whose pledge father was Bill.

At times, it was hard to believe they were related, let alone twins. Beyond their lean and lanky frames, the brothers really didn't look too much alike. Bill had white-blond hair and a pale complexion, while his brother had darker features. Neither of the brothers gave any indication that they hailed from great wealth. ("Billy was kind of a goofus. He was not sophisticated," said someone who knew him during his MIT years.) "They never flaunted it, they never spent a lot of money, and they never dressed differently than anybody else," remembered Tom Burns, an MIT friend.

The only real giveaway that they came from money was the fact that David owned a car (unlike most of his other classmates), a red Sunbeam Alpine convertible that he parked behind the Beta house.

The heated rivalry between the brothers had cooled considerably by the time they arrived at MIT. Boarding school, and with it some years apart from David, had mellowed Bill. At Culver Military Academy, Bill wasn't locked in constant competition with his more athletic and outgoing twin. This allowed him to cultivate his own persona and focus on what he was good at: academics. "He was very ambitious as far as his studies," said his Culver classmate Robert Lindgren. "He was industrious, didn't play much—all work." He added, "He wasn't much of a ladies' man, and he didn't pretend to be."

Classmates remember Bill as a quiet, shy, and analytical teenager, who ran cross-country and boxed, but who had little interest in the military-style order of Culver. "We used to consider ourselves, Bill and I, kind of renegades," said Bruce Lassman, a Culver friend. "We didn't do anything to be outcasts. Here's a school where if you excelled you were a lieutenant or captain, but both Bill and I were corporals." (Bill still ranked above his rebellious brother Charles, who graduated Culver as a private.)

"He pretty much went his own way. He knew what he wanted and did it," said Bertram Beach Culver III, another classmate and a member of the family who founded the school. "He was not unpopular but kind of set the terms on things like friendships. He decided if he wanted to be around you."

At Culver, Bill began to accept the ways he differed from his brother, if not fully embrace them. But at MIT, they were once again thrown back together, living in the same house, attending the same classes, sharing the same group of friends. When old animosities flared, it was typically on the basketball court. The brothers' towering size—both of them were verging on six feet five—made them ideal recruits, and they joined MIT's junior varsity team as freshmen.

"Bill was always trying to keep up with Dave. He always felt inferior and always felt that Dave got the best of things," recalled Bill Bloebaum, an MIT friend and teammate of the brothers. "If they bumped into each other at practice, Bill would quickly get verbal on it, but it wouldn't bother Dave that much. Bill was the more emotional guy. He wore his emotions on his shoulder."

A top rebounder with a deadly jump shot, David quickly emerged as the team's star player, and one of the finer athletes ever to pass through the university. (He even set the freshman pole-vaulting record.) Bill was a second-stringer, who occasionally subbed for his brother and was better known for his on-court tussles than his basketball prowess.

MIT's basketball team had a dismal track record—a 3 and 13 season was an average performance. They were called, after all, the Engineers, as if to highlight the fact that their skill lay off the court. During the 1959–1960 season, Jack Barry, MIT's varsity basketball coach, inherited a team composed largely of sophomores, including David and Bill. Recognizing their inexperience, he drilled the players on a single formation. "He always said that our team was not good enough to have more than one play, so we ran that one play all the time," said Burns, who played the high post (David played the low post) in this formation.

Both David and Bill remember their charismatic coach fondly. "He organized the team to compensate for everybody's weaknesses," Bill recalled. "One guy couldn't dribble, so he said, 'You just stand here.' Another guy could shoot from the outside but not the inside, so he said, 'O.K., your job is shooting over here.'... He emphasized complete teamwork and instilled in us the attitude that we MIT nerds could win." (David later donated $2 million to endow the head coach position at MIT.)

In December 1959, during Bill and David's sophomore year, the Engineers piled onto the team bus for the hour-and-a-half trip to Hartford, Connecticut, to face off against Trinity College, where they were handed their first double-digit loss of the season. The next game—a highly anticipated matchup with their Cambridge rivals, Harvard—was a 50-point blowout so humiliating that the Crimson's contrite coach apologized to Barry after the game. Just before Christmas break, though, things began to look up. The Engineers eked out a 1-point victory over Worcester Polytechnic Institute, when David drained the deciding basket. The team was riding high off that victory when they faced Springfield in early January. By the second half, David had scored 23 points.

Then disaster struck.

With minutes on the clock, he aggravated an old knee injury that sidelined him for the rest of the season. He watched from the bench as the team embarked on a dispiriting losing streak that netted the Engineers a 2 and 20 record.

"We were basically a disaster," said Mead Wyman, a teammate and Beta brother, who remains close with David. "It was a long season."

Things turned around the following year, when David returned to the court. Averaging 24 points a game, he ranked among the top 30 scorers nationwide and won a spot on the All New England team. "His moves were just so good," Wyman recalled. At the conclusion of the Engineers' impressive 11 and 8 season, MIT's newspaper reported: "The backbone of the team on the floor was Dave Koch."

Bill dropped off the team their senior year, while David was elected its captain, a role he had been passed over for as a junior. ("It was an attitude thing," one of his teammates said. "He was more focused on himself junior year.") David described his squad that year as "hustling, fighting, aggressive," and he predicted at the start of the season that the 1962 team would be MIT's best ever.

It was. The Engineers went on a 15-game winning streak to end the season, boasting a 17 and 4 record. David set a longstanding MIT record of his own that season, scoring 41 points during one game against Middlebury College. His record remained intact for 46 years, until it was surpassed by MIT's Jimmy Bartolotta, who went on to play pro basketball in Europe.

On the final game of the 1962 season, against the University of Chicago, David walked off the court to a standing ovation. But the record-breaking season still ended in disappointment. The players and their coach believed the team was a shoo-in for the NCAA tournament. New Hampshire's Saint Anselm College was selected instead.

The season was filled with highs and lows, but one of the most memorable moments occurred earlier that year at a home game in MIT's Rockwell Cage. The tall, beefy player guarding David had pushed him around for most of the game. The referees seemed oblivious, which made the opposing player that much more brazen in his manhandling of the Engineers' star player. At one point, dispensing with any pretense of finesse, he roughly shoved David to the ground. Moments later, a lanky form suddenly leapt from the stands and charged David's startled opponent, leveling the big player with a single blow.

"Bill went out and knocked the guy flat," remembered Bill Bloebaum.

Tom Burns recalled: "Bill was not going to let anybody push David around like that." He added, "I think everybody was thinking, 'well, that's Bill. You can't stop him once he gets going.'"

The Engineers received a technical foul, and Bill was promptly ejected from the Rockwell Cage.

Charles remained in Boston after completing his bachelor's degree in 1957. He occasionally dropped by the Beta house to look in on his brothers and watched their basketball games from the bleachers. David and Bill attended parties at Charles's apartment, and the three brothers sometimes dated together. They were closer than ever.

Like the twins, Charles thrived at MIT, where the environment was a welcome change from the highly regimented gulag of military school. "We didn't even have to attend class—all we had to do was do the work. I felt liberated," Charles has said.

Similar to his younger brothers, he displayed no pretensions of privilege. "You had no idea of the wealth he represented," said Ellis Braman, a fraternity brother. "He was a great guy, very personable, very friendly. He charmed the girls. He was a good looking fellow—tall, blonde."

The challenging engineering classes at MIT came easily to Charles, and on the nights before big exams, when his friends crammed, he'd often repair to a local beer and pizza joint and kick back. "Just smart as a whip," Braman said.

Outside of academics, Charles's primary passion was rugby. His legendary competitive streak truly flared on the rugby pitch, though he even played games of flag football with an unusual level of intensity. "It was like he was playing the Super Bowl," recalled an MIT graduate who refereed games Charles played in.

He attended graduate school at MIT directly after college, and completed a master's degree in nuclear engineering in 1958. Charles had contemplated making a career in this fledgling industry, but he soon thought better of it. The federal government tightly regulated the nuclear sector. Working in the industry, he would be at the perpetual mercy of Washington bureaucrats. His budding libertarian sensibilities were repulsed by the notion. So he took a second master's, this one in chemical engineering. By 1959, Charles was working as an engineer for the Boston-based consulting firm Arthur D. Little. He enjoyed living in Boston, and moreover, he loved his job. In Wichita he was Fred Koch's son, but in New England, Charles had found a way to step out of his father's shadow.

A year went by, then two. Back home in Wichita, Fred Koch grew restless. He wanted Charles home. He was in poor health. His blood pressure was sky high and he had a family history of heart problems. His mother had died of congestive heart failure. A heart attack had also claimed his older brother in the 1950s, after which Fred helped to pay the private school tuitions of his nieces and nephews and gave them a small bloc of stock in his company.

Fred had grown forgetful and gone was the great vigor and drive of his younger years. In a letter to his friend Robert Welch, intended to nudge the aging John Birch Society leader to consider stepping aside for the good of the movement, Fred confided that while he had always intended to "remain in business until I died," his failing memory and waning energy had forced him to reconsider. "Regretfully, I came to the conclusion that the time had come for me to gradually withdraw from business and to turn it over to someone else," Fred wrote. "I suppose what this all means is a gradual hardening of the arteries and a reduced supply of blood to the brain so the gray matter just doesn't function like it should."

There was never much doubt about Fred's choice of successor. His artistic eldest son had no interest in the engineering field, or the family business. "MIT is not for you, Frederick. I think Harvard is for you," Frederick recalled his father counseling him. Ever since his arrival in Cambridge in the early 1950s, he pursued a very different life and very different interests than his three younger brothers.

At Harvard, Frederick studied English literature and acted in theater productions. His fondest memories are of singing in the Glee Club. The Boston Symphony Orchestra's conductor, Charles Munch, enlisted the Glee Club to perform as the chorus in a series of concerts featuring the symphonies of Berlioz. RCA Victor recorded the performances, enabling Frederick to proudly play an LP for his parents in which he sang in *Romeo and Juliet* and the *Damnation of Faust*. "I had a wonderful time there," Frederick said of his Harvard years.

The eldest Koch brother left the faintest of impressions on his dorm mates in Harvard's Adams House. They remember him as a thin, pale boy and recall that he was unfailingly polite and arrived at school with an enormous collection of opera LPs. Based on Fredericks's affect, they guessed at his sexuality.

After graduation, Frederick attended Harvard Law School for a year, before abandoning the program to enlist in the U.S. Naval Reserve in the fall of 1956. His first duty station was in Millington, Tennessee. The young petty officer, first class, was attached to a technical training unit, then transferred to a logistical command, where he oversaw officer personnel records. This was "far more interesting work than what was required of me" in his prior post, he reported to Harvard classmates in an alumni update. In 1958, before his discharge from the Navy, Frederick served aboard the USS *Saratoga* in the Atlantic fleet.

After returning to civilian life, Frederick attended the Yale School of Drama, majoring in playwriting. For his master's thesis, he collaborated with Clark Gesner (later known for composing *You're a Good Man, Charlie Brown*) on a musical theater adaptation of the 1941 book *No Bed for Bacon*. Set in the Elizabethan era, the comedic book was later cited for inspiring some of the plotlines in the Academy Award–winning film *Shakespeare in Love*.

Frederick, in these years, explored the gay lifestyle, at least from an academic perspective. In the late 1950s, he became a follower of the ONE Institute of Homophile Studies, an organization for gays and lesbians founded in 1956, and a subscriber to its quarterly journal. In a July 1959 letter to the organization, requesting a copy of a book it had published called *Homosexuals Today*, he also inquired whether the institute was "familiar with a booklet or pamphlet listing, by name and address, the gay bars and restaurants in various European cities?...If you are aware of the title and editorial address of this publication, I should appreciate receiving this information."

A fellow Yale classmate, Bob Murray, remembered Frederick for his "prim campus haberdashery," which usually included a coat and tie, and for the fact that he often kept to himself and was occasionally ridiculed because of his priggish appearance. "His mark," Murray said, "seemed limited to his...aloofness, his marginal presence, his formal dress, his 'aloneness.'" Frederick appeared to have few friends, nor much of a social life.

Murray recalled his surprise when, before Christmas recess in 1960 or 1961, Frederick threw a large party at his off-campus apartment, located across the street from New Haven's Shubert Theater. When Murray and his wife arrived, students spilled into the hallway and down a stairway leading to the apartment. A refrigerator stocked with champagne was ajar and partygoers were handing bottle after bottle into the crowd.

"The host was not seen in the crowd and the crowd was simply helping itself, some stuffing several bottles into their coat pockets and leaving the premises for a private party of their own," Murray said. Murray and his wife finally located Frederick "in a far corner of his dark living room looking, we decided later, lost and baffled by being caught in a riot. We left after having acknowledged the host, feeling even more sorry than before for 'the poor little rich boy.'"

Frederick moved from New Haven to New York City after completing his master's program in 1961. He taught script writing for a semester at New York's New School and apprenticed with theater producer Charles Hollerith Jr., but he mostly lived off a trust fund Fred Koch had established for his son the year Frederick graduated from Yale. "The arrangement," Frederick recalled, "was that I would receive dividends on a quarterly basis and this would continue until the age of 45," when he could access the principal. The Koch patriarch structured it in this way because he feared Frederick, left to his own devices, would blow through his trust fund on ill-advised theater productions. "My father was quite concerned about my having chosen a very risky profession," Frederick said. "And he was particularly concerned about the temptation I might have to invest my own capital in plays that I would produce. And he wanted...me to have some assurance that I would have an income quite apart from the theater."

Mary Koch lamented in a 1986 interview that her eldest son had an "inferiority complex" that prevented him from achieving more with his life. "Freddie never composed anything himself and his father was upset that he never earned a living. Fred felt Freddie just indulged his pleasures in art, music, and literature when he could have created something."

Even though his immediate family lacked confidence in his ability to make a living in the arts, Frederick was popular among his parents' circle of friends, with whom he seemed more at ease than his contemporaries. On periodic visits home to Wichita for holidays or other special occasions, he often joined his mother on the weekly cocktail party circuit. (Fred was rarely if ever seen at these confabs.) "Freddie used to love to go to those cocktail parties and gatherings," remembered one fellow partygoer. "He was very good at conversation and always interested in what other people were doing." He added: "Other people outside the family from Wichita were very impressed with Freddie, by the things that he'd done and the good causes he'd supported. In Wichita, Freddie was the most liked of all the four brothers, in the sense that he often went to those cocktail parties. He socialized more with our parents' generation."

Charles resisted his father's first few attempts to lure him home to Wichita. Finally, Fred gave his son an ultimatum: "He told me either you come back here and take over the company or I'm going to sell it," Charles recalled. So Charles dutifully returned home in late 1961 to begin learning the ropes of his father's company.

Fred had always seen great leadership potential in Charles. Even so, when Charles went to work for the family company, Fred didn't want to build up his twenty-six-year-old son's confidence too much. "I hope your first deal is a loser," he told him, "otherwise you will think you're a lot smarter than you are."

Fred put Charles to work as the vice president of Koch Engineering, the company he had spun off when Winkler-Koch disbanded in the 1940s. The company, which composed only a small part of Fred's business empire, was just scraping by. Most of its customers were overseas, and the fact that the company had no international manufacturing presence was part of the problem. One of Charles's early assignments entailed surveying possible locations in Europe to site a manufacturing plant for the production of Koch FLEXI-TRAYs, used for separating (or "fractionating") oil. After scouring Europe, the young executive settled on a site in Bergamo, Italy. Fred was convinced that this was the money-losing deal he had warned his son about. "I have tried to discourage him," he told a friend in a letter, "but he won't listen to papa." Fred's aversion to Italy stemmed from his experience there in 1958, during national elections, when he witnessed "how strong the Communists were."

"Personally," he confided to the friend, "I think we are going to pour the money down the drain, but it's his baby so I am going to let him go ahead."

It turned out to be the first in a series of astute business moves by Charles, who, by 1965, had doubled Koch Engineering's sales. Fred named Charles president of Koch Engineering in 1963 and made him a vice president of his main company, Rock Island Oil and Refining. Working closely with Fred's right-hand man, Sterling Varner, an Oklahoma native who seemed to have a countrified expression for every occasion, Charles moved aggressively to expand the firm's crude oil gathering business. They acquired pipelines and small trucking companies—undervalued and unwanted assets that Varner lovingly referred to as "the junk."

Varner worked for L. B. Simmons when Fred bought his uncle's Rock Island Oil pipeline and refinery assets in the 1940s. Varner came along as part of the deal. The son of an Oklahoma oil field worker, he had started out as a crude oil purchasing clerk, rising steadily through the ranks to become an indispensable executive. It was quite a reversal from Varner's early days with Fred's company, when he made $2,400 a year and had some reason to believe he was expendable. One summer early in Varner's tenure, Fred asked him to oversee the drilling of water wells at Beaverhead Ranch. Summer came and went without the industrialist issuing Varner a new assignment, so finally, as Thanksgiving neared, he called his boss.

"Who?" Fred asked, when Varner announced who was calling. Fred had forgotten about him, though he would eventually recognize great promise in Varner and take him under his wing. It wasn't just Varner's knack for sussing out good deals, but his ability to connect with people. He was the kind of guy who put a hand on your shoulder when he reached out to shake your hand. He could relate just as easily to an oil field roughneck as he could to a Wichita banker. He did both with a colloquial charm, peppering his speech with oil patch bon mots that fellow executives fondly referred to as "Sterlingisms."

By the time Charles arrived on the scene, Varner, sixteen years his senior, knew every nook and cranny of Fred's business empire. He became the young businessman's tutor as Charles learned the ropes and, in later years, his most trusted advisor. Varner was the perfect foil for Charles, who like so many ambitious young men tended to overlook the human details. Charles's mathematical mind adapted easily to the big picture and the bottom line, but he could be woefully inept at dealing with people. Varner, who did not come from a world of quarterly reviews and profit plans, understood there was more to success than merely business acumen. Charm was a crucial ingredient, and Varner had it in surplus. "He really taught me a lot about the importance of people... and being people-oriented," Charles would later say. With Charles serving as the company's brain and Varner as its soul, the pair became a formidable management team—and occasional partners in crime.

While Charles pushed for expansion, his father focused on conserving capital to pay his estate taxes. In one case, when Charles sought his father's sign off to buy two North Dakota trucking companies, Fred approved the purchase of just one of them. When Fred left on a trip, Charles and Varner went ahead and bought both companies anyway. "When I informed him of this," Charles recalled, "my father was initially furious, but eventually forgave us since both acquisitions ended up being highly profitable." In 1966, Fred named Charles president of Rock Island Oil and Refining "so that, as he put it, if something happened to him, I would be in charge."

During the mid-1960s, Fred had been in and out of the hospital with heart trouble. He suffered a major heart attack in mid-1967 that left him hospitalized for two months. Not long after he was released, the industrialist cajoled his doctor for clearance to go hunting, which the physician finally granted.

That November, Fred accompanied his close friend R. C. "Mac" McCormick, owner of Wichita's Broadview Hotel, on a hunting excursion to Utah. On November 17, Fred was in a duck blind near the Bear River, accompanied by a gun loader. He hadn't shot well all day. When a solitary duck flew overhead, Fred tracked the bird with the muzzle of his shotgun. He aimed, then squeezed the trigger. The bird stopped in mid-flight and fell from the sky.

"Boy, that was a magnificent shot," the industrialist managed to say. Then he collapsed.

CHAPTER FIVE

Successor

"His death threw responsibility for his interests on one of his four sons, Charles," read Fred's obituary, two days later, in *The Wichita Eagle*. The claim was accurate, but it understated the reality. In an instant, Charles had hurtled from his father's protégé to his successor. Now Charles, who had just turned thirty-two, ruled the empire. He was petrified.

Fred had effectively turned the company over to his son a year earlier, but had remained close at hand to provide advice and instruction, even if Charles ignored it. He had been his son's backstop and sounding board. Now Charles alone held the family's future in his hands.

The Monday after Fred's death was clear and temperate. Shortly before 2:30 p.m. mourners gathered in the chapel of the sterile-looking Downing & Lahey Mortuary, a short drive from the Koch family's home. Friends, family, and business associates packed the pews. Some of Fred's John Birch Society pals, including Clarence Manion, onetime dean of Notre Dame's law school and a popular right-wing radio host, traveled from out of town to pay their respects.

"A man of modesty, he was never impressed with flattery," eulogized Pastor Rang Morgan, of Wichita's Sharon Baptist Church, at the service. "He used to say to me, 'Rang, flattery is much like perfume. It's o.k. to inhale it; but don't ever swallow it.'"

The pastor referred briefly to Fred's crusade against communism, saying, "I'm sure that Fred Koch had enemies for no man makes such a stand for that which is right as he did, without making enemies along the way.

"One had only to be associated with this man for a short while to know how he felt about his business," he went on. "He felt that there were no short cuts to success; and that no business could be successful unless there was a total loyalty from all associated with it."

After their father's funeral, Bill, Charles, and David boarded a small plane, flew up above the Flint Hills, and scattered their father's ashes above the rolling acreage of his beloved Spring Creek Ranch.

Later, while setting his father's affairs in order, Charles unearthed a letter Fred had written on a cold January day in 1936, two months after Charles's birth and when Frederick was three. He told his sons that they would one day inherit a "large sum" of money and he imparted his wisdom regarding their inheritance:

It may be either a blessing or a curse. You can use it as a valuable tool for accomplishment or you can squander it foolishly.

If you choose to let this money destroy your initiative and independence then it will be a curse to you and my action in giving it to you will have been a mistake. I should regret very much to have you miss the glorious feeling of accomplishment and I know you are not going to let me down.

Remember that often adversity is a blessing in disguise and is certainly the greatest character builder. Be kind and generous to one another and be good to your mother.

Despite his words about being "kind and generous to one another," the terms of the businessman's will planted the seeds of resentment. Almost a year to the day before he died, Fred had scrawled his signature on an updated version that excluded Frederick from the same inheritance as his three younger brothers. Fred didn't leave his eldest son a pauper; he had created two trust funds for him, one in 1961 and the other in 1966. But Fred was determined that he receive nothing more.

Their father removed Frederick from his will, according to Charles, because he had repeatedly stolen from him in the years before his death "and then lied about it when confronted with the evidence." Frederick lifted traveler's checks, cash, and an "air travel card" from their dad, Charles said; in one case, he alleged, his older brother forged his signature on their father's Brooks Brothers charge account.

According to Charles, on the first occasion Fred caught his son stealing, he forgave Frederick. Indeed, Fred included Frederick in a previous version of his will, drafted in June 1966. But later that year, after Fred had created trusts for each of his sons, the industrialist discovered that Frederick had again stolen from him. "The fact that…he in the face of that would steal from him again was the final straw," Charles said. ("I refute all of Charles' allegations as a calculated campaign of vilification," Frederick said. "He who would cast aspersions should be beyond reproach.")

Frederick learned of his disinheritance when he returned home for Fred's funeral. His grief-stricken mother—unaware of Frederick's removal until she read her husband's will—broke the news to him in the library of the family's home. Frederick recalled that she asked him not to contest the will and "said that she would never favor one son over the other when it came time for her to write her will and that all her sons would be treated equally." Deeply embittered, he pressured his mother in the years ahead to make things right. "I have never forgotten your saying, shortly after father died, that you intended to leave me a share in your estate equal to that of my brothers," he wrote Mary in May 1972. "You asked me at that time not to contest father's will." He'd obliged, believing his mother "would set things straight eventually." But this had yet to happen. Frederick asked Mary to create a second trust to put him on a more even footing with his younger brothers. Doing so, he said, would "no longer perpetuate an imbalance that reflected father's unequal affection for his children."

Mary resisted Frederick's efforts to extract more money from the family, replying by letter that his father had left him an "adequate" trust. Though he was left out of Fred's will, Frederick still owned a little more than 14 percent of the stock in his father's company and 16 percent of the shares in a charitable foundation Fred had established in 1953. Charles, David, and Bill each inherited 20-plus percent stakes in the company (the rest was owned by other family members, including the descendants of L. B. Simmons) and nearly 23 percent apiece of the foundation. Fred left to his wife their property and all of his possessions, including their art collection.

Though they owned an equal share of their father's company, Charles, David, and Bill were not equals in the family business. Fred anointed Charles as his professional heir. He had control of the company, and he could run it as he pleased. After Fred's death, a number of the industrialist's friends counseled Charles to sell his father's corporate assets, believing there was a good market for them. At the time Fred's holdings included four ranches; a crude oil gathering and refining business; some minor oil exploration interests; and Koch Engineering Company, the outfit Charles had turned around in the early 1960s, which sold equipment to international oil industry customers.

Charles politely refused those who advised him to sell. "Charles told me that he wasn't going to do that," Sterling Varner recalled, "that he'd seen a lot of companies in the second generation disappear. They would either go broke or sell out....So he set his mind to make this company grow and prosper, and he told me that he was going to devote his life to it."

Charles remembered: "I was scared, but I also thought we had a lot of opportunities." He planned to "take the foundation we had, particularly the spirit, the attitude, and the values, and compete with major oil companies—compete with all the major...companies that were in the businesses that we were in."

Charles had inherited not just the reins of the company, but also his father's reticent, press-shy nature. The beauty of running a private company, Charles often pointed out, was that you didn't have to bare your soul to the public and financial regulators, tipping off your competition to your strengths and weaknesses in the process. ("We don't typically want to broadcast what we're doing," he once explained.) But on June 27, 1968, Charles did something that seemed unthinkable: He convened New York City's financial media for a press conference, where he announced that he planned to consolidate Fred Koch's business empire and rename the company Koch Industries in his father's honor. In another first, Charles also unveiled the company's impressive size. With $250 million in annual sales (roughly $1.7 billion in today's dollars), it ranked among the largest privately owned companies in America. And it was aggressively growing.

"Our change of corporate identity, and the corporate realignment accompanying this change, symbolize the new thrusts of activity within all divisions and subsidiaries of Koch Industries Inc., which will add at least $30 million in gross sales in 1968," the executive said.

The following year, Charles engineered one of the most important deals in the company's history, an acquisition that powered the businessman's expansion plans for years to come. A decade earlier in 1959, when a 35 percent interest in the Great Northern Oil Company had come on the market, Charles's father had plunked down nearly $5 million without hesitation. It was a wise investment. The company owned a lucrative 40,000-barrels-per-day refinery, known as Pine Bend, near the Twin Cities. It had easy access to a steady supply of Canadian crude and little in the way of competition in the upper Midwestern market.

Fred's investment would ultimately lead to a longstanding relationship between the Koch family and one of its most important business allies, the Marshall clan. J. Howard Marshall II was an oilman and attorney who had cofounded Great Northern in 1954. Fred had gotten to know him during World War II, when Marshall served as chief counsel to the Petroleum Administration for War. (Marshall today is better remembered for his marriage, at age eighty-nine, to *Playboy* playmate and stripper Anna Nicole Smith.) Marshall, whose friendship with Fred solidified when the Wichita businessman bought into Great Northern, owned 16 percent of the company.

In the late 1960s, Union Oil Company of California, owner of a 49 percent stake in Great Northern, was sniffing around for a buyer, and Charles glimpsed an opening to consolidate control. "Charles had all of his father's ability plus some," Marshall remembered.

Charles knew the Pine Bend refinery well; he had worked there in his mid-twenties. He approached Marshall with a plan to exchange his Great Northern stock for Koch Industries shares; then, with 51 percent owned by Koch Industries, he acquired Union Oil's shares for $30.5 million, giving Koch Industries total control of the company.

"I generally do not like partners, but Howard Marshall is an exception," Charles told the veteran oilman after the stock swap, according to Marshall. In this case, the upside of controlling Pine Bend outweighed the perils of bringing an outsider into the strictly family-owned company. The ideally located refinery was a cash cow—as Koch executives themselves later described it—that fueled subsequent acquisitions.

Charles wanted to branch out beyond the traditional businesses in which his father had operated. "Charles had been pressing for a long time to get into the chemical business," Varner recalled. He also positioned the company, which had hewed strictly to the oil business, to enter related sectors including natural gas and gas liquids, such as butane and propane. Before long, Varner said, "we were handling around a fifth of all the propane in the United States."

The key with all these products was transporting them, so Koch Industries concentrated on building its pipeline and trucking capacity. And the company's healthy appetite for risk enabled it to beat out competitors vying for access to the product. "We were willing to build a pipeline into a new field without a commitment from the producers as soon as there was any indication it would be economic," Charles recalled. "Other pipeline companies typically attempted to reduce their risk by requiring a commitment, a reserve study, and a fixed tariff."

In the years to follow, Koch Industries followed a business model that might have appeared scattershot to outsiders: Koch would move into animal feed and agriculture, highway and tennis court surfaces, and telecommunications. Koch was perceived as an oil company, but Charles viewed the enterprise through a different lens. He made investments based purely on the company's core capabilities—the ability to transport, process, and trade commodities.

Executives who had worked for his father quickly noticed their differing styles. Fred occasionally allowed sentimentality to influence his business decisions, whereas his son focused relentlessly on profit margins. Fred's move into ranching—based partly on the natural beauty of the tracts he was buying and his frontier childhood—was one example of this. On one occasion, faced with the decision of buying a ranch that neighbored Beaverhead in Montana, or spending the same amount on an industrial Caterpillar tractor, Fred opted for the tractor, even though he realized that purchasing the land made more business sense. "I have wanted one of those big tractors all my life, so let's buy it anyway," Fred explained.

Faced with the same choice, Charles would have made a different calculation, though he did have a certain soft spot for the ranches where he had toiled during his youth. On a few occasions, Charles resolved to sell off the properties, which were less profitable than other businesses Koch Industries was involved in. But in the end, "he always priced them way above the market so they would not sell," Varner said.

Charles's business sense wasn't always on target, and in his first years of running Koch Industries, he occasionally steered the company into blunders. The most memorable occurred in the early 1970s when Koch Industries, following the lead of its competitors in the oil market, gambled big on supertankers. It bought five tankers and chartered a host of others just as the market cratered, leaving Koch on the hook for millions—nearly $500 million, one board member told *Fortune*—as the company scrambled to extricate itself from the collapsing business. All that remained of the disastrous endeavor was the ship's bell from the *Mary R. Koch*, the tanker Charles had named after his mother, which he later presented to her after the vessel was sold at a huge loss.

Charles's emphasis on growth and laser-like focus on profit were not rooted in a desire to become one of the world's richest men. The spark that drove him to build his company and keep building it came from a different place. "He doesn't do it to make money, never has," said Tony Woodlief, the former Koch Industries management consultant. "It's always just been a great, big fascinating puzzle. He's most excited when they've solved some problem. 'Golly, we buy this shipping terminal and start producing this product and holy cow, we now have an international distribution network. That stumped everybody for fifty years and we figured it out.' That's what he likes."

"It's always been the discovery that turns him on," he continued. "And that's why he made all the money....He just loves the discovery and the wealth followed."

Pursuing expansion with his signature intensity, Charles worked six, sometimes seven days a week and expected the same of his inner circle. He grew so accustomed to fielding middle-of-the-night calls from employees operating in different time zones that one evening he awoke from a deep sleep believing the phone was ringing and walked out of his bedroom to answer it. He realized a few moments later that he had dreamt the call—and was now standing in the hallway of his apartment building in his underwear. Charles even designed his exercise regimen—he ran a few miles several days a week—so it wouldn't detract from his productivity. "My objective," he once said, "is to get the most exercise in the shortest possible time."

Charles often seemed oblivious to the demands he placed on his employees. In August 1968, in an episode executives still shook their heads at years after the fact, he convened a meeting on a Sunday afternoon that ran until midnight.

But his methods worked. The company was growing at a head-spinning pace. Charles had inherited an enterprise with 650 employees and a value of about $50 million. Over the next fifteen years, Koch Industries' value rose to $1.5 billion and the company employed 7,000 people. Its small group of shareholders reaped the rewards of this growth in dividend checks that kept adding zeros, increasing from the thousands into the millions; the year of Fred Koch's death, the company paid out less than $300,000 a year. By the early 1980s, the Koch brothers and the other shareholders divided up a pot of close to $28 million.

Even though Charles, as Koch's chairman and CEO, charted the direction of the company, it remained a family enterprise. By the late 1960s, Bill and David had joined the company's board of directors and took a more active role in plotting its future course.

At the time, Bill was still in Boston, completing a doctorate in chemical engineering at MIT; David had moved to New York City, where he worked as a junior engineer at a chemical company.

Frederick, as in childhood, remained the odd man out. His 14 percent interest in the company entitled him to a board position of his own, but he elected not to get involved with the management of Koch Industries. This was just fine with Charles, whose relationship with his older brother was distant at best. "Frederick and I had quite different interests, so we were never close," he once explained. But this was an understatement. Charles held his bon vivant brother in contempt. "Over the years," Charles once said, "I had accepted my father's analysis of Freddie of not really being a whole person, of being a person who was amoral and not capable of true feelings towards other people."

As Charles had made clear to J. Howard Marshall, he disliked partnerships, especially with people he didn't trust—like Frederick, a wild card. He displayed no interest in the company's affairs now, but what about in the future?

Eight months after their father's death, Charles made a play for Frederick's shares, but in doing so he badly underestimated his older brother. During the summer of 1968, Charles made an appointment to visit Frederick to discuss the possibility of acquiring his stake. Befitting their cool relationship, they convened in formal fashion at the midtown office of Frederick's attorney S. Hazard Gillespie, a partner with the white-shoe law firm of Davis, Polk & Wardwell.

Gillespie was a legal legend, who in the late 1950s and early 1960s served as the U.S. Attorney for the Southern District of New York, where he was known for his aggressive prosecution of securities fraud and for unsuccessfully making the government's obscenity case against *Lady Chatterley's Lover*. In private practice, the bow-tie-wearing litigator represented a string of high-profile clients, including actresses Mary Pickford and Tallulah Bankhead.

Charles had worked out what he considered a fair price for Frederick's holdings, $120 per share. He handed Gillespie a document on which he had calculated how much annual interest the proceeds would accrue if invested in various mutual funds—that is, how much yearly income Frederick would have to live on. Why keep his money tied up in a private company like Koch Industries, Charles seemed to be suggesting, when Frederick could make a tidy living investing in the public markets?

Frederick heard Charles out, but found his brother's effort to separate him from the stock their father had gifted him rather brazen. "I thought it was presumptuous of a younger brother to map out my financial future for me," Frederick recalled.

Gillespie had commissioned a study of Frederick's holdings, based on years of financial statements, in advance of the meeting. The lawyer told Charles that this review had determined that Frederick's stock could be worth up to three times what Charles was offering. With that, Gillespie picked up the document Charles had handed him, and, with the young executive watching, theatrically dropped it in a waste bin.

"Goodbye," the lawyer said coolly.

David officially joined the family company in 1970, taking a mid-level position, at a salary of $16,000 a year, as the technical service manager at Koch Engineering, the same division where Charles got his feet wet in the family business. Unlike his older brother, who was summoned home to learn the ropes, David was spared from returning to Wichita; he established an office in Manhattan.

After college, David and Bill each earned master's degrees in chemical engineering from MIT. From there, David entered the working world, while Bill remained in graduate school. David's first job, in 1963, was as a research engineer for a Cambridge-based company called Amicon. He went on to spend three years at Arthur D. Little, the consulting firm where Charles had gotten his start, developing cigarette filters and conducting engineering feasibility studies.

David had a reputation as a hardworking playboy, who enjoyed regaling friends and dates with tales of exotic travel—polar bear hunting in the Arctic Circle, stalking boar in the Hungarian countryside. *The Boston Globe*'s "Hobbledehoy" column captured his globe-trotting persona in 1967: "Dave Koch of Cambridge, who works at Arthur D. Little and plays just about everywhere, just returned from three weeks of traveling in Switzerland and Germany with a store of gamesman-like remarks." Among his Gatsbyesque pronouncements: "St. Moritz is to the Alps as St. Tropez is to the Riviera." And: "Kitzbuhl's where the swingers are, but the good skiing is at St. Anton."

Later that year, David left the Boston area for the more glamorous metropolis of New York, a city crowded with other wealthy heirs who held their own turgid opinions on St. Moritz and Kitzbühel. He went to work for the chemical company Halcon International, and its subsidiary, Scientific Design. Some of his coworkers knew of his wealthy background, but he didn't seem to possess a noticeable air of entitlement. What colleagues noticed most was his intellect and work ethic.

"David was a sponge for information," one of them recalled. "He came knowing almost nothing. And he tried to learn everything he could possibly learn. He worked as hard as anybody, in fact probably harder than anybody."

David often worked late into the evenings. During the summer months, his Park Avenue office building shut off the air-conditioning at 5:00 p.m. As the sun went down, David could often be found in his office, stripped down to his boxer shorts and a T-shirt, plunking away at his calculator. In 1970, after the company denied David's request for a transfer to the company's sales department ("he wasn't the sophisticated man he now is," the colleague said), he joined Koch Engineering, where before long he was selling products to his former employer.

Charles had put the once-struggling engineering subsidiary firmly into the black, but Sterling Varner credited David ("very technical, but also sales oriented") with transforming Koch Engineering from a relatively small company into a "world-wide business." Rising over the next decade to vice president and then president of Koch Engineering, David expanded its limited repertoire to include a host of product lines that catered to the petrochemical industry, including an assortment of internal components for the fractionation towers used by oil and chemical companies.

In 1977, David's responsibilities expanded to include running Koch Membrane Systems, a company that specialized in wastewater treatment technology. The subsidiary was located in Wilmington, Massachusetts, a northern suburb of Boston. Originally called Abcor, the company had been started by MIT professors, including Ray Baddour, one of Bill's chemical engineering teachers. Bill had convinced Charles to invest in the business, which Koch Industries later acquired outright.

Running Koch Membrane required David to spend at least a couple days a week in the Boston area. When he was in town, he typically bunked with Bill, who had remained in Massachusetts after completing a doctorate in chemical engineering. Bill had joined the family business in the mid-1970s; by now he ran a new subsidiary called Koch Carbon, through which Koch Industries hoped to gain a foothold in coal mining and the trading of petroleum coke. Known within the energy industry as "petcoke," the carbon residue created through the refining process had a market of its own as a coal-like fuel source. "I took great pride in working in my father's company with my brothers," Bill recalled.

The three brothers were working together, expanding their father's business in ways that he couldn't have imagined. They were tasting the "glorious feeling of accomplishment" Fred Koch had always wanted his sons to experience for themselves. It was, for the moment, exactly how Fred would have wanted it.

In late 1972, a wave of relief rippled through the senior ranks at Koch Industries as word spread that Charles, then thirty-seven, had gotten engaged. This meant that overworked executives might finally get to spend a little more time with their families.

To say that Charles was a workaholic underplayed the depth of his addiction. He spent what spare time he had studying heady books on economics, philosophy, and organizational psychology, amassing knowledge that he could channel into Koch Industries. Charles wanted to show the world that he wasn't just a trust fund kid who had been handed the keys to the kingdom; he was an empire builder in his own right.

"He almost killed us, because this was his whole soul," Varner remembered. "He worked long hours, weekends, holidays. He finally got married, and we were delighted to see that because he stopped working weekends."

Elizabeth Buzzi was nine years younger than Charles. When they met in 1967, the twenty-three-year-old had already been married once before. A petite, pretty blonde, Liz had a feisty nature and the profanity-laden vocabulary of a longshoreman. She had attended Catholic school in Wichita and an all-women's college in Columbia, Missouri. She hailed from a well-off family of her own, though nothing like the Kochs. The Buzzis owned a chain of department stores called Hinkel's, which, from its flagship location in downtown Wichita, had expanded into Texas, Oklahoma, and New Mexico.

Their engagement wasn't exactly storybook. Charles delivered his marriage proposal with businesslike efficiency, over the phone and while paging through his calendar for an opening in his schedule. The couple had dated for five years. Charles and Liz had decided, family friend Nestor Weigand explained, "Well, within five years, we're either going to be married or we'll break up." In 1972, when their fifth anniversary approached, "They had a private discussion. 'This is the fifth year. Are you a person of your word or what is this?' Bang! They were married like that." The couple, who married two days before Christmas, wed so quickly that an already-planned ski vacation to Vail with Weigand and other friends doubled as their honeymoon.

After their marriage, the couple moved into a five-bedroom, nine-bath contemporary-style house that Charles built on the compound where he grew up, near his childhood home, where his mother still lived. Charles's friends credit Liz with drawing him out of himself, and opening the aperture on his narrow life, in which there had been room for little other than Koch Industries business. "Charles would no question have been very successful if he hadn't met Liz, if he'd remained a bachelor, but Liz brought a sense of reality, if you will, to him," his friend Leslie Rudd said. "She brought Charles down to earth. I think he lived a normal life because of Liz.... She's important to making him the kind of person he is."

Charles has said: "I am so goal-oriented that I can get withdrawn from relationships, and Liz really taught me how to have a close, loving relationship."

The birth of their children, Elizabeth Robinson in October 1975 and Charles Chase in June 1977, also added a new emotional dimension to his life. Like his own father, he worried that privilege would corrupt the initiative of his children; he lectured them often about his value system, including on Sunday afternoons, when Charles subjected his kids to lengthy discourses on economics.

"Whatever they participated in, they needed to participate the best they could," Weigand said. "And it didn't mean that they had to be the best at it, but they had to work to the maximum of their own abilities." But Charles was not his father. He was the kind of dad who didn't miss Chase's Biddy Basketball games at the local YMCA and encouraged Elizabeth's interest in literature. Charles's kids, Weigand said, got the kind of love "that Fred, being the John Wayne that he was, didn't have the ability to articulate or to express. Because [Charles's] kids understood the love part."

Outside of the firm and his family, there was a third crucial influence on the CEO's life. It not only changed the way Charles saw the world, but it inspired him to embark on a lifelong crusade to change the world itself.

CHAPTER SIX

Rise of the Kochtopus

On a summer day in the early 1960s, Charles drove up a rutted dirt road that climbed into the heavily wooded foothills of the Rampart Mountain Range. Dense with second-growth Douglas firs and Ponderosa pines, the steep terrain rose 1,000 feet in elevation in the space of a quarter-mile. Nestled into this pastoral tableau, located midway between Colorado Springs and Denver, were a handful of log cabins sited near a long, three-story lodge.

With its gurgling brook, horse stables, and walking trails, the compound looked like a sleep-away camp. In fact, it was a libertarian mecca, where freedom seekers from around the world made pilgrimages to learn at the feet of a gray-haired, bolo-tie-wearing guru. More than a few attendees of the intensive two-week sessions at Robert LeFevre's Freedom School, who prior to their enrollment had perhaps experienced faint stirrings of libertarian identity, emerged as fierce free-market crusaders.

Though LeFevre was the primary instructor, the school's cast of guest lecturers during the 1960s included movement luminaries such as University of Chicago economist and future Nobel Prize winner Milton Friedman, a vocal foe of the Keynesian approach to economics, in which government plays a central role in guiding the economy; Leonard Read, founder of the Foundation for Economic Education, a pioneering free-market think tank; and the journalist Rose Wilder Lane (daughter of Laura Ingalls Wilder of

Little House on the Prairie notoriety), whose broadsides against socialism, Social Security, and the income tax elevated her to a libertarian heroine on par with Ayn Rand. The campus's three-story lodge, where classes were taught, was named in her honor.

LeFevre established the Freedom School in late 1956. In those early years, he had spent mornings churning out libertarian-tinged editorials for his employer, the *Colorado Springs Gazette*, and the remainder of his days building, often by hand, what he hoped would become the world's premier institution for disseminating the gospel of free enterprise and unbridled liberty.

LeFevre was tall, with the melodious voice of a radio announcer (which he had once been). He had the theatrical flair of a showman—or a charlatan. Though he was married, LeFevre's "family" included three other women who had moved with him from California to Colorado in search of a refuge from the oppressive reach of government. He was a onetime devotee of the cultish "I Am" movement, which at its peak in the late 1930s had as many as 1 million followers. It was a theosophical sect that believed in a collection of supernatural beings called the Ascended Masters, a group that supposedly included Jesus, Confucius, and St. Germain, whose souls were reincarnated into new human forms throughout the ages. The movement's cofounder, a former mining engineer named Guy Ballard, claimed he had encountered St. Germain while hiking California's Mount Shasta; Ballard also professed to be the reembodiment of George Washington, among other ancient souls.

LeFevre, who coauthored a 1940 book titled *I Am: America's Destiny*, told of undergoing a religious experience of his own in which he heard a voice intoning, "with the power of thunder," the mantra "I Am." He also spoke of having an out-of-body experience in which he floated through the air to Mount Shasta and of driving a car while asleep with the divine assistance of his "higher mental body." LeFevre worked his way into the upper echelons of the I Am movement, and when the Justice Department targeted the group's leaders for mail fraud—for sending books containing outlandish claims, including that Ballard, his wife, and their son could cure diseases using supernatural powers—he was among those who were indicted. (The charges were later dropped.)

LeFevre's motley background ran the gamut: He had been an actor, soldier, restaurateur, real estate broker, hotel owner, traveling salesman, TV anchorman, congressional candidate, and newspaper columnist. His experiences dealing with city bureaucrats and union bosses as a landlord and restaurant owner in San Francisco had ultimately soured LeFevre on government. In the 1950s, he aligned himself with a variety of antiunion and anticommunist causes, hitting the lecture circuit to decry the nexus between organized labor and the Communist Party. He worked with right-wing groups including the Wage Earners Committee, which picketed Hollywood films and targeted studio bosses and producers for their supposed communist sympathies.

LeFevre grew into such an ardent foe of government that he refused to vote lest he legitimize it. "Voting is the method for obtaining legal power to coerce others," he argued. He held that any rights government conferred on its citizens it had already robbed them of, and he taught his students that "slavery is rationalized, under the name of government and politics, because of the belief that if we didn't enslave others, the others would enslave us. Thus, we practice slavery on some in order that others should be free." As Brian Doherty detailed in his definitive history of libertarianism, *Radicals for Capitalism*, LeFevre was so puritanical in his philosophy that he "held it to be an impermissible violation of the property rights of an assailant to destroy the ropes he'd tied you up with (just so long as they were his ropes) and just as bad to take a necklace back from a blackguard who stole it from you as it was for the blackguard to take it from you in the first place." His belief in pacifism was equally uncompromising: Once, in the face of a physical confrontation, he'd simply lain down on the ground and played possum.

By the early sixties, LeFevre had found a receptive audience at the top tier of the John Birch Society by way of Wisconsin steel magnate William Grede, who became an early financial backer of the Freedom School. Grede was a founding member of the Birch Society who, along with Fred Koch, had been present at the organization's birth in Indianapolis.

Bob Love, the Koch family friend with whom Charles had opened a Birch Society bookstore, became deeply involved with LeFevre's school. So did Charles, who was so taken with LeFevre that he roped David into enrolling with him in a two-week Freedom School session.

Charles was an ideal pupil for LeFevre's teachings, which played an important role in shaping the businessman's political views. Not long after he returned home to Wichita from Boston, while browsing his father's wood-paneled library, its shelves crowded with tomes on history and free enterprise, he discovered Austrian economics. He had grown up with his father's dinner-table disquisitions about the depredations of government, the serpentine creep of socialism and communism into American society, so Charles was well primed to receive the wisdom of the Austrians. This school of thought, which formed one of the intellectual pillars of libertarianism, held that economics could be understood only through the prism of human behavior, and its adherents opposed government efforts to meddle with the "spontaneous order" of the markets.

A voracious reader like his father, Charles was driven by a burning curiosity to understand the mechanics of society, the hidden order of things that caused some cultures to founder where others flourished. In his free time, Charles often sequestered himself in his North Woodlawn Street apartment among precarious stacks of books, living a "hermit"-like existence, he has said. With classical music playing faintly in the background, Charles devoured the works of Austrian economists Friedrich Hayek and Ludwig von Mises, read classical liberal thinkers such as Milton Friedman and Joseph Schumpeter, and he studied the theories of Hungarian polymath Michael Polanyi, who pioneered the concept of spontaneous order.

While Charles read widely across an array of disciplines—from political theory to psychology—he credited two works in particular with launching his intellectual odyssey. The first was the bible of the Austrian school, Mises's *Human Action*, in which the economist wrote that "economics is not about goods and services; it is about human choice and action." Mises, whose controversial views were often condemned by his economic contemporaries, stated in this treatise that "a society that chooses between capitalism and socialism does not choose between two social systems; it chooses between social cooperation and the disintegration of society."

The second, and perhaps more formative tract when it came to Charles's worldview, was F. A. "Baldy" Harper's *Why Wages Rise*. In this slim volume, first published in 1957, the Cornell-trained economist made the case that unions and government intervention do not lead to wage increases, which come solely through "increased output per hour of work." Harper argued that the "greatest opportunity...for a quick increase in wages is to reduce the cost of governing ourselves," and suggested that "compulsory employment devices, such as child labor laws" cause societal ills such as "juvenile delinquency." Harper's book provoked a realization in Charles that he likened to a "peak experience," the term coined by psychologist Abraham Maslow (another thinker Charles admired) for a near religious state of harmony and understanding. Imbued with this euphoric clarity, he later said, "I've never looked back."

His scholarship reinforced his belief, instilled during his

boyhood, that "societal well being was only possible in a system of economic freedom." By his late twenties, Charles had become a full-throated libertarian evangelist. It was an extreme ideology, in which the role of government was nearly nonexistent, and one that fell well outside the traditional left-right poles of political thought.

His appearance in December 1965 at Kansas University's "minority opinions forum" typified his thinking. At a moment when The Byrds' "Turn, Turn, Turn" was topping the charts, this young, square-jawed businessman, who wore thick Buddy Holly–style glasses, blasted the federal government for nurturing a welfare state through "interventionist" policies. The government's sole role in the capitalist system, he told the two-dozen audience members, should be "only to keep a check on those who might attempt to interfere with the laws of supply and demand."

His belief in the cold logic of capitalism was absolute and unforgiving, without room for equivocation or shades of gray. For those businessmen who did not adhere to the laws of the market—who did not create value—he had not a shred of pity. "Every time I hear of an entrepreneur going out of business I cheer," Charles said. "He did not serve the consumer and for that he should be a janitor or a worker."

LeFevre encouraged attendees of his libertarian retreats to pack Western wear and "sturdy shoes." Students bunked in austere wood-paneled rooms, and an outdoor "barbecue breakfast" was held on Sundays. During these two-week sessions, students had mornings to themselves to ride horseback on the mountain trails, pitch horseshoes, play volleyball or badminton, or peruse the school's 3,000-volume library. Classes began after lunch and ran until 9:00 p.m., with a two-hour break for dinner.

Courses delved into the "banalities of socialism" and the "philosophy of freedom," and workshops explored topics including "Education in a Free Society" and "Explorations on Freedom."

LeFevre held a special seminar, "Explorations in Human Action," for business executives that focused on "management and labor relations problems." The school invited participants to bring their wives, but warned that "they would be excluded from class discussions, though they may sit in as observers." (They weren't the only ones excluded from participation. In 1965, LeFevre told *The New York Times* that his school had yet to admit a black person; finding accommodations for them, he said, might prove challenging because of the segregationists among the student body.) LeFevre awarded his students a "certificate of proficiency" at the completion of their courses.

After attending Freedom School classes, Charles joined the school's board of trustees, along with fellow Birchers Bob Love and William Grede. In 1964, Charles became one of six officers at the school, and he personally donated nearly $7,000 to LeFevre's institution—among the largest contributions the Freedom School received that year. Later, he became a trustee of Rampart College, an unaccredited four-year school LeFevre founded on the Freedom School campus.

By the late 1960s, there was no longer room to be both a Bircher and a LeFevre acolyte. Birch Society founder Robert Welch, who demanded absolute loyalty from his followers, disapproved of LeFevre's offbeat teachings and his approach—which focused on steering clear of government, not engaging it via a quasi-political movement.

The two spheres coexisted uneasily for a time, but Vietnam forced a schism, which was part of a larger split between conservatives and antiwar libertarians. Welch had taken a tortuous position on the war. He at first opposed U.S. involvement, believing America was being lured into a communist trap. But faced with alienating the flag-waving conservatives within the society's fraying ranks, he adopted a more nuanced stance. "Victory, Then Peace" became the society's slogan.

Charles and Bob Love, steeped in LeFevre's pacifist teachings, took a different view, thoroughly opposing the war. In May 1968, they took out a full-page antiwar ad that ran in *The Wichita Eagle*. "Let's Get Out of Vietnam Now," it demanded. Coming from two high-profile John Birch Society members, this was no minor act of defiance. In a May 31, 1968, letter to Charles, William Grede called the advertisement "almost sabotage from within the Society." Charles and Love ultimately parted ways with the Birch Society over Vietnam. Later, in a letter Welch asked Grede to personally deliver to Charles, the Birch Society founder begged him to return to the society: "You belong with us in this fight, Charles, and we need you." But the young CEO was now on a different path.

Many years later, Koch Industries sought to distance Charles and David from Freedom School founder Robert LeFevre, a controversial figure even within his own movement. After *The New Yorker* ran a 2010 article critical of the brothers, describing them as "devotees" of LeFevre, the company responded with an extensive rebuttal. It noted that "while Charles and David Koch both have met LeFevre, they were never 'devotees' of LeFevre..."

Perhaps this was true of David, who followed his brother down the libertarian path and never became the ardent believer Charles was. But it seriously obscured the true nature of Charles's association with LeFevre and the Freedom School, of which he was not just a graduate but a donor and board member. Under LeFevre's tutelage, Charles drifted farther from his conservative roots into new, radical ideological terrain.

By the late 1960s, antiwar protests raged in the streets, schools across the South were being desegregated, and President Richard Nixon was paving the way for closer relations between the United States and Communist China and expanding the federal bureaucracy to include the Environmental Protection Agency, the Occupational Health and Safety Administration, and a government-led War on Drugs. Meanwhile, members of the embryonic libertarian movement, composed of a small, unruly cadre of radical thinkers from Left and Right, were doing what they did best: disagreeing about almost everything other than their mutual disdain for government.

Charles increasingly immersed himself in this volatile stew of anarchists, Ayn Rand disciples, laissez-faire economists, disaffected Students for a Democratic Society members, and others on the political fringe. In 1969, Charles hired the first of a series of political adjutants—George Pearson, who joined Koch Industries to oversee Charles's political and philanthropic endeavors. Pearson, who grew up in the small city of Beaver Falls, outside of Pittsburgh, had been a student of Hans Sennholz (a protégé of Austrian economist Ludwig von Mises) at Pennsylvania's Grove City College. Pearson called the economist's class "a defining moment in my life," and he devoted his career to promoting the libertarian ideas Sennholz had awoken him to.

Together Charles and Pearson, then in his late twenties, formed a libertarian supper club in Wichita, where they invited notable speakers to lecture. These events featured the Freedom School's LeFevre on at least one occasion; one attendee recalled that the libertarian guru "converted" his wife "to anarchy in about 30 minutes."

His eyes opened, Charles was not content that the precepts of the libertarian philosophy stay confined to supper clubs, or discussion groups, or Rampart Mountain redoubts. "I was looking for ways to develop, apply, and spread the ideas I was learning," he recalled. The problem was that "no one was familiar with these ideas."

Charles took every opportunity he could to groom like-minded thinkers and identify libertarian converts. Gus diZerega recalled meeting Charles in the mid-1960s at his Bircher bookstore. A politically precocious high school student, diZerega had attended Birch Society meetings with his mother and he had started a local chapter of Young Americans for Freedom. Spotting diZerega and a friend browsing in the store, Charles led them away from the anti-communist broadsides and over to the special section that he had filled with tracts on Austrian economics and classical liberalism. "Charles said, 'You should start reading this kind of thing,' and then he bought us some books that we could never have afforded," diZerega remembered.

Charles later invited diZerega and his fellow YAF members over to his parents' mansion for long, philosophical talks in the basement. "At that time," diZerega said, "Charles was a very committed libertarian, possibly even what we call an anarcho-capitalist"—that is, someone who believes that virtually every function of society can be privately funded, eliminating the need for government. "He was very interested in ideas, very interested in talking about ideas, the implications of ideas, where they would lead, not just interested in power or money." DiZerega—whose Freedom School education was also bankrolled by Charles—went on to get his Ph.D. in political science from Berkeley and credits the industrialist with setting him on the path to his career in academia. "I would never have gotten into serious academic work, I think, absent his influence."

At the time when diZerega met Charles, there existed little infrastructure to incubate, let alone broadcast, libertarian dogma. Charles assessed the libertarian movement as if sizing up a failing business. In the marketplace of ideas, libertarianism was a product that few Americans wanted to buy, let alone finance, and its intellectuals were held at arm's length by academia. Enraptured by the libertarian philosophy, Charles decided that advancing its precepts would form the backbone of his philanthropic legacy: He became libertarianism's primary sugar daddy.

In 1974, Charles's ideological aide-de-camp George Pearson offered a rare glimpse into the strategic thinking behind his boss's philanthropy at a gathering of nonprofit directors. Pearson was now running the newly formed Charles Koch Foundation, a nonprofit created to finance Charles's libertarian projects.

"We did not see politicians as setting the prevalent ideology but as reflecting it," he noted, explaining that "[Friedrich] Hayek contends that the prevalent ideology is set by the intellectuals.... They are the teachers, preachers, journalists, lecturers, publicists, news writers and commentators, writers of fiction, cartoonists, artists, and all others who disseminate ideas."

Charles's strategy focused on grooming the intellectual class—through education, research funding, and other efforts—who would, in turn, shape public opinion and influence lawmakers. The "intellectual war," Pearson said, would not be won overnight. "It took years to bring this country around to believing that government could solve problems better than the market, and it will take years to get rid of that destructive notion. Belief that government participation is necessary or helpful and that governments are beneficial needs [to be] challenged."

Charles began to invest in institution building. Myriad libertarian and free-market organizations would later thrive because of his largesse. "None of these free market and policy institutions would have survived and prospered without Charles Koch," said libertarian economist Dominick Armentano, an emeritus professor at the University of Hartford, who worked closely over the years with institutions that Charles funded.

In addition to his involvement with the Freedom School in the 1960s, Charles became a board member and key benefactor of the Institute for Humane Studies, which Baldy Harper had initially run out of his Menlo Park, California, garage. Its goal, then as now, was to mentor libertarian scholars, nurture the next generation of thought leaders, and "further the science of a free society."

When Harper died suddenly of a heart attack in 1973, Charles stepped in briefly to helm the organization, vowing to continue Harper's work and keep alive his vision. At the funeral, he tenderly eulogized his friend. "He taught us about liberty which was, in his words, 'the absence of coercion of a human being by any other human being.'...Of all the teachers of liberty, none was as well beloved as Baldy, for it was he who taught the teachers and, in teaching, taught them humility and gentleness."

Just as Charles focused intently, methodically, obsessively on growth at Koch Industries, he had similarly grand aspirations for libertarianism. He often grappled with the question of how to expand libertarianism beyond its ragtag confines. By its very nature, this philosophy had attracted a combustible mix of free thinkers, from sober-minded academics to black-flag-waving anarchists, and from buttoned-down executives to survivalists, sci-fi geeks, and eccentrics seeking to establish a floating libertarian utopia on the high seas.

Charles sought a coherent strategy, not the ad hoc approach that had characterized the movement up until then. There was plenty of informal parlor talk about how to elevate libertarianism to a genuine mass movement, but it was Murray Rothbard, another student of Mises's, who wrote the manifesto that distilled the movement's guiding principles and showed a path forward to greater acceptance. Part of the debate among libertarian thinkers centered on whether to advance the cause through an intellectual or an activist approach. To Rothbard, the Bronx-born son of Eastern European Jews who had received his Ph.D. in economics from Columbia University, the answer was both. Rothbard, known for his fiery, stem-winding diatribes against "statism," captured Charles's imagination.

During the winter of 1976, Charles invited the Brillo-haired and bespectacled economist, who was then forty-nine, to spend the weekend strategizing at a ski lodge in Vail, one of the businessman's favorite vacation destinations. A fire crackled in a stone fireplace as the two men bantered for hours about how to coalesce their fellow believers and attract new recruits to their freedom-fighting ranks. Prior to this retreat, Charles and Rothbard had outlined a strategy modeled closely on the John Birch Society. (For all its flaws, Welch's group had managed to grow into a bona fide movement with an estimated 100,000 members at its peak.)

Their plan called for the formation of a Libertarian Society, replete with Bircheresque bookstores around the country. As they strategized in Vail, Charles and Rothbard came up with a handful of candidates to lead this new organization. Edward Crane III, a San Francisco–based financial advisor who, at thirty, had become the national chairman of the fledgling Libertarian Party, topped the list. Crane, the son of a Republican doctor, grew up in the suburbs of Los Angeles and he enjoyed going against the grain. Attending Berkeley during the turbulent 1960s, Crane ran for student government on a pledge to abolish it. During Barry Goldwater's 1964 presidential campaign, he stumped for the conservative Arizona senator as precinct captain in this predominately left-wing enclave. Disillusioned by the Goldwater campaign, Crane drifted toward libertarianism. He was tough and opinionated, a contrarian who spoke his mind freely—even, and perhaps especially, to powerful business titans.

In May 1976, Rothbard approached Crane, who was then running the campaign of Libertarian presidential candidate Roger MacBride, to gauge his interest in heading the Libertarian Society. "Now, we have quite a few scholars in the libertarian movement (although not as much, of course, as we should have), and we have a large, amorphous, and often nutty rank-and-file; but we have no one with organizing ability," Rothbard wrote to Crane. "This makes you, Ed, a unique and extremely scarce resource; not only are you the best person to head a Libertarian Society effort, but you are also the *only* one, and I know that Charles feels the same way."

Crane and Charles had met during the 1976 campaign, when Charles threw a fund-raiser for MacBride at his midcentury modern home in Wichita, with its floor-to-ceiling windows and recessed living room. Crane's candidate had become a libertarian hero four years earlier, when, as a Republican Electoral College elector in Virginia, MacBride refused to give his vote to Richard Nixon and Spiro Agnew, and instead cast a symbolic ballot for the Libertarian Party's nominees. MacBride was also the "adopted grandson" of libertarian icon Rose Wilder Lane—namesake of the Freedom School's lodge; upon her death, he became the literary heir to her mother's *Little House* series, and as such was the cocreator of the long-running NBC television show.

Chatting with Charles, Crane was immediately struck by the depth of the businessman's libertarian fervor. "He was more hardcore than I was," Crane recalled. Crane's commitment to the cause and competence similarly impressed Charles.

Following the election, where MacBride received a little less than 173,000 votes, a disheartened Crane considered leaving the Libertarian Party altogether and returning to his native California and a comfortable finance job. But Charles urged him to reconsider. The movement couldn't afford to lose talent of Crane's caliber. Its biggest weakness, as Charles saw it, was a lack of professionalism. He had tired of throwing money away on flaky activists and scholars who failed to deliver. To Charles, libertarianism wasn't just theoretical. He wanted action. Wholesale political and social change. And he wanted to see it within his lifetime.

"What would it take to keep you in the movement?" Charles probed.

Crane considered the question. While running MacBride's campaign, he had grown acquainted with the Beltway public policy shops such as Brookings and the American Enterprise Institute and marveled at their influence. Brookings, for its part, had managed to get a powerful new government division created in the form of the Congressional Budget Office—then have one of its scholars appointed as its director.

Crane had daydreamed of a libertarian answer to the liberal and conservative organizations that dominated the think tank world, a goal long advocated and heartily endorsed by economist Murray Rothbard.

"It would be nice to have a libertarian think tank," Crane replied.

The Cato Institute opened in early 1977, with Crane as its leader, Rothbard its intellectual muse and top scholar, and Charles the organization's wallet. The think tank, at Rothbard's suggestion, took its name from a series of eighteenth-century pseudonymous essays, signed Cato, that advocated freedom from government tyranny. They established the institute, at Charles's insistence, under the laws of Kansas, which allowed nonprofit entities to issue stock. Unlike a typical corporation, these shares held no real monetary value, but they did offer a mechanism of control. Cato's shareholders (among them, Charles, Crane, and Rothbard) had the ability to appoint the think tank's board members, and in this way they could ensure that the think tank remained tethered to its founding mission.

Cato's plush, wainscoted offices occupied half of the second floor of a three-story, redbrick building at 1700 Montgomery Street, at the foot of San Francisco's Telegraph Hill. Portraits of what the Catoites called the "dead libertarians"—John Stuart Mill, Lysander Spooner, Benjamin R. Tucker, H. L. Mencken— lined the walls. Cato had headquartered in San Francisco because, first and foremost, this was where Crane wanted to live. But there was also something apropos about establishing the libertarian beachhead far from the den of corruption and compromise that was Washington.

A converted warehouse down the street, where Rachmaninoff

concertos boomed from a stereo and scruffy libertarian activists huddled over secondhand desks, housed the distinctly shabbier offices of two other Koch-funded operations, along with the California headquarters of the Libertarian Party: Modeled on Students for a Democratic Society, the newly established Students for a Libertarian Society had ambitions of fomenting a similar movement of campus activism around libertarian issues. *Libertarian Review*, a magazine that Charles had purchased in early 1977, also occupied the warehouse space.

Charles had placed the magazine under the editorship of Roy Childs, a keen libertarian thinker and erudite essayist (and the source of the earsplitting Rachmaninoff). Childs had first struck up a correspondence with Charles's philanthropic gatekeeper George Pearson in 1969, when he was a twenty-year-old college student at S.U.N.Y. Buffalo. He later managed to convince Charles to buy *Libertarian Review* and install him as editor, even though Cato had already started publishing a magazine of its own called *Inquiry*. While *Inquiry*'s target audience was libertarian allies on the Left, who shared similar views on issues such as civil liberties and foreign policy, Childs pitched a libertarian answer to *National Review*. "Roy's message to Charles," recalled Jeff Riggenbach, *Libertarian Review*'s executive editor in the late 1970s and early 1980s, "was that it takes a while to do this, but in *National Review* we see the benefits of doing it. If you stick with it and build the magazine gradually it will over time make a difference in the culture, it will over time turn people's minds around."

Almost overnight, San Francisco became a hub of libertarian organizing, and the movement's orbit now revolved largely around Charles Koch's seemingly bottomless bank account. Charles closely monitored the operations he funded to ensure his investments would eventually yield the dividends he sought in transforming the political culture. "His rationale was that if he was funding an organization, he had the right to see that it was effective," said Richard Wilcke, who in the late 1970s and early 1980s ran the Koch-created free-market advocacy group Council for a Competitive Economy. "It was not the intention to create sinecures for shiftless ideologues." Charles jetted to San Francisco regularly to tour the offices of the outfits he was underwriting and to strategize with department heads. When he was in Wichita, he remained in daily contact with Crane.

"His whole idea was that these institutions would become self-sustaining," said Justin Raimondo, who worked for *Libertarian Review* and Students for a Libertarian Society. "They had to start making some money back. He was giving them seed money. He was pretty penurious, given the scale of his wealth, which of course was huge. He was watching pennies." (In one case, Charles grew angry with Crane for approving a $300-per-month pay increase for Childs, which he viewed as exorbitant.)

Charles's libertarian comrades learned quickly that he was not a typical corporate fat cat. During the first board meeting of the Cato Institute, the participants broke for lunch at the Rusty Scupper, an upscale seafood restaurant nearby. Notably absent was Charles, who was spotted at the greasy spoon down the street, where Cato's young, thrifty staffers frequently congregated for lunch. Charles sat alone at a corner table with his burger, Coke, and fries. He was lost in a copy of Hayek's *The Constitution of Liberty*.

Charles's everyman persona surprised fellow libertarians in different ways as well. During a small conference on Austrian economics held in Scotland, Charles, the economist Walter Block, and their wives were chatting on a street corner when a surly drunk stumbled up. *Sidewalks are for walking, not standing*, he growled. A stunned Block watched as Charles calmly and wordlessly stepped out in front of the trio and raised his fists in the boxing stance.

But it wasn't just Charles's down-to-earth demeanor that intrigued libertarians; it was also the fact that one of America's wealthiest men shared their radical views. "I was used to the idea that anyone who ran a big business and had a lot of money was a Republican," Riggenbach said. "And of course, in recent years, Charles has looked more and more like that profile. Back then he seemed to me to be just as radical as Murray Rothbard or Ed Crane. He seemed to me to be an anarchist."

"He was contemptuous of government on every level," Riggenbach continued. "It was not just on economic issues. He was not disposed to look on the people who later formed the Tea Party as his allies. He was instead disposed to look on them as people who were too terrified of the results of their thinking to pursue their ideas where they naturally led"—that is, to a worldview closer to anarchism than conservatism.

Charles certainly talked the talk. Asked during a gathering of Wichita Rotarians in the late 1970s to describe his view of government, he responded, "It is to serve as a night watchman, to protect individuals and property from outside threat, including fraud. That is the maximum." When Childs put together an issue of *Libertarian Review* devoted to strategy in August 1978 ("Toward the Second American Revolution," was splashed on the cover), Charles contributed an impassioned, four-page essay that served as a libertarian call to arms to the business community, which he chided for hypocrisy. "How discrediting it is for us to request welfare for ourselves while attacking welfare for the poor," he wrote. "Our critics rightfully claim that we want socialism only for the rich."

He decried corporate leaders who preached "freedom in voluntary economic activities," but simultaneously called for "the full force of the law against voluntary sexual or other personal activities." And he blasted the business community for buying into "the fallacious concept that the corporation has a broad 'social responsibility' beyond its duty to its shareholders."

He urged businessmen to resist the temptation to seek change via the Republican Party. "If this is our only hope then we are doomed," he wrote. "The Republican Party is the party of 'business' in the *worse* [sic] sense—in the sense of business accommodation and partnership with government." There was no way to "destroy the prevalent statist paradigm" through a political party that had helped to perpetuate it.

Just as in the early 1960s, when the John Birch Society's Robert Welch and his conspiracy-crazed followers caused hand-wringing among influential conservatives, the radical philosophy espoused by Charles, Murray Rothbard, and their fellow libertarians provoked similar unease on the Right. Once again, William Buckley's *National Review* took it upon itself to protect the virtue of conservatism.

In 1979, the year after Charles's jeremiad against establishment conservatives, the magazine took aim at the movement and its main benefactor in a pair of articles devoted to eviscerating libertarianism.

"Who is against liberty? Or prosperity, which, we are told, comes as a bonus with it?" wrote social critic Ernest Van Den Haag in the magazine's cover story. "But how to get, and keep, both? The libertarian answer is beguilingly simple: The government is the problem, not the solution. Do away with it, and we will all be free and prosperous. Society has been wrong for the last few thousand years in making laws and demanding obedience to them. Murray Rothbard will put it right.

"The character of the libertarian movement," Van Den Haag concluded, "is now such that all true lovers of liberty must oppose it."

A separate article focused on Cato, which the magazine derided for falling in with the New Left foreign policy milieu, and it took a swipe at the sanity of the fellow bankrolling the whole mad endeavor, describing Charles as "a man whose wealth and devotion to privacy are straight out of the Howard Hughes legend."

By now Charles had begun to come under attack not just from outside the libertarian movement, but from within it as well. One of his most vocal critics was a mustachioed gadfly named Samuel Konkin III, who dressed in black in solidarity with his anarchist forefathers. A Dungeons & Dragons enthusiast, he embodied the movement's sci-fi-geek side—the kind of eccentric activist getting in the way of Charles's efforts to bring respectability to libertarianism.

Konkin had watched in horror as his compatriots slavishly cozied up to the Wichita businessman in pursuit of funding. To Konkin, these Koch supplicants risked sullying the movement as the tool of an oil baron. He saw glaring hypocrisy in a movement of individualists, whose primary goals included rolling back a culture of government dependency and control, subjugating themselves to the dependency and control of a business mogul. He coined the term "Kochtopus" to describe the many-tentacled operation funded by Charles, whom he accused of trying to "buy the major Libertarian institutions—not just the Party—and run the movement as other plutocrats run all the other political parties in capitalist states."

The libertarian denizens of Montgomery Street paid little heed to such crankery, which they attributed mostly to the jealousy of those who had not managed to ingratiate themselves with Charles. This crowd of activists, scholars, and journalists considered themselves proud appendages of the "Kochtopus" and even adopted Konkin's derisive term as their own.

By the late 1970s, the movement—once small enough to squeeze into the living room of Murray Rothbard's Upper West Side apartment—seemed finally on the march. "It was an exciting time, indeed," remembered the economist Dominick Armentano. "There was plenty of debate about ideas and policy to be sure but most of the concern was over strategy. How aggressively do you push ideas, especially radical ones like libertarianism? Which alliances advance your cause and which ones should be avoided?"

Gaining a firmer toehold in politics seemed the next logical step for Charles and his allies. And there was some evidence that libertarian ideas were resounding with the electorate. In California's 1978 gubernatorial race, which pitted Democratic incumbent Jerry "Moonbeam" Brown against the state's Republican attorney general, a libertarian candidate managed to capture almost 400,000 votes, more than 5 percent of the total. Thanks to his impressive showing, Ed Clark, a wonkish and somewhat stiff oil industry attorney, became an early favorite as the Libertarian Party's presidential candidate in 1980. Charles and Cato's Ed Crane—who now ran both the think tank and the Libertarian Party—saw the upcoming election as an opportunity to showcase libertarianism to a national audience on a scale that hadn't been seen before.

Ahead of the party's 1979 nominating convention, Charles was asked to join a possible Ed Clark ticket as the Libertarian Party's vice presidential nominee. With a company to run—and a deep aversion to publicity—Charles declined, but he cajoled Bill and David, both thirty-nine and working for Koch Industries, to consider running. Neither had gotten very involved with libertarianism, but because of Charles's passion for the movement, they had both donated to the causes he supported.

There was an ulterior motive to running a Koch. A loophole in the Federal Election Campaign Act allowed candidates to donate unlimited funds to their campaigns, circumventing individual contribution limits (which libertarians didn't believe in to begin with). Staked by one of the Koch brothers, the Libertarian Party could mount a true national campaign.

Bill considered the proposition, but ultimately begged off. David, however, went for the idea, inspired by the 1976 presidential campaign of Roger MacBride. "Here was a great guy, advocating all the things I believed in," David said in 1980. "He wanted less government and taxes and was talking about repealing all these victimless-crime laws that had accumulated on the books. I have friends who smoke pot. I know many homosexuals. It's ridiculous to treat them as criminals—and here was someone running for president, saying just that."

In mid-August 1979, a few weeks before the party's nominating convention, David circulated a letter to the more than 500 Libertarian Party delegates announcing his candidacy and openly acknowledging it would allow him to pour money (he pledged "several hundred thousand dollars" to start) into the campaign.

David's candidacy caused some grumbling in the movement among libertarians who, though grateful for the Kochs' support, feared being viewed as a subsidiary of Koch Industries. Some also expressed concern about the optics of a businessman effectively buying the Libertarian Party's nomination. "I was disturbed by it," said Robert Poole, then the editor of the libertarian *Reason* magazine. "David Koch has not been active in the party. But everyone made the calculations.... He was a Libertarian, he agreed with us, he was offering money we couldn't otherwise get."

In early September 1979, the Libertarian Party's nominating convention kicked off in Los Angeles, as a thick shroud of smog enveloped the city. The Bonaventure Hotel, a futuristic-looking trio of cylindrical skyscrapers in downtown L.A., teemed with hundreds of libertarians from every strain of the eclectic movement: Miseians and Hayekians, anarcho-capitalists, shaggy-haired peaceniks, and black-clad anarchists.

It wasn't Madison Square Garden, where the following year Ted Kennedy would deliver a Camelot-worthy concession speech, or Detroit's Joe Louis Arena, where at the last minute Ronald Reagan selected George H. W. Bush as his running mate after entertaining a "co-presidency" with Gerald Ford, but the libertarian convention was momentous in its own way. Donning patriotic skimmer hats and waving CLARK FOR PRESIDENT signs, here were more than two thousand people committed to eviscerating the political status quo and, in some cases, the government itself.

On September 9, Roy Childs, the heavyset and bearded editor of Charles's *Libertarian Review*, looked out on the audience from the dais in the ballroom. He was among a trio of speakers who would be endorsing David's candidacy. Unifying libertarians was like herding cats, and the lingering reservations about David had to be confronted head on.

"We are no longer at the stage where the movement can be 'bought.' And certainly Ed Clark can't be bought," Childs told the crowd. "The government says we can't spend our own money defending our own rights. Well, I say nuts to that, and so does David Koch. Let's get to work!"

Three other VP candidates were in contention, but David won the balloting in a landslide. It didn't hurt his chances that David had made it known that he had decided to up the ante on his contribution pledge to a half-million dollars and was leaving open the possibility that he might chip in even more.

Hoots and applause echoed in the ballroom as David nervously strolled in to claim the nomination. He broke the ice with a joke. "Delegates and visitors, my speech today will be like my candidacy—short but very valuable."

"As I said in my letter to you announcing my candidacy," David went on, over peals of laughter, "you have done an incredibly good job in bringing the Libertarian Party from obscurity to the point where today we represent the best hope for human freedom since the American Revolution.... I feel particularly as a businessman, who's run a successful company, who's had to deal with the harassment and the ridiculous interference of government in the affairs of my business, that I can be particularly effective at communicating the libertarian ideas and concepts to businessmen.

"With Ed Clark as our standard-bearer," he concluded, "the

two-party system is in grave danger." Smiling broadly, David raised his right fist aloft and locked hands with his running mate, who had joined him on the stage.

Winning wasn't the point. No one was that naïve. The real goal of the endeavor was taking on the entrenched political system and using the presidential campaign, and accompanying media attention, to disseminate the libertarian message. "Before you can teach, you have to get people's attention," David told a group of Texas Libertarian Party members as the campaign got under way. "The ideas are so persuasive that once people hear about them they will be willing to accept them."

When it came to selling the libertarian brand, the Clark-Koch campaign, and its chief architect, Cato's Ed Crane, understood that Americans might have difficulty wrapping their minds around their radical ideas in undiluted form. This was an ongoing and thorny debate within the movement—how to stick to their core principles and expand their base, while neither selling out libertarianism nor scaring the American electorate.

Crane himself had declared in 1974: "The real threat to the [Libertarian Party] lies in the temptation to make the big time through compromise of our principles to gain votes immediately. The fact is that the only hope we have for continued success is to stick to our principles and never compromise."

During a 1978 *Reason* magazine roundtable, Charles expressed a similar view: "Our greatest strength is that our philosophy is a consistent world view and will appeal to the brightest, most enthusiastic, most capable people, particularly young people." He worried that watering down their "radical philosophy" would "destroy the movement."

As the 1980 campaign wore on, it began to seem to libertarian purists that the Clark-Koch campaign had taken precisely the path that Crane and Charles Koch had once warned against. Ed Clark, for instance, had stopped short of calling for the wholesale abolition of the income tax. And he was flirting dangerously with the Left on the subject of opposing nuclear power.

Halfway through the campaign, David Nolan, one of the Libertarian Party's founders, sent a terse missive to Clark begging for a course correction. Though just thirty-six, the mustachioed activist was one of the movement's elder statesmen, driven to cofound the party in 1971 by outrage over Richard Nixon's imposition of wage and price controls and abandonment of the gold standard. Before the nominating convention convened, Clark met with Nolan and other influential party leaders to lock down their support; the candidate had assured them of the ideological purity of his platform—and his running mate. Nolan had therefore not opposed David's vice presidential nomination, though he and other prominent libertarians had doubts about the businessman's libertarian bona fides. Now, Nolan fumed, the Clark-Koch faction was "pushing the party into a stance which is radically different from the traditional libertarian posture on certain key issues, and which is dangerously out of touch with the temper of the times."

Rothbard, increasingly agitated by the direction Charles Koch and Ed Crane were taking his beloved movement, had come to a similar conclusion. He sensed "a paradigm shift in all parts of the 'Kochtopus,' " he told a libertarian colleague. "Koch," he said, "explicitly wants to run the movement like a corporation, where orders are given, dissidents are fired, etc. Crane ditto."

As Election Day neared, Rothbard's private denunciations about the movement's ideological drift exploded into open hostility. He reached his breaking point in the final weeks of the election. Clark had landed a primetime appearance on ABC's *Nightline*, a key opportunity to expose millions of TV viewers to libertarianism. Yet instead of articulating their core beliefs, Clark had described their philosophy as "low-tax liberalism" and said "we want to get back immediately to the kind of government that President Kennedy had back in the early 1960s." *Low-tax liberalism? Kennedy?* Rothbard and his loyal followers boiled over.

On Election Day, the nation decisively swept Ronald Reagan into power and the Clark-Koch campaign claimed a little under 1 million votes, about 1 percent of the total cast. Thanks largely to repeated cash infusions from David, who ended up larding his campaign coffers with a little more than $2 million, the Libertarian Party made it on the ballot in all fifty states and the District of Columbia. The 1980 campaign would later be viewed as a high water mark for the Libertarian Party, which only during the 2012 election surpassed the Clark-Koch ticket's vote tally (though not its share of the popular vote) in a presidential campaign. David reflected on the campaign as a personal triumph, listing his vice presidential candidacy years later under "proudest achievement" on an MIT alumni questionnaire.

But the outcome at the time was viewed as a disappointment, since the campaign had early on estimated that the Libertarian Party ticket would garner 4 or 5 percent of the electorate, on par with Ed Clark's showing in the California gubernatorial race. The campaign's lackluster performance frustrated Charles, according to Clark. "He was not awfully pleased," he recalled. "I think he thought it could have been better in the number of votes and building the movement."

Rothbard penned a scathing postmortem after the election in a newsletter he edited called *The Libertarian Forum*. "The Clark/Koch campaign was a fourfold disaster, on the following counts: betrayal of principle; failure to educate or build cadre; fiscal irresponsibility; and lack of votes." Far from taking libertarianism to new heights, the 1980 election reduced it to new lows as infighting and factional feuds engulfed the movement. SMASH THE CRANE MACHINE buttons now adorned the jackets of some Libertarian Party activists.

Adding insult to injury, the ringleader of the revolt was Rothbard, for whom Charles had built a comfortable academic perch and whose strategy he had tried to put into play. Tensions between Rothbard and Ed Crane—or as the economist preferred, Boss Crane—had begun to flare by the spring of 1979, and relations between the men had rapidly devolved from there. Even so, in early March 1981, Rothbard was floored to reach into his mailbox and retrieve a letter from Crane requesting that he relinquish his shares in the Cato Institute. Citing Rothbard's "deep-seated" antagonism, Crane wrote that "we believe it would be difficult, if not impossible, for you to objectively evaluate ongoing and future Cato projects as a Board member."

A few weeks later, when Cato held its quarterly board meeting, Rothbard, still seething, entered the think tank's conference room with a lawyer in tow. When the meeting began, Rothbard's attorney addressed the group, arguing for his client's right to continue serving on the board.

Charles coolly explained that Cato's shareholders—meaning himself and Crane—had convened the previous night and dissolved the board, re-forming it minus Rothbard. The irascible economist, his fury building, objected. He was, after all, a Cato shareholder, yet had not been informed of the session.

Charles told Rothbard that he was, in fact, no longer a Cato shareholder either. His shares had been canceled. "This action is illegal," Rothbard sputtered as he and his lawyer stormed out. "Therefore any further decisions taken at this meeting are illegal!"

Following the 1980 election and amid the intraparty feuding, other big changes were under way within the Kochtopus. In his ongoing mission to create social change, Charles rethought his strategy, shutting down some of his libertarian projects. He cut off funding to Students for a Libertarian Society, which had angered its benefactor with the publication of a monograph that glorified San Francisco's White Night riots—a series of violent uprisings in reaction to the lenient sentence given to Dan White, the San Francisco Board of Supervisors member who assassinated Mayor George Moscone and fellow supervisor Harvey Milk. Titled "In Praise of Outlaws: Rebuilding Gay Liberation," its cover featured a row of burning police cars—precisely the type of radical imagery that relegated libertarianism to the fringe. Hemorrhaging money and making little inroads in movement building, *Libertarian Review* was folded into *Inquiry*, which itself ceased publication after a couple of years.

By late 1981, as if fleeing the upheaval on Montgomery Street, Cato uprooted from San Francisco to a historic town house on Capitol Hill. Rothbard, who had taken a position with the newly founded Ludwig von Mises Institute, saw the move as a sign that he'd been right all along, that Ed Crane and Charles Koch were willing to sell out libertarianism if it brought them closer to mainstream acceptance and political influence. "The massive shift of the Kochtopus to D.C. symbolized and physically embodied the shift of the Kochtopusian Line toward the State and toward Respectability," wrote Rothbard, the embers of his grudge still smoldering.

Even as the libertarian movement imploded, devolving into internecine battles and turning some of Charles's onetime allies into lifelong enemies, conflict brewed on another front, this one much closer to home.

CHAPTER SEVEN

The Divorce

On Christmas Day 1979, the four Koch brothers gathered in the wood-paneled dining room of their childhood home, where their mother had set the long table with lace placemats, gold-rimmed crystal wineglasses, and an arrangement of white poinsettias. Also at the table were Charles's wife, Liz, and Joan Granlund, the ex-model who doubled as Bill's secretary and live-in girlfriend.

Mary was hosting Christmas dinner, as was the family custom, and the Koch patriarch was never far from mind as he peered down from an oil painting on a nearby wall. Over the course of the evening, the festive mood evaporated thanks to Bill, who chose the occasion to unload years of emotional baggage.

Bill was Mary's *enfant terrible*. As long as anyone could remember, he'd been excitable and tempestuous. He never outgrew the feeling of being slighted by Charles. Since joining the firm in 1974, he'd felt like the third and lesser wheel in the brotherly triumvirate that controlled Koch Industries. He brooded over his role within the company, as well as over how Mary, who had just turned seventy-two, planned to distribute her estate among her sons. As in his boyhood, Bill's inner swirl of emotions whipped into a maelstrom with little warning. This storm had been building for some time.

Seated across from his mother, Bill vented a series of grievances.

Growing up, he had perceived Mary as cool and distant, more interested in society gatherings than child rearing. He now blamed her for laying the foundation for the emotional turmoil that had ebbed and flowed throughout his life. She had not loved him as she did his brothers; she had treated him unfairly. According to Charles, Bill also pressed her on the disposition of the family's art collection. Their father had given Charles some paintings before his death; Bill insisted Mary "equalize" the brothers by leaving more of the art collection to him in her will.

"Billy," Charles said, "just leave her alone." Charles tried to calm his brother down. "I'm not going to fight you over any property, but just leave Mama alone."

Bill laid into Charles, too, whom he faulted for running their father's company like a dictator. Fred may have selected Charles as his successor, but Koch Industries belonged to all of them. One recent episode in particular had made Bill suspicious of his brother's motives. That November, at Charles's request, a company lawyer had presented Bill with a draft estate plan. It specified that on his death, Bill's stock in Koch Industries would automatically be sold back to the company at a predetermined—and in Bill's view, laughably discounted—price. Under the plan, the IRS might wipe out much of his wealth, while Koch Industries took control of his lucrative holdings. It was a plan designed to further the company's interests, not his. Bill had no heirs yet (though he and Joan would later have a son), but he viewed the episode as symbolic of Charles's controlling nature. His brother was trying to cheat him out of his birthright, even in death.

Mary struggled to hold back tears. The discord, occurring on one of the few occasions when the Kochs still gathered as a family, finally overcame her. Sobbing, she pushed back from the table and hurried from the room.

It was the last Christmas the Kochs spent together.

Bill lingered at MIT long after his brothers entered the working world, spending a leisurely eight years completing his doctoral work. He finally received his degree at age thirty-one. During that time, David had begun referring to his twin as "the student," and Charles had started to wonder whether their wayward brother would ever enter the real world. "He had a country-club attitude," David told an interviewer. "Boston was a wonderful place to be. Billy got distracted. He lost his direction."

In 1968, as Bill completed his Ph.D., Charles began easing him into the family business, asking him to establish a small venture capital fund to both invest in high-tech start-ups and identify potential acquisitions for Koch Industries. MIT's Cambridge campus, a hub of innovation, seemed an ideal perch from which to do this. But the endeavor was ultimately a bust, eventually bleeding $90,000, according to Charles. Mistakes and occasional bad investments were part of doing business, but what bothered Charles more was the feeling that Bill didn't approach the project with the drive he expected from Koch employees. "Bill couldn't get to work on time," he said. "Couldn't get himself out of bed." In 1973, Charles shut down the operation.

Bill officially joined the family company, in 1974, as a salesman for a Wellesley, Massachusetts–based Koch subsidiary that specialized in buying and selling agricultural chemicals and other products in China. Affable and able to dial up the charm with customers, he displayed a talent for sales and deal making. In a complex transaction that impressed Charles and Koch Industries' upper management, Bill, on his own initiative, engineered a deal to provide Louisiana natural gas to a Texas sulfur plant, and Texas sulfur to the company's Chinese customers. The deal netted Koch $5 million. Charles soon promoted Bill to run the subsidiary. By 1976, Bill was running Koch Carbon, the company's newly established mining and petroleum coke subsidiary.

Still, Bill's style at times clashed with the aggressive, streamlined ethos that Charles cultivated. Koch had grown into a large company, but its success lay in the fact that it could still operate like a small one, without the layers of cumbersome bureaucracy that hindered its competitors. Where its rivals lumbered along, Koch moved swiftly and decisively. Part of this was because it was a private company and largely family owned, meaning deals and strategic decisions didn't require a laborious board approval process.

Like Charles, Bill was highly analytical. But in meticulously studying every facet of an issue, Koch executives felt he could waffle. He sought the opinions of high-priced consultants, commissioned studies, and snowed Koch managers in with reports and memoranda. He asked endless questions, many of them astute, but to what end? At Koch, it was results that mattered. Profits. And under Bill's leadership, according to Charles, Koch Carbon did not fare well.

Bill nevertheless pressed for more and more responsibility, petitioning Charles to elevate him to vice president for corporate development in charge of identifying strategic acquisitions. "Bill was never happy running a division," Sterling Varner, who'd risen to company president, once observed. "He wanted to get more involved in the overall management of the company."

William Hanna, the Koch Industries executive to whom Bill reported (and who later succeeded Varner), noted: "It was important for Bill to be important."

Charles reluctantly gave Bill the promotion, despite doubts about whether he deserved it. Once in his new position, Bill pushed for more, requesting a large budget and a sizable staff to analyze potential deals. "He wanted unilateral authority to spend $25 million a year investing in acquisitions and other deals of his choice," David recalled. "And Charles and Sterling felt, as I did, that this was way too excessive. He hadn't proved that he could manage investments of that magnitude properly." As part of his new position, which hadn't existed at the company previously, Bill also requested to undertake evaluations of Koch business units in order to identify their strengths and weaknesses.

Ahead of a March 1980 board meeting, Bill flew in from his home in Massachusetts to plead his case to Charles. The evaluations seemed to Charles like a surefire morale killer—his managers would feel as if they were being second-guessed. Charles's management philosophy centered on investing his employees with as much decision-making authority as they could handle and letting the results speak for themselves. Charles considered the acquisition budget Bill proposed overkill. He told Bill he couldn't endorse the proposal and urged his brother to start small, go slow: "We don't want to go out and acquire the world."

But when the board meeting arrived, Bill bypassed Charles, handing out bound copies of his proposal and appealing directly to the company's seven directors, which in addition to the three Koch brothers, included Sterling Varner; Tom Carey, the company's chief financial officer; Texas oilman J. Howard Marshall II, who'd helped Charles gain control of the Great Northern Oil Company; and Fred Koch's cousin Marjorie Simmons Gray, the daughter of L. B. Simmons, whose Oklahoma-based refinery and pipeline Fred had acquired in 1946.

The directors were dubious of Bill's proposal and ultimately sided with Charles. Struggling to persuade them, Bill grew more and more distraught. David, who was in town from New York for the board meeting, recalled him beginning to sob; he cringed at the sight of his brother embarrassing himself. "He was very upset, and I thought he presented his case tremendously badly," David said.

Bill's behavior concerned David, and after the meeting ended, he pulled his twin aside.

"Bill, you didn't handle that at all well," David said.

By then Bill had regained his composure. "Yeah, I was too emotional, I agree with you," he responded, according to David. "I just didn't do a good job. My emotions carried me away."

* * *

By college, the boyhood animosities between Bill and Charles had largely dissipated. Or so Charles thought. Beginning in late 1979 and continuing through 1980, tensions between the brothers built, then built some more until relations between them were worse than ever. Bill was openly dismissive of Charles in front of David and, worse, other Koch employees. Behind his back, Bill referred to him as "Prince Charles" and derisively compared his stewardship of Koch to a member of royalty lording over his court and kingdom. Over dinner at Boston's Algonquin Club with David and Wichita real estate developer and family friend George Ablah in early 1980, Bill trashed Charles. The Kochs had recently joined with Ablah in a $195-million deal to purchase Chrysler's real estate holdings. As the three men sat beneath the pewter chandelier in the dining room of the McKim, Mead & White clubhouse, Bill commented that Koch had a reputation for screwing over its business partners, David recalled. David was outraged. "You've got to retract that statement," he said.

Bill was not terribly discreet. Nor did he seem to care. Word of his belligerent comments soon got back to Charles, who in late April 1980 angrily scrawled out a note to his brother: "What is the purpose of these attacks on me? I hear from all over the country that you're constantly criticizing me." Lately, Charles went on, Bill had gone out of his way to criticize his management during reports to the board and his memos carried "accusatory" undertones. Charles warned his brother that he was on a "destructive" path. "Whatever I've done to make you so bitter toward me is in the past," he wrote, adding that if the brothers could not work together "in friendship," they should at least do so "civilly."

Bill's criticisms of Charles—intemperate as they could sometimes be—were not merely rooted in sour grapes or in a bitter sibling rivalry. Bill and other Koch Industries shareholders had developed some legitimate worries about the direction the company had taken under Charles's management.

Koch's record of growth was unassailable. That wasn't the issue. What concerned Bill and other shareholders was the company's increasing run-ins with the government. Lately Koch Industries had managed to run afoul of agencies ranging from the Department of Energy to the Internal Revenue Service. The company faced not just civil penalties, but criminal prosecution.

In early 1980, the Justice Department empaneled a federal grand jury to investigate whether Koch Industries and a half-dozen employees of Koch's oil exploration division, based in Denver, had conspired to rig a Bureau of Land Management lottery for federal oil and gas leases. By June, the grand jury had returned criminal indictments against Koch Industries and its employees.

The Department of Energy, meanwhile, was auditing Koch (along with other oil and gas companies) for violating federal controls on the price of oil and overcharging customers. In the worst-case scenario, the company's top accountant confided to Bill, Koch could be liable for more than $1 billion. Perhaps enough to sink the company. (Just a few years earlier, federal regulators had accused Koch of overcharging on sales of propane by $10 million.)

Bill initially supported Charles's libertarian projects, but he had grown troubled by the increasing amounts of company money Charles diverted to his "libertarian revolution causes"—causes Bill now considered loony.

"No shareholders had any influence over how the company was being run and large contributions and corporate assets were being used to further the political philosophy of one man," Bill said later.

Charles's activism had drawn unwanted attention to the company and the family. Their father had loathed publicity, scrupulously guarding the family's privacy, especially after his John Birch Society involvement landed his name in the paper. Now that Charles had coaxed David into running as the Libertarian Party's vice presidential candidate, the family was in the media spotlight as never before.

Bill and other Koch shareholders—who by now included Marjorie Simmons Gray's daughters, second cousins to the Koch brothers, and the two sons of J. Howard Marshall II—also had concerns about liquidity. Bill was one of the richest men in America, worth hundreds of millions of dollars. But only on paper. He had needed to borrow money to buy a mansion in the tony town of Dover, on Massachusetts's South Shore, which seemed ludicrous given the scale of his wealth. Nearly all of his net worth was locked up in a closely held, private company. Unlike a publicly traded company, the market value of Koch stock was opaque and there were strict rules over to whom the shares could be sold. If any of Koch's shareholders wanted to cash in their holdings, they would likely be forced to do so at an extreme discount.

Koch shares did pay a dividend (about 6 percent of the company's earnings), but Bill considered it stingy. The growth-obsessed operating style of Charles and his right-hand man, Sterling Varner, called for plowing almost all of Koch Industries' earnings back into the company. "That was our religion...to make things grow...to push, push, push," according to Varner. This strategy expanded Koch Industries, though not the bank accounts of its shareholders, at least not immediately.

Bill's brothers, meanwhile, considered his appetite for money "insatiable." He earned nearly $4 million in annual dividends and another $1 million in salary and bonuses—how much was enough? To Bill's mind, though, what was the point of being filthy rich if you couldn't enjoy it? He had other interests he wanted to pursue outside the firm: art, fine wine, yachting. And he wasn't getting any younger. In May 1980, he had turned forty.

Frustrated with his role at Koch and the paltry dividends he received—and frightened by the government investigations looming ominously over the company—Bill began furtively meeting with Koch shareholders, including the Marshall brothers, Pierce and Howard III, to discuss the liquidity problem and other issues of concern. Some of them, it turned out, shared his frustrations. The most obvious solution was taking the company public. But Charles vehemently opposed this option. (Koch Industries would go public "literally over my dead body," he later emphasized.) He preferred keeping a tight rein on Koch; the last thing he wanted was more oversight and interference from government bureaucrats. When Bill raised the possibility of going public with Koch's top lawyer, Don Cordes, he immediately shot the idea down. "This should never be a public company. If this were a public company, all the officers and directors would be in jail," Cordes told him without elaborating, according to Bill.

Charles had maintained that the oil-lottery-rigging mess which resulted in criminal charges and fines for the company and three employees was the fault of a few bad apples working in the company's Denver office. But knowing that his brother kept close tabs on every aspect of the business, Bill wondered whether Charles—and perhaps even Sterling Varner—had known about the illegal activities that had led to the charges. (His suspicions were never proven.)

On Thursday, July 3, 1980, an eleven-page single-spaced letter landed on Charles's desk. He had learned to greet Bill's frequent, overheated missives with a mixture of dread, annoyance, and mild anxiety. His blood pressure rose as he read. This wasn't a memo. It was an indictment that blasted Charles on everything from his supposedly autocratic management style to his libertarian activism and his role in pushing David's vice presidential candidacy. Though the letter was addressed solely to Charles, he soon discovered that Bill had circulated it to some of the shareholders. Bill had taken Charles to task on several fronts—his lack of concern about regulatory violations and his insensitivity to shareholders' demands for dividends, among them.

Bill accused Charles of keeping the board in the dark about key corporate matters, including "the pricing policies and activities" that "resulted in the government alleging both civil and criminal violations" of wage and price control regulations. "As a result... the directors and the shareholders must look on helplessly as the corporation's good name is dragged through the mud by one set of indictments and is threatened by more such actions."

Bill delved into the "extremely frustrating" liquidity issue, complaining that it was "absurd" that shareholders who were "extremely wealthy on paper" had almost no ability to utilize their assets. "What is the purpose of having wealth if you cannot do anything with it, especially when under our present tax laws on death they will undoubtedly end up in the hands of the government and politicians?" he asked. Bill accused Charles of "creating Koch Industries as a monument to business success" and neglecting the "desires of the shareholders" in the process.

Then he threw down the gauntlet. "Since I'm not alone in these concerns, failure to solve them...will be destructive to everyone concerned. Indeed if they are not solved, the company will probably have to be sold or taken public."

The memo Charles held incredulously in his hands was nothing short of a declaration of war.

Six days later, on July 9, 1980, Charles took his customary place at the head of the long, polished table in Koch Industries' conference room. A large world map, pinpointing the locations of Koch's global operations, hung on the wall behind him. As usual, David sat to Charles's right, and Sterling Varner to his left.

Charles was not someone who allowed his emotions to color his judgment. He was better known for his inscrutable impassiveness. But that afternoon, as the directors gathered for a board meeting, he was visibly angry. Charles had added a last-minute item to the agenda: "W.I.K. Has Leveled Serious Charges."

Once the seven directors had assembled, Charles explained that Bill's letter had finally convinced him that his brother's behavior and allegations were so serious that they needed to be addressed by the full board. To Charles, Bill's continued attacks and behind-the-scenes rabble-rousing posed a mortal threat to the company, perhaps the most serious peril it had faced since their father had fended off Universal Oil Products and the oil majors.

During the contentious four-hour meeting, the CEO went point by point through Bill's memo, eventually coming out with his suspicions: He accused his brother of angling for his job, or possibly Sterling Varner's. Charles ultimately unveiled a resolution giving him the authority to terminate Bill from the company, should he continue to attack the management and cause unrest.

"Charles Koch is the boss and will always be so long as he's the chairman, and he won't hesitate to run anyone off—anyone off—if that's indicated," Varner told the board. Varner had received complaints from middle managers, who felt Bill meddled in aspects of the business outside of his purview and expressed alarm at his hostility toward Charles. "You can't refer to the management group, Bill, as the prince and his court," Varner chastised. "Middle management thinks you are unfair to Charles, and they are upset. They like you, but they can't figure out what you're up to."

Marjorie Simmons Gray, their father's cousin, spoke up. The in-fighting had gotten out of hand, she said, urging Charles to table the resolution. "I don't believe I have misread Bill's intention," she said. "He's got the company's best interest at heart." Gray said that a mountain had been made out of a molehill, that past hostilities should be forgotten and forgiven, and that everyone should go on working for the company.

J. Howard Marshall II, a lawyer by training who prided himself on his skills as a mediator, also implored Charles to back off. Sometimes family blowups, he said, were beneficial, resulting in better relationships once the air was cleared.

Charles relented. He would allow Bill to stay on at the company under one condition. Bill would have to formally pledge to discontinue his attacks and to cease fomenting dissent among the shareholders. "I said I would live up to the rules of the corporation, but I would not give up my rights as a shareholder and as an individual," Bill recalled. Charles, for his part, agreed to convene a committee to explore liquidity concerns.

Watching the escalating strife between Bill and Charles anguished David. The last thing he wanted was for Bill to be cast out of the company. He just wanted his brother to keep himself in check, to stop stirring up trouble and antagonizing Charles.

Following the board meeting, David felt a temporary sense of relief, even optimism. It had been tense, but the issues were now all out on the table. He thought "progress had been made in clearing up these harsh feelings, that we were back on the same page, and that Billy would continue to work in the company and make contributions, and that it was a very healthy experience to have opened up and discussed all these things very frankly."

Bill, however, came away with a different feeling. He was as uneasy as ever about Koch Industries and his future there. He didn't trust Charles. And he had no intention of backing down.

By the following month, Bill was back to jousting with Charles, writing in an August 18 letter, "If you have irrevocably decided that you cannot tolerate me in the company simply because I disagreed with some of your management practices, then you should directly and forthrightly state it to me personally, man to man and brother to brother...rather than to fire me on the grounds that I may be disloyal...." He told Charles that under no conditions would he be "subservient to somebody else's autocratic desires."

In August and September, Charles dispatched emissaries, including Varner, to test the waters with Bill on whether he might consider selling his Koch shares. Bill declined. During the summer and into the fall, he had quietly lined up a coalition among Koch's small circle of shareholders who agreed that the company's board should expand from seven to nine members in order to more accurately reflect their full spectrum of interests. "Corporate democracy," Bill called it. He had argued in his July letter to Charles that the board should take a "stronger and...more active role" in the management of the company, and this would be their mechanism for doing so. His allies included the Simmons clan. These cousins held a sizable 13.1 percent bloc of Koch voting shares. Also in Bill's corner was J. Howard Marshall's eldest son, J. Howard Marshall III, who owned 4.1 percent of the company. When Marshall's sons had married, their father had gifted them the bulk of his prized Koch stock—what the elderly businessman referred to as the "family jewels."

Most important, Bill had persuaded his oldest brother, Frederick, to back his cause. Though partially disinherited by their father, a slight whose sting never truly went away, he still owned 14.2 percent of the company. Next to his brothers, who held 20.7 percent apiece, Frederick was the largest shareholder. Armed with Frederick's shares, Bill's consortium would technically control a little more than 52 percent of Koch Industries, enough to push through whatever changes they wished. Charles and David, meanwhile, together held 41.4 percent of the company's stock; Pierce Marshall and his father owned 4.5 percent; and Sterling Varner and other veteran employees controlled 2 percent of the company's shares. That brought the combined holdings of Charles's loyalists to a little under 48 percent.

Though Frederick's stake in Koch Industries entitled him to representation on the board, he had never exercised this right. The extent of his involvement with the company consisted of attending a handful of shareholder meetings in the early 1970s.

Frederick, who was already away at boarding school when his siblings were growing up, was perhaps closest with Bill, with whom he shared a love of fine art. The two were logical allies. Frederick had his own tensions with Charles. His younger brother's attempt to buy him out of the company after their father's death had angered him. And when that effort failed, Bill alleged, Charles later resorted to more devious means—what Bill described as a homosexual blackmail attempt to force Frederick to sell his shares, a charge Charles has denied. ("Charles' 'homosexual blackmail' to get control of my shares did not succeed for the simple reason that I am not homosexual," Frederick said.)

Like Bill, Frederick's lack of control over his wealth—all of it tied up in Koch Industries shares—frustrated him. He had ambitions as a collector of art and antiques, and as a patron of the theater. Frederick strongly favored taking the company public in order to unlock their assets.

Bill's coup attempt, which had evolved over the months, hinged on calling a special shareholders meeting, its purpose to both expand the board and elect a new slate of directors, a move that would require first dissolving the existing board. Together, Bill and his alliance controlled a small majority of Koch stock and enough votes to elect five directors. Since Charles refused to accede to shareholder wishes, they would have to force his hand. Taking over the board would give them control over the direction of the company; they could marshal their influence to take the company public, raise dividends, or make whatever other strategic (or management) changes they desired.

They had agreed to vote their shares to elect Bill, Marjorie Simmons Gray, J. Howard Marshall III, Frederick's longtime lawyer S. Hazard Gillespie, and Jimmy Linn, a prominent Oklahoma City attorney who was also Marjorie Simmons Gray's son-in-law. Charles and David and their backers would possess the votes to elect four board members. Charles and David were a given, but the chances were good that in this shake-up, J. Howard Marshall II, who had passed the majority of his shares down to his sons, might lose his seat, while Sterling Varner and Koch's chief financial officer, Tom Carey, retained theirs.

Sensing dissension—though unaware of any plans afoot to expand the board—Charles circulated a strongly worded, four-and-a-half-page letter to shareholders on November 18, 1980, less than three weeks before Bill and his faction planned to convene their meeting. "My primary effort has been and will continue to be to assure the ongoing profitability and growth of the company," he wrote. "Some have alluded to this objective as a desire to build a monument to Charles Koch, but this is an unfair assertion and reflects a lack of understanding of economics and human nature. A company cannot remain viable if its management objectives are confined to staying even."

Failing to follow a growth-oriented mission, Charles noted, would make it impossible to retain and recruit top talent and doom the company in the long run. "That, in any event, is my firm conviction, and it is a conviction I will continue to follow." He warned that he would "resist any efforts to impede our efficiency by the imposition of any…bureaucratic committee or board structure."

Bill, meanwhile, had called the First National Bank of Wichita, which administered his and Frederick's trusts. He requested proxies to vote the Koch Industries shares held in trust. After swearing a bank official to secrecy, Bill explained that he wanted to call a stockholders meeting in order to elect a board that would more accurately represent the interests of shareholders. He described his brother's maddening obstinacy and failure to address shareholder desires. To underscore his point, he told the banker a parable involving a farmer and his prize mule.

"He couldn't train him because the mule would never listen to him," Bill explained, "so he took him to the best mule trainer in the world and negotiated a price with the mule trainer to train him, and the price came up to be $1,000. And the farmer said,

'My God, $1,000. Hell, the mule is only worth $5,000.' He said, 'Well, I'm the best in the world.' So, he paid it. First thing the mule trainer did was to pick up a two by four and swat that mule by the side of the head. And the farmer said, 'What the hell did you do that for? That is a prize mule. You hurt it.' The mule trainer said, 'If I'm going to train him, I got to get his attention.'" The implication was clear: Charles needed a blow to the head for the good of Koch Industries.

On November 25, 1980, as dusk spilled across the plains surrounding Koch's Wichita headquarters, Bill stepped into Charles's office. It was the Tuesday before Thanksgiving and the brothers had scheduled a meeting to discuss liquidity, but Bill had other matters on his mind. He told Charles that he and other stockholders wanted him to call a special shareholders meeting to, among other things, discuss Bill's role in the company.

Charles was stunned. "You're embarking on a program that's going to destroy the company," he seethed. "You're out for revenge against me. You won't get your self-respect from attacking me. You and the shareholders should be cheering on what I've done for the company instead of complaining."

"Charles, let's talk about what we want to do here."

Charles laughed sarcastically. "Billy, you're the type of person that if the bullet is ricocheting around the room and I say duck, you want to debate the merits of the bullet."

"Charles, all I want to talk to you about is how to improve the company."

"Well, Billy, you hate me, you're out to get me."

"No, Charles, that's not true."

There was no sense forestalling the inevitable. If Charles and Bill could not get along as brothers, how could they continue on as business partners?

"We need a divorce," Charles said finally. They would have

to divide the company, or one brother would need to buy out the other.

"Well, Charles, if you're not going to call the meeting, then I'll call it," Bill said. He walked out of Charles's office, leaving the shell-shocked CEO to fume and fret.

"One piece of advice my father gave me was that, 'If you want someone to hate you, make him a lot of money,'" Charles reflected later. "I didn't understand it at the time. I understand it now."

As Charles anxiously spent the holiday in Wichita with his family, David celebrated Thanksgiving in New York with Frederick, dining in the tenants-only restaurant located off the lobby in Frederick's residence at 825 Fifth Avenue. The prewar co-op, designed in the 1920s by J. E. R. Carpenter, was one of the jewels of Fifth Avenue. It had a striking double-gabled roof of red terra-cotta tile, and a roster of upper-crust tenants.

David lived in a U.N. Plaza duplex overlooking the East River, perhaps a ten-minute cab ride from Frederick, but the brothers tended to see each other only when their mother visited. Today, however, David had an agenda. Charles had told him about his conversation with Bill, and the possibility that their brother might call a shareholders meeting. He wanted to gauge where Frederick stood.

David turned up at Frederick's apartment 40 minutes early, before the other guests had arrived, and he filled him in on the recent strife between Bill and Charles. He incorrectly assumed his eldest brother was in the dark about developments at their family company. "Fred listened attentively," David recalled, "and I thought I was educating him for the first time about what was happening.... Obviously, I was very naïve." According to Frederick, he remained quiet because "at this point in time William had asked that I not reveal my reaction to the proxy fight."

Charles had told David to keep an eye out for a letter announcing a shareholders meeting, and David fished it out of the mail at his office the Friday after Thanksgiving. "Enclosed is a notice for a special stockholders meeting of Koch Industries that a number of Koch stockholders are calling to consider increasing the Board of Directors of Koch Industries to nine members..." the cover letter read. "This broader representation will be important in making decisions on stockholder liquidity and dividend issues which will be decided by the board."

David phoned Charles in Wichita, reading him sections of the letter in disbelief. Bill's name was on the announcement. Even more alarming, so was Frederick's. David had spent hours with his oldest brother the previous day; Frederick had played dumb, never mentioning the plan they had set in motion. It seemed plain to Charles and David that a hostile takeover attempt was under way and that Bill might be angling to oust Charles.

When he hung up with Charles, David phoned Frederick. "I got this notice, Freddie, what's going on?"

"Well, I think it's time for a change in management of Koch Industries," Frederick responded.

"Why do you want to fire Charles? He's done a great job."

"Well," Frederick said, "are you surprised?" It was no secret that Frederick and Charles disliked one another. (Frederick would later say that the goal was not to remove Charles as CEO, but as board chairman.)

On Saturday, David tracked down Bill, who was spending the weekend in Oklahoma City with members of the Simmons family.

"Are you going to fire Charles?" David demanded when Bill came on the line.

"No we're not," Bill said. "We have no intentions to."

David didn't buy it. "You're lying," he said. "You're no brother of mine. I never want to have anything to do with you again." He slammed down the phone.

*　　*　　*

That day, Charles heard from J. Howard Marshall II. The elderly oil tycoon, then seventy-five, had been friends with Fred Koch and was fiercely loyal to Charles. Marshall considered his decision to swap his interest in Great Northern Oil for Koch stock "either the smartest or the luckiest thing I ever did, and maybe a combination of both. It turned out to be the best deal I ever made."

Earlier in the week, when Charles informed him of Bill's machinations, Marshall had reassured Koch's worried CEO that neither of his sons, who together controlled a little over 8 percent of the company stock, would be involved; they'd never cross their father. By Saturday of Thanksgiving weekend, Marshall, however, was shocked to learn that this was precisely what his elder son, Howard III, intended to do. When Marshall finally spoke to his son, who confirmed his role in the unfolding proxy fight, Howard II pleaded with him, making "a case based on family obligation and loyalty," but Howard III remained committed to Bill's plan.

"What do we do now?" Charles asked after Marshall had explained the situation.

"Well," Marshall said, "there's one thing that Howard III understands, and that's money." Marshall would attempt to buy his stock back from his son. Without Howard III's small, yet decisive, percentage of voting stock, the dissident shareholders would lack the shares necessary to ram through the changes to the board they desired.

The next day, Sunday, Charles and Koch's general counsel Don Cordes flew from Wichita to Houston, where they picked up Howard Marshall, and continued on to Los Angeles, to present an offer to Howard III. It was less than a week before Bill's shareholder meeting was scheduled to commence, on Friday, December 5.

"I'm going to offer Howard III $8 million, take it or leave it," Marshall said as they were en route.

When Bill learned of Marshall's offer to his son, he offered to double it. A few agonizing days passed in Los Angeles, as Howard III pondered his next move—selling out to his dad or going against him. He had underestimated his father's reaction to the shareholder insurrection. The prospect that his son might betray Charles had brought the old man to tears. Marshall looked so frail as he laid out an $8 million cashier's check in front of his son. It was as if the dispute was sapping the very life force out of him.

Family loyalty eventually won out. Howard III rejected Bill's offer. He accompanied Marshall Senior and Koch's lawyer, Don Cordes, to his bank, where he relinquished his Koch shares, stored in a safety-deposit box. The balance of power had abruptly shifted: With the Marshall family's shares, along with a small amount of stock owned by longtime Koch Industries executives, Charles controlled 51 percent of the company.

With Bill's rebellion falling apart, he called off the shareholders meeting scheduled for that Friday. But Koch's board did convene that day: its purpose to decide Bill's fate. He'd crossed a line. His scheming had sparked a wildfire of panic among Koch employees. Bill had lost the trust of Koch's senior managers. How could he continue on with the company's employees wondering what he might do next?

Charles had wanted to fire Bill that summer. The narrowly averted putsch confirmed to him that he shouldn't have relented. Charles entrusted Varner, with his gentle though direct manner, with the task of convincing Bill to resign quietly. But Bill refused, forcing Varner to make a formal motion to the board calling for his ouster. In the dark-paneled boardroom, one by one four hands went up.

But David's wasn't among them.

Over the past year, David had been torn apart, between loyalty to his twin and fealty to his older brother. He was furious with Bill for throwing the company into turmoil; in a surge of anger he had even told his brother that he wanted nothing to do with him. But that wasn't true. David wanted desperately to maintain a connection to Bill. Charles, in raising his hand in support of Bill's firing, had made a choice not just to excommunicate his brother from the company, but to sever him from his life. David couldn't bring himself to do the same, and thankfully he didn't need to. The vote carried without him taking sides.

The following week, on December 10, Koch's general counsel met with members of the dissident shareholders group at the Oklahoma City law offices of Jimmy Linn to begin negotiations between the opposing factions. Cordes floated an offer to buy out the dissidents at $140 a share (which would have made Bill's stake worth about $329 million). He also delivered a warning—or was it a threat? He cautioned that Bill and his shareholder allies should steer clear of Wichita. The dissidents had stirred up such hostilities, the lawyer said, that their safety could not be guaranteed.

As Christmas 1980 approached, Bill sent gifts to his niece and nephew, Elizabeth and Chase, who were then five and three, respectively. Even this seemingly harmless gesture filled Charles with suspicion. He sent the presents back. When Bill called his brother to wish him a Merry Christmas, Charles refused to come to the phone. Mary, as usual, had invited her sons to spend the holidays in Wichita, but Charles told his mother that he and his family would not attend Christmas dinner at her home if Bill and Frederick were there. Because of the discord, Mary told Bill and Frederick not to come home for Christmas. (Frederick doesn't recall being disinvited. If the brothers "chose not to come, the decision was theirs.")

Bill's efforts to assert himself had failed spectacularly. If he had felt like an outcast before, now he truly was the family's black sheep. Since childhood, when Fred and Mary Koch sent their tantrum-prone son to a psychologist to get over his intense resentment of Charles, Bill had periodically lapsed into deep depressions.

But the six months after his firing from Koch were among his darkest. Cloistered in his Dover, Massachusetts, mansion, he spent his days plotting with his lawyers and vegetating in front of the television. "This was the worst time I'd ever seen him in his life," David recalled. "He was almost paralyzed, almost lifeless."

David tried to help his brother get back on his feet. In late 1981, Bill and his girlfriend Joan urged him to visit a Boston psychiatrist they'd been seeing; they believed this would help to improve communication between the twins. David, who made weekly business trips to Massachusetts, warily obliged.

The experience was surreal. The psychiatrist "spoke for about an hour and a half on why I needed psychiatric care," David remembered. Growing angry that he had been lured to the psychiatrist's office under false pretenses, David finally forced the conversation back to Bill. "I asked a number of questions...to the psychiatrist and one was why was Billy so angry and nasty to our mother and made her cry all the time, upset her so much, and he said, 'Well, that's a very positive sign because people with your brother's problems have to climb out of their depression on the backs of the people they love the most.'...I asked him about why Billy...started this fight to get control of Koch Industries and he said, 'Well, Billy has a secret desire to fail' and that he knew that when he started this fight with Charles that he couldn't win. I asked the doctor what I could do to help my brother and get him out of this depression and terribly unhappy state that he was in, and he said, '...there is nothing that you can do...until you straighten yourself out.'"

David left the two-and-a-half-hour session deeply shaken, and with the suspicion that this shrink had prodded Bill to take a stand against Charles. The experience shocked him so much that he wrote everything down. According to David, when he spoke to Bill a few days later, Bill reported that the psychiatrist had told him that his twin was "totally under the control of Charles."

*   *   *

Back at Koch Industries, Bill's firing had removed one threat to Charles's hegemony. But Bill, Frederick, and the dissident shareholders (all of them family members) still controlled nearly half of the company. Like his father, Charles demanded loyalty from his business associates and employees, and he couldn't pursue his plans for Koch Industries always looking over his shoulder for the next coup attempt by malcontented stockholders. The company and the dissidents needed a "divorce," as Charles had put it. And it would be a messy one.

All options were now on the table, including taking the company public. In early 1981, Koch entered preliminary merger talks with Kerr-McGee, a publicly traded oil and gas company. The deal would have exchanged Koch shares for Kerr holdings, solving shareholder liquidity problems. But the companies could not reach any middle ground on a valuation of Koch.

Meanwhile, Koch hired Morgan Stanley and Lehman Brothers to conduct parallel valuations of the company. Both investment banks determined that Koch shares should fetch in the vicinity of $160 a share, a price Bill (who stood to net about $376 million) and his allies deemed far too low. Bill subsequently retained Goldman Sachs and the Boston-based consulting firm Bain & Company (where a young Mitt Romney was cutting his teeth) to conduct their own analyses. As was his style, Bill was not a passive client; he grilled his advisors and pressed them to scrutinize every corner of the sprawling conglomerate. "Bill was a very demanding client," remembered Alfred Eckert, who led the Goldman Sachs team evaluating Koch Industries, "very involved, asked very good questions, spent a lot of time making sure that no stone would be left unturned."

By 1982, with negotiations faltering, Bill hired a New York lawyer named Arthur Liman, a high-profile litigator who had served as the chief counsel on the Senate's Iran-Contra investigation. Bill realized that the threat of litigation might goose Koch to raise its offer, and Liman's hiring alone sent a clear signal. Another pressure point was publicity, a powerful motivator for a company that played it very close to the vest. Charles, Bill observed, "was very sensitive to publicity at that time."

Both sides had agreed to keep the delicate negotiations confidential, and the company had so far managed to keep news of the boardroom acrimony out of the media. Koch Industries did not want to spook its already worried employees or allow its competitors and business partners to smell weakness. But in July 1982, the corporate discord spilled into the press when *Fortune* magazine ran a feature story titled "Family Feud at a Corporate Colossus." Charles and David had given interviews for the story without mentioning the tense talks under way, but Bill and his allies had violated the family's vow of *omerta*, anonymously disclosing information about the rift among Koch's owners.

"Keeping a company with estimated annual revenues of more than $14 billion out of the public eye is a task that one of its principal owners describes as 'sort of like trying to hide an elephant behind a telephone pole,'" the article began. "...But these days the shy elephant is stomping around in a traumatic fit. A family feud has erupted among the four Koch brothers, who own 75% of the company, dividing them into two rival camps. Blood and money, that most volatile of mixtures, makes their fight over the corporation's future especially bitter."

Charles, predictably, was horrified by the story, which quoted an anonymous member of the dissident faction—who later turned out to be Bill—saying: "It's a classic dispute between stockholders who want yield and liquidity and a management that wants power and authority."

That October, when negotiations had still failed to progress, Bill finally unleashed a suit against Koch Industries and his brothers. He alleged a laundry list of mismanagement, including Charles's lavishing of company funds on libertarian causes. Frederick, under intense pressure from their mother to do his part to deescalate the family hostilities, declined to join the lawsuit.

Charles and David retaliated with a $400 million countersuit, claiming that Bill and his supporters had used *Fortune* to defame Charles by portraying him as "no less maliciously creative than the willful J. R. Ewing of the television show 'Dallas' in devising ways to control his brothers and the family fortune."

Through the end of 1982 and into early 1983, the two sides remained far apart on a buyout. In November, Koch had offered $160 (the valuation suggested by Morgan Stanley and Lehman); Bill's team countered with $240. But as discovery in the lawsuit began to heat up, so, too, did the pace of negotiations.

On May 25, 1983, the dissident shareholders, accompanied by a phalanx of lawyers and investment bankers, convened at the Marriott Hotel near New York's LaGuardia Airport. Desperate to rid itself of the suit and the problem shareholders, Koch had substantially raised its bid to $200 a share, plus an interest in an oil concession off the coast of Santa Barbara, California.

Bill thought he could still squeeze more out of his brothers. Nevertheless, as he opened the meeting, he stressed that it was "very important for our group to stick together. We came into this fight together, we should go out together."

Lawyer Arthur Liman, Bill recalled, told the shareholders that Koch Industries "was our heritage and we had to decide whether we wanted to keep our heritage or get away from it and pursue our own endeavors in life and he viewed that as the essence of the decision.... He said this was a good opportunity to get away from Charles, who in his opinion was going to run the company in his own way for his benefit without regard for anybody else."

A consensus emerged, as the rest of the advisors chimed in: *Take the offer.* The shareholders asked the gaggle of lawyers and bankers to clear the room so they could deliberate. Hopeful of restoring family peace, Marjorie Simmons Gray, whose close relationship with Mary Koch had suffered because the Koch matriarch blamed her for siding against Charles, urged that they settle. Frederick agreed, telling the group he had better things to do in life than get dragged into a long and nasty lawsuit. When the shareholders took a vote, Bill was the lone holdout.

"I advocated going back at a higher number and then horse trading to around $220," Bill recalled. "That was the number I was shooting for." But keeping their coalition together had been a struggle as it was. He likened his role to Dwight Eisenhower's during World War II: The general had spent most of his time simply holding the Allies together. In the interest of maintaining a united front, Bill reluctantly agreed to accept the deal.

But he wanted it to happen quickly, before Koch could pull the offer or attempt to chisel on the price. The company was equally eager to settle the matter. By the following day, May 26, the company had sent a draft agreement to Liman. "Bullshit," Bill told his lawyer, "I'm not going to go with their draft." Bill so thoroughly distrusted Charles by this point that he insisted Liman's firm draft the agreement. Koch tried to "slip things by the other side" in contracts, Bill told his lawyer.

Over two days in early June, lawyers for both sides completed a marathon of contract negotiations in the midtown Manhattan offices of Liman's firm, Paul, Weiss, Rifkind, Wharton & Garrison. Near midnight on June 4, 1983, the finalized agreement sat before Charles in the law firm's large conference room, where Bill was also seated. (David and Frederick were not present.) Under the terms of the deal, Koch would buy out the dissident shareholders for $1.1 billion, of which Bill would receive $470 million and Frederick $330 million. Such was the price of peace at Koch Industries. Charles signed. So did Bill.

The deal completed, Bill stood up from the conference table and smiled. "We've got our business affairs separated, and the war is over," he told his brother. They were after all relatively young men—Bill was forty-three and Charles forty-seven—with many years ahead of them. "We're still brothers, and I care about you." Bill extended his hand. Charles ignored the gesture. He turned and strode briskly out of the conference room, trailed by his lawyers. After he left, Bill crumpled heavily into his chair and buried his face in his hands. Tears were in his eyes.

Closing this acrimonious chapter brought a wave of relief to Koch employees, who had experienced several years of uncertainty about the company's future. At the 1984 annual stockholders meeting, fifty-six of Koch's top managers signed onto a symbolic resolution celebrating Charles for navigating the company through the recent tumult. Noting that "1983 saw the conclusion of one of the most traumatic periods in the Company's history," it lauded Charles "for the leadership abilities, high principles and strength of character which he displayed not only in leading the Company to its outstanding success over the years but in leading the company through its recent crisis without sacrificing the principles for which he and the Company have stood."

But the testing of Charles's mettle had just begun. The long war between the Koch brothers was only starting.

CHAPTER EIGHT

Mighty Mary

Since the feuding between Mary Koch's sons had begun, the anniversary of Fred's death, on November 17, had arrived each year freighted with additional melancholy. She felt his absence most acutely because the battle among their boys, in all likelihood, never would have erupted had he not died young.

Fred would have snuffed out any hint of family unrest; on his watch, a brother-versus-brother legal skirmish was unthinkable. But without his firm hand to keep them in check, his sons ignored their father's beyond-the-grave admonition to "be kind and generous to one another."

The feud that had engulfed the clan—making family gatherings impossible and maintaining good relations with each of her four sons an act of emotional contortionism—had wounded Mary deeply. "She was the meat in the middle of the sandwich, and she was getting pounded on both sides," says one of her closest confidantes during this period.

Alone in the dark, sprawling stone mansion off 13th Street, she lay awake nights trying to figure out how to heal the divisions that were tearing her family apart. Mary saw much of her late husband in Bill and Charles—especially in their bullheadedness; like Fred, they were "made of stubborn Dutch stock that won't give in."

The negative publicity (and whispers in Wichita society) that the dispute generated added to Mary's distress. The 1982 *For-*

tune article that first lifted the curtain on the Kochs' private melo-
drama dealt a particularly heavy blow. It upset her all the more
because she had read the story directly after returning to Wichita
from a trip to see Bill and his girlfriend Joan in Massachusetts.
During her visit, Bill had wined and dined Mary and her friends
in Boston, where some of his art collection was on display at the
Museum of Fine Arts. And he had even hired a mariachi band
to serenade them during a luncheon at his Dover manse. Flipping
anxiously through the pages of *Fortune*, Mary saw the family rift
become a chasm before her eyes. She blamed Bill for the "distaste-
ful" article, which she considered a sickening act of "character
assassination" against Charles.

Mary loved her sons equally—or tried to. Bill was generous,
and he could be utterly charming when he chose to be. David was
sensible and easygoing, the kind of son a mother didn't need to
worry about, though she did wish he'd give up his bachelor ways
and settle down. She was deeply proud of Charles for shouldering
the responsibility for his father's company at such a young age,
and for the incredible wealth he had brought to the family. And
Frederick—he was an artistic soul just like she was.

Mary had tried to adopt an air of neutrality, but her true alle-
giance seemed clear enough—it was to Charles and the company
he'd built from the patchwork of his father's holdings. Instead of
rebelling, she felt the dissident shareholders should bow down to
Charles for what he'd accomplished. Knowing Bill's temperamen-
tal streak and the grudge he had nursed against Charles since boyhood, Mary had a difficult time seeing the strife—at least Bill's
part in it—as anything other than the unsettling continuation of a
childhood vendetta. "You have judged Charles in a cruel & jealous
manner instead of appreciating the way he has worked to make
the company grow & give all of the stockholders more dividends,"
she wrote Bill in October 1982. Had he been "more rational" and
"less emotional," Mary continued, Bill "could have accomplished

a great deal" at Koch Industries. She called her son's decision to file suit against his brothers "unforgivable" and she feared her family would never spend another Christmas together, because "instead of joy & love there would be bitterness & hatred."

Mary had exerted every ounce of her maternal influence to hasten a settlement, even calling Koch Industries' general counsel Don Cordes to implore him to speed things along. She wrote Frederick to plead with him to "help me to mend bridges not destroy them." (Her persistent guilt tripping had kept Frederick from joining Bill's 1982 lawsuit.) Unable to get through to Bill by other means, she resorted to emotional blackmail. "This conflict is tearing me down & affecting my health," she wrote him as the feud escalated. "I am a nervous wreck & dissolve in tears when I think or talk about this terrible war going on between my sons."

"The only thing I want before I die is reconciliation," she wrote in another letter, signing off: "Please listen to me before I die!"

After the settlement, Mary allowed herself a flicker of hope that family harmony might finally be within reach. "I never was so relieved in my life & I am sure you must be too," she wrote Frederick shortly after the deal had closed.

To Bill, who Mary learned had continued to stew after the two sides had untangled their business affairs, she wrote: "I trust & pray that you can find some business that will interest you enough to get your teeth in it & get over your brooding & bitterness." Mary's siding with Charles and David confirmed what Bill had always felt—that she favored his brothers. Their relationship deteriorated rapidly after Bill filed suit, until mother and son barely communicated.

Bill felt remorse for the toll the rift had taken on his mother. He found her pleas "emotionally wrenching," he told an interviewer, but he ignored them in his single-minded quest to squeeze every last penny out of his brothers. In June 1983, as lawyers finalized the stock purchase agreement at the offices of Paul, Weiss, Rifkind, Wharton & Garrison, Bill had beckoned over Bob Howard, a Wichita attorney who represented Koch Industries and the Koch family. "Howard, I want you to do something for me. When you get home please tell Mama I still love her." Howard dutifully conveyed the message. The gesture "touched" Mary, but there were still raw feelings. "My heart aches over all the past trouble," she told Bill in a July 1983 letter. But she hoped "in time there can be peace in our family."

Peace among her sons proved elusive, but there was a brief period of détente. Newly flush with cash, Bill and Frederick busied themselves spending some of their enormous wealth.

Frederick became a voracious collector, hoovering up rare manuscripts, musical scores, and paintings. Though he often deployed third-party agents to keep his role in the purchases anonymous, the frenetic pace of his buying turned heads on the international auction scene. "Almost every day, in London, New York, Paris or Monte Carlo a picture is bought by Mr. Koch or by dealers acting on his behalf," London's *Daily Telegraph* reported in the 1980s, noting that he was said to be shelling out £18 million annually on art purchases. "The buying goes on relentlessly. Koch is said by an associate to be 'unimpressed by cost.' There's been nothing quite like it since Pierpont Morgan."

Frederick's buying habits mystified the art world not only because of the scale of his spending and the secrecy surrounding his purchases, but because his ravenous collecting seemed to lack a through-line. "As befits a man who has used his wealth to buy himself complete privacy," the *Telegraph* noted, "the nature of Mr. Koch's taste remains something of a secret. It is certainly eclectic. He likes Symbolism, the aesthetic movement, the ancient Greek and Roman painters between 1860 and 1910, the ornate and baroque, the male subject."

One former Sotheby's employee recalled that Frederick "was known as kind of the vacuum cleaner of Madison Avenue"—where the auction house was then situated. "He bought everything and anything, some of which was really terrific, some of which not so much. He was very interested in Pre-Raphaelite thought, and everything that went along with it, music, poetry, paintings, drawings, sculpture, and so acquired a lot of things from that era. I think pretty much anything that came his way, he bought."

Frederick also splurged on historic abodes, which he then lovingly restored, often with the help of his architect, Charles Young, who had worked with I. M. Pei. On the French Riviera near Monaco, he scooped up Villa Torre Clementina, its lavish gardens designed to guide visitors, as if passing through the rooms of a home, to the shore of the Mediterranean. Near Salzburg, Frederick acquired Schloss Blühnbach, the palatial hunting lodge of Archduke Franz Ferdinand. To house his massive nineteenth-century art collection, he selected Sutton Place, a sixteenth-century Tudor masterpiece outside London, which had once been owned by John Paul Getty and was infamous as the illicit trysting spot of Henry VIII and Anne Boleyn. In the United States, he purchased Elm Court, a Gothic mansion in western Pennsylvania with a loggia that evoked the architecture of the Ivy League; and just off Manhattan's Fifth Avenue on East 80th Street, he acquired an ornate, six-floor French Regency–style town house, which had once belonged to one of the daughters of dime store magnate Frank Winfield Woolworth.

The odd thing about his obsession with historic houses is that he rarely stayed in them, even when he visited. He kept an apartment in Monte Carlo, near Villa Torre Clementina. When he visited Elm Court, according to one of his guests, he slept not in the main house but in a smaller residence on the property. He never spent a night at Sutton Place (and under tax rules he technically couldn't, because he purchased it through a charitable foundation). And when in New York, he lived in a two-bedroom apartment on Fifth Avenue, a fifteen-minute walk from the large, spectacular town house that he almost never slept in. It was as if he viewed his collection of homes as objects of art, to be appreciated but not sullied by human contact.

Frederick's life had a hermetic quality to it, but the same could not be said of Bill's. Feeling "like a kid let out of reform school," he indulged in his own flamboyant way. Advised by the executive director of the Getty Museum, he binged on expensive art. He rapidly accumulated a series of multimillion-dollar properties, including a Fifth Avenue duplex, and two Cape Cod compounds. In a cavernous, climate-controlled cellar beneath Homeport, one of his Cape estates, he amassed a 30,000-plus-bottle wine collection, including an incredibly rare 150-year vertical of Château Lafite, which *Wine Spectator* would (in 1996) dub the finest in America. Bill took up sailing, a sport that appealed to his analytical mind and love of nature. When a local yacht club rejected his application—Bill had offended the delicate sensibilities of Cape Cod's blue bloods by noisily choppering to and from the peninsula, among other lapses in decorum—he built his own marina. Though he enjoyed throwing around millions like they were sawbucks, Bill quickly tired of his life of leisure. He'd become the quintessential "country club bum" Fred Koch so despised. "After eating so many gourmet meals and drinking so much good wine, I knew I needed to do something," he said.

So in late 1983, Bill formed an energy company called Oxbow, the term for a sharp, U-shaped bend in a river. It was a poetic nod to Bill's own new direction. At Koch Industries, he led the company's move into coal mining and petroleum coke—a valuable refining by-product. Now he steered Oxbow into the same sector, making him a competitor (albeit a minor one) of his brothers' company. But he also branched out into geothermal power, real estate, and even bought a stake in *CFO* magazine. The publication, he liked to point out, was started by Neil Goldhirsh, who had been in business with his brother Bernard, the founder of *Inc.* magazine. Neil had parted ways with Bernard over brotherly disagreements, a scenario Bill could relate to.

Bill was very much his father's son, a shrewd and innovative businessman, and over the years Oxbow grew into a multimillion- (and later, multibillion-) dollar business. Bill had something to prove—and he was proving it. "The best thing that ever could have happened to me was leaving the company," he said in the late 1980s. "I didn't have big mother to protect me. The whole process was very painful, but a lot of good comes out of a lot of bad. When I was working there, my whole image, everything I was doing was all wrapped up in the company."

But as he tried to move on with his life, Bill remained anchored to the past. Less than a year after the brothers had sealed their drawn-out corporate divorce, Bill commenced an investigation into whether Charles and his allies had cheated the dissident sharehold- ers into selling their shares cheaply. Koch Industries had borrowed more than $800 million to finance the buyout. Bill and his bankers calculated that it would take years for the company to free itself of the debt, but somehow it did so in just two. "How could they have so much cash?" Bill wondered. The buyout should have hobbled the company, but Koch Industries was growing faster than ever.

In June 1985, Bill again filed suit against his brothers and Koch Industries; the Simmons clan joined him. They alleged that Charles and his allies had hidden or misrepresented lucrative assets, includ- ing oil and gas concessions in Qatar and a pair of wells in Utah, and had intentionally downplayed the financial prospects of the company's Minnesota-based refinery, Pine Bend. The plaintiffs soon augmented the complaint to tack on allegations of fraud and racketeering. After remaining on the sidelines of the legal dispute, Frederick, to his mother's tearful dismay, signed on to the case as well, convinced by his attorney to do so.

The suit alleged that Charles "had mislead [sic] plaintiffs as to the profitability, worth, and future prospects of KII"—Koch Industries Inc.—"by a course of action which included distributing misinformation" and contended Bill, Frederick, and the other dissidents were deceived by "Charles Koch's actions which suggested that he was irresponsible and that his lack of judgment had and would continue to adversely affect the value, profitability and prospects of KII. Representative of his irresponsible conduct was his fettish [sic] with Libertarian causes, which included wasting in excess of $5 million of KII funds on such causes" and "his exposure of KII to potentially large money judgments on account of his disregard of government regulations and laws." They charged that this had been part of a pattern of fraudulent behavior intended to "encourage plaintiffs and others not supportive of Charles Koch to give up their stock ownership interests in KII and to do so for less than fair value." (The company denied the allegations. "I don't think the lawsuit has anything to do with money," Don Cordes, Koch's top lawyer, retorted at the time.)

Once again, the Koch brothers were at war. The rift was so total that representatives of Charles and David approached *Forbes* that year to request that their entry in the magazine's annual roundup of America's richest citizens "be severed from Fred and William, their deeply alienated brothers," the magazine noted. "Now, that's sibling rivalry."

Mary's family was imploding. She found respite from her despair in the company of a younger man whose marriage was unraveling.

In the early 1980s, Mary met Michael Oliver at the Wichita Art Association, where she was a long-serving board member and major benefactor. A young, free-spirited assistant art professor at Friends University, a Christian liberal arts college in Wichita, Oliver specialized in pewter smithing. He had grown up poor in Mary's hometown of Kansas City, working his way through junior college and eventually earning an MFA from the University of Kansas. As she reached out her delicate hand to take his, Oliver was awed to be in the presence of a member of Wichita royalty. "The way she stood, the way her eyes sparkled, her kindness, her inner-self was so genuine and pleasant," he recalled. "She could remember names like you wouldn't believe. My lord. I'm sure it was cultural, that cultural idea that you need to remember everyone's names."

Following their first meeting, Mary grew close with Oliver and his then-wife, inviting them to spend the weekend at Spring Creek, the Koch family's ranch in the Flint Hills. Oliver's marriage was on the rocks, and by 1984, the couple had filed for divorce. As the news spread through the city's close-knit arts scene, Oliver bumped into Mary at a gala at the Wichita Art Museum. She teared up when she spotted him. He began crying, too.

"Oh, you were such a lovely couple, why is this happening?" she asked. "Don't worry about it, Michael, I'll take care of you."

Soon she invited him to dinner at her home. Oliver was petrified as he pulled his beat-up Honda through the security gate and up the circle drive. That night they sipped vodka tonics with a twist of lemon, Mary's favorite cocktail, and in amusing contrast to her aristocratic image, she served Stouffer's macaroni and cheese. ("David said these are nourishing," she told Oliver matter-of-factly.)

"I knew there was an attraction between both of us, and I just enjoyed being with her," Oliver remembered. Their friendship soon evolved into something more. "It was a natural progression, because she was lonely and I was lonely. She was very lonely."

Mary had sought companionship with a handful of (often much younger) men after Fred's death. Though her courtship with Fred and their honeymoon were the stuff of storybooks, their marriage had not always been a happy one. She had loved Fred but also feared him, according to Bill. "My father was fairly tough with my mother," Bill once told *Vanity Fair*. "When she would irritate him, he wouldn't speak to her for two weeks....My mother was afraid of my father."

One member of the extended Koch family described Mary as "a beautiful bird in a cage." This relative noted, "She lived, by modern female standards, the life of a princess in a tower. She was kind of held captive by history and by the men in her life....She was Fred's trophy. So what was she going to do? Maybe that's why she chose to live her final days the way she did, in this kind of I'll-be-damned-what-you-think-of-me, I'm-going-to-do-what-I-want-and-have-Michael-in-[my]-life" way.

Oliver was half Mary's age, and five years younger than her youngest sons, David and Bill. Their relationship became grist for the local gossip mill, as members of her social circle speculated about the gold-digging motives of Mary's handsome consort.

"I got a lot of criticism," Oliver recalled. "I was everything from a gigolo to whatever you want. But she didn't care, and I didn't care. And I said, 'You know, it takes a younger man to keep up with you.' It was just exciting. It was like you dream when you are a little child, and you always wanted to be the prince living in the castle. Well, I got that. That happened."

David and Charles were initially suspicious. But as Oliver chauffeured Mary around Wichita, prepared meals with her at night, and escorted her on long walks around the Koch compound, the family—and particularly David, with whom Oliver occasionally played tennis—gradually warmed to him. Charles was always polite, but Oliver felt intimidated by him and he noticed that Mary occasionally seemed apprehensive around her son. "Charles has a lot of his dad in him," Oliver said. "So she was a little afraid of him."

Mary had two sides. One was the elegant, patrician *grand dame* of Wichita high society, who draped herself in fur and jewels and affected a mild air of *noblesse oblige*—a "woman from a different era," the member of the extended family put it. But she was also an avid outdoorswoman, as comfortable in waders as she was in couture, and as at home in a hunting blind as in an opera box.

One longtime family friend, Constance Witterman, described her as "a woman of all seasons. She was cultured, refined, intellectual, athletic…she was everything all rolled up into one." Charles's friends nicknamed her "Mighty Mary" for her indomitable style.

"She loved to party, loved to dance, loved to fish, loved to shoot, loved to hunt," Oliver said. Together, they cruised the Flint Hills by four-wheeler, fly-fishing in the creeks and lakes around the Koch family ranch. Mary, whose deadly marksmanship was the stuff of local legend, taught Oliver how to shoot skeet. They traveled a couple times a year to hunt and fish at the Rolling Rock Club, the exclusive sportsman's retreat in western Pennsylvania owned by the Mellon family.

One of Mary's favorite summer pastimes was hunting bullfrogs. She was part of what Oliver half-jokingly described as a "secret society" of frog hunters among the local elite ("we're talking about some of the richest people in all of Wichita") who on summer evenings, after a few libations, waded into nearby ponds and streams scanning the shore with flashlights and scooping the amphibians—temporarily immobilized by the light—into canvas sacks. This group contributed their bounty to the chef at the Wichita Country Club, across the street from the Koch compound, getting dressed up in tuxes and dinner gowns to feast on frog's legs and champagne in one of the club's private dining rooms.

Oliver accompanied Mary on a hunt one night, sneaking onto the golf course to scour for bullfrogs in the water hazards. After an hour, they had harvested fifteen and Oliver followed Mary, both of them splattered with mud, up to the house with a noisy, pulsating gunnysack slung over his shoulder. When they reached the house and set the sack in the double stainless steel sink in the kitchen, it was no longer moving. There wasn't a sound.

"Mary, do you think they're dead?" Oliver asked.

Together they opened the bag and cautiously peered in. Petrified bullfrogs exploded out of the sack. Covered in mud and slipping on the floor, the pair chased after the escapees. "They were all over the house!" remembered Oliver. "All over the damn house. You'd catch one and then the next day she'd catch another one. It was a couple of days that they were around!"

For all the happy memories Oliver shared with Mary, there were morose ones as well. He spent many days lifting her out of the doldrums, as she wallowed in despair over the battle playing out between her sons. "Mary was in a turmoil," Oliver said. "She was extremely upset most of the time." He noted, "She tried to be the peacemaker that she was, but Bill and Charles were having nothing of it."

After Bill and Frederick sued in 1985, it seemed every family dispute was now destined for the courts. In 1988, Charles and David successfully sued Bill to compel him to follow through on an agreement for Bill to trade his share of their childhood home for their interest in their father's gold coin collection. Bill and Frederick, meanwhile, had launched another legal campaign against their brothers over control of the charitable foundation their father had created.

The contours of the foundation dispute were similar to those that had caused Bill to launch a proxy fight against Charles. By the late 1970s, Bill and Frederick had grown upset with how the foundation distributed its contributions. Administered by Charles's philanthropic and political lieutenant, George Pearson, it channeled a large portion of its annual disbursements to libertarian causes, particularly the Institute for Humane Studies, instead of the primarily arts-related charities the rest of the family favored. "Charles was running the Foundation for his own benefit and not for the benefit of the shareholders," Bill claimed in a deposition.

As Frederick noted in his own deposition, "I was dissatisfied by the large amounts of money that were going from the Foundation to the Institute for Humane Studies, which I didn't feel represented all of the shareholders' wishes." Frederick was getting deluged with donation requests from the various cultural organizations he supported—including the Metropolitan Opera, the New York City Ballet, the Royal Shakespeare Theatre, Caramoor (a center for music and the arts in Katonah, New York), and many others— but was increasingly unable to fulfill them at the level he desired.

In March 1979, before a meeting of the foundation's directors, Bill told Charles that there had been a "palace revolt"; he and his brothers had decided that, going forward, each family member should allocate funds to the causes of their choice based on the percentage of shares they held in the foundation. (Charles, David, and Bill owned a little more than 22 percent apiece; Mary and Frederick each possessed 16 percent.) Charles went along with the proposal until the mid-1980s, when he and David decided that they wanted to rename the foundation to include their mother and place her in control of it. Bill and Frederick refused.

Mary tried to keep the peace. "Please don't be angry with Charles over the Fred C. Koch Fdt.," she wrote Frederick in May 1985. The annual income his trusts generated—some $20 million—should be more than sufficient to cover his philanthropic endeavors, she pointed out. "It upsets me very much for you to fight this."

But fight it he did. And when, in 1988, Frederick and Bill filed suit over the foundation, they named Mary as a defendant along with Charles and David. As they pursued the case, Bill's lawyer dredged up Murray Rothbard, the economist cofounder of the Cato Institute whom Charles had driven out of that think tank. Rothbard was more than happy to pontificate on Charles's despotic rule over nonprofit entities. A memo summarizing Rothbard's expected testimony stated that "Charles Koch involves

himself in the minutest details related to the non-profit foundations with which he is associated," including matters as picayune
as "stationery design and color of offices."

Rothbard intended to testify that Charles "cannot tolerate dissent" and "will go to any end to acquire/retain control over the
non-profit foundations with which he is associated." The memo
alleged that "Charles Koch wants absolute control of the nonprofit foundations, but wants to be able to spend other people's
money." And it charged that he used these foundations to "acquire
access to, and respect from, influential people in government."

In March 1989, a little more than a month before the case went to
trial, Mary suffered a mild stroke, which affected her balance and
caused bouts of dizziness. Her blood pressure had also been spik-
ing, and her doctor prescribed medication for hypertension. Bill
and Frederick, nevertheless, subpoenaed Mary to testify.

A surreal courtroom scene played out in Wichita district court
that April, as Mary's doctor took the stand to back David and
Charles's position that, owing to her condition, their ailing mother
not be forced to endure the ordeal of providing courtroom testimony. The case had already been difficult enough on her. Mary
had broken down while being questioned about her correspondence with Frederick during one deposition.

"I don't think she is ready for this sort of thing," her physician,
Dr. Albert Michelbach, testified. The court proceedings, he added,
had affected "her physical and mental health." And "the stress is
going to cause her blood pressure to get out of control."

Attempting to make the case that Mary was healthy enough to
provide testimony, the opposing counsel grilled her doctor about
her tennis playing—("So, to the best of your knowledge, she's still
playing tennis on occasion?")—implying that if she could play tennis, she could testify in a courtroom.

llousness of counsel and of the plaintiffs," marveled the
ily's longtime lawyer, Bob Howard, "is almost beyond
my experience."

Later that summer, Howard, a partner with Kansas's largest law firm, Foulston Siefkin, strolled up to the heavy wooden door at Mary's home and rang the bell. He had managed to keep her off the stand, and they had easily won the case.

"Have you seen this?" Mary asked as she opened the door. Her eyes were bloodshot and she was clutching a two-day-old copy of the *Wall Street Journal*, its front page splashed with a story titled "Blood Feud."

"To hear William Koch tell it," the August 9, 1989, article began, "his brother Charles is a liar, a cheater and a racketeer. Charles responds that William has 'various psychiatric ailments' and is dead set on ruining the family business."

The article disclosed the humiliating news that Mary's sons had tried to force her to testify. ("She was able to play tennis with her stroke," Bill's lawyer griped to the reporter.) Bill told the *Journal*, "When you go into battle, the only way to do it is to assume you are going to fight to the finish."

The story was salt in an already painful wound. "In light of what they're saying, I don't think I want to leave anything to Bill and Fred," Mary told Howard, the lawyer recalled. He was carrying with him the new version of the will she had asked his law firm to prepare.

"You know, Mary," he counseled, "this is just more of the same thing that's been going on, it's just a current piece of publicity about the same litigation. Do you really want to cut Frederick and William out of your will?"

Mary, who would turn eighty-two in October, had come to the difficult realization that she might not live to see peace in her family. But perhaps her death could put an end to the war. At her request, Howard had drafted up a new clause to her will stating that "in the event that any of my said sons is involved in litigation at the time of my death as a plaintiff against me or any of my other sons," they would be disinherited if the litigation wasn't dismissed within six weeks of her death.

Howard convinced her to leave the will as it was—the anti-litigation provision would serve the same purpose if Bill and Frederick refused to cease their legal campaign. They retreated through the formal dining room to the sun porch at the rear of the house, taking seats at a glass-topped patio table with the three people the lawyer had brought to witness the signing. The air was sticky with humidity, and the low, gathering clouds foretold a storm.

The fighting, Mary said heavily as they reviewed her final bequests, was "killing Charles."

She looked down and signed.

Mary's health deteriorated. She showed signs of dementia, possibly exhibiting the early symptoms of Alzheimer's disease. She stared blankly, before snapping back to reality. And she experienced spells of confusion, sometimes trying to eat using two knives. She also began night walking, climbing up and down the stairs of her home as if in a trance. To keep her from injuring herself, Oliver began sleeping near her bed, snapping awake when he heard her stir.

"She started failing," he recalled. "And I think it was due to a lot of the stress, especially after the instigation of the war."

Since college, Mary had remained close with her Wellesley roommate Betty Bowersock, whose twin daughters were Mary's godchildren. Bowersock and her husband belonged to the Hemlock Society, the national right-to-die organization, and they planned to kill themselves before they grew infirm. In 1990, as Mary's medical condition worsened and she grew increasingly despondent over the quarrel between her sons, the Bowersocks invited Mary to join them in a suicide pact. According to Oliver,

Mary considered ending her life with a pharmaceutical cocktail rather than watch helplessly as a civil war destroyed her family. Alarmed, Oliver, together with Charles's wife, Liz, dissuaded Mary from further entertaining the proposition. Bowersock and her eighty-two-year-old husband ultimately followed through in April 1990, downing Darvocet and Seconal in their Middleburg, Virginia, home.

Sensing her time was drawing near, Mary issued a final request. "All I want to do is see my children one more time," she told Oliver. "I'd just like to see them and talk with them and see Wyatt"— Bill's three-year-old son.

This was no simple matter. "I was told by Liz that Mary was not to see them anymore because of the lawsuits," Oliver said. While Charles ran Koch Industries, Liz handled domestic affairs on the large compound, including making sure that Mary was looked after. Both were strong-minded women, and they occasionally butted heads. "They were not the best of the best friends," Oliver said. "Mary had her way of doing things, and Liz had her way of doing things. They were both Libras."

At the risk of angering Liz and Charles, Oliver quietly arranged for Mary to visit with her estranged sons, on separate occasions in the winter and summer of 1990.

"Mary was enamored with the child," Oliver remembered of Mary's dinner with Bill, Joan, and Wyatt, when her toddler grandson had scampered around the house in plaid coveralls and a clip-on bow tie. "He had red hair and Fred had reddish hair, and curly. Mary had an excellent night that night."

In the final months of Mary's life, Oliver said he had to seek Liz's permission before taking Mary off the premises. ("You certainly wouldn't want to embarrass the Koch family.") If Mary required medical attention, he had standing orders not to call 911. "My instructions were to call Liz before the police," Oliver remembered. "I wasn't to call the ambulance or anything. They wanted to be in control of the ambulance, the press, et cetera."

On Wednesday, December 19, 1990, Mary's fragile health declined drastically. The previous weekend, Michael Oliver, with the Kochs' permission, had escorted Mary to a Christmas party at the home of her friend Lucy Deck. It had been like old times. "She moved around the cocktail party with grace and elegance," Oliver said, "and had her vodka and tonic with lemon and talked to everybody and remembered everybody's name." By Wednesday night, she struggled to breathe and clung to consciousness. Liz summoned an ambulance. Oliver, holding Mary's hand, walked alongside the gurney as EMTs carefully wheeled her out of her home. As Oliver stepped into the back of the ambulance to accompany Mary to the hospital, Liz grabbed his shoulder.

"Michael, Mary doesn't need you now, but I do," she said, according to Oliver.

For the first time in his five-year relationship with Mary, he almost felt like a member of the family. The ambulance, its siren blaring, pulled out the front gate; together, he and Liz drove out the back to meet Mary at the hospital.

On Friday morning, Liz called Oliver at home. "Michael," she said, "Mary's gone." It was December 21, Oliver's forty-fifth birthday.

Liz called back the following day, an edge in her voice. She couldn't find one of Mary's diamond rings. *Where was it?* The unspoken implication was that Oliver had stolen it. "Go through her bedroom, go to her makeup table, and to your left, the third ring down is the ring you want," he told her testily. They were changing the locks on Mary's home, she told him, and asked him to return his set of keys and the remote control for the security gate. "You understand that this is just common procedure," she said, Oliver recalled. His time in the Koch family had come to an end.

*   *   *

Tragedies bring some families closer. But Mary's death did not cause even a momentary thaw between her sons. At their mother's funeral, Bill tried to greet Charles, offering a handshake, but Charles once again rebuffed the gesture, behaving as if Bill weren't even in the room.

After the funeral, the brothers held a wake at Mary's home. (Frederick was unable to attend, after an ice storm kept his plane grounded in Chicago.) Needing a moment to himself to mourn, Oliver descended a back staircase to the downstairs trophy room. He passed a pair of upright elephant tusks—from a bull Fred had bagged on safari—that framed the brass bell from the supertanker Charles had named for Mary. As he stood alone among polar bear and lion pelts, and the heads of water buffalo, dik-dik, and ibex, Bill entered the room from another staircase carrying an armload of files and papers. He looked surprised to see Oliver. "These are my personal papers that I wanted to make sure I get back, because I know I won't ever see them again," he hastily explained, according to Oliver.

Oliver thought little of it as Bill hurried past, but he said Charles and David's lawyers later told him that the stack of documents Bill carried off contained Mary's calendars and other personal papers. Bill had learned that he and Frederick would be disinherited from Mary's estate if they refused to drop their suit against Charles, David, and Koch Industries—something Bill had no intention of doing. He was presumably gathering ammunition for another fight. Far from ending the legal hostilities, Mary's will sparked another round of litigation.

CHAPTER NINE

"My God, I'm Going to Die!"

His shoes were off, his suit jacket folded neatly on the aisle seat beside him. The sunset streaked the sky in pastels, as the sprawl of Los Angeles twinkled into view outside David's window in the first-class cabin of USAir Flight 1493. It was February 1, 1991, less than two months after his mother's death. He had just completed two days of business meetings in Ohio and caught a 4:15 p.m. flight from Columbus to LAX.

Over the weekend, he planned to attend the fiftieth birthday party of a friend, as well as a board of directors meeting for the libertarian Reason Foundation, publisher of *Reason* magazine, scheduled for Saturday afternoon in Santa Monica. That evening, a Friday, David had a date with an on-again-off-again girlfriend, one of the revolving cast of lithe, leggy model types that he always seemed to have on his arm. Blond, green-eyed, and twenty years younger than David, Julie Hayek had been crowned Miss USA in 1983 and had nearly won the Miss Universe title later that year. An aspiring actress, her credits included bit roles on *Matlock*, *Dallas*, and *Days of Our Lives*.

The flight, two-thirds full, was scheduled to touch down at LAX at 6:11 p.m. Pacific time. That would leave him just enough time to check into his room at the Four Seasons in Beverly Hills, freshen up, and meet his date for dinner—and whatever came afterward.

Flight 1493 descended from the east, touching down gently

on runway 24L with a faint squeal of the tires. Seconds later, the plane reverberated with the teeth-gnashing crunch of metal on metal. A shower of sparks cascaded past David's window. Then a ball of fire. Terrified shrieks rose from the back of the plane.

"Stay down, stay down, stay down!" a stewardess shouted over the intercom.

The Boeing 737 had collided with a small, SkyWest commuter plane headed to Palmdale, California. A frazzled air traffic controller had mistakenly held the SkyWest plane for takeoff on the same runway on which she had cleared the USAir flight to land. The twelve people aboard the smaller aircraft died on impact, and the out-of-control 737, engulfed in flames, careened wildly across an active taxiway and toward a stand of maintenance buildings, dragging what remained of the mangled propeller plane.

Flight 1493 skidded into an abandoned firehouse at 60 miles per hour. The impact hurled David, who had unbuckled his seatbelt after the initial collision to make a dash for an exit, over a row of seats and into the bulkhead. The cabin lights flickered and went out. Thick, caustic smoke poured into the cabin. As panicked passengers trampled over him, David, on his hands and knees, scoured the floor for his loafers. They were gone. He felt for his jacket, hoping to use it to cover his face, but couldn't locate it.

David crawled toward the exit at the rear of the plane, his fellow passengers barely discernible through the smoke. He made it only a few rows; a frenzied mob of passengers clogged the aisle. David was at the back of the panicked scrum. He would never make it. He stood up and turned back.

As David gagged on toxic fumes from the burning jet fuel, an odd sensation overcame him. It wasn't panic. It wasn't fear. It wasn't desperation.

He felt…curious.

"My God," he thought to himself, "I'm going to die! What an interesting experience!"

It was as if he had momentarily taken leave of his body and was now a mere spectator to his ordeal. Overcome by an odd calm, he wondered about the experience of death, and standing in the aisle, his consciousness slipping away, he prepared himself to greet it.

Then his survival instinct kicked in. The smoke must be entering the plane through some opening, he reasoned. A crack in the fuselage? Other passengers had massed at the rear of the plane, but David felt his way toward the front. An inferno blazed outside the main cabin door. To David's right, though, he glimpsed a sliver of light around the galley exit. It was open several inches. Jolted with adrenaline, he pried the door open a few more inches and stuck his head out, gulping the murky air. He yanked on the door again. It moved a couple feet.

David stood in the doorway. Flames licked up from below. He could barely make out the ground through the billowing smoke. "Oh, what the hell!" he thought. He leapt to the tarmac. He picked himself up and hurried away from the burning plane in his socks. When he finally looked back, he saw a nightmare of wreckage strewn across the runway leading to the blackened, burning carcass of USAir 1493. Passengers spilled out of the plane's right rear exit and dazed survivors wandered, zombie-like, around the tarmac.

Of the 89 passengers and crew members aboard David's plane, 22 people perished and 30 were injured. A bus ferried the survivors to a nearby terminal. David was a bit banged up, his knees skinned and his right heel bruised, but he otherwise felt okay. If he hurried, maybe he could still make his date with Hayek. When David tried to leave the terminal, a guard brusquely turned him back. It was a good thing. Though he felt fine, his lungs were badly damaged. Later, after a doctor examined him, he was sent by ambulance with another injured passenger to a hospital in Marina del Rey to be treated for smoke inhalation. As David walked to the entrance, a CNN reporter, who had staked out the hospital, approached him. His voice hoarse and clothes charred, the executive gamely recounted the crash. Many of David's friends learned of his brush with death from seeing this interview, which was replayed dozens of times over the next couple days. So many well-wishers called David's Manhattan apartment that the answering machine ran out of tape after recording 58 messages.

David spent the next two days in the intensive care unit, where he was fed intravenously and intubated with a tube that delivered pure oxygen to his lungs. He could only communicate by writing notes. Morphine dulled the physical pain, but not the emotional aftershocks of David's near-death experience. The calm façade he had managed the day of the crash crumbled by the following morning. He could still picture the faces of people who had died on his flight, including Deanna Bethea, the sweet, twenty-two-year-old stewardess who had waited on him in first class. Also dead was the older couple seated directly across the aisle from him, George and Rosemary Weth.

In the days after the tragedy, David had flashbacks of the crash and relived it in his dreams. He felt a crushing sense of guilt. After opening the galley door, why hadn't he helped other passengers— perhaps the Weths—to safety? Why had he merely saved himself while others had slowly suffocated? Close to passing out when he jumped to the tarmac, David might have perished himself had he tried to be a hero. This, at least, was what he told himself.

David left the hospital that Sunday, assisted by Charles and Liz, who'd flown to L.A. to look after him. The David Koch who had jetted to L.A. for a tryst with a beauty queen was a different man from the one who hobbled out of the hospital that Sunday, short of breath; still coughing black, bloody mucus; and aware more than ever of his own fragile mortality.

"This may sound odd," he said years later, "but I felt this experience was very spiritual. That I was saved when all those others died. I felt that the good Lord spared my life for a purpose. And since then, I've been busy doing all the good works I can think of."

* * *

At the time of the crash, David, then fifty, was one of New York City's most eligible bachelors. And he had been enjoying every second of it.

The Ferrari-driving business titan, more than a few female admirers had noticed, bore a resemblance to the actor Michael Caine. Fun loving and gregarious, David had a trademark laugh— loud and honking, it easily rose above the din of cocktail parties. He was an endearing figure on the New York society scene: Though a member of the elite, he somehow managed to project the aura of a guileless Kansas farm boy—albeit one who had grown up in a home decorated with Renoirs and Thomas Hart Bentons. ("He doesn't have a mean streak in him," one New York friend remarked.)

David lived at 870 U.N. Plaza—once home to Truman Capote, Walter Cronkite, and many other New York notables—in a penthouse duplex with leather couches, a 1970s vibe, and a wall of windows overlooking the East River and Roosevelt Island. He spent summer weekends at his 15,000-square-foot oceanfront mansion in Southampton, and jetted off during the winter months to his ski lodge in Aspen. He enjoyed cruising the Mediterranean by chartered yacht and had a taste for exotic travel, journeying to places such as the Galapagos Islands and Olduvai Gorge in the eastern Serengeti, a mecca for paleoanthropologists studying the origins of man—a subject of particular fascination to David and an early focus of his philanthropy.

It didn't hurt his appeal among Manhattan's eligible women that his name regularly turned up on *Forbes*'s annual list of America's wealthiest people. But he was a catch who didn't want to get caught. "He was having a good time *not* being married," said John Damgard, who met David on the basketball court at Deerfield and remains one of his closest friends. "He had no difficulty attracting incredibly attractive women. If you're tall, handsome, and rich, lots of fun, a good athlete, you can go skiing, play tennis, you can do all these things anywhere in the world—it's not surprising. And when he went places, he didn't have to stay at a youth hostel, let's just put it that way."

When he visited New York on business, Damgard, then the head of the Futures Industry Association, was David's wingman. They hit the town together, dining at Le Cirque and other Manhattan hotspots, where, to impress their dates, David invariably ordered the most expensive bottle of wine on the menu. Afterward, they would keep the party going at one of New York's exclusive, velvet-rope-lined nightclubs. "We ran hard together as bachelors," Damgard recalled.

David "liked having a lot of women around," according to one of his 1980s-era girlfriends. He at one point had his eye on Marla Maples, whom Donald Trump left his first wife to marry. ("Marla's a babe," David told *New York* magazine in 1990. "I wish Donald hadn't gotten there first.")

His incessant dating—sometimes he juggled multiple love interests over the course of a day—earned him a reputation as an incorrigible playboy. The Hugh Hefner–esque bacchanals he threw at his sprawling seven-bedroom, nine-bathroom Southampton beach house were legend. He "plays harder than anyone I know," one of David's close friends noted during his bachelor days, adding that the executive was also the "hardest working guy I know."

With the roster of invitees running to a thousand or more—"a third of which were beautiful, wild, single women," David once boasted—the parties featured six different types of champagne. Scantily clad women danced poolside and gyrated on the tennis court. Some of David's parties went so late that he served guests two meals, dinner and breakfast. "Those were the best parties I've ever been to," one friend, and frequent party guest, said. His annual New Year's Eve blowouts in Aspen—which on occasion featured strippers—were similarly grandiose. "People really got in the mood," the friend said. "A lot of the crowd were these L.A.

chicks who had just bought a new pair of tits and wanted to make sure that they did not go unnoticed—those parties got pretty wild. There were bands and hot tubs and it was fun."

As David entered his fifties, the idea of having a family increasingly appealed to him, but he remained "gun-shy" about the prospect of marriage, referring to past relationships that could have ended in matrimony as "close calls." The ongoing battle with Bill and Frederick worsened his fear of commitment. If such a bitter, bare-knuckled legal brawl could break out among brothers, imagine the kind of ugliness that could erupt between a married couple in the midst of a divorce.

Then David met Julia Flesher, a statuesque twenty-seven-year-old who hailed from humble Midwestern origins. Born in Indianola, Iowa, and raised outside of Little Rock, Arkansas, she had worked her way into the exalted world of Upper East Side society by way of her job as a $200-a-week assistant to the fashion designer Adolfo. (During the 1980s, she occasionally accompanied her boss to the White House to fit Nancy Reagan.) Mutual friends set the pair up, and on their first date, in early 1991, David escorted Julia to Le Club, an exclusive, members-only haunt on East 55th Street frequented by business tycoons. ("It was the sort of place where you were likely to see a wealthy seventy-five-year-old guy walk in with three blondes from Sweden," Donald Trump, a member, once put it.)

The evening did not go well.

"I was a little too, how should I say it, forward with my humor," David recalled of their evening together. "Julia was smiling, but weakly." She remembered the date this way: "Afterward we shook hands and I said, 'I'm glad I met that man because now I know I never want to go out with him.'"

Three days after their date, David lay prone in a hospital bed, his body a pin cushion of tubes and wires, after barely escaping the burning carnage of Flight 1493.

*　　*　　*

Six months after surviving the crash, David bumped into Julia at a party. Their second encounter started out about as smoothly as their first. He introduced himself to the willowy, six-foot blonde as if the pair had never met. "She said, 'David, we went out together,' " he recalled. "And I pulled out my trusty black book and said, 'Oh, my God.' "

Despite this rocky start, he managed to persuade Julia to go out with him again. This time, instead of a club frequented by lecherous bigwigs, he took her to the U.S. Open. "Julia was the ideal," Damgard said. "That was it. He knew that was the woman he was going to marry." She had come into his life at just the right time. The plane crash had awoken him to the capriciousness of life—how it could be taken from you in an instant, leaving so much unfulfilled. He was ready to put his days of empty pleasure seeking behind him; Julia, for her part, preferred to ignore David's playboy past.

As Julia and David began dating, members of his social circle remained unconvinced that she could tame him. Indeed, David required some firm prodding in order to make the ultimate commitment. "After four and a half years, Julia gave me two choices," he remembered. "I would be a live husband or a dead bachelor."

After an extended courtship, David proposed to her on Christmas Eve in 1995, giving Julia the triple emerald cut diamond ring that had belonged to his mother. They wed over Memorial Day weekend in 1996 at David's Meadow Lane mansion in Southampton (which he dubbed "Aspen East"). Two years later she gave birth to David Jr., followed by Mary Julia (in 2001) and John Mark (in 2006).

Fatherhood suited David and it also changed his public persona as a cad. "That was the old David," said one of his close friends. "David is now a great dad, loves going home and being with the kids, dotes on those children." Yet as a first-time father at fifty-eight, "he's not able to kind of get down on all fours and go 'ga ga goo goo,' so there's help around there." This friend added: "Julia is a great mother and a great wife....David's an older father to have little kids. And she's figured it all out. It's made his life 100 percent better."

The New York society columnist David Patrick Columbia noted: "When he finally married Julia...many thought she'd be his trophy wife. She has taken on the role, however of Wife and Mother in an ideal form: she is his consort; his life changed and so did his image."

While David's marriage gave him a new aura of respectability among New York's social elite, the transition to being Mrs. Koch—what Columbia called "the construction of Julia Koch"—did not go seamlessly for her. Along the Upper East Side–Southampton social axis, there were expectations of a billionaire's wife that didn't exist for a girlfriend, a Byzantine social code that neophytes were somehow supposed to deduce on their own. There were black-tie galas to chair, fund-raisers to organize, parties to host-ess, not to mention decorators to audition for their new fifteen-room apartment at 1040 Fifth Avenue, which had once belonged to Jackie Kennedy Onassis. David had bought the apartment for $9.5 million in 1995, shortly after Onassis's death, and the couple spent the next three years renovating it.

The doyennes of the Upper East Side carefully dissected every move she made as the new bride of New York's second-richest man (Michael Bloomberg, at that point, was the richest). "She was averse to making mistakes and she didn't want to do anything that might be interpreted as not winning the seal of approval," said a family friend. "She is very private." To Julia's dismay, her awk-ward entrée into New York's *beau monde* played out in the press. "She looked dazed, like a gazelle caught in the strobe lights," *The New York Times*'s Elisabeth Bumiller riffed in a less-than-flattering assessment of Julia's formal New York society debut in 1997, when she cochaired the Metropolitan Museum's annual benefit for the Costume Institute.

The *New York Post* later ran a lengthy article called "How New York Rejected Its Leading Socialite," which chronicled Julia's supposed high-society faux pas. "Julia thought it was all about having a lot of money, but it isn't," one acquaintance sniped. "She didn't have the sophistication to carry it off, and New York can be very cruel to people who set themselves up like that." The story noted that Julia had run afoul of Pat Buckley, wife of the *National Review*'s William F. Buckley, a prodigious charity fund-raiser and den mother to aspiring socialites. Buckley felt Julia shirked the "hard, hard slogging" required for charity work; David's wife irritated her further when, during one benefit, Julia had talked to a tablemate during Buckley's speech.

It seemed like she could not do anything right in the eyes of her critics. She was even criticized for barring *W* magazine from photographing the recently renovated interior of their new apartment, on the grounds that she didn't "want people judging our taste." But didn't she understand that, as a socialite, her *raison d'être* was taste making and trendsetting? Julia was also accused of toning down David's once-raucous shindigs by aggrieved B-listers who no longer made the slimmed-down invite list. When one year the couple dared to throw a subdued version of David's annual New Year's Eve bash—inviting some 200 guests instead of the typical 800-plus—one miffed socialite fumed that "Julia's fingerprints were all over it."

Given the cattiness, it was no surprise when, in the late 1990s, Julia temporarily fled New York for the more welcoming social scene of Palm Beach, where in 1998 the Kochs purchased Villa el Sarmiento, designed by Addison Mizner, the architect responsible for numerous Gold Coast landmarks, including The Breakers Hotel. "She decided that she wasn't going to put herself in a position where somebody could have the opportunity to criticize her for no particular reason," said the family friend.

Julia eventually settled more comfortably into the role of society wife, despite the cold shoulder from Pat Buckley, turning up at all the places where it was important to be seen, clinging gracefully to David's arm at galas and benefits, and presiding over parties at their home, where guests such as Glenn Close, Princess Firyal of Jordan, and Barbara Walters mingled over Dom Perignon and caviar.

Barely had they settled into Jackie O's old pad when, in 2004, David plunked down $17 million for a 9,000-square-foot duplex in 740 Park Avenue, the Upper East Side apartment building where, coincidentally, Jackie O grew up. The expanding family, David explained, couldn't possibly squeeze another child (and another nanny) into their old apartment, which spanned the entire fifteenth floor of 1040 Fifth Avenue. In a nod to their Oz-like surroundings, a plaque in the marble entryway to their current digs reminds visitors: TOTO, I DON'T THINK WE'RE IN KANSAS ANYMORE.

Not long into his courtship with Julia, David faced a second brush with death. In 1992, at the age of fifty-two, a routine blood test showed elevated prostate antigens, and his doctor soon diagnosed him with an advanced form of prostate cancer. He believed that he was again staring down death. "That puts the fear of God in you!" he recalled. "I thought I was going to die, certainly in months, if not in weeks."

Treated with radiation at Sloan-Kettering, David was handed a reprieve when his cancer went into remission. In his exuberant style, he celebrated twice-cheating death with an extravagant, champagne-fueled Southampton soiree on a clear August evening in 1993, with music by Michael Carney's orchestra and a $100,000 fireworks display put on by Long Island's Grucci family. But the cancer soon returned, requiring more radical treatment. In 1995, he underwent prostate surgery.

Once again, the cancer vanished only to reappear. Though each of his brothers was later successfully treated for prostate cancer,

David's cancer was incurable. He could only try to forestall the slow-moving disease as long as possible. He was treated with hormones to stop the production of testosterone that fuels prostate cancer, a therapy that kept his cancer in check but sapped his sex drive and enlarged his breasts. When eventually that treatment began to falter, he joined a clinical trial for an experimental drug called Zytiga. "The side effects," he quipped to a reporter, "are minor compared to dying."

After Flight 1493, David had become an outspoken airplane safety advocate, drafting up a detailed list of technical recommendations to prevent future tragedies, testifying before a congressional committee probing "aircraft cabin safety and fire survivability." ("I'm a chemical engineer, and I'm trained to analyze things in a technical fashion," he told the assembled members of the House Government Activities and Transportation Committee.) He attacked cancer with a similar analytical intensity. David took the approach, said his friend John Damgard, that "cancer was just something he had to outsmart."

David had begun serving on hospital boards in the 1980s, but his experience with cancer inspired him to make medical research a main thrust of his philanthropy. "Discovering that I had cancer and the terrible fear that it generated in me turned me into a crusader," he once said, "a crusader to provide financing to many different centers to develop cures—not only for prostate cancer but for other kinds of cancer as well." He would eventually spend at least a half-billion dollars on projects like these, including underwriting the construction of the sleek, glass-walled David H. Koch Institute for Integrative Cancer Research at MIT, where world-class biologists and engineers collaborate on innovative cancer treatments.

By pouring hundreds of millions into cancer research, David hoped to promote advances that would prolong, if not save, thousands of lives—including his. One by one, he knew, his treatments would fail, requiring him to have a new therapy at the ready. His life depended on financing breakthroughs that would keep him one step ahead of the disease that's trying to kill him. He likened his philanthropic approach to the one time he attended the Kentucky Derby and managed to place a bet on the winner. His strategy entailed betting on every horse in the race.

Where David had once calmly prepared himself for death in the smoke-choked cabin of USAir 1493, he was now doing all he could to buy more time. For a man for whom money was no object, he recognized the harsh irony that his billions could not purchase the thing that he desired most after becoming a father—to live long enough to see his three children graduate from college. "I can't have what you have and what no amount of money can buy," he once lamented to Damgard, "the assurance that you'll watch your children grow up and your grandchildren. But I'm going to make goddamn sure that I give it my very, very best shot."

CHAPTER TEN

The Art of War

Bill did nothing in a small way, as his ongoing battle with Koch Industries had shown. But even some of his closest friends, well acquainted with his take-no-prisoners temperament, thought Bill was delusional when, in 1990, he announced an audacious bid for the yachting world's most coveted prize, the America's Cup.

"Let me make sure I have this straight," his friend and Cape Cod neighbor Louis Cabot deadpanned when Bill broke the news to him. "You're thinking of entering the America's Cup, where you have had no experience. You're thinking of starting from scratch, finding designers and builders to put together this new boat that nobody has ever sailed, and hiring maybe a couple hundred people to run dozens of different departments in what will amount to a small corporation. You're thinking of moving the whole show to San Diego and building what will amount to a small waterfront village.... And you're thinking of doing all this in just seventeen months. Is that what you're thinking?"

The smile that crept across Bill's face answered the question; this was precisely what he had in mind.

Bill first learned to sail as a teenager aboard a 19-foot Lightning at Culver Military Academy. After he was cast out of Koch Industries, sailing became a sort of therapy for his estrangement from David, Charles, and their mother. Bill felt like a man without a family, like the umbilical cord had been unceremoniously clipped, but on the water with his crewmates, he discovered a new kind of brotherhood. "In a way," he said in 1991, "this organization replaces the family harmony I never had."

The America's Cup is held every three to five years at the yacht club of its last victor; 1992's was to be hosted by the San Diego Yacht Club, whose *Stars & Stripes*, with sailing legend Dennis Conner at the helm, had won back the America's Cup from an Australian team in 1987. To build his racing syndicate, Bill took up residence in a $30,000-a-month bay-front rental in San Diego's Point Loma. His world-class art collection, as usual, traveled with him. The house featured paintings by Monet and Cézanne, but the Boteros drew the most attention. The two large bronze sculptures that Bill showcased on his lawn included a rotund, cigar-smoking nude that locals unkindly dubbed "Roseanne," after the comedienne and sitcom actress.

By then, Bill had relocated the corporate headquarters of Oxbow to Palm Beach, Florida, from Dover, Massachusetts, following a lengthy dispute with the Massachusetts tax authorities, who had slapped him with a massive tax bill following the buyout of his shares in Koch Industries. Bill took the Massachusetts Commissioner of Revenue to court, ultimately extracting a massive refund of more than $46 million, but the experience embittered him and he began looking around for a more tax-friendly locale in which to settle. Florida fit the bill.

In between bouts of litigation with Charles and David (and many other adversaries), Bill had spent the past six-plus years building Oxbow into a successful enterprise, with a focus on the development of alternative energy sources and a handful of geothermal power plants in the Western United States and abroad. By 1990, Oxbow claimed annual sales in excess of $1 billion. As Bill set his mind to building his racing syndicate, he handed day-to-day control of Oxbow to a trio of trusted executives. Bill's friend Louis Cabot had pointed out that creating this sailing team would be very much akin to constructing a company from scratch. The team, which the mathematically minded businessman called America[3]—a nod to his motto of "teamwork, technology, talent"—would eventually employ some 200 people.

A contrarian by nature, Bill eschewed the conventions of sailing from the outset as he built his syndicate. He passed over yachting's most esteemed shipbuilders for a team of MIT scientists and recruited his crew largely from the sport's less headstrong second string. Bill also had no intention of being the crew's seventeenth man, an honorary slot reserved for boat owners living vicariously through their teams. He instituted an unusual rotation at the helm, in which he took a turn piloting the 70-plus-foot vessel.

Few thought the neophyte from landlocked Kansas, who spoke poetically of glimpsing a virtual ocean as a boy in the undulating prairie tall grass, had a shot at winning the vaunted international sailing race. His fellow yachtsmen viewed him as a dilettante, even a buffoon. "The bespectacled Koch was at various times during the competition referred to as clownish, arrogant and zany, and as the Gerald Ford of sailing," *Sports Illustrated* reported at the time, noting that he was "so prone to on-board pratfalls that after twice being bonked on the head by a swinging boom he was presented with a San Diego Charger helmet by a local disc jockey."

Annoyed by the less-than-warm reception he received from the locals and the yachting elite—especially supporters of Dennis Conner, with whom Bill was vying for the honor of defending the Cup—Bill at one point threatened to spin "Roseanne" 180 degrees. That way the Botero sculpture would have its backside pointed directly at the snobbish San Diego Yacht Club.

But nothing did more to quiet his critics than vanquishing Conner and his crew in a nail-biting series of races, the final of which, on May 1, 1992, was a blowout. That day, Bill's gleaming white yacht sped so far ahead of *Stars & Stripes* that he couldn't even make out the ads on Conner's sails. When Bill had first announced his America's Cup bid, the Las Vegas bookmakers had placed his odds at 100-to-1. Now he was defending the trophy against the Italian racing syndicate Il Moro di Venezia and its thirty-two-year-old skipper, Paul Cayard.

The month after defeating Conner, Bill and America[3] edged past Il Moro in what had been a neck-and-neck race and cruised across the finish line 44 seconds ahead of the Italian crew. Reaching this euphoric moment had consumed nearly a year-and-a-half of Bill's life and $68.5 million of his then-$650 million fortune. Moët rained down from every direction and family, friends, and America[3] back office staff swarmed the yacht in zodiacs. As Bill's boat cruised back into the harbor and passed the San Diego Yacht Club, he spotted the Cup on the dock; moments later he flung himself into the water and swam toward his prize, lifting the sterling silver trophy above his head when he reached it. The experience was life altering. "I learned a lot about myself," Bill once said. "I learned I could do a lot more than I thought I could."

Bill's obsessive, single-minded quest for the trophy struck some of his fellow sailors as a pursuit rooted not in a love of sailing, but in his bitter, long-running rivalry with Charles and David. "The real issue is why did he want the Cup," pondered Gary Jobson, a sailing legend who was one of Bill's most trusted advisors as he assembled the America[3] team. "I don't think it has anything to do with sailing. I think it had to do with proving himself to his brothers."

To David's great surprise, Bill invited him to San Diego to sail with his team in a few early races. David turned down the offer—how could he go sailing with an estranged brother who had named him as a defendant in an ongoing lawsuit?—but he also declined an opportunity to chair Team Conner. "I can't bet against my brother," he said. Whatever Bill's reasons for battling for the Cup, David was relieved that his twin had won it. Bill's need to show the world his worth seemed so profound, so all-consuming—imagine how he would have reacted if he'd lost.

During the competition, *The Wichita Eagle* carried regular wire dispatches about Bill's exploits, and he wasted no time making the most of his new fame in his hometown, a city where he hadn't lived full-time since middle school. With the court docket ballooning in *Koch v. Koch Industries*, Bill and Frederick's ongoing lawsuit over the stock buyout, Bill began lavishing money on Kansas in a not-so-subtle campaign to burnish his image among potential jurors. The month after the race, he displayed the trophy in the lobby of Wichita's city hall. Later that summer Bill pledged $500,000 to create a 15,000-square-foot boathouse in Wichita on the east bank of the Arkansas River (in the same building where Fred Koch's first office had been located), where *Jayhawk*, one of the racing yachts the America[3] team had sailed, would be on permanent display outside. This was just the start of a philanthropic blitzkrieg. In the years to follow, he sponsored festivals and 5Ks. He footed the bill for the Reverend Jesse Jackson to address employees of the Wichita school district, and twice loaned his art collection to the local museum.

He also became an anticrime crusader. In 1994, after Bill and his son, Wyatt, then eight years old, attended a July Fourth fireworks display in Wichita where gang violence had erupted, he bankrolled a commission to study the state's crime problem and develop recommendations to help at-risk youth.

"I'm a celebrity in Kansas," he boasted. "I walk down the street and people ask for my autograph." He grew close to the state's Democratic governor, Joan Finney, who conferred on him the honorary title of admiral of the Kansas Navy. Bill—whose relationship with Joan Granlund, Wyatt's mother, was on and off during their more than twenty years together—also began casually dating the state's attractive attorney general, Carla Stovall, causing a minor scandal when he gifted her with a $5,000 diamond tennis bracelet that she was later forced to return.

Bill's flashy style made him a hit with the Kansas press and helped him to cultivate local journalists. He had provided Kansas reporters with all-expenses-paid junkets to watch him compete in the America's Cup. Two years later, in 1994, he offered local news outlets heavily subsidized trips to San Diego to cover his announcement of the formation of the first-ever all-female America's Cup team, which would sail aboard a yacht he'd christened the *Mighty Mary*, after his late mother. ("She took my brothers' side in all the legal fights, and I guess this is my way of forgiving her and asking her forgiveness," he told reporters. "Corny, huh?") The endeavor seemed to combine two of Bill's passions: sailing—and fit, young women. There was surely some irony in the fact that, in the course of his tribute to female empowerment, he impregnated Marie Beard, a six-foot Texan who had tried out for the America's Cup team (and in 1996 gave birth to Bill's daughter, Charlotte).

The zany adventures of "Wild Bill," as he came to be called, were far more appealing to local reporters than his brothers' latest pipeline purchase or refinery expansion. The year he unveiled his female sailing syndicate, Bill appeared as the celebrity mystery guest at the Wichita Gridiron Club's annual show, where as "Captain Koch" he donned a superhero costume in a comedy sketch about his efforts to "save" Kansas. Afterward, he footed the bill for local journalists and their spouses at an upscale Wichita restaurant, which one Kansas journalism professor considered part of Bill's efforts to purchase "the best coverage money can buy."

"Bill spent some time in Wichita and just delighted in saying scurrilous things—not for publication—but for people he partied with, and he partied with the press a great deal of the time," said one veteran Wichita journalist. "The young reporters would come back with stories about what great fun he was. He was obviously courting them and doing one heck of a job of it, too, buying champagne by the magnums, et cetera. The parties went late into the night at the local pubs and they thought he was terrific. Of course, on the other side, here's buttoned up Charles. The contrast couldn't have been greater."

By 1997, Bill's stature had risen to such heights in Kansas that he was floated as a possible Democratic challenger to Republican Senator Sam Brownback—a prospect that must have made Charles shudder. He fueled rumors of a potential Senate bid by telling the *Lawrence Journal-World* that he was "listening to the suitors" and found the prospect of elected office "very seductive." Focus groups Bill commissioned showed that, second to Bob Dole, Bill Koch was America's best-known Kansan.

The fawning recognition Bill received for his philanthropy infuriated Charles and his supporters. "Billy's brought his toys to town, shared them and people love it," Sterling Varner fumed. "Meanwhile Charles has worked his butt off here. He put his heart into building this company. He's given millions to charity and never said anything. Billy comes to town and builds a little boathouse and he's a hero. We must be doing something wrong. If it weren't for Charles, Billy wouldn't even have a rowboat."

In the mid-1990s, according to a former senior Wichita official, Koch Industries quietly complained about the boathouse—an aggravating monument to Bill's sailing prowess—dispatching a lobbyist to city hall to express the company's displeasure.

"Can you imagine how Charles feels when he drives through downtown Wichita on his way to the airport and has to see that every time?" the lobbyist asked. According to the former official, the lobbyist was told that Charles should consider taking another route, because the boathouse was there to stay. When in 1997 the state opted against reauthorizing Bill's crime commission, the *Topeka Capital-Journal* cited sources (including Bill) who said that Charles had leaned on Kansas's new governor, Bill Graves, to shutter the outfit.

It was all the state's nonprofit community could do to stay out of the crossfire of the family feud. In one episode, the Kansas Sports Hall of Fame rejected a $50,000 contribution from Bill—along with a model of his America's Cup–winning yacht for display—after learning that accepting the donation might jeopardize its funding from Koch Industries.

Bill knew his local involvement chafed Charles, and he was candid about the strategic motives behind his generosity. "I've had a lot of bad PR in Kansas and part of this is to level the playing field."

Bill's aggressive PR machine forced Charles and his notoriously closemouthed company to ramp up their own publicity efforts. In charity, as in everything else he did, Charles preferred to keep a low profile. He didn't care about seeing his name enshrined on a plaque or memorialized on a building (at least one that didn't belong to Koch Industries); in fact, he found that sort of attention embarrassing. For years, Charles and Liz Koch, along with Koch Industries itself, had donated generously, but quietly, to a variety of local causes. They paid for the Twilight Pops Concert at the annual Wichita River Festival, contributed to the city's Institute of Logopedics (which focuses on speech disorders), gave to the local Boys & Girls Club and United Way, and provided a grant to fund a mobile mammography van. They bankrolled Shakespeare in the Park and underwrote a performance by Ray Charles to benefit the Wichita Center for the Arts. Charles also formed his own nonprofit, Youth Entrepreneurs, to educate Kansas students in business and economics.

As Bill splashed money around and nabbed headlines, Charles and Koch Industries had little choice but to respond in kind. "They became just much more engaged locally," said the former city official. "I think they consciously wanted to build their local image. Bill Koch really smoked them out." The more conspicuous tenor of their giving was evident in the combined $2 million gift Charles and Liz Koch and the company made to the local Salvation Army in 1994 for the construction of a new headquarters, dubbed the Koch Center.

But other factors may have influenced their effort at image building. One September evening in 1993, the Kochs' sixteen-year-old son, Chase, blew through a red light as he sped down Wichita's East Douglas Road on the way to a local mall. The teenager's Ford Explorer barreled through the intersection just as twelve-year-old Zachary Seibert, listening to Kris Kross on his headphones, crossed the street. Seibert died at a local hospital about an hour later.

Rumors circulated that the Kochs would use their power and influence to make any charges disappear, but Charles and his family instead seemed determined that their billionaire status not become an issue. Instead of retreating behind the gates of their Wichita compound and leaving lawyers and crisis management professionals to handle the fallout, the enigmatic family made a public showing of support for the Seiberts. The Kochs escorted their traumatized son to the boy's funeral, "where every eye in that church was on them," one attendee remembered. Chase later pleaded guilty to a misdemeanor charge of vehicular manslaughter and was sentenced to 100 hours of community service and 18 months of probation. The judge also imposed a 9:00 p.m. curfew for 10 months. (This was a fairly harsh sentence, according to the special prosecutor in the case, who said an adult would have probably gotten off easier.)

"That was a tough deal to go through," said Charles's friend Nestor Weigand. "It was just a very, very painful time. I think it was one of those things that families do. They just do whatever they can to try to survive it."

After his son's accident, in addition to becoming more visible in his charitable giving, Charles and his company permitted the local paper rare access to write one of the first in-depth profiles of Koch Industries, its chief executive, and his family. It marked a new era of cautious public engagement for the company. "Before, our whole strategy was that no one needed to know anything," Paul Brooks, a Koch senior vice president, said at the time.

Despite Charles's best efforts, however, his estranged brother continued to enjoy widespread popularity, especially among state and local officials. The fact that they persisted in lauding Bill for his generosity stung Charles and others at Koch Industries. The company employed thousands of people in Kansas. Didn't Bill's friends in government realize that he was on a revenge-fueled crusade to destroy everything Charles had built?

Finally, in 1997, Koch Industries sent the state a subtle but unmistakable message when it announced plans to expand—in Houston, not Wichita.

"Billy is going to take five years off Charles' life," Nestor Weigand complained to *The Wichita Eagle*, telling the paper that the Koch family was aggrieved by a "lack of insight" into Bill's motives. "Everything Billy does Charles feels deeply."

"The only thing I do know," Weigand said, "is the day this is over, Billy is gone. You won't even see his smoke."

Another layer of the conflict played out in the shadows. This war, like most, had its covert aspect, with allegations of espionage and skullduggery on both sides. Bill, especially, seemed to relish the use of cloak-and-dagger tactics, which over the years he employed not just against his brothers but against a wide range of rivals, including sailing competitors, employees, at least one former girl-friend, and the second of his three wives.

In the 1980s and 1990s, the brothers unleashed a small army of private investigators on each other. "We're up against a very secretive company that operates like a cult," Oxbow's spokesman, Brad Goldstein, once told *The New York Times*, explaining the company's heavy reliance on PIs.

The elaborate operations hatched by Bill's operatives seemed right out of the CIA playbook. In one case, *Vanity Fair* reported, his crafty investigators established a phony company and posed as corporate headhunters in order to glean intelligence from ex–Koch Industries employees, donning body mics to secretly record their interviews.

Former Oxbow employees claim Bill's investigators resorted to underhanded electronic surveillance techniques, including buggings and wiretaps. "He has bragged to me that he has had his brothers and other people tracked by private investigators and he has wiretapped their discussions," one former Oxbow executive, Michael Aquilina, said in a 1988 lawsuit against Bill and his company. (Aquilina was fired from Oxbow after Bill accused him of submitting fraudulent financial statements.) Though Bill denied having his brothers followed or conducting any illegal surveillance—"I didn't authorize using it, and never will," he once said—he did acknowledge that he had on one occasion worn a bug, tucked into his breast pocket, to a meeting with J. Howard Marshall II. ("The recording wasn't worth shit," Bill said.)

Bill's investigators also engaged in more low-tech methods: Seeking intelligence and clues to Koch Industries' legal strategy, they pilfered trash from the homes and offices of Charles, David, and three of their lawyers, bribing janitors and trash collectors to gain access to their garbage, according to the brothers' attorneys. (The Dumpster-diving operation resulted in a temporary restraining order in 1992 that prevented Bill and his legal team from "invading or interfering with the privacy and confidentiality of the defendants, their counsel, and their immediate families, either through efforts to obtain the trash from the personal residences or the offices" of the brothers or their lawyers.)

In Bill's case, there was often little need to riffle through his garbage cans to dig up dirt, though perhaps Koch's detectives tried it. He was, as *Vanity Fair*'s Bryan Burrough put it in a 1994 profile, "a man whose closet is free of skeletons in large part because they all seem to be turning somersaults in his living room." Bill left a turbulent wake of controversy and litigation wherever he went, and his misadventures provided plenty of ammunition for Koch Industries. In its effort to discredit Bill as hyperlitigious, mentally unbalanced, and fueled by vengeance, the company's PR shop created a dossier of Bill's more memorable debacles. "Koch had done a bunch of opposition research on Bill Koch—a fact-based summary of litigation he'd been involved in, and what he'd done and said," explained a former Koch executive. The company distributed this fifty-page opposition research file, titled "The Truth About *Koch v. Koch Industries*," widely to reporters covering the legal drama.

The juiciest scuttlebutt often concerned Bill's stormy personal life (he would eventually sire five children by four women: Wyatt with first wife Joan, Charlotte with girlfriend Marie Beard, William Jr. and Robin with second wife Angela Gauntt, and Kaitlin with third wife Bridget Rooney Koch). The tawdriest of his soap-operatic travails was revealed, as were so many of the Koch clan's most intimate moments, in a drab courtroom, where in November 1995 Bill faced off against a former Ford model named Catherine de Castelbajac. He'd installed her in his seldom-used, $2.5 million pied-à-terre in the apartment section of Boston's Four Seasons, but wanted to evict her now that their romance had cooled. (De Castelbajac, the wife of a French nobleman when they began their affair, also became a target of Bill's detectives when she refused to vacate his apartment. They in turn uncovered her modest origins as, in Bill's words, a "Santa Barbara surfing girl.")

As Bill wooed de Castelbajac, he simultaneously juggled at least three other women, including Joan, whom he married in April 1994 to legitimize Wyatt for estate-planning purposes. He and Joan divorced not long after.

The sensational nine-day trial over de Castelbajac's housing arrangements made news on both sides of the Atlantic, with tabloid editors one-upping each other with headline puns (such as, BEAUTY AND THE LEASE and JUST ONE OF THOSE FLINGS). It's unlikely such titillating testimony had ever been heard in Boston housing court, where lurid details about the couple's courtship were revealed ("She started kissing me quite passionately. I must admit I did not resist.") and a series of steamy transcontinental faxes that passed between the pair were entered into evidence.

"Hot Love From Your X-rated Protestant Princess," de Castelbajac signed one of the racy messages. She referred to herself in a separate fax as a "wet orchid" who yearned for warm honey to be drizzled on her body. In another, she wrote: "My poor nerve endings are already hungry. You are creating such a wanton woman. I can feel those kisses, and every inch of my body misses you."

Bill's far-less-sensuous facsimiles displayed the MIT-trained engineer's geeky side: "I cannot describe how much I look forward to seeing you again," he wrote. "It is beyond calculation by the largest computers." In another fax, he jotted an equation to express his devotion, ending with a hand-drawn heart and, within it, the mathematical symbol for infinity.

In late November 1995, Bill won the court's approval to evict the ex-model. Less than two weeks after the verdict was read, Bill's newest love interest, thirty-two-year-old Marie Beard, announced she was three months pregnant with his child—and that she was moving into his Palm Beach mansion.

In the mid-1990s, an aura of Cold War–esque vigilance enveloped both Oxbow and Koch Industries. In addition to concerns about Dumpster-diving detectives and electronic eavesdropping, both factions also believed the other had slipped informants into their midst.

"We were all paranoid because of the tactics that were in use," said a former Koch executive. "There was a paranoia at some point that my secretary was a Bill Koch plant. You saw something at every turn."

Bill grew increasingly distrustful of everyone around him. "There were moles and spies all over," he has said. He feared his brothers had tapped his phones and believed that Koch operatives had stolen documents from his offices. Once, in an effort to prove Koch spies had infiltrated Oxbow, Bill's in-house counsel drafted a bogus memo and left it sitting conspicuously on his desk over-night. This fictitious document later turned up in a filing made by Koch Industries, according to Bill and his lawyers.

Bill had taken to furtively recording some of his phone calls on a Norelco Dictaphone, and he employed a shadowy security operator, Marc Nezer, to sweep for bugs and smoke out possible Koch moles. Employees occasionally spotted Nezer at the Oxbow offices on weekends slithering through the heating ducts. It was unclear whether he was combing for listening devices—or perhaps planting them.

Former employees say Bill had them surveilled in an effort to uncover those who might have betrayed him. Among them was Paul Siu, an Oxbow executive and close friend of Bill's in the 1970s and 1980s. Suspected of spying for Bill's brothers, he was canned from Oxbow. Afterward, Siu alleged that Bill had him tailed and bugged his phones. "After the proxy fight, he changed completely," he noted. "...Bill was in the first stage of Howard Hughes syndrome. Very paranoid."

Spy games became a way of life for Bill, and he used them pro-digiously during his bid for the America's Cup. The race has long had a reputation for a certain amount of espionage. Bill's com-petitors, however, accused him of taking things to an absurd and unsportsmanlike extreme. He was unapologetic. "This is more than the gentlemanly sport it used to be," he said. "This is war."

Guzzini, a 30-foot Bayliner speed boat with blacked out win-dows and a full complement of electronics gear, became the emblem of Bill's spy operation. As much for psychological warfare purposes as for intelligence gathering, it cruised the waters around

San Diego, shadowing rival boats as crew members pointed hand-held lasers at their quarry to record speed and telemetry data. The ever-present boat caused an uproar after a *Guzzini* deck hand, in a cheeky display of America³'s surveillance powers, spotted a group of rival sailors playing poker through long-range binoculars and radioed over to advise: "Keep the King. Discard the Jack."

Bill's team dispatched helicopters to track and photograph competitors and deployed divers (using rebreathers so the telltale bubbles wouldn't arouse suspicion) to study the keels of rival yachts. ("I wasn't alone," Bill told the *Palm Beach Post*.) Nezer, Bill's security specialist, who liked to cultivate a 007-esque mystique, also periodically materialized at the America³ team's San Diego compound. "He just seemed to come and go," said Gary Jobson, the syndicate's tactician. "Nobody knew what he was doing. Somebody said he was a Mossad agent. I stayed away from him." According to Jobson, Bill hired Italian speakers to lurk around the Italian team, and his investigators combed through the trash of rival syndicates seeking any morsel of information that might provide an advantage.

"They probably have a good idea of how many times we go to the bathroom, how many times I make phone calls," huffed Il Moro's skipper Paul Cayard.

Bill's team was ultimately said to have spent more than $2 million on its intelligence and counterespionage activities. Following the race, America's Cup officials, alarmed by the widespread spying, instituted a new regulation to curb future espionage. It was known informally as "the Bill Koch rule."

"That's been his whole life—private investigators with his brothers and trying to get an edge in all kinds of nefarious ways. The America's Cup was right there for him," said Jobson, who experienced his own harrowing brush with Bill's security apparatus.

A decorated sailor who had won the America's Cup aboard Ted Turner's *Courageous* in 1977, Jobson began sailing with Bill in 1984. He had helped to convince the businessman to make an attempt on the Cup. With "his technical mind and my pragmatic strategic experience, we actually blended pretty well," Jobson recalled.

At least for a time. A year into their America's Cup bid, Jobson grew uncomfortable with Bill's management style. "Bill is a guy that likes to have competitions between his people," he explained. "You don't know you're in a competition, but he kind of likes to throw stuff out there—'that guy is saying something about you' and then he says the same thing to another guy. Then he sits back and watches the show." In 1991, after receiving a job offer from ESPN, where Jobson saw a brighter future, he abruptly resigned from the team. Bill was incensed. "People don't leave Bill Koch," Jobson said.

After Jobson quit, Bill became convinced that his onetime tactician had turned on him and was leaking technical secrets to his America's Cup opponents. Bill sicced private investigators on the sailor.

Jobson had an inkling something was amiss. "I had a bad vibe," he remembered. "I'd put the garbage out, and the garbage can would be on the other side of the driveway the next morning and the garbageman hadn't come yet. And my phone seemed to be tapped. I can't prove it, but you would hear funny clicking noises when I talked on the phone. Something felt weird."

Then Jobson arrived home one day to find a thick envelope on the doorstep of his rented home in Point Loma. It contained a 150-page surveillance report from the detective agency Bill had hired to track him—leaked, he surmised, by a member of the America[3] organization who had taken pity on him.

"Holy Christ," Jobson thought as he paged through the report, finding a terrifyingly detailed account of his comings and goings, "these guys have been following me around for months." Later, as if in some spy thriller cliché, he peered out his window to see men snapping photographs of his house. Jobson hired a lawyer, who contacted Bill's attorney, making clear that his client had hard evidence that Bill was having him watched. Soon after, Jobson said, the surveillance ceased.

Sailing rivals were one thing, but Bill reserved some of his most bellicose tactics for his brothers. His 1983 settlement with Charles and David had netted nearly a half-billion dollars, but not the respect—not even the handshake one competitor gives to a worthy adversary at the end of a hard-fought match—that he craved from Charles. Since then, Bill, often joined by Frederick, had taken his brothers to court repeatedly.

In 1985 Bill filed a lawsuit, *Koch v. Koch Industries*, in federal district court in Wichita, alleging that Koch Industries had obscured assets during the settlement talks. Not long afterward, Bill and Frederick battled their brothers over control of their father's foundation. In 1991, they contested their mother's will, which included a clause cutting any of Mary Koch's children out of her estate if they did not drop pending litigation against each other within a certain time frame; the provision was aimed squarely at Bill and Frederick. The clause, Bill and Frederick argued, was the underhanded work of Charles, and the will itself was tainted because it had been drafted by the law firm representing Koch Industries. (A judge disagreed, finding that Mary was not subject to undue influence; Bill and Frederick also lost their case over the foundation.)

In Bill's ongoing psychodrama with Charles, nothing was off the table. If he had to drag the family name out of the shadows and through the mud to achieve closure, then so be it.

In the mid-to-late 1980s, PIs working for Bill and his legal team swarmed over windswept towns across the Midwest chasing rumors that Koch Industries had stolen oil at the wellhead from remote production sites, some of them located on Native

American reservations. His investigators deposed dozens of former employees, collecting handwritten affidavits and frequently offering as much as $300 per interview in compensation (a fact that would later allow Koch's lawyers to argue their testimony had been purchased).

The ex-employees were salt-of-the-earth types who wore handlebar mustaches and had names like Harley. Many had worked as Koch oil gaugers, responsible for measuring the quantity and quality of the crude the company purchased. The process was not cut and dry. Petroleum contracts or expands based on the temperature. It ranges in density, and the amount of sediment and impurities in the product also affects the measurement. The job entailed taking a variety of measurements and readings to accurately calculate how much oil was being purchased. But the numbers could easily be adjusted or fudged, especially at far-flung lease sites that operated on the honor system, where a handwritten "run ticket" filled out by the gauger was the only record of the sale.

Koch gaugers, and others involved in the company's oil gathering operations, described receiving instruction in how to manipulate measurements—shave an inch here, add one there, goose a temperature reading by 10 degrees—that ensured the company carted off more crude than it paid for. The process, these gaugers said, was known internally as the "Koch method."

By adjusting various measurements, Bob Gould, who worked for the company for nearly two decades, explained that "on an average I would gain from 3 to 4 barrels of oil that Koch Oil Co. didn't buy on each tank of oil" he processed. This didn't sound like much. But multiplied by ten tanks a day, five days a week, and the overages would add up. And Gould was just one of dozens of Koch oil gaugers.

The gaugers said their superiors never told them explicitly to steal; rather they described coming under relentless pressure from higher-ups to "work the oil" in the company's favor. "Let's help

Charlie out. That was a big phrase. Always help Charlie out, referring to Charles Koch," remembered David Toliver, one former
Koch gauger. Some of the company's employees joked that Koch
really stood for "Keep Old Charlie Happy."

Bill's self-initiated oil-theft probe was fortuitously timed. In
1987, the Senate had created a special investigative committee,
chaired by Arizona Democrat Dennis DeConcini, to look into
fraud and mismanagement afflicting Native American lands and
institutions. With assistance from Bill, who opened up his files to
the congressional investigators and teed up witnesses, the investigation expanded to include allegations of oil theft from tribal
lands. If Charles treasured his reputation as a man of high principle and integrity, this would be an ideal opportunity to demolish
it, Bill must have thought.

In 1988, an FBI agent named Richard J. "Jim" Elroy led a team
of committee investigators into Oklahoma's Indian country in the
hopes of catching Koch and other oil companies in the act of stealing oil. Elroy, who was on loan from the bureau to assist with
the committee's investigation, was in his late forties, his dark hair
graying at the temples. The tenacious FBI veteran could tell a good
yarn, of which he had many from his eighteen years working public corruption cases, largely from the bureau's Oklahoma City field
office. Soon he would have another tale to tell.

Elroy and his team staked out eight randomly selected oil leases,
struggling to find cover in the flat, wide-open terrain. The investigators crouched in ditches, behind cedar bushes, and in one case,
hid among a herd of Hereford cattle, training a camera with a
600-millimeter lens on gaugers as they came and went. Once a
gauger had pulled away, an investigator hurried out to conduct
his own measurements of how much oil had been extracted. He
compared that to how much oil the gauger said he'd taken on a
handwritten "run ticket."

A year later, on an overcast May morning in the nation's capital, the committee held a widely covered hearing in the Dirksen Senate Office Building, where the panel's chief counsel, Ken Ballen, questioned Elroy. (In a sign of just how closely Bill worked with the Senate investigators, he would later develop close ties to Ballen and Elroy. After retiring from the FBI, Elroy joined Bill's retinue of private eyes.)

"Agent Elroy," Ballen asked, "could you provide to the members of the committee...the results of the surveillance on the eight leases that was conducted by committee investigators?"

"On six of the eight we found they were stealing oil," the FBI agent responded. "Two of the leases we found they were quite accurate."

In each of the six cases where theft had occurred, Elroy testified, Koch Industries had been the purchaser.

Charles had told committee investigators earlier that year that gauging was "a very uncertain art" practiced by people who "aren't rocket scientists." Elroy had a different take: "I don't know how you could draw any other conclusion but that this is top management-directed theft," he told the committee.

Blindsided by the allegations, Koch Industries entered crisis mode. It hastily released a 57-page statement rebutting the charges and claiming that they were the product of Bill's "vendetta." The company's general counsel, Don Cordes, alleged that the company had become the object of "political skullduggery."

Koch Industries enlisted a quartet of current and former senators from Kansas and Oklahoma to complain to their colleagues on the committee about the "reliability" of the evidence and testimony investigators had gathered. And it hired a group of high-powered Democratic lobbyists, including the wife of Iowa Senator Tom Harkin, in an effort to soften the language in the committee report released later that year.

These overtures had no effect. The Senate panel's scathing report accused Koch Industries of "systematic theft" and of engaging "in a widespread and sophisticated scheme to steal crude oil from Indians and others through fraudulent mismeasuring and reporting." Based on documents subpoenaed from Koch, the committee reported that the company had stolen at least $31 million worth of oil in the previous three years alone.

The scandal played out a year before Mary Koch's death, forcing her to bear witness to another wave of negative publicity concerning the family. After the Senate report's release, Frederick, who left the investigations and legal maneuvering to Bill, sent an extract of the report to his mother with the most damning passages neatly underlined in red pen. It was an apparent effort to illustrate the righteousness of their legal battle against Charles and David, and to convince Mary that if Charles was capable of stealing from Native Americans, he had it in him to cheat his brothers. In a letter that accompanied the report, Frederick wrote that "the pattern of oil theft is so pervasive against Koch Industries" and the "evidence is too overwhelming" for Charles's denial of wrongdoing to be taken seriously. "You must agree that Father would be appalled to observe the way his company reveals to the world today a callow lack of respect for those values which he held in high esteem—honesty and integrity."

As if allegations of rampant larceny weren't bad enough, the report also accused Koch Industries of investigating the private lives of committee staff. "One Koch employee in Oklahoma even went so far as to interview the ex-wife of a Committee investigator about the circumstances of their divorce," the Senate report stated. In a separate episode, Elroy claimed that he had nabbed one of Koch's investigators tailing him in Oklahoma City. He pulled the man from his car at gunpoint and snapped open his FBI credentials. "You might take a message back to your employer," Elroy growled. "Your next person might come back in a body bag."

Based on the committee's investigation, the Justice Department opened a criminal probe into the oil-theft allegations, a case that it later closed without issuing indictments. Bill, meanwhile, launched another front in his legal bombardment. Since the alleged oil thefts had occurred on federal lands, depriving the government of royalties, he filed a whistleblower lawsuit under the False Claims Act for which he could claim a percentage of any money recovered.

Charles seemed caught off guard by Bill's scorched earth tactics. "Why," he wondered, "would someone in your own family try to get the U.S. government to brand you as a racketeer?"

In Bill's bare-knuckled world the answer was simple: The charges "have a sting," he said. "They bring people to the negotiating table sooner." He admitted, "I was cold-blooded and Machiavellian about coming up with it....I don't want to see my brothers in jail. But I'm at war."

Over the course of the litigation with his brothers, Bill often stressed that he was not acting based on emotion. This was business. He was merely a ruthless tactician plotting his way through a corporate conflict using every weapon (litigation, publicity, PIs) in his arsenal. But then, almost in the same breath, he expounded on grievances that went back to childhood—his absentee parents, poor self-image, the bully of an older brother who instigated fights between the twins, and who every time Bill neared the top of the storm cellar during games of King of the Hill, shoved him roughly to the ground. Bill seemed to consider the brutal legal in-fighting an adult version of King of the Hill. A game of dominance. "I almost wish," he once said of Charles, "I would have started a fight with him 30 years ago."

Sam Crow, the World War II veteran and onetime military judge shepherding the *Koch v. Koch Industries* litigation, saw clearly that congressional hearing rooms and courtrooms, especially his, had "become the stage for the unraveling of a family."

In August 1997, after nearly a decade-and-a-half of legal skirmishing, Crow finally scheduled the case for trial the following

April. He had whittled the suit, initially loaded with charges of secret Swiss bank accounts, hidden assets, and widespread racketeering, down to two claims: Koch had used devious accounting gimmicks, the plaintiffs alleged, to artificially understate its assets and operating profits as the company and the dissident shareholders brokered the buyout. The other charge was that Charles and the company's management had deceived Bill, Frederick, and the Simmons family about expansion plans at Koch's Pine Bend refinery in Minnesota and an associated pipeline deal that vastly improved Koch's competitive position in the Midwest. Because of these alleged deceptions, the plaintiffs believed Koch Industries had defrauded them by as much as $2 billion, adjusting for inflation and interest.

Motions piled up on Judge Crow's desk in the months leading up to the trial, both sides jousting over what evidence he should permit. Koch fought efforts by Bill's legal team to present information that it had destroyed incriminating documents during discovery. Bill's lawyers, meanwhile, battled to keep the defendants from highlighting their client's "lifelong history of feelings of inferiority," "obsessive hatred" toward his brothers, and background of psychoanalysis. Citing Bill and Frederick's attempt to drag their late mother into court against the advice of her doctor, Charles and David's attorneys argued that these topics were indeed fair game. "These are not the acts of rational men; these are the acts of a man consumed by hatred and willingly followed by his weaker brother."

The public relations war also heated up in anticipation of the trial. Both sides traded accusations that the other had tried to unduly influence the jury pool through media interviews, television ads, and sly public opinion polls, including one testing the waters for Bill's nascent Senate candidacy.

Judge Crow, feeling much like a parent disciplining squabbling children, finally intervened. "The court almost forgets that this complex litigation involves claims for hundreds of millions of dollars," he wrote in a ruling that silenced both sides with a gag order. "Unfortunately, the court is instead reminded of a childhood tussle on the school playground—followed by the inevitable volley of finger pointing accompanied by a chorus of participants shouting the defensive retort of 'He started it,' as the teacher approaches to break up the fray."

On a warm, clear afternoon in early April 1998, the four Koch brothers arrived at the Frank Carlson Federal Building in Topeka. It was a bitter kind of reunion, the first time in years they had all been in the same place—even the same time zone. When they saw each other at all anymore, the venue was always a sterile courtroom.

A scrum of reporters and TV crews had converged in front of the charmless, redbrick building to catch the feuding brothers as they arrived. Dodging the press, Bill and Frederick slipped into the courthouse through a rear entrance. Charles and David, accompanied by their fashionably dressed wives, parked in a nearby garage, strode past the media, and entered through the front door.

Inside the courtroom, the two sets of brothers avoided eye contact. They chatted quietly among themselves, doing their best to appear impassive. The seating had even been arranged so the warring siblings could avoid each other. Steering clear entirely, however, was impossible. When in the weeks ahead the brothers occasionally passed one another in the narrow corridors of the courthouse, they did so as ghosts, leaving nothing in their wake but a tingling, combustible tension in the air.

The court summoned a pool of sixty potential jurors at the start of the trial. At least as many lawyers and paralegals seemed to be buzzing around the courtroom at times. Led by the esteemed Chicago trial lawyer Fred Bartlit Jr., who a couple of years later would help George W. Bush litigate his way to the Oval Office, the plaintiffs' legal entourage alone occupied three floors at the Ramada in downtown Topeka (the trial had been moved there from Wichita in order to find jurors untainted by opinions on the Koch brothers). By one estimate, Bill's legal tab had surpassed $200,000 per week.

Working-class farmers, truck drivers, teachers, and retirees composed the bulk of the jury pool. They were the kind of people who settled family disputes in the living room, not the courtroom. For them, a legal feud of these dimensions was unfathomable, as was the ten-figure sum involved. It would be hard to paint the brothers, especially Bill and Frederick, in any sympathetic light. "There's no poor people in this case," Bartlit told one potential juror. "Everybody's rich. That's just the way it is."

As the lawyers weeded them out, they asked jury candidates for their reactions to a particular statement. "Business is war and anything goes." Agree or disagree?

"Let me take you back and tell you the story of a truly fascinating Kansas family." A silk handkerchief peaked neatly from the pocket of his tailored suit. Not a gray hair was out of place. His ramrod posture recalled his military training as a West Point cadet and Army Ranger. Surveying the six-man, six-woman jury with an eyebrow cocked, Fred Bartlit looked every inch the power lawyer as he delivered his opening statement in a forceful, booming voice.

"This family was unusual," he continued, "because they grew up in a very litigious atmosphere. Fred Koch, the patriarch, invented ways of refining very heavy oil, very heavy, thick oil.... The major oil companies took him to court, and he had many, many long years of court fights and he sometimes was on the verge of losing, but he was a fighter. Around the family dinner table, it was unusual, because the talk was of litigation, the talk was of you've got to stick up for your rights, and you never, never quit no matter what. That's what these boys—these men—learned from their dad. They grew up hearing about court fights, and in this family, this unusual family, conflict got to mean going to court."

Continuing his portrait of a family that gave new meaning to dysfunction, Bartlit told the jury that the case "was about a man's driving need for total control and total power." It was about how "Charles Koch went above the law in this country and also how he went above the ordinary rules that we live by in dealing with our own family.

"No verdict is going to fix this family at this point," the lawyer said. "...Fortunately, your job as jurors is not to fix the family, but to sort out the hard evidence, look at the proof...and that's much easier than figuring out where a family went wrong."

Where Bill had flown in a shock troop of legal heavy hitters, Charles stayed the course with his family's longtime lawyer Bob Howard and the local Wichita law firm of Foulston Siefkin. The contrasts between Howard and Bartlit were hard to miss. A native Kansan, Howard wore a slightly rumpled suit, spoke in nasal tones, and had a mild, folksy manner. Howard's unassuming appearance belied a masterful legal tactician, and one who knew the Koch clan inside and out. Having represented Charles, David, and their late mother since the 1980s, the sixty-seven-year-old lawyer knew most of the skeletons in the family's closet.

"The plaintiffs in this case seek to label this a pure business dispute," Howard told the jury, flipping through his notes. "It isn't. It's a dispute that arose of family strife and family conflict." At its root were "deteriorating...interpersonal relationships" and money-hungry family members who, unlike Charles, did not want to grow Koch Industries but to loot it of its profits.

"That's what this lawsuit is about," Howard said, "a continuation of a bitter family fight that should have been settled in 1983 when we paid $1.1 billion for peace that has never come to Kansas."

*   *   *

David Koch took the stand in mid-April, the first of the four Koch brothers to testify. The fifty-seven-year-old executive vice president of Koch Industries endured three days of questioning. His testimony veered from impenetrable technical matters about the refinery expansion to details about the brothers' boyhood rivalry: "We were strong-minded, head-strong individuals," he said at one point. "Of course, yeah, we competed, but I don't think it was excessive."

Bill's lawyer asked him one afternoon about his twin's firing. Why in the boardroom that day had David abstained from voting to kick his brother out of the company? His face flushed. "Well," he began. "I have very strong feelings for my brother, and I wanted…" He trailed off, bringing his hand to his forehead. "This is tough to talk about. Boy."

David tried to fight through the deep well of emotion that had pooled within. "Bill had acted very badly in the company," he said, his voice breaking. "He'd done some terrible things." The businessman began to sob, his sorrow amplified throughout the rapt courtroom by the microphone clipped to his tie. Across the room, Charles lifted his glasses to dab a tear. Bill stared down at the table in front of him.

"Mr. Koch, do you want a recess?" the judge asked.

"I think I can get through it here." David paused to collect himself. "I just didn't want him to act this way. I wanted him to behave himself, do a good job, and he wouldn't, and he deceived me, but I wanted to help him out. I wanted to maintain my relationship with him. I just couldn't vote against him, but I knew he couldn't work in the company anymore, so it was my desperate desire to try to maintain a relationship with him."

Frederick took the stand on May 1. Provincial Topeka, surrounded by brothers he had almost nothing in common with, was surely the last place he wanted to be. Give him London, New York, or Monte Carlo—anywhere with a whiff of sophistication and a thriving auction scene. Shorter than his six-foot-plus brothers, with the delicate features of his mother, the sixty-four-year-old had sat quietly through the proceedings, a curiosity to the members of the press covering the trial. "He was so quiet and so almost like a nonfactor, like he didn't want to be there," remembered someone who attended the trial.

Frederick had a reputation as a recluse, based largely on his preference for staying out of the media, not sequestering himself at home. He was active with various arts and cultural organizations, including the Metropolitan Opera, the Royal Shakespeare Company, and the Pierpont Morgan Library, and he was a regular at New York galas and fund-raisers. But even some people who had known him for years considered him an enigma. Of all of the Koch brothers, even Charles, he was the most relentlessly private. Frederick made his employees sign strict nondisclosure agreements, vowing that they would not divulge anything about their employer to anyone, and especially the press.

He was hard to read—most in his element when talking about art or literature or theater—and his genteel demeanor could turn frigid without warning. A man of contradictions, he thought little about dropping six figures at Sotheby's, but could also be bizarrely frugal, growing angry at his staff if they added too much postage to letters and packages. He spared no expense when it came to refurbishing his homes, but he preferred taking the public bus in New York and typically flew commercial.

One associate recalled strolling down East 80th Street with Frederick on a sweltering summer afternoon in the mid-1990s. Crossing Fifth Avenue, Frederick noticed a nickel in the middle of the crosswalk; it had been run over so many times that it was embedded in the asphalt. His companion looked on in shock as Frederick stooped down, took out his keys, and began trying to pry the coin loose. The multi-millionaire continued to work as the traffic light changed. Traffic bore down and horns blared, but Frederick kept digging, finally dislodging the nickel. "I got it," he said, holding the coin up with a beatific expression on his face. "I just was dumb-founded," his companion recalled. ("I never pick up coins in the street," Frederick said, "despite this apocryphal account.")

"Today I'm largely involved in charitable activities," Frederick told the court. He affected a noticeable British accent from the time he had spent in England overseeing the ten-year renovation of Sutton Place, where Frederick had displayed his collection of nineteenth-century paintings. "The house is now open to the pub-lic. It's one of the most popular attractions within the environ-ments of London. We're completely sold out two years in advance."

The eldest Koch brother's testimony was relatively brief. He knew nothing of the oil business or the inner workings of the fam-ily company. In the court drama, Frederick and David were the supporting actors. Charles and Bill were the trial's star witnesses.

Bill was suffering from a cold when he began the first of seven grueling days of testimony. Bartlit launched his examination of his client with a series of rapid-fire questions designed to dispense with the notion that Bill had staged a boardroom coup with the aim of deposing Charles.

"First, did you ever want your brother, Charles, out of Koch Industries?"

"Never," Bill replied, his voice slightly hoarse.

"Did you ever want him removed as CEO of Koch?"

"No."

"Did you have any feelings of jealousy towards your brother Charles?"

"No."

"Now," Bartlit said, "let's talk about the 1980 proposal to expand the board of directors. What was the purpose of that proposal?"

"The purpose," Bill replied, "was to create a democratic board that represented all of the shareholders proportionally, one man, one vote."

Bill portrayed his brother as a dictatorial chief executive who didn't tolerate dissent and whose management practices and anti-government philosophy had caused Koch Industries to run afoul of regulators. "I didn't want to see the company go down for legal problems or ethical problems," he testified.

When Howard's turn came, the attorney chiseled away at Bill's testimony.

Wasn't it true that Bill had voted in 1982, when he still had a seat on Koch's board, to oust Charles as the company's CEO?

"Yes." So he had, in fact, tried to depose his brother, even if this hadn't been the original goal of his boardroom putsch.

And hadn't he also voted against David continuing on as an executive officer of the company?

"I may have."

Question by question, Howard highlighted Bill's efforts to extract money from Koch Industries at any cost, even if it meant breaking up the company his father had started by selling his holdings to a corporate raider, such as T. Boone Pickens, or Saudi investors.

"You wanted to continue to grow the company, or you wanted to put it up for grabs to corporate raiders and corporate takeover artists to see if you couldn't get the highest possible dollar to your shares?" Howard probed.

"I had mixed feelings. My feelings were, on the one hand, I wanted to be purely an economic man, get the best economic deal; and on the other hand, I had a lot of emotional attachment to the company.... There came a time when those feelings shifted, however."

"And in the competition between the two halves of your-self," Howard asked, "what won out was get the highest price, wasn't it?"

"Oh, eventually, that's what won out," Bill acknowledged.

When Charles testified in late May, Bill looked away from the witness stand. During the proceedings, one trial attendee recalled, Bill "was like a caged animal. He was ready to attack."

Charles may have been the CEO of a large, multinational company, but he was nevertheless uncomfortable with public speaking. "Work for Koch Industries," he said quietly when asked to state his profession. It was classic Charles. He didn't say that he ran Koch Industries, that he was the company's chairman and chief executive. He just worked there, like thousands of others.

Charles testified haltingly, sometimes fumbling for words, but he ceded little ground. Early on, he upended the notion, advanced by Bartlit, that Fred Koch had taught his sons that "if you can't work things out around the table...you go to court and you fight and fight and fight."

"What I recall is the opposite," Charles said. "My father had gone through a nightmare of litigation from 1929 to 1952, and as part of that, he'd countersued, which lasted a number of years. His saying about that is, 'That was a mistake, that was a terrible mistake.' He said, 'Never sue.' He said, 'Out of those lawsuits, I finally settled. I settled for a million and a half dollars. The lawyers got a third, the government got a third, and I got a third, and I ended up with my business destroyed.' So he said, 'never sue,' those were his words."

Later, as he recounted the family's last Christmas together in 1979, when Bill had launched into a tirade that had brought their mother to tears, Charles appeared to stare directly at his brother as he spoke: "He accused her of being a bad mother, of not loving him, and that whatever problems he had were largely her fault."

Bill never looked up from the table in front of him.

Week after week, as the trial slogged on, Charles and David, sometimes accompanied by their wives, flew to Topeka on Sundays, returning home for at best a few days at the end of the week—Charles to Wichita, David to New York. Then they began the whole exhausting ritual all over again.

During the trial, the brothers rented a Topeka mansion that had belonged to a member of the Menninger family, who had founded a famous psychiatric clinic and sanitarium in the city. Charles and David's daily routine varied little. The brothers convened for breakfast with their lawyers and advisors to prep for trial, then caravanned over to the courthouse in black SUVs. They concluded the day in a similar fashion, debriefing with their lawyers and advisors over dinner.

The long legal battle had taken a noticeable toll on each of the brothers, but perhaps none more so than Charles. The typically energetic CEO wasn't sleeping well. He looked drawn and haggard. It was not just his company but his values that were under assault.

"No question—that was the hardest period of Charles' life. Beyond anything I could describe," said Leslie Rudd, Charles's close friend.

Gerald O'Shaughnessy, another close friend, observed that he had "never quite seen him so…distracted and preoccupied."

In the months before the trial, Charles was aloof and withdrawn. Perhaps for the first time since he had gone to work for his father's company in 1961, he seemed disengaged from the business. "I frankly didn't think he was that focused on the company then," said a former Koch executive. "During that period there were a bunch of questionable deals."

Exhibit A was Koch's $670 million acquisition of Purina Mills, completed several weeks before *Koch v. Koch Industries* went to trial. Before year's end, the feed company filed for Chapter 11, inflicting major losses on Koch Industries. And by April 1999, this and other bad bets on its agriculture businesses forced hundreds of layoffs at the company, as Charles and the company's management

struggled to turn around money-losing divisions or extricate themselves entirely. "The company had a couple of people who are gone
now who just shouldn't have had as much authority as they did,"
recalled Tony Woodlief, who went to work as a Koch management
consultant in March 1997 and later became a vice president of
Charles's charitable foundation. "They talked a good game and
then they made some really stupid decisions....Charles, you cannot get an ounce of bullshit past him, but at that time he was so
checked out."

Throughout the eleven-week trial, Charles watched the proceedings almost expressionless, even while Liz, his fiercely loyal wife,
struggled to stifle her anger as Bill and Frederick's lawyers painted
her husband as a tyrant and a cheat. His wooden demeanor
masked the inner tumult of watching his family's private drama
splayed out for the world to see. The litigation, the former Koch
executive said, was "crushing" Charles. "You could see a side of
Charles that no one had ever seen before and no one will likely
ever see again. That trial—destroyed him is not the right word. It
was as if he had aged 40 years."

On Tuesday, June 16, after two-and-a-half months of testimony,
Bartlit and Howard delivered their closing arguments. "The only
thing that people like this recognize, unfortunately, is money,"
Bartlit told the jury, arguing that Koch's management had displayed the "attitude of somebody who will do it again unless they
get more than a slap on the wrist."

Howard called the case a "modern parable. And the moral is,
beware of a brother driven by the need for more money, by greed,
and by the desire to rule or ruin, because if you don't, you're in for
20 years of corporate warfare."

Koch Industries had hired Courtroom Sciences Inc., the consulting firm cofounded by "Dr. Phil" McGraw, to advise on the case
and empanel a shadow jury, who reported daily on their impressions of the evidence and testimony presented at trial. The shadow

jurors were told that their participation was solely for research purposes, but the electronic keypad lock on the room they were interviewed in and the anti-eavesdropping devices affixed to its walls suggested the endeavor was not just academic. Their true purpose was to give Charles and David's legal team a glimpse into the psyche of the jury and the arguments and evidence they had been swayed by.

While the real jury deliberated, the CSI consultants delivered their verdict to Charles and David at the Menninger house. The brothers, the consultants said, needed to prepare themselves for the worst. "The CSI guys said you need to focus on loss—you guys have lost," said someone familiar with this conversation. "David shut down." In the event of a loss, one of the brothers might have to make a statement to the press. "Fuck it," David said. "I'm not doing it."

At 9:45 a.m. on June 19, when the jury sent a message to Judge Crow that they had reached a verdict, Charles and David were far from Topeka. David had returned to New York, where Julia was expecting the birth of their first child later that summer. Charles was trying to occupy himself with work in Wichita. Frederick, too, was MIA; he had flown back to Europe.

But Bill had remained in Topeka to anxiously await the verdict. It was only natural, since he had invested so much of his time and money into the case.

Judge Crow recessed the court and summoned the lawyers into his chambers to review the verdict. Bartlit emerged grim-faced not long after. "They're guilty of misrepresentation," he told Bill, "but it's not material." The jurors, in other words, believed that Koch Industries had concealed some facts during negotiations with the shareholders, but determined these omissions did not significantly affect the sale price. There would be no damages. Charles and David had prevailed.

Word of the victory spread quickly at Koch's Wichita headquarters, where an e-mail circulated late Friday morning informing the staff that "the jury unanimously ruled, as we've always known, that Bill Koch and the other shareholders were treated fairly when their stock was purchased for more than $1.1 billion." Charles delivered the news to David by phone. The trauma of the trial behind them, the brothers both wept with relief.

Charles and David knew their battle with Bill was nowhere near over; Charles had resigned himself to the fact that Bill would keep coming at him as long as he had "breath or money." But they had won a key battle.

Bill's team, offering its own spin on the trial's outcome, trumpeted in a press release that "Jury Finds Koch Industries Guilty of Misrepresentation." Bill called the verdict a "moral victory." But symbolic triumphs mattered little to the America's Cup–winning skipper. In reality, he was shattered, and in the coming months a familiar gloom shrouded his life.

After the verdict, reporters cornered Bill outside the Topeka courthouse and peppered him with questions. Defiant, Bill announced that he would appeal. "These guys are crooks. In my opinion," he said, "this is the 10th round of a 15-round championship fight."

CHAPTER ELEVEN

There Will Be Blood

On August 24, 1996, in a rural subdivision fifty miles southeast of Dallas, an acrid smell wafted into the small trailer home Danny Smalley shared with his two daughters. The odor was mild at first, as if the pilot light of a stove had blown out. After Smalley's seventeen-year-old daughter, Danielle, complained, the forty-year-old mechanic went outside to investigate and checked the propane tank behind their trailer. It wasn't leaking, so he went back to watching the Little League World Series in his bedroom.

Danielle, meanwhile, buzzed around the house, packing and tidying up. Her friend Jason Stone had come by, and the teenagers were discussing plans for her farewell party that night. Danielle was the president of her high school theater club, and had won a drama scholarship to a nearby community college. The following day she planned to move into the dorms. A pretty girl with a bright smile, bangs, and long dark hair that fell past her shoulders, she had dreams of pop stardom. Once she was rich and famous, Danielle had told her father, she planned to buy him a new Harley.

The smell had gotten worse. Danielle felt queasy.

The Smalleys didn't own a telephone, but she and Jason volunteered to drive over to a neighbor's home to call in a report of a possible gas leak. A little after 3:30 p.m., Danny walked the teenagers outside and watched for a moment as Danielle backed his 1964 Chevy pickup truck out of the driveway, looped around a telephone pole, and drove for the main road. A couple hundred yards from the house, the pickup stalled as it crossed a dry creek bed. Danielle turned the ignition. Nothing. She turned the key again.

The thunderous explosion spewed a geyser of flame hundreds of feet in the air. George York, the local constable, felt the concussion a couple miles away. He'd heard chatter about a gas leak over the radio. He raced toward the scene.

As York entered the Oak Trail Estates subdivision where the Smalleys lived, he saw terrified families fleeing into the road toward him. The tops of trees were charred and smoking. A picnic table was in flames. The area looked "like it was strafed by Napalm," York recalled.

York spotted a man running toward him wearing nothing but athletic shorts and a demented expression. Tears streamed down Danny Smalley's face; his trembling hands were raised to the sky. "You're no God!" he bellowed. "You're the devil!" Everything was on fire; it appeared to Smalley as if hell itself had opened up to claim his daughter and Jason Stone.

Their bodies lay about 50 feet apart. The teenagers had been on fire as they tried to run from the truck. Both were on their backs, in the fetal position. "They were still bubbling from the ears and the nose and the eyes," York recalled. They were unrecognizable, their hair and clothes incinerated. The only way to tell them apart was by examining their genitals. York helped Smalley—still cursing God for stealing his daughter—cover their smoldering bodies.

At 3:09 p.m., in the dimly lit pipeline control center at Koch Industries' Wichita headquarters, an alert flashed red on one of the six screens Danny Mills was monitoring. This was the nerve center of the company's pipeline system, where a bank of computer consoles, arrayed in a semicircle, displayed the constantly updating vital signs of Koch's 40,000-mile network, which Charles and David had built over the last few decades into one of the largest in the nation.

The pressure in the Sterling I pipeline had dropped to zero. It stretched 570 miles, from Medford, Oklahoma, to Mount Belvieu, Texas. Unknown to Danny Smalley and most of his neighbors, it ran within several hundred feet of their homes, coursing with a thousand barrels an hour of highly volatile liquid butane. (The clear gas is used to fuel cigarette lighters, as an aerosol propellant, and is also blended into gasoline and propane.)

The pressure reading couldn't be right. A malfunction, Mills assumed. Perhaps one of the transmitters that relayed data back to the control center was on the fritz.

Twenty minutes later another alert blinked on his screen, this one showing abnormally low suction at a pumping station. Mills beckoned a coworker over, who peered at the monitor. "It looks like you have a problem," he said.

A ringing telephone interrupted Mills as he tried to diagnose what had gone wrong with Sterling I. On the line was Rick Burgett, a former Koch contractor who happened to live in the same subdivision as the Smalleys. "You have a major leak in this area," Burgett told Mills.

A few minutes later, Mills was on the phone with the Kaufman County Sheriff's Office. He needed to get a technician out to the site immediately. "This is Danny with Koch Industries. The pipeline that ruptured, I need to know where this place is."

After being transferred a few times, a dispatcher finally gave Mills directions to Oak Trail. "You'll see it when you get there. They said that the flames are about 200 feet."

"Flames?" Mills started to panic; he thought there was just a leak.

"Yeah."

"What caught fire?" he asked.

"It's a gas main broke, blew up," the dispatcher said.

"Good God."

The clear liquid gushing from the ground looked at first like water. But it quickly vaporized after hitting the air. Danielle and Jason had unwittingly driven directly into a cloud of butane that had drifted down the creek bed. All it had taken was a single ignition spark to set off a massive explosion that scorched more than a dozen acres of land.

Following the tragedy, Danny Smalley descended into a vortex of despair. Diagnosed with post-traumatic stress disorder, he needed pills to sleep; even when he drifted off, he often woke up mid-scream, as he dreamt night after night about the explosion. While out driving, sometimes a song came on the radio that reminded him of Danielle. But he couldn't picture her anymore. All he saw was her burnt corpse.

Smalley blamed himself for his daughter's death—he should have been the one in that truck—and became suicidal. A year after the explosion, friends discovered Smalley in the cemetery where he buried his daughter. He had doused himself in gasoline and was preparing to take his life, as Danielle's had been taken.

By 1998, the Stone family had settled with Koch, as had Danielle's mother, Judy, who split with Danny in 1990. Danny pressed forward with a lawsuit, holding out even as Koch's lawyers threw out higher and higher figures, eventually offering $10 million on the day the case went to trial. Smalley sought something more valuable. He wanted the opportunity to sit on the witness stand and stare down the company that had robbed him of his daughter. He wanted Charles and David Koch to understand just what they had taken from him. He wanted his day in court.

Smalley had hired Ted Lyon, a well-known Texas trial lawyer. A veteran of state politics, Lyon had served for fourteen years as a Democratic legislator in the Texas House and Senate. With a surplus of folksy charm, he was a master at courting juries, as his history of winning record-setting verdicts could attest.

Whenever Lyon took on a personal injury case, he insisted on pacing the accident scene. When he represented parents who had lost a son or a daughter, he made a point of calling on them at home, where he would inevitably find a shrine to the child. In court, he was a storyteller. The details brought the narrative to life; the narrative swayed the jury.

Koch Industries retained its own retinue of legal heavy-hitters to represent the company, including attorneys from the high-powered Houston-based law firm of Fulbright & Jaworski. During one early deposition in the case, Koch's representatives numbered at least a dozen. On the other side of the conference table sat Lyon and Marquette Wolf, a fresh-faced associate who had recently graduated from Southern Methodist University's law school. The intimidating display of legal firepower spooked the young lawyer. But it wasn't Lyon's first showdown with a powerful corporation trying to flex its muscles. Turning to Wolf, Lyon invoked the catchphrase of the Texas Rangers, the legendary frontier lawmen. "One riot," he drawled, "one Ranger."

Meanwhile, in Washington, a dogged, platinum-haired prosecutor named Angela O'Connell was also taking on Koch Industries. She had grown up in the DC area and joined the Justice Department in 1982, after graduating from Georgetown Law School. She was now the lead attorney on one of the largest environmental cases in the agency's history. In 1995, the federal government had filed suit against Koch under the Clean Water Act, alleging that the company's pipelines and storage facilities had leaked millions of gallons of oil into the waters of six states across the South and the Midwest. One of the reasons for these spills, the agency believed, was the decrepit state of the company's pipeline system. Koch had grown into a business behemoth by shrewdly buying up under-valued oil assets that Sterling Varner called "junk"—and in some cases it was now starting to show.

The Justice Department had documented over 300 spills since 1990. The worst of them had occurred in October 1994, when a pipeline in southern Texas disgorged nearly 100,000 gallons of crude and painted a 12-mile oil slick on Nueces and Corpus Christi Bays.

Spills happen in the oil business, but the scope of Koch's violations and the company's disregard for the environmental consequences had attracted federal scrutiny. In the event of a spill in U.S. waters, oil companies are required by law to report the estimated amount to the Coast Guard, which marshals resources accordingly and responds to the scene. But Koch "repeatedly lied about the amount to avoid penalties," O'Connell said. "These guys would call in two barrels when they had something that was a shocking amount of oil." (In the case of the Corpus Christi spill, the company had originally reported that just 420 gallons of oil had spilled.) Asked by government lawyers whether they had ever knowingly downplayed the size of spills, several Koch officials pleaded the Fifth Amendment.

"Many of Koch's spills...occurred in remote areas and were never reported to any authorities. Many of these were in the amount of 5 to 6 barrels, although I estimate that there were dozens of spills of over 50 barrels which entered the water," noted Phil Dubose, who worked for Koch Industries for twenty-six years, rising to become a division manager of its marine subsidiary.

When the authorities did respond, Dubose said, Koch employees were instructed to cover up the extent of the accident by using techniques like "wheel washing," in which a boat's engine blade churns up the oil slick to mask it. "It was understood that we should either 'wheel wash' the spill, or to cover it up with soil if it was on land," he noted. " 'Wheel washing' was a standard practice for Koch in my division. Crews often did so on their own initiative, since they wanted to protect their jobs."

Bill Koch had warned years earlier about the company's knack for getting into trouble with regulators. Now the government was scrutinizing Koch Industries as never before—and behind the scenes, Bill and his lawyers were providing information to the Justice Department to assist the agency in its investigation.

During O'Connell's twenty-five-year career at Justice, she had prosecuted nearly every oil company out there—but none, she said, like Koch. "They're always operating outside of the system. It's kind of like what they used to call Texas Justice, only it's happening in Wichita."

O'Connell began to suspect that Koch had placed her under surveillance. "I thought that my trash can was taken outside my house several days," she recalled. "I was upset enough about it at the time to report what I thought was a bugging and what I thought was the trash being taken—a number of incidents." The Justice Department was never able to prove that Koch had targeted one of its prosecutors, but for the first time in her career, O'Connell operated as if everything she said and did was being monitored.

She was especially careful during visits to Koch's Wichita headquarters, an edifice of sleek brown granite rising incongruously from the Kansas prairie. "When I was in their headquarters and they'd say, 'Oh, feel free to use the phone, feel free to talk in this office'—we never said anything inside those offices," O'Connell said. "I never made a phone call inside that place."

In 1999, as Ted Lyon worked on the Smalley case, he hired a security firm to sweep for listening devices in his offices, located on the fifth floor of an office tower in the Dallas exurb of Mesquite. He suspected that he and other lawyers at his firm were being spied on, perhaps by investigators working for Koch Industries. "There were things during the case that no else would have known about, but somehow they knew about it," he said.

"We had a lot of different witnesses we had to run down," Lyon added, "people who had formerly worked for them and things of that nature. We would be talking about them on the phone with an investigator or we'd be talking about them between Marquette and I, and they would suddenly be visited by Koch representatives."

The security consultants discovered that transmitters had been planted in the firm's offices and set to broadcast to an FM frequency. "I'm not saying that the Kochs did it," Lyon said carefully. "I just thought it was very interesting that it happened during the time we were litigating that case."

Lyon also discovered that the company was having Danny Smalley tailed. He said he turned the tables by hiring a private detective of his own to follow Koch's investigator, then subpoenaing the PI once he discovered his identity. Koch also attempted to track down witnesses who would chisel away at Smalley's credibility at trial. According to Lyon, they dug up one woman who was prepared to testify that the grieving father was an alcoholic who beat his daughters; it turned out, though, that she wasn't much of a character witness. She was a paranoid schizophrenic who had been in and out of a mental institution, where she underwent repeated shock therapy treatments.

"They did everything they could to intimidate us," Lyon said. "It was battle after battle after battle." The only option was to match the company's aggressive legal strategy with their own.

"Unrelenting," Wolf noted, "was the only way with them."

Document by document, deposition by deposition, a picture began to emerge of an unusually profit-obsessed corporate culture in which almost everything came second to the bottom line.

"They weren't just corporate guys trying to hide corporate wrongdoing," Lyon said. "They did not give a darn about hurting people.... They didn't care about anything but money."

Bill, Charles, and David Koch in Lincoln, Massachusetts, in 1968, the year after their father's death. Charles was then running the family company. Bill was earning a Ph.D. and overseeing a family venture capital fund, and David was working in New York City for the chemical company Halcon International. *Photo Credit: ©Mikki Ansin*

Mr. Fred C. Koch

Wichita,
Kansas

Mr. Koch was born in Quanah, Texas, on September 23, 1900. He received his B.S. degree from the Massachusetts Institute of Technology in 1922, and soon thereafter became Chief Engineer of the Midway Oil and Storage Company in England, as well as Vice President of the Winkler-Koch Engineering Company in Wichita, Kansas. The latter company was building oil refining plants all over the world, including the U.S.S.R. from 1929 to 1932.

It was Fred Koch's personal knowledge of Communism, from his own experiences and observations in Soviet Russia, which made him such an ardent anti-Communist. He later recorded these experiences in a small book, *A Businessman Looks At Communism*, of which 2,600,000 copies have been sold.

He is currently Chairman of Rock Island Oil and Refining Company, Inc., and of Koch Engineering Co., Inc., both of Wichita, Kansas; and is on the board of a number of other corporations. He is a member of the American Petroleum Institute, and the American Institute of Chemical Engineers. He and Mrs. Koch have three sons, Charles, William, and David. Fred has traveled extensively on every continent, and has hunted big game in Canada, Mexico, India, Africa, and the Arctic.

Patriarch Fred C. Koch's biographical entry in a John Birch Society pamphlet from the 1960s. Curiously, the bio only mentions Fred having three sons, leaving out his namesake Frederick.

(Top) A 1935 Russian-language advertisement for the Winkler-Koch Engineering Co. His work in the Soviet Union made Fred Koch a millionaire, but his experiences there convinced him of communism's evils. (Bottom) The cover of his 1960 anti-communist polemic.

A compilation of home movies and photos was introduced as evidence in a 1991 legal battle over the will of the family matriarch, Mary Robinson Koch. (Top) Mary with David, Charles, Bill, and Frederick at the family compound in Wichita. (Middle) The box shows Bill, Charles, David, and Frederick as boys. (Bottom) David lands a punch on his twin brother Bill. Briefly captain of the MIT boxing team, Fred taught his sons the finer points of pugilism. *Credit for film stills: Courtesy of Michael Oliver*

Charles, the second-born son, grew Koch Industries into America's second-largest private company. (Bottom) Frederick, seen here with his mother in 1990, had little interest in the family business, and became a patron of the arts. *Photo Credit for Charles photo: © Bo Rader/ Wichita Eagle/MCT via Getty Images. Photo Credit for Frederick photo: Courtesy of Michael Oliver*

When he was a bachelor, David Koch threw legendary parties. Here he rings in New Year's Eve in Aspen. (Bottom) Twin brother Bill celebrates his 1992 America's Cup win in San Diego, California. *Credit for David photo: ©Dafydd Jones. Credit for Bill photo: ©Vince Bucci/AFP/Getty Images*

(At top) David, who ran as the Libertarian Party's vice presidential candidate in 1980, appears on stage in Los Angeles with the party's presidential nominee Ed Clark. (Middle) David, seated with Koch Industries top political advisor Richard Fink, at a November 2011 Americans For Prosperity summit. (Bottom) David and wife Julia at the January 2013 groundbreaking of the David H. Koch Plaza at New York's Metropolitan Museum of Art. *David Libertarian Party photo: ©AP Photo/Randy Rasmussen. David and Richard Fink: ©Chip Somodevilla/Getty Images. David and Julia at the Met: ©Astrid Stawiarz/Getty Images*

On August 24, 1996, teenagers Jason Stone and Danielle Smalley drove into a cloud of butane leaking from a Koch Industries pipeline. Both were killed in the explosion. This is what remained of Smalley's truck.

Greenpeace's airship circles over Rancho Mirage, California, in January 2011 ahead of a private meeting of Charles and David's political donor network. *Photo Credit for Greenpeace photo: ©Gus Ruelas*

Kenoth Whitstine, who had resigned in 1994 as a Koch pipeline manager in southern Texas, testified in a deposition that the company had taken a shockingly cavalier approach to pipeline safety. He recalled taking his supervisor out to inspect one stretch of pipeline that he believed posed a hazard. Portions of the once-buried pipeline were now fully exposed, and Whitstine worried that it could be punctured. "You know," Whitstine said, "one of them logging trucks could drive over this line here and it could very possibly drag the Dresser off or something and cause a blowout and possibly burn, catch on fire, and kill...whoever might be in the logging truck."

The supervisor's callous response chilled him. He said "that I needed to understand that money spent on certain projects could make a lot more money than on other projects and that they could come back and pay off a lawsuit from an incident and still be money ahead." The message was that it was more profitable "to take a gamble of something happening later and handle that situation when it arose," even when human lives might be at stake.

"Given the time-value of money and the rate of return on money invested, Koch made a profit from its repeated decisions to delay implementing standard maintenance procedures and necessary repairs," said Texas's onetime deputy attorney general Linda Eads, who joined forces with the Justice Department in prosecuting the Clean Water Act case.

Lyon and Wolf discovered that the section of pipeline that had ruptured near the Smalleys' home was part of a 70-mile stretch of Sterling I that Koch Industries had taken offline in early 1993, after a newer pipeline, known as Sterling II, had gone into operation. But as demand grew, the company realized it could reap an additional $8 million annually by placing this section back into service.

Constructed in the early 1980s, Sterling I had a history of corrosion problems almost from the outset. It had been constructed in wet conditions, and its anticorrosion coating had started to erode in some sections not long after the pipeline was installed. Before the company brought the decommissioned section back online, it threaded a cylindrical device through it called a "smart pig," whose magnetic sensors recorded detailed data about the pipeline's structural integrity. It discovered evidence of corrosion in 583 locations—just within the 46-mile length of line spanning Kaufman County. When the company had previously tested the pipeline, flooding it with water, it ruptured a mile and a half from Danny Smalley's trailer.

Koch maintenance workers repaired the pipeline and patched up the spots displaying the most damage, but left other corroded areas untended to. In January 1996, after the line passed a second hydrostatic test, liquid butane once again began flowing through it.

Less than eight months later, Danielle Smalley and Jason Stone were burned alive.

"I will tell you Koch Industries is definitely responsible for the death of Danielle Smalley," Bill Caffey, an executive vice president and board member of Koch Industries, acknowledged during one combative deposition. "We made mistakes."

On October 6, 1999, when the case went to trial, Lyon displayed a large aerial map of Kaufman County marked with the route of the pipeline, which bisected the county from north to south; it was hard to go anywhere without crossing it. He wanted the jurors to think about the pipeline each morning as they drove to the courthouse, how perhaps it could have been them or their children who had been killed in a butane inferno.

Lyon saved Smalley as his final witness. During the trial, some of the testimony had been so gruesome that the lawyer had periodically asked his client to step out of the room to avoid needlessly subjecting him to it. As Smalley testified, the forty-four-year-old father summoned every ounce of rage within him. "Money to them is blood," he seethed. "That's all it is. That's their life force, is money. That's all they care about. They're so greedy, you know. It's just greed. They put the value of a human life to a piece of paper that says this is money. I choose the life, not the paper. But that's the only way that I can hurt them, is to take them for every penny that I can get."

During his closing statement, Lyon projected a clock on a screen and paused theatrically for 60 seconds to give jurors a concept of the agonizing length of time in which it had taken Danielle to die. "There is no more horrible death than a burn death," he said. "There is no more horrible way to lose somebody than to see them burn to death in front of your eyes."

Lyon asked the jury to return a massive verdict—$100 million. Instead, on October 22, they awarded an amount nearly three times that. As the $296 million verdict was read, Marquette Wolf, who for more than two years had poured his life into the case, dropped to his knees. On the other side of the courtroom, Koch's lawyers looked physically ill. The jury had heeded Smalley's entreaty to send a message to the company. It was, at that point, the largest wrongful death award in U.S. history.

For Charles and David, it was hard to fully digest this blow. Their focus was on Tulsa, Oklahoma, where, a little more than a year after the Topeka trial that was decided in their favor, Bill had dragged them into another bruising court fight. A federal investigation into allegations that Koch Industries stole oil from Native American lands had concluded in 1992 without returning indictments. Inquiries by the U.S. Bureau of Land Management and the Osage Tribal Council in Oklahoma had likewise failed to corroborate the charges. But to bring the allegations before a jury, Bill Koch had cleverly utilized the False Claims Act, allowing a private citizen to sue on the government's behalf as a whistleblower in instances where alleged fraud had occurred. It was a civil case—not a criminal one, like the Justice Department had contemplated—so the standard of proof was lower than the beyond-a-reasonable-doubt threshold required for a criminal conviction.

Bill wasn't a typical whistleblower. He'd brought the case for tactical reasons. It was another avenue for the out-for-blood Koch brother to apply pressure to Charles and David in his ongoing campaign to force them to pay up for allegedly scamming him and his allies over the sale of their Koch Industries stock.

In early September, a month before the trial, Charles was diagnosed with prostate cancer and underwent surgery later that month. Bill wished him a "speedy recovery" in the pages of *The Wichita Eagle.* Even though in a few weeks Bill would take Charles to court in an attempt to prove him a corporate scofflaw, he told a reporter that he still held out hope for a reconciliation. "In spite of all that has happened, when this is over, I would like to take Charles for a sail" and "share several bottles of my best wine with him."

The notion received an incredulous reply from Koch Industries: "Bill Koch has been attacking Charles, David and Koch Industries for 20 years. That attack is continuing, and now he says he wants to share a bottle of wine and take them sailing?"

The same week that testimony in the Danielle Smalley case began, Bill's whistleblower suit went to trial in Tulsa. The normally dull courtroom had been outfitted for a spectacle: It featured a 20-foot-projection TV screen and so much multimedia gadgetry that the room plunged into darkness on several occasions when the equipment overwhelmed the turn-of-the-century building's circuit breakers.

As the proceedings got under way, Roy Bell, a mustache-wearing Vietnam veteran who was Bill's longtime lawyer, told the jury that Koch Industries had engaged in a "deliberate pattern of fraud" that netted as much as $230 million in overages between 1980 and 1989—"overages" being benign oil industry lingo for crude a company didn't pay for. Bell displayed a pyramid of photographs. At the bottom were the lowly oil gaugers who, the attorney said, had copped to oil theft. The pyramid rose through the company's hierarchy until it reached Charles Koch, giving the impression that the bespectacled, white-haired businessman sat atop a criminal enterprise. One might have expected similar imagery at the trial of a Mafia don.

In the weeks that followed, a parade of former Koch employees testified, in person and via videotaped depositions displayed on the large screen facing the jury. Seeking to stoke negative coverage of Koch Industries ahead of the trial, a Dallas-based detective working for an investigative firm hired by Bill circulated a highlight reel of the depositions to a host of Midwestern journalists. The investigator, Jack Taylor, also sent copies of the tape—dubbed "The Koch Method"—to trial lawyers suing Koch Industries, including Ted Lyon and Marquette Wolf, enclosing articles detailing the company's legal entanglements and environmental misdeeds.

Seated at the cramped counsel's table, Bill scribbled notes and cracked an occasional smile as the gaugers testified. Hailing from at least a dozen different states, these ex-employees (some of whom had been fired or laid off by the company) told of learning to gauge oil the "Koch way," by adjusting their measurements to "bring home the barrel"—make sure, in other words, that if Koch paid for a barrel at the wellhead, that much crude or more arrived at the transfer station.

"I felt that it was stealing oil," Dana Ehrhart, an ex-Koch gauger in Texas, testified.

"It was enough to bother my conscience," admitted James Spalding, who'd gauged oil for Koch in New Mexico in the 1980s before becoming an evangelist.

"I feel like I'm up here telling the whole world I was a thief, and at the time I thought what I was doing was the right thing," Curtis Henson, a twenty-five-year Koch veteran, tearfully told the court.

"I had to do what they said to do," noted former gauger L. B. Perry, "or I wouldn't have a job."

The company's lawyers countered with the testimony of oil producers who had no qualms with Koch's measuring practices and Koch employees who explained the inexactitudes of gauging. "I made what I felt were necessary and fair adjustments to get to the station with the number of barrels that I bought," gauger Dale Sanders testified.

In December, as the trial drew to a close, Charles Koch himself finally took the stand. Liz, along with David and Julia, accompanied him to Tulsa for moral support. They watched from the gallery as he related when he had first learned about the vagaries of oil measurement during one of those backbreaking summers of manual labor in his teens. Fred Koch had put his son to work digging pipeline trenches near his refinery in Duncan, Oklahoma. One day, Charles recalled, a couple of oil producers teased him about his father's "overages." Their comments—calling his father's ironclad integrity into question—concerned him enough to bring them up with the company's pipeline managers. They "explained to me the nature of the crude oil measuring business and how a company like ours would tend to be over." This was "accepted on both sides—by the producers and the purchasers." But the rampant oil skimming that Bill had accused the company of simply wouldn't fly in the industry, he said. "If the producers believe your measurements are not as accurate as somebody else's, they're going to take volume away from you."

The deliberations slogged on well into December. As Christmas neared, the judge mercifully gave the jury a half-day reprieve to complete last-minute shopping. The verdict arrived on December 23, as Charles and his family headed to Colorado for the holidays. The jury found Koch guilty of nearly 25,000 false claims against the government and the company faced a potential penalty of more than $200 million. JURY FINDS KOCH CHEATED, and variations of this headline, screamed from the pages of newspapers across the country on Christmas Eve.

Koch's chief spokesman, Jay Rosser, who'd spent the past few years attempting to douse the public relations brush fires Bill had started, described the verdict as "another unfortunate manifestation of Billy's obsessive, 19-year campaign against the company and his brothers. Billy has stalked his brothers, suing them for imagined wrongs of every kind." He hastened to add that the excommunicated Koch brother had "even sued his mother in the years before her death."

Publicly, the company maintained a veneer of confidence that the verdict would be overturned. Privately, the brothers and their advisors were shell-shocked. "It was a huge loss," a former Koch Industries executive said.

Bill had finally scored a big win against his brothers. And he took a victory lap. "This shows they are the biggest crooks in the oil industry," he told a reporter. In the late 1980s, he had described the case as a Machiavellian tactic to bring his brothers to the bargaining table, but he now framed it as an effort to restore honor to the Koch family name and their father's legacy. Fred Koch had built the company "on honesty and integrity. After he died, my brother took it over and it became a company that practiced organized, white-collar crime." So much, it seemed, for reconciliation.

Charles and his company were under siege. By his brother. By the government. By trial lawyers. By an avalanche of bad publicity. In the space of just a few months in late 1999, the company not only suffered a pair of damaging legal defeats, but also pleaded guilty to an array of environmental infractions in Minnesota—the site of the company's Pine Bend oil refinery, which had been under investigation by the EPA and the FBI. The federal government fined the company $8 million for illegally dumping a million gallons of ammonia-laced wastewater and spilling some 600,000 gallons of fuel into a wetland and the nearby Mississippi River. This was in addition to a $6.9 million fine the company had already paid to settle a suit with the Minnesota Pollution Control Agency over some of the same violations.

Once again allegations surfaced that Koch Industries had tried to conceal its environmental offenses, for example, by dumping pollutants under the cover of darkness and falsifying records. "There were times when…yeah, we lied," Thomas Holton, an ex-employee who worked in the leak detection unit at Koch's Pine Bend refinery outside the Twin Cities, told the *Minnesota Star Tribune*. "We did do that. And I won't cover that up."

Morale at the company plummeted. Employees worried about the fate of Koch Industries, and Charles had done little to assuage those fears. What his employees needed was a pep talk, some reassurance that Koch would navigate this traumatic period, but Charles remained closemouthed about the assorted legal threats facing the company. In 1999, as tensions within the company mounted, Tony Woodlief, the Koch management consultant, poked his head into Charles's third-floor office. Its built-in bookshelves were lined with the twenty-volume *Oxford English Dictionary* and books by his favorite economic and political thinkers, including Thomas Sowell, Friedrich Hayek, Ludwig von Mises, and Joseph Schumpeter.

When Woodlief first met Charles in 1997, he had been completing his doctorate in political science at the University of Michigan. They were introduced at a conference sponsored by the Institute for Humane Studies, a libertarian organization where Charles had served on the board since the 1960s. The businessman had given a presentation on his management philosophy, which was steeped in libertarian concepts; his goal was to replicate a free-market society within his firm. To Woodlief, then a thirty-year-old academic, Charles's management system sounded good in theory, but he was skeptical that it could work. Charles liked being challenged on his views, and he enjoyed debate, so he invited Woodlief to Wichita for a firsthand look at his operation. Woodlief took him up on his offer and left with a job.

With many Koch employees on edge, Woodlief asked his distracted boss for a word. They repaired to the company's large cafeteria, where Charles usually ate lunch, and sat down with their trays. "I think you ought to have an all-company meeting and just talk to them about the struggles we're facing and reassure them," Woodlief said. "People respect you and right now they want to hear from you. They don't expect you to have all the answers. They just want to know that you know they're worried about the future of the company. They just want to hear from you."

Charles thanked Woodlief for his advice, but said he wasn't going to follow it. There were too many unknowns and open questions. If the company didn't fully understand the regulatory onslaught it faced, how could he tell his employees that everything was going to be okay?

Charles later realized his mistake. Months later, after some of Koch's regulatory troubles had begun to clear up, he left an apologetic voice mail for Woodlief: "You were right. I should have talked to them."

As 1999 drew to a close, Koch Industries faced the prospect of still another headline-grabbing trial. In the space of less than two years, it had been dragged into court three times—first by Bill, Frederick, and the Simmons family, alleging the company duped them on the sale of their Koch Industries holdings; then by the grieving father of Danielle Smalley; and then yet again by Bill Koch, billionaire whistleblower. Now, after more than four years, the Clean Water Act case that Angela O'Connell and her Justice Department colleagues had pursued was poised to go before a jury. The case hinged on the accusation that Koch Industries had fouled the environment by leaking millions of gallons of oil from its pipelines and storage tanks, and that the company frequently sought to cover up these accidents by masking or minimizing its spills. During the fall of 1999, the case came so close to going to trial that Justice Department attorneys began looking for hotel accommodations. At the last minute, the company entered into a series of tense negotiating sessions with federal prosecutors and lawyers at the Texas Attorney General's Office, also party to the case.

Shortly after the New Year, the Justice Department and EPA announced that Koch had agreed to pay a $35 million fine, the largest ever levied under the Clean Water Act up to that point. Accusing Koch of "egregious violations," EPA Administrator Carol Browner said that the landmark fine "sends a strong message that those who try to profit from polluting our environment will pay the price." Despite the record fine, some of the lawyers working on the case felt Koch Industries got off lightly, especially given what former Texas Deputy Attorney General Linda Eads described as the "willfulness" of its behavior. "I didn't feel like it was a win. I didn't," she said. "I felt like it was a draw. I wasn't sitting there giving high fives to everybody."

Koch Industries, with ample help from Bill along the way, had by now developed a reputation as a corporate outlaw—a company that placed profits over safety, stole from oil producers, and flouted government regulations.

In many ways, the company was an extension of Charles, a reflection of his values, beliefs, and persona. His humble, taciturn style was its humble, taciturn style. His rigid free-market philosophy was its rigid free-market philosophy. If the company had taken an antagonistic view toward government regulation, it had flowed from him.

"We should *not* cave in the moment a regulator sets foot on our doorstep," he once thundered in a call to arms to the business community, penned in 1978 at the height of his libertarian fervor. "Do not cooperate voluntarily; instead, resist wherever and to whatever extent you legally can. And do so in the name of *justice*."

But during the recent legal onslaught, Charles had received a wake-up call. The world he lived in was not the libertarian paradise he wanted it to be. "It was a seminal moment in his life, because he finally began to understand the costs of what they now call public sector," said one Koch veteran. "There's a cost—a high cost—for not being a world-class company.

"These were learning points that turned the culture around," he added. "They went on a multi-year crash course to overhaul the company. It was probably one of the most grandiose turnarounds ever."

In a reversal of the defiant message Charles had once sent to business leaders, his corporate mantra became "10,000% compliance with all laws and regulations." This meant that he expected 100 percent compliance from 100 percent of his employees. "While business was becoming increasingly regulated, we kept thinking and acting as if we lived in a pure market economy," Charles acknowledged. "The reality was far different. The laws of economics seemed less and less relevant in a world where the uncertainty of politics had replaced the uncertainty of the marketplace."

During this period, as the company tried to navigate its thorny relationship with the federal government, especially on environmental matters, it lured away the EPA's assistant administrator Donald Clay. It also hired Alex Beehler, a top trial attorney in the Justice Department's Environment and Natural Resources Division—the same section that had aggressively prosecuted the company. Meanwhile, Richard Fink, a Rutgers- and New York University–trained economist who had risen to become one of Charles's most trusted deputies, led a dramatic reshuffling and integration of the company's public affairs, government relations, and legal departments into a "public sector" division.

The company also began offloading large swaths of its troublesome pipeline system, eventually downsizing its network from some 40,000 miles to 4,000. Koch pivoted from some of its core businesses to focus on the far-less-regulated energy and commodities trading markets, competing with the likes of Enron.

"We've learned from the nineties we have to be on top of our game and that one of our biggest customers is in fact the government," said Mark Holden, Koch's general counsel. "We deal with them every day, so if that's one of your customers in that sense you need to build relationships with them like you would a commercial enterprise or entity." He added, "We learned a lot in the nineties, and if we hadn't, I don't know what would have happened because the road we were on wasn't going to be productive."

By the spring of 2001, a new era was dawning for Koch Industries. It had emerged from the hellfire of scandal and litigation as a more modern and less politically tone deaf company, though with an institutional bunker mentality forged by years of bitter legal warfare. At the same time, there was also a budding armistice in the 20-year feud between the Koch brothers. Despite his courtroom triumph, 2000 had been a tumultuous year for Bill.

Around 11:00 p.m. on July 17, 2000, a Barnstable police car pulled down the driveway at 177 Seapuit River Road and stopped in front of Homeport, Bill's nine-bedroom Cape Cod colonial-style mansion. White with hunter green shutters, the 8,600-square-foot waterfront home was located on the private island of Oyster Harbors, one of the Cape's most exclusive communities. It was situated on 1.5 acres and featured a deepwater dock and a gunite pool. On the front lawn sat a handful of curvaceous Botero sculptures, and Bill's art collection crammed the interior of the home.

Bill had remarried in November 1996. His new wife, the former Angela Gauntt, was nineteen years younger. She hailed from Montgomery, Alabama, though when they met, via a mutual friend, she lived in New Orleans and worked as a fund-raiser for

Tulane University. The couple had been out on only a handful of dates when Bill popped the question. Given the state of his personal life at the time they met, it was hard to imagine that Bill was in the market for marriage. He had just battled to evict his former mistress Catherine de Castelbajac—she of the not-safe-for-work faxes—and he was also expecting a child with Marie Beard, whom Bill had met when she tried out for his all-female America's Cup team.

After their marriage, Angela added two more children, William Jr. and Robin, to his brood, which now numbered four. But soon their relationship began to unravel, particularly after Bill lost his lawsuit against his brothers over the sale of his Koch Industries stock. "It was something he could not get over—it just ate him up," Angela said. "After that, everything just took a turn for the worse. He was depressed and despondent." Bill already had a reputation for swilling copious amounts of pricey French wine—after contracting hepatitis in grad school, he could no longer stomach beer or hard alcohol—and Angela claimed he had developed a drinking problem. "He was not fun to be around when he drank too much," she said.

Late on the evening of July 17, Angela frantically summoned the Barnstable police, accusing her husband of domestic violence. Wyatt, Bill's red-haired fourteen-year-old son, was staying with them, and Angela alleged that her enraged husband had threatened "to beat his whole family to death with his belt." She claimed Bill had also punched her in the stomach. Based on her allegations, which Bill strenuously denied, the police arrested him and charged him with domestic assault and threatening to commit murder.

Angela was granted a restraining order, forcing Bill to live in the guest quarters of their Cape compound and stipulating that he had to refrain from drinking 24 hours before visiting their children. It also included an eyebrow-raising proviso allowing Bill to be in Angela's proximity only if the couple was entertaining.

After the incident, they attended counseling and tried to reconcile. Then Angela learned that Bill had hired a private investigator to follow her. "It was frightening, and embarrassing," she said at the time. "At that point, I knew there was no hope of reconciling. I had become the enemy." She filed for divorce that September. Bill approached the dissolution of their marriage in his customarily pugilistic style. According to Angela's lawyer, he told his wife, "I'll litigate you into the ground." But Angela could play hard ball, too: The pace of their negotiations heated up after she attempted to have court records unsealed in Bill's divorce from his first wife, Joan Granlund. By November, she dropped a civil suit against Bill and recanted her accusation that he had threatened to kill her and his son Wyatt, though she maintained that an assault had taken place. (Several witnesses, including Wyatt, backed Bill's account that no physical altercation occurred.) Soon thereafter they entered into a $16 million divorce settlement.

For a time, their acrimonious split made it difficult for Bill to gaze on one of his favorite paintings, Amedeo Modigliani's sensuous *Reclining Nude*, which hung in his Palm Beach living room nearby a Matisse and a Picasso. "I liked looking at it when I was happily married, right before I would go to bed with my wife," he told a reporter wistfully a couple weeks after the divorce was finalized. "You can't tell what she's feeling. Is she pensive? Is she happy? Bored? Is she looking to get out of there? In a way, this painting combines the sensuality of women and the elegance of their bodies with the mystery of their souls."

Bill had begun to do some soul-searching of his own. The Koch brothers had entered their sixties. In the time that Bill had spent battling his brothers, Charles's children had grown up and graduated from college. David had gotten married and started a family of his own. Bill didn't know their children; they didn't know his. The brothers had spent a third of their lives—more if you count the explosive fights during their childhood—at one another's throats.

In October 2000, in the midst of Bill's messy divorce, the long-running lawsuit among the four Koch brothers reached the end of the road when the Supreme Court declined to hear Bill and Frederick's last-ditch appeal. A few months earlier, the federal judge who heard Koch Industries' oil theft case in Tulsa had denied the company's motion requesting that he overturn the jury verdict. The company eventually settled for $25 million, of which $7.4 million went to Bill and the rest to the federal government. (Koch Industries also paid Bill's formidable legal bills, estimated at $25 million.)

During the summer of 2000, as their legal travails wound down, Bill initiated a cautious rapprochement with his brothers—conveying, through his lawyers, that he was ready to begin the process of deescalating their feud. The fight between the Koch brothers—at least as far as Bill, David, and Charles were concerned—had always had to do with much more than money.

As negotiations quietly commenced, the most contentious talks had nothing to do with dollar figures, but how the brothers would divide their father's possessions. "During the settlement discussions," Bill recalled, "we were dealing with large sums of money but the biggest thing we argued about was who was going to get what painting out of my father's collection. The most valuable painting he had in there was worth peanuts compared to what we were talking about. It wasn't the money, it was the emotional stake." He said at another point, "We ended up in a heated argument, almost fisticuffs, over my father's art collection."

The talks continued for nine months, persisting even after *60 Minutes II* aired a story that Bill had tried to dissuade the show from running, which featured a previously taped interview in which he accused Koch Industries of "organized crime. And management-driven from the top down."

The peace treaty that ended two decades of family warfare was signed on a balmy spring evening in Palm Beach. On May

23, 2001, a light, salt-air breeze blew off the Atlantic, as Charles and David arrived at Bill's Anglo-Caribbean-style mansion, which evoked the plantation of some Colonial viceroy and straddled a lush, four-acre property that stretched from the ocean to the Inter-coastal Waterway. The home featured an open-roofed courtyard in the center, a 35,000-bottle wine cellar with a groin-vaulted ceiling crafted from 150-year-old bricks, and room after room of the kind of art rarely seen outside of the world's finest museums— paintings by Dali, Degas, Matisse, Winslow Homer, Frederic Remington. Bill and David, it turned out, were practically neighbors. About two miles up the road, David owned the equally glorious Villa el Sarmiento, an architectural masterpiece built in 1923 that featured a Mediterranean-style terra-cotta roof.

Bill had put together a small dinner party for the settlement signing. The agreement, in addition to dividing their father's property and providing an undisclosed payout to Bill, included a non-disparagement clause and significant financial penalties if either side breached the peace accord.

The three brothers had not shared a meal together in nearly twenty years. During that time, almost every word that had passed between them had filtered through attorneys. The lawyers, as always, were present, as the brothers awkwardly reconnected. They chatted about their families, about their lousy knees.

David still felt a powerful kinship with his twin, even though he had made his life hellish for years. Charles was cordial, but there was a limit to what he could forgive. Bill and he were no longer mortal enemies, but that was the extent of their détente. The brothers did manage a few laughs, as they told old stories. Everyone chuckled at the memory of when Bill, always the hothead, had subbed in for David during an MIT basketball game, only to get ejected within seconds for brawling with the opposing team.

"My dad used to say it takes two to fight," Bill reflected after the settlement. "So many punches get thrown, you lose track of who threw the first one. No one in this whole event wears the white hat, and nobody wears the black hat."

He added, "There's nothing more explosive or worse than blood and money."

Not too long after the brothers formally ended their feud, Julia picked up her son, David Jr., at his Palm Beach preschool. (Before their children were elementary school age, Julia, not a fan of the cold weather, spent much of the winter with their kids in Florida.) She noticed David Jr. with his arm around another child. This was his new best friend, David Jr. informed his mother. Out of all the other children at the preschool, the blond-haired toddler had befriended his cousin William Jr.

In time, David and Bill began to rebuild their relationship. By now Bill had a new woman in his life. After divorcing Angela, he began dating Bridget Rooney, the granddaughter of the late Art Rooney, the founding owner of the Pittsburgh Steelers football franchise. A prominent socialite on the Palm Beach–Aspen circuit, Rooney had previously been romantically linked to actor Kevin Costner, with whom she had a son named Liam. She would later become Bill's third wife, and in 2006 they had a daughter together, Kaitlin.

Rooney, along with David's wife, Julia, paved the way for the brothers' cautious reconciliation, according to John Damgard, David's longtime friend. "I give a lot of credit to those wives for bringing those boys back together," he said. Bridget and Julia were around the same age, as were the brothers' children. Both owned homes near each other in Palm Beach and Aspen. The couples and their kids began getting together.

In May 2002, Bill and Bridget invited David and Julia to a joint 1970s-themed birthday bash they threw at Bill's home, where men in powder blue tuxedos and women with teased-up hair dined on new potatoes stuffed with caviar and lamb wrapped in phyllo dough. (Bill was turning sixty-two, Bridget forty.)

The following year, David and Julia hosted Bill and Bridget at Villa el Sarmiento for a party over Thanksgiving weekend. "Welcome to El Sarmiento," five-year-old David Jr. greeted guests, with a flourish of his hand, as they pulled up to the oceanfront home.

Kent Groninger, a fraternity brother of the twins and one of their teammates on the MIT basketball squad, recalled attending a more intimate gathering with the brothers a couple years later. David, who remains close with his MIT teammates, periodically hosts reunions of the squad in Aspen. During one of these get-togethers in the mid-2000s, Groninger and about five other members of the team attended. "David had asked Billy to come by, and we were all a little nervous about that," he said. "And Dave was so deferential to Billy. I mean, Dave was actually subdued that evening. He just let Billy do the talking. And Billy was talking a little bit about his America's Cup experience. And I could just see that Dave was tiptoeing around Billy. It was kind of a big moment where the two were in the same room and Dave for once was stepping back and letting Billy be the center of attention."

"There were friends of both of them there," Groninger added. "And they kind of made up, shook hands."

When Bill married Bridget in February 2005, he asked David to be his best man. At the rehearsal dinner, where guests dined on New Zealand elk and sipped $500-a-bottle 1996 Château Latour, David warmly toasted his brother. "Who would have thought 10 years ago that we'd be friends," he marveled, "much less that I'd be the best man at my brother's wedding."

Years after their improbable reconciliation, Bill calls David his "very best friend." His relationship with Charles, however, never recovered. Only in recent years has there been the mildest of thaws. A turning point came in May 2010, when Julia threw a lavish seventieth birthday party for David at the Everglades Club in Palm Beach.

Located at the west end of Palm Beach's main commercial drag,

Worth Avenue, the club doesn't look like much from the street. But once visitors step inside, they are transported back in time, strolling through a reception hall that looks as if it belongs in a Spanish castle. A courtyard leads to a golf course and striking views of the Intercoastal Waterway. The Addison Mizner architecture is a stark contrast to the starched, Waspy membership: A member was once reportedly rebuked for hosting Estée Lauder (a Jew) on the premises.

The party was held in the club's orange tree–lined ballroom, known as the Orange Garden, which features a retractable roof. On this evening, it had been opened to the sky, so guests could dine and dance under the stars.

Friends and family, including Charles and Liz, flew in from around the country to attend the *Wizard of Oz*–themed bash—"Come to the Emerald City," the invitation read. A yellow brick road and actors in costume greeted them when they arrived. What guests remember most, other than the performance by Lionel Richie and the massive birthday cake fashioned into a fairytale castle, were the speeches—Bill's in particular.

Bill had asked Julia if he could toast his brother, and she in turn had consulted Charles, who was in charge of the speaking agenda, according to a family friend. The family politics, even after nearly a decade, remained fraught. "I think Julia just knew that this could be an ugly moment and that Billy's kind of unpredictable and he might get up there and put a turd in the punch bowl," a family friend said. "So I think it was Charles' decision, in Julia's view, of whether this would be good or not." Charles, the family friend said, gave his permission, but, he added, "I'm sure he was holding his breath the whole evening about what Billy was going to say in front of all their friends."

When Bill took the microphone, a mild air of apprehension gripped those who knew the brothers best. For better and for worse, Bill had always been guided by emotion and he quickly entered sensitive terrain, but only alluded to the brothers' twenty-year battle in the vaguest of terms. Instead, Bill spoke of his childhood jealousy of his handsome and talented twin. David had always scored the most girls, the most points on the basketball court. "He said," according to John Damgard, " 'I consider David, and always have, my closest and best friend, not just my brother and I am so pleased we are now able to treat each other in a more civilized manner.' It was very, very touching."

During his emotional speech, Bill burst into tears. "I actually shed tears listening to this, as did a lot of people in the room," said Kent Groninger. "There were a lot of wet eyes."

After his speech, Bill returned to his table, where he was seated with a half-dozen of the twins' fraternity brothers. Groninger, still choked up, clapped Bill on the shoulder. "That was a wonderful speech," he said. A few minutes later, Charles appeared next to Bill at the table. Bill stood up, rising a couple inches taller than his brother, and they chatted quietly. "We were all trying to keep our eyes off of it," Groninger remembered. "It was such an awkward moment. They were kind of kissing and making up, I think. Charlie was quite taken by what Billy had said." The following day, Charles and Liz accepted a brunch invitation at Bill and Bridget's home.

While the brothers may have shared a moment of warmth in Palm Beach, the scars of the past run too deep to fully heal, Charles's close friends say. "I don't think he necessarily wants to rekindle whole relationships. I think he just wishes [it] would go away," one of them said.

"In Palm Beach," said Nestor Weigand, "[Charles] was very respectful to Billy. He didn't ignore him. He didn't punch him, but he was there, then he was gone. I don't think that there's a tremendous amount of conversation between times." He added, "They're definitely not friends." Charles seems to have difficulty even uttering Bill's name, let alone calling him a brother. He referred to Bill in one 2012 interview as "the brother of the twin."

Bill describes his relationship with Charles as one of "peaceful coexistence." But the peace between the brothers remains a delicate one. Bill's longtime spokesman, Brad Goldstein, mixing military metaphors, suggested that it would not take much—an errant interview perhaps—to reignite "the war between the north and the south" or provoke a "nuclear escalation."

CHAPTER TWELVE

Planet Koch

Unshackled from the bitter feud that had consumed the Koch family for two decades, and with the onslaught of prosecutions by environmental regulators behind him, Charles led Koch Industries into a period of explosive growth. It was an unprecedented spurt even for a company that had expanded by more than a thousandfold since the early 1960s. Charles attributed this expansion to a management system that blended his libertarian ideology into all aspects of the business. Just as General Electric has Six Sigma, Koch Industries runs according to the precepts of Market-Based Management.

In April 2004, the rapidly growing company completed its largest-ever acquisition, buying the textile-maker Invista—owner of such trademarked brands as Lycra and Stainmaster—from DuPont for $4.2 billion. Soon Charles pursued an even more ambitious deal. The negotiations played out during the fall of 2005, heating up over a weekend in early November when he was supposed to have been kicking back with a small group of friends and family. The occasion was Charles's seventieth birthday and the Kochs had invited their guests to celebrate the milestone with them in Indian Wells, the resort town near Palm Springs where they own a 7,500-square-foot vacation home. The five-bedroom, eight-bathroom mansion sits behind the unmarked gates of the Vintage Club, an exclusive community where neighbors include Bill Gates, Lee Iacocca, and Phil Anschutz; before a new member can even fork over the $300,000 initiation fee, a sponsor and three other members must attest to his or her bona fides.

Charles is an avid golfer who regularly shoots his age, and he often unwinds by hitting the links at one of the local courses, but that weekend he was sidelined by an injury. He nevertheless accompanied David, John Damgard, and other friends on a golf outing at The Reserve, a nearby country club where Charles belongs, if only to satisfy the course rule that members accompany their guests at all times. While adhering to that regulation, Charles violated another: He was glued to his cell phone as he watched his guests play from the shade of a golf cart.

"You're not very good company, Charles! You're on the goddamn cell phone!" Damgard called out.

It wasn't just Charles's friends who noticed he was constantly on the phone. Before long, a member of the security staff drove up to remind him of the course's no cell phone policy. "It's my job to make sure people obey the rules out here," he told Charles apologetically. Charles put his phone away. But after the guard left, he pulled it out again, glancing around occasionally with his ear to the receiver.

Soon, the security staffer came back to issue the billionaire another warning. "You're putting me in a tough position, Mr. Koch—that's the second time I warned you about that cell phone."

"Okay, okay," Charles said. The phone went away, but moments later he had it back at his ear.

The irritated guard later drove up a third time: "Mr. Koch, the rules are the rules. I'm really sorry but I have to turn you in, you're going to get a letter"—a formal reprimand from the club's management.

This time Charles shrugged, and kept the phone to his ear.

"Charles, what in the hell could be so goddamn important?" Damgard asked after the guard sped off.

"I can't tell you," he replied sheepishly.

This piqued Damgard's interest. Something big was up. When he later pressed Charles again about the cell phone episode on the golf course, the CEO came clean. He'd been monitoring Koch's bid for a Fortune 500 company.

"I just bought Georgia-Pacific," Charles said.

Offering $48 per share, a 39 percent premium above where Georgia-Pacific's stock was trading, Koch paid $13.2 billion in cash for the company and assumed $7.8 billion in debt. At the time of the $21 billion buyout, Koch Industries had some 30,000 employees scattered across the world, 18,000 of whom had been absorbed through the Invista deal. The massive acquisition of Atlanta-based Georgia-Pacific, with 50,000-plus workers and some $20 billion in annual sales, nearly tripled Koch's workforce and catapulted the company to America's largest private corporation (at least until the spot was reclaimed by Cargill). The company now boasted a population larger than some island nations.

The deal also had a sentimental dimension to it, completing an arc of history connecting the Koch brothers' future to their past. It added to their extensive holdings a battered industrial plant located a few miles outside of Quanah, Texas, Fred Koch's birthplace. Generations of Quanahans had pulverized gypsum into plaster there, and they now produce joint compound and slabs of wallboard bound for Home Depot, Lowes, and beyond. Fred himself had toiled at the plant one summer as a teenager.

At first glance, Georgia-Pacific seemed an odd fit for the satellite of companies that composed the Koch universe. It was a marquee-name paper, pulp, and forest products conglomerate that retailed popular consumer brands. Moreover, until Charles took Georgia-Pacific private, it was a publicly traded concern. Koch Industries, by contrast, was militantly private and, with the exception of its ranch holdings, had labored largely as a middleman in the oil and petrochemical industries, leaving the extraction and retailing to others but handling everything in between. What use would a petrochemical company that prized its under-the-radar status have with the maker of Brawny paper towels, Dixie cups, and Angel Soft toilet paper?

The answer lay in Koch's unique operating style. The company did not define itself by the products it peddled, but by the capabilities it possessed. "We thought we were in the oil business," a Koch executive once put it, "but we found out our real expertise is in the gathering, transportation, processing, and trading business."

Viewed through this lens, Koch and Georgia-Pacific complemented each other in many ways. At their essence, both were conglomerates that excelled in processing raw materials—whether timber or gypsum or petroleum—into a wide range of products.

Few CEOs would have seen the wisdom of acquiring Georgia-Pacific, a company saddled with tens of thousands of asbestos-related lawsuits and billions of dollars of debt. But this was precisely the type of deal that Charles and his fellow executives sought out, involving a troubled company with the potential for a dramatic turnaround. They hoped that taking the company private would relieve quarterly earnings pressure and help refocus Georgia-Pacific on creating long-term profits. Koch Industries' strong cash position would help reduce Georgia-Pacific's debt load, enabling it to reinvest more of its earnings into the company's manufacturing operations.

Charles possessed an uncanny ability to sniff out profitable ventures, and when he occasionally mired the company in money-losing deals, he quickly cut his losses. The results of his leadership spoke for themselves. Between 1960 and 2006, the company's revenues increased from $70 million to $90 *billion*. During that timeframe, an original investment of $1,000 in Koch Industries would have swelled to $2 million, a rate of growth that outperformed the S&P 500 by a factor of 16. This was not just dumb luck. Charles had a formula.

*　　*　　*

Charles is not a religious man, but he is devout. He once read the Old Testament cover to cover, but his purpose wasn't worship but to glean the secrets of its power and influence. He adheres to an economic theology; his prophets are free-market thinkers. He learned to see the world through an economic prism—a series of transactions, each one guided by the innate laws of human behavior, a ballet of consumption. It didn't matter whether you peddled formaldehyde or free-market dogma itself, the same rules applied.

One of the aspects of Charles's personality that friends and colleagues comment on most, aside from his competitiveness, is how consistently his belief system permeates every corner of his life. "Whatever switch the rest of us have where we choose whether to integrate what we believe with what we do, he doesn't have that switch," said Tony Woodlief, the onetime Koch management consultant and a former vice president at Charles's charitable foundation. "He just doesn't have room to believe something and not act on it."

This explains the libertarian-tinged ethos of Koch Industries, which traces back to the 1960s, when Charles earned the autodidact's equivalent of a Ph.D. in Austrian economics in his book-strewn apartment. One thing that irked him about the budding libertarian movement, which he would spend so much time and money working to cultivate, was its reliance on untested theories. Theory interested Charles only insofar as it informed action. Koch Industries became his real-world laboratory.

Within the microcosm of his company, Charles worked to conjure the free-market utopia that the millions of dollars in contributions he channeled to think tanks, pressure groups, universities, and politicians had failed to bring about in the world beyond his control. It wasn't until the 1990s, when Charles hit upon a name for his management philosophy, that he began a systematic effort to diffuse it through every strata of his business empire, from boardroom to mail room. He developed Market-Based Management, he said, through the study of the conditions that allow free societies to prosper—what Charles called the "science of liberty."

First he flattened Koch Industries' management structure. Wherever possible, he decentralized decision making and pushed it down to the lowest levels. In lieu of property rights, the company granted its workers "decision rights"—the authority to manage the assets under their command. This extended not just to managers or supervisors, but to mechanics, factory workers, and mail clerks, who often possessed valuable, but untapped, knowledge their superiors up the food chain did not. Employees who had previously kept their heads down and did their jobs now had the ability to modify equipment to operate more quickly or tweak refinery output on their own initiative.

"I went out and interviewed people and they were tearful," Woodlief said. "We're talking people without high school degrees, getting paid by the hour, no air-conditioning, at a manufacturing plant, but for these people their lives really had changed. Like one guy, he points out his work area with pride because now he is in charge of it. He decides how the work will come through it. He has authority."

Charles's management regime encouraged employees to challenge ideas, even those of their superiors. It deemphasized job titles—and in some cases eliminated them entirely—and the responsibilities and authority of people who held the same positions varied widely based on their strengths and ability. Koch's employees were taught to think of themselves as business owners and drilled repeatedly on the imperative to create value in everything they did. The company removed salary caps and aligned incentives to harness employees' entrepreneurial instincts; the company limited employees in their earning power only by the "value" they brought to Koch Industries. At the company's highest echelons, executives often received six- and seven-figure bonuses.

An especially capable employee could sometimes pull down more than his or her supervisor, after the company awarded incentive compensation.

The widespread application of Market-Based Management quickly upended the paradigm of the ideal Koch employee. "What was fascinating was that some people who had been exemplary employees in the old regime, where you kept your mouth shut and did what you were told, a lot of them didn't make it," Woodlief said. "Some of the troublemakers became exemplary employees, because when you think about an entrepreneur, that's somebody who's perpetually frustrated, who always sees a better way of doing it and gets really pissed off."

Charles ran his company as a meritocracy; degrees and credentials often mattered little. High school–educated farm boys from Oklahoma ran multimillion-dollar divisions and ambitious twenty-somethings skyrocketed through the ranks. "If they find somebody who's really going to do well, they give him every opportunity to grow as fast as he can grow," said one former Koch employee who managed a division. "There's no, 'Oh you have to be around for five years before you do this' type of thing. If you do well, your next step comes pretty fast."

But in cultivating a free-market atmosphere within his company, Charles inevitably invited in some of its more carnivorous aspects. A cutthroat culture developed. Internal rivalries formed. "Everybody's after everybody else's throat," one ex-employee told *The Wichita Eagle*.

As the new corporate culture took root, morale suffered initially and middle managers feared for their jobs. During that period, in the late 1990s, Koch Industries faced a wave of discrimination lawsuits by middle-aged employees who claimed, in some cases, that the company used Market-Based Management as a pretext to sweep them out the door to make room for younger, hungrier employees. One suit, brought by a forty-eight-year-old Koch lawyer who alleged he'd been unfairly demoted and subsequently fired, accused the company of "generally hiring one type of 'clone' that fit Koch's image of itself—young, white male, sharp, aggressive, and consistent with Koch's management philosophy."

As Charles and his inner circle tried to simulate market conditions within the company, the road away from serfdom was not without its share of wrecks. Taking the Austrian model to its logical extreme, the company created internal markets through which business units purchased and traded for services. Part of the idea was to curb the overconsumption of company resources by putting a price tag on the use of a lawyer or lobbyist or the commissioning of a market research report. "Accountants started billing people in 15-minute segments for paperclips and pencils," sighed a senior Koch executive. "It was a disaster. The whole system broke down."

With Market-Based Management came a buzzword-laden vernacular—"Kochspeak," as some employees called it with a roll of the eyes. Terms like "comparative advantage" (the ability to produce something at a lower cost than competitors), "creative destruction" (Joseph Schumpeter's term for the sometimes messy process of innovation, where old methods are obliterated so new ones can rise up), and "fatal conceit" (Hayek's notion that the premise of socialism is logically flawed) were soon on the lips of Koch managers. The company encouraged executives to read Mises and Hayek, and in some cases they drew just enough knowledge from these free-market thinkers to be destructive with it; while fluent in the esoteric language of Market-Based Management, they misapplied it completely. "The concepts became little more than buzzwords," Charles acknowledged. "Employees used them to justify what they were already doing, or worse, what they wanted to do."

Market-Based Management hinged on measuring performance, especially employee performance, and the company placed a major emphasis on quantifying in granular detail each worker's contributions to the company. Koch based its incentive system—what employees called "I-Comp"—on these evaluations. Assessing how much money an employee had earned for the company was a relatively straightforward task when it came to, say, a commodities trader in Koch's financial division or a refinery manager, but there were many other workers whose economic value was harder to compute. What about the employees who maintained the company's pipelines? Technically, the more diligently they did their jobs, the more they sliced into the company's profits.

The former manager of a Koch research group recalled his boss once asking him to evaluate the members of his staff "based on their contribution to the bottom line"—the literal dollars and cents they had earned for the company. He balked. "I said, 'I can't do that. I can't tell you how much value in terms of sales and profit a particular technician does. It's an outrageous question. He's too far from the action. He has too little control. I can't tell you that this particular employee earns this much for the company and thus should get this amount of money.'"

A few months later, the manager attended a Market-Based Management seminar in Wichita led by Charles. After the CEO's spiel, he asked for questions. The manager raised his hand.

"Charles," he said, "I'm having difficulty relating what my technicians do to the company's bottom line. My problem is, they don't have any real control. There are all kinds of decision makers in between them—their supervisors, me, the product managers, salespeople, pricing."

Charles seemed perplexed by the question. "Why," he asked, "are you trying to do that?"

The impression that had filtered down from upper management was that Charles had wanted all employees to be evaluated based on their individual return to the company—but, in actuality, the CEO's definition of "value" was more expansive. "We'd all been doing something that had been misunderstood from something Charles had said," the manager recalled. "There's a lot of stuff that goes on in Koch because of Market-Based Management [that] doesn't always reflect what Charles wants."

Whether or not employees misinterpreted Charles's management edicts, his relentless emphasis on profits and value creation may have had dangerous, even deadly, consequences. In the Danielle Smalley case, as well as other lawsuits involving Koch's dilapidated pipelines and environmental negligence, lawyers repeatedly cited Charles's management philosophy as a key factor.

"Koch has a pattern of delaying needed repairs and maintenance, often neglecting them entirely," Linda Eads, the former Texas deputy attorney general, noted in a 2001 affidavit. "One reason for this failure to operate safe pipelines comes from Koch's so-called Market-Based Management approach. For example, under this management philosophy, each section of the Koch pipeline must show a profit, and this profit must increase every quarter. Environmental and safety compliance does not pay off quarter by fiscal quarter, and thus employees are not rewarded or encouraged to strive for safety or compliance. Indeed, safety improvements are regularly delayed or ignored even when recommended by employees. Employees at Koch are told that every decision has to be judged by its economic effect and how the decision will affect the company's profitability."

Market-Based Management caused controversy in other areas, too, as Charles and his ideological lieutenants attempted to apply the technique to the constellation of nonprofits he funded. "If I get a concept in my head that I think is the way the world works," Charles admitted, "I apply it to everything." There even came a point when Charles tried to impose his management philosophy on the private school his children attended.

Located nearly across the street from the Koch compound, the

Wichita Collegiate School was cofounded by Bob Love, Fred Koch's John Birch Society sidekick and later Charles's libertarian compatriot. A generous benefactor of the school, Charles chaired its executive council in the early 1990s. In 1993, the billionaire ignited an acrimonious uprising at the school, after its well-liked headmaster abruptly resigned due to efforts by Charles and other trustees to foist Market-Based Management on Wichita Collegiate and meddle with hiring decisions. Incensed parents threatened to pull their children from the school; faculty members quit; students wore black in protest. Charles stepped down from the board of trustees citing, among other reasons, the school's refusal to integrate his management style. But in a sign of just how much influence he exerted over the school, Richard Fink, one of Charles's key advisors and an architect of Market-Based Management, was installed as Collegiate's interim head. The outrage ran so deep that, as Fink tried to tamp down the uproar, he was hung in effigy around campus.

A couple years later, similar discontent roiled the Institute for Humane Studies, which had relocated from California to the Arlington, Virginia, campus of George Mason University, where in the 1980s, Charles and Fink had established a beachhead of free-market research and scholarship. The mission of IHS is to groom libertarian intellectuals by doling out scholarships, sponsoring seminars, and placing students in internships at like-minded organizations. The impact of the institute's work was not easy to discern. Charles nevertheless grew intent on measuring the intellectual dividends of the institute's programs, as if manufacturing libertarian ideologues and widgets were one and the same.

"Koch, evidently beginning to despair at the prospects of achieving political goals in his lifetime, became obsessed with a quick fix and decided that IHS needed to have 'quantifiable results,' " noted Auburn University philosophy professor Roderick Long, who was affiliated with the Institute for Humane Studies. "Massive micromanagement ensued."

Professor Long recalled that "the management began to do things like increasing the size of student seminars, packing them in, and then giving the students a political questionnaire at the beginning of the week and another one at the end, to measure how much their political beliefs had shifted over the course of the week. (Woe betide any student who needs more than a week to mull new ideas prior to conversion.) They also started running scholarship application essays through a computer to measure how many times the 'right names' (Mises, Hayek, Friedman, Rand, Bastiat, etc.) were mentioned—regardless of what was said about them!"

"These," he noted, "were the days that my friends and I used to refer to as 'the Shadow falling on Rivendell' "—an allusion to the evil pall Sauron casts over the elven stronghold of Rivendell in J. R. R. Tolkien's *The Lord of the Rings* trilogy.

While efforts to impose Market-Based Management outside of Koch Industries faltered, it eventually flourished within the company. "You couldn't avoid it," a former Koch executive said. A copy of Charles's 2007 management manifesto, *The Science of Success*, is standard reading for new employees, and the company's ubiquitous ten "Guiding Principles" ("integrity," "principled entrepreneurship," and "value creation," among others) are stamped on the time cards of factory workers and printed on coffee cups. Koch employees at every level attend a two-day Market-Based Management Academy. Managers, meanwhile, receive additional instruction on how to identify the characteristics of an ideal Koch hire—that is, someone who will be receptive to the Market-Based Management–driven culture.

"They have a very rigid selection and development process," the former executive said, noting that more than a dozen Koch employees screened him before the company made him an offer. "They want to make sure they're hiring the right people with the right ethics and the right business orientation." He added, "I never met a dumb person at Koch. Everyone was brilliant." The company's interview process relies heavily on SBO—situation, behavior, outcome—questions to identify candidates in the Koch mold. "Have you ever made a mistake at work?" is one typical interview question. Another: "Tell me about a time that you failed."

The company went through a phase of recruiting talent from elite universities, including University of Chicago–trained MBAs, but it found that many of these hires—often headstrong and overconfident—didn't survive long within Koch's corporate ecosystem. Instead, Koch has largely built its business with men and women who share its Midwestern roots, drawn from the University of Kansas, Oklahoma State, and other nearby state schools.

"They're always looking for what's called an 'upper right quadrant' person," noted Nancy Pfotenhauer, who once ran Koch Industries' Washington lobbying operation and is a veteran of a handful of Koch-funded nonprofits. "If you have humility on one axis and ability on another, they're looking for that combination."

It also helps if you fall in the right quadrant politically and buy into the libertarian ideology that is so deeply embedded in Koch's corporate DNA. Fully embracing the Koch mind-set means believing, as Charles does, in the self-regulating powers of the market and the socialistic evils of big government. It requires sharing the company's Adam Smith–inspired philosophy that acting in one's self (or corporate) interest benefits society as a whole in the long run.

Even the company's quarterly newsletter, *Discovery*, is an overtly political organ that contains editorials promoting climate change skepticism ("much of this 'information' is discredited science") and jeremiads about the tyranny of regulation, federal spending, and unwarranted government intrusions into the marketplace.

"A growing government is often the worst enemy of liberty," Charles warned in one *Discovery* column during the 2008 presidential race. "Judging from what we've heard from the presidential campaigns so far, we could be facing the greatest loss of liberty and prosperity since the 1930s." On the eve of the 2008 election, another Koch executive stressed "the importance of keeping our principles in mind and being an informed voter in this election....Imagine what our world could be like if every candidate for public office was measured by the standards of our MBM® Guiding Principles."

People of all political persuasions work for Koch, but given the company's strong institutional perspective, some employees with liberal beliefs tend not to advertise their politics.

"You either drink the Kool-Aid or you keep your mouth shut and walk the line," said Randy Rathbun, a Wichita lawyer and former U.S. attorney in Kansas who has many friends who work for the company. When Rathbun ran for Congress in 1996 as a Democrat, his campaign received numerous contributions from supporters at Koch Industries, but the donations were uniformly small, he said. He appreciated the support, but the relatively diminutive size of the contributions puzzled him. Rathbun later learned that Koch employees had intentionally contributed low-dollar amounts in order to skate under state campaign contribution reporting limits. They feared the consequences if the company discovered them supporting a Democrat, especially one that Koch Industries' political action committee along with top Koch executives had targeted for defeat. "I have never seen a place where people are afraid like this where they work," Rathbun said, noting that some of his friends who work for Koch jokingly refer to it as the "evil empire." He added, "There's a culture of fear out there."

Because of the company's insistence that its employees conform to the Market-Based Management model, some have complained of a cultlike atmosphere. "Everyone is walking around like they are in the George Orwell book, *1984*," commented one former employee.

In contrast to his brother David, who is respected by the company's rank-and-file but not seen as the driving force behind the company's success, Charles is viewed as a near-mythic figure, a man of preternatural intellect and economic prowess, whose mystique is only intensified by his quotidian persona. He is unquestionably powerful, but unfailingly humble; elusive, but uncomplicated; cosmopolitan, yet thoroughly Kansan. Although Charles could have his lunch flown in daily from Paris if he chose, employees often spot him in the cafeteria, tray in hand and waiting patiently in line at the "healthy choice" station.

Charles has been described as a businessman so shrewd that "in a fifty-fifty deal, he keeps the hyphen," but he projects the image of a brainy professor, not a cutthroat mogul. "I am Charles Koch," he once introduced himself to a classroom of junior executives who had gathered for training in Market-Based Management. "I'm in the philosophy department."

He's known by friends and colleagues alike as a voracious consumer of knowledge. Even on the short commute between his home and office, a drive of no more than fifteen minutes, he pops in heady audiobooks such as Thomas Sowell's *Ethnic America* or Eric Foner's *Reconstruction*. Every conversation is an opportunity to profit intellectually, and when Charles hits upon a subject that fascinates him, he drills for details. "If he's even in the elevator with you," said Pfotenhauer, the former Koch lobbyist, "he's trying to learn from you. He doesn't waste a minute."

Charles is a true believer, whose free-market beliefs are unquestionably self-interested—but also undeniably sincere. His value system is apparent in all aspects of his company, including Koch's lobbying operation. Until the early 1990s, the company didn't have a Washington presence; this, one former Koch lobbyist said, reflected Charles's inherent distrust of politicians and his antigovernment bent. Once it did open a Washington office, prompted by the wave of government investigations and the bad PR stirred up

by Bill Koch, the company's lobbyists operated differenت
the K Street–hired guns that stalk the halls of Congress foۭ
corporate clients.

Koch's lobbyists don't shift their positions based on the politicۭ
headwinds. According to one Senate Republican leadership aide,
they won't be found pressing for subsidies in one bill and opposing
them in another. "They're not rent seekers," he said. The overrid-
ing factor guiding the company's lobbying agenda is not whether
a legislative proposal will be good or bad for Koch Industries, but
whether it is consistent with Charles's libertarian beliefs.

Richard Fink, Charles's top advisor, enforces ideological con-
sistency across the spectrum of Koch business units, and he
frequently intercedes to prevent them from inadvertently trans-
gressing Charles's free-market creed. Such was the case when one
Koch business unit, which had developed an environmentally sensitive incinerator, sought permission to work with government
regulators to strengthen environmental rules. This might have
improved the company's competitive position, but it went against
Charles's overarching philosophy. Fink spiked the idea.

Charles's goals have always been larger than building a business.
He created a free-market society in miniature at Koch Industries,
but his decades-long effort, and David's, to catalyze social change
on a broader scale has proven far more difficult. The brothers are
"driven by their feeling that the way they run their company is the
way the country should be run," the former Koch manager said.
As the Obama era dawned, the brothers felt America desperately
needed a Koch-style turnaround.

CHAPTER THIRTEEN

Out of the Shadows

In late January 2009, as Richard Fink strode into Koch Industries' imposing dark-glass-and-granite headquarters on the outskirts of Wichita, the nation's economy was in free fall. The stock market had cratered. Credit markets had seized. There was talk of bank nationalization, another Great Depression.

The Bush administration had responded by throwing open the national vault: It rescued failing banks and financial firms with a $700 billion bailout and doled out $17.4 billion to save America's ailing automakers. Additional billions would soon be on the way to Detroit. The incoming Obama administration, just a few days in office, was meanwhile pressing forward with plans for another massive outlay of federal cash via a stimulus package of close to a trillion dollars.

There was nothing free about this market, in which U.S. taxpayers kept foundering businesses on life support and the government injected the economy with money the country didn't have to spend. General Motors had in effect been nationalized. It was Keynesian economics on steroids. The Austrians were spinning in their graves.

In the 1930s, under similar economic conditions, FDR had ushered in the New Deal, reshaping the scope of government in ways that conservatives had been fighting to roll back ever since. Under the new administration, Fink believed, there was no telling how large the bureaucracy might balloon, how expansive and entrenched government programs might grow, how much economic freedom might be robbed from the private sector in a federal power grab. There was a Democratic House. A Democratic Senate. A Democratic president. To Fink and his bosses, Charles and David Koch, this augured a trifecta of doom. The last time a Democrat had sat in the White House, the company had weathered one of the rockiest periods in its history, as environmental regulators and Justice Department lawyers mercilessly besieged Koch Industries.

Fink had been considering retirement, hoping to play more golf and spend time unwinding at his vacation home in Delaware's Bethany Beach. The silver-haired strategist had spent more than thirty years in the ideological trenches. He oversaw Charles's multifarious philanthropic, political, and public policy endeavors, as well as the whole of Koch Industries' public sector group, which encompassed its lobbying, communications, and legal divisions.

Now the country, as far as Fink could see it, had reached a crossroads. It faced not just an economic crisis but an ideological one. He and the Kochs had spent decades trying to turn the tide, fighting their own kind of culture war to remake America into their free-market, small-government ideal, a place of unfettered capitalism where the market's "invisible hand" would always guide society in the right direction. The progressive administration of Barack Obama threatened to roll back much of what they had achieved. Fink was a veteran of many political street fights, and he had at least one more left in him. Retirement could wait.

That day in Wichita, Fink huddled with Charles and David to discuss the political climate and plot their next moves. Just a few days earlier, Obama had taken the oath of office, placing his hand on the same velvet-bound Bible that Abraham Lincoln had used in 1861. Already the Kochs and their top political advisor were looking ahead to Obama's defeat.

Though Charles and David had supported George W. Bush—and a host of Koch employees had joined his administration—they were no big fans of his presidency. Bush had led the country into two costly wars, assailed civil liberties in the name of national security, expanded the size of government, and run up the federal deficit. If that was compassionate conservatism, they preferred the original, tough-love variety. But from their perspective, at least Bush's policies had fostered a more hospitable regulatory environment.

Obama was a different story. He talked of overhauling health care, tackling global warming, reforming the financial system. Charles considered him a "dedicated egalitarian" who had "internalized some Marxist models." David, the more bombastic of the pair, declared him "the most radical president we've ever had as a nation," a leader steeped in the "hard core economic socialist" politics of his Kenyan father.

The Obama administration, Fink told the brothers, was poised to push the country over the precipice. Labor unions, social programs, regulation, tax hikes—nearly everything the administration stood for, they stood against. The brothers had two choices, Fink said. They could keep their heads down and watch the country slide into oblivion, or they could come out swinging. Fink counseled jihad.

"If we are going to do this, we should do it right or not at all," Fink told the brothers. "But if we don't do it right or if we don't do it at all, we will be insignificant and we will just waste a lot of time, and I would rather play golf."

The risks were clear. Fink and others at Koch Industries feared political retribution of the kind they believed the Clinton administration had targeted them with. Back then, the Koch brothers, through an advocacy group called Citizens for a Sound Economy, had fought health care reform and other key pieces of Clinton's agenda. After years of prosecutorial scrutiny, the Clinton administration's parting shot, a little more than a month before the 2000 election, was a 97-count felony indictment against Koch Industries and four of its employees. It accused the company of releasing at least 91 metric tons of the cancer-causing pollutant benzene from its Corpus Christi oil refinery, which it alleged Koch officials had tried to conceal. The case fell apart, and the company ultimately pleaded guilty to a single charge of "covering up environmental violations" and paid a $20 million fine (the equivalent of a parking ticket for a company that earned in excess of $30 billion in revenues that year).

But this finale to the traumatic Clinton years was still fresh on the brothers' minds. When a still-embittered David had once visited the Clinton presidential library in Little Rock, where he was visiting his in-laws over the Christmas holiday, he had sarcastically asked a docent where he could find Monica Lewinsky's famous blue dress. Informed this presidential artifact was not part of its collection, he half-jokingly accused the library of whitewashing history.

The Justice Department wasn't the only arrow in a president's quiver. The White House had other, subtler means at its disposal. Koch and its subsidiaries sought thousands of federal permits annually—what if the Obama administration made some of them especially difficult to obtain?

By taking on the Obama administration, Charles and David would also jeopardize their privacy. Despite the scale of their wealth and the scope of their political activity over the years, they and their company were not household names. In the past, they had often tried whenever possible to keep Koch Industries out of the public eye. "In their minds, the bigger you get the more public scrutiny you invite," explained an ex–Koch executive. The same rule applied, only doubly so, in the rough-and-tumble world of politics. Though David did enjoy the accolades that came with his medical and cultural philanthropy, Charles was so publicity averse that he had to be cajoled into lending his name to the basketball arena at Wichita State University that he underwrote. He was fond of the expression—one his father also used—that "it's the whale who surfaces to spout off that gets harpooned."

Fink warned the brothers that they would be placing not just their company but their legacy on the line. "If we do it right," Fink cautioned, "then it is going to get very, very ugly."

Richard Fink's rise within Koch Industries provides a road map to the brothers' decades-long ascendance from libertarian outsiders to influential conservative powerbrokers. It connects the dots on the brothers' journey from backers of the ideologically driven libertarian movement to reputed kingpins of the hell-raising Tea Party juggernaut.

Considering how poorly their first meeting had gone, Fink still finds it hard to believe that Charles chose to work with him. In 1978, Fink was a twenty-seven-year-old doctoral student at New York University, which at the time had the country's lone graduate program focused on Austrian economics. Fink had done his undergrad work at Rutgers University, not far from his hometown of Maplewood, New Jersey. There, he'd come under the tutelage of several libertarian economists. As he worked toward his Ph.D., Fink taught part-time at Rutgers, and he began investigating the possibility of founding a dedicated Austrian economics program there. The idea horrified faculty members schooled in traditional economics, but Rutgers's dean and the chairman of the economics department told Fink they would not stand in his way if he could scare up the necessary capital on his own.

Charles, then developing a reputation as the moneybags bankrolling the libertarian movement, was on Fink's shortlist of possible funders. The young economist phoned his Wichita office obsessively until one day the businessman's mild Midwestern twang came on the line. Charles, always scouting for new talent, invited Fink to Wichita to make his pitch in person.

Fink was thrilled, but what would he wear to his big meeting? He purchased what he considered a snazzy suit—his first—for the occasion. It was made of black polyester and accented with white piping. Underneath, he wore a checkered shirt and a bright blue tie. With his long hair and unruly beard, Fink looked like he was trying out for the Bee Gees, not auditioning for a man who could make or break his future with the stroke of a pen.

When they met, Charles flipped impassively through Fink's proposal. He said little, but seemed unimpressed. Fink returned home to New Jersey assuming Charles wasn't interested. But not long after the meeting, he came through with $150,000 to fund Fink's program.

Thinking back years later on the impression he must have made, Fink once commented to Charles that he was surprised the businessman had even given him a single dollar. "If a guy came up to me with a black polyester suit, white piping, dressed like that with a beard and hair down to his shoulders, I don't think I would probably meet with him let alone give him the equivalent of about $500,000 in inflation-adjusted dollars."

"Why," he asked, "did you do that?"

"I like polyester," Charles deadpanned. "It's petroleum based."

Something had impressed Charles about Fink—and it wasn't the suit. He wasn't one of the flaky libertarian activists Charles normally encountered, who had grand notions but little follow-through. "There are a lot of people who have ideas but they don't know how to get it done," Charles later reflected. "Rich always had a sense for how to get something done and make it effective."

Starting with Charles's seed funding, Fink's Austrian program—its initial goal to provide a handful of undergraduate economics students with an alternative to the predominant Keynesian model—bloomed into one of the nation's preeminent centers of free-market scholarship and advocacy. In 1980, Fink moved the program, along with four of the five students who had enrolled in it, from Rutgers to the campus of George Mason University, then a little-known, state-run school in the Virginia suburbs outside of Washington. At the time, the university had a small cadre of Austrian economists on staff, who had urged Fink to relocate there after hearing that he was shopping around for a new home for his program. At George Mason, he folded the program into a broader research outfit that was at first called the Center for Market Processes and later renamed the Mercatus Center, after the Latin word for "markets."

As the center grew in stature, and as George Mason itself became a magnet for students interested in Austrian economics, Charles poured millions into Mercatus and other programs at the university. The center became home to such eminent free-market economists as Nobel Prize winner Vernon Smith and Tyler Cowen, an author and *New York Times* contributor who was one of the students who had moved with Fink from Rutgers to George Mason in 1980. Slowly, Mercatus grew into an influential and feisty bastion of deregulatory policy. A testament to its clout: Mercatus recommended 14 of the 23 federal rules targeted on the incoming Bush administration's regulatory "hit list."

By then Fink (who, with Charles, remains a Mercatus board member) had ascended through a series of positions within the Koch brothers' ideological and corporate empire. "He is almost like a fireman in the sense that he is often called upon by the Kochs to address issues that pop up that need attention," said James Miller III, the White House budget director during the Reagan administration, who has served on the boards of Koch-funded organizations since the late 1980s. "So he is frequently involved with some of the nonprofits when issues come up." More than just a fixer, Miller noted, Fink is also a "grand strategist in the sense of seeing how the pieces fit together, seeing how opportunities for affecting outcomes are emerging."

Fink's strategic vision dazzled Charles. "He had a game plan and a master plan for how they were going to get from point A to point B, which was influencing national politics," said a political operative who worked with Fink in the 1990s. Based on his plan for lifting their free-market worldview out of the intellectual ghetto, Fink very quickly worked his way into the CEO's inner circle. "Richie got Charles' ear big time and convinced Charles that he, Richie, was the strategist that he needed," said Richard Wilcke, who ran the Council for a Competitive Economy, a short-lived organization Charles founded in the late 1970s that focused on pressuring the business community to forsake subsidies and other government handouts. "[Fink] convinced [Charles] that he was really the guy who understood the strategy and what needed to be done. And Charles bought it. He was enamored with Fink."

At the time Fink came on the scene, the Cato Institute's Ed Crane was Charles's chief political advisor. But a falling-out between the CEO and the sometimes-acerbic think-tank president provided an opening for Fink to claim the mantle of ideological consigliere. Fink's rapid rise also displaced George Pearson, who since 1969 had overseen Charles's libertarian philanthropy and who had grown so close to the Koch family that he even received a $10,000 bequest in Mary Koch's will.

"Fink is a mover," said a libertarian activist who knew him well. "And sometimes you have to move people if you're a mover."

Fink is Charles's gatekeeper, one of few people within the Koch empire who unfailingly have his ear. He created lasting enmity among the many people—most of them ideological allies—he tangled with on his path to power. His detractors describe him in Rasputinesque terms: sharp-elbowed, ruthless, backstabbing. One of his critics is George Mason University economics professor Charles Rowley, who said he has "fought an increasingly lonely battle against Charles Koch's growing influence over the Economics Department and the Mercatus Center at George Mason

University since the late 1990s," including efforts to meddle with hiring decisions at the school. Rowley called Fink "a third-rate political hack" and "a man who is very appropriately named."

Fink made enemies as he did battle on the Koch brothers' behalf, but he also produced results. His three-decade partnership with Charles changed the face of American politics—and it changed the public image of Koch Industries from a little-known energy conglomerate into a quasi-political corporate entity.

"Charles is a passionate free-market guy," noted a former Koch executive. "Rich Fink is his soulmate on all of this. The arrival of Rich Fink changed a lot of stuff. They didn't face the public sector threat. They weren't involved in change-the-world stuff then."

In the early 1980s, Charles asked Fink to study a handful of libertarian outfits he supported with a view toward recalibrating his strategy to bring about a free-market revolution. The plan they hatched culminated some 30 years later in the creation of a powerful political fiefdom within the broader Republican firmament that threatened the GOP establishment itself. Their strategy helped lay the intellectual and organizational groundwork for the Tea Party and other Obama antagonists.

Charles and Fink put into motion a Friedrich Hayek–inspired plan they called a "Structure of Social Change"—a three-tiered model in which the production, packaging, and marketing of ideas was akin to the manufacturing of Lycra. Their plan for bringing about a free-market epoch and Koch Industries' business model—gathering raw materials and refining them into more valuable products consumers desire—were basically one and the same. As Fink once explained, in clinical fashion:

When we apply this model to the realm of ideas and social change, at the higher stages we have the investment in the intellectual raw materials, that is, the exploration and production of abstract concepts and theories. In the public policy arena, these still come primarily (though not exclusively) from the research done by scholars at our universities.

To facilitate the production of these raw materials, Charles pumped millions of dollars into hundreds of universities around the country. These contributions—which totaled nearly $31 million between 2007 and 2011 alone—have gone to endow professorships, underwrite free-market economics programs, and sponsor conferences and lecture series for libertarian thinkers. (Charles was not a passive investor: When his foundation provided $1.5 million to hire a pair of economics professors at Florida State University, his representatives insisted on a contract with the school giving them veto power over job candidates.)

Step two of the process, Fink explained, entailed taking the intellectual output of these academic programs, ideas "often unintelligible to the layperson and seemingly unrelated to real-world problems," and refining them into a "useable form."

In the middle stages, ideas are applied to a relevant context and molded into needed solutions for real-world problems. This is the work of the think tanks and policy institutions. Without these organizations, theory or abstract thought would have less value and less impact on our society.

This was the domain of the Cato Institute, Mercatus, and the dozens of other free-market, antiregulatory policy shops that Charles, David, and their foundations have supported over the years. Organizations like these churned out reports, position papers, and op-eds arguing for the privatization of Social Security; fingering public employee unions for causing state budget crises; attempting to debunk climate science; and making the case for slashing the welfare system and Medicaid.

Charles and Fink also concentrated on grooming an intellectual class of research scholars, journalists, and others to articulate these policies to the masses. One of the vehicles for this was the Institute for Humane Studies, the incubator of libertarian thought that economist Baldy Harper founded in the 1960s. The institute offers a range of educational opportunities for budding libertarian thinkers at the graduate and undergraduate level, holding summer seminars and awarding generous scholarships, grants, and fellowships to the next generation of Charles Kochs. Charles's foundation provided another avenue for cultivating young ideological allies, offering an internship program that places students at an assortment of right-leaning public policy organizations.

The third piece of the master plan was mobilizing citizen-activists—or at least creating the illusion of a grassroots groundswell. These activists would agitate for the same policies the academics had conceptualized and the think tanks had refined into talking points and policy prescriptions.

Citizen activist or implementation groups are needed in the final stage to take the policy ideas from the think tanks and translate them into proposals that citizens can understand and act upon. These groups are also able to build diverse coalitions of individual citizens and special interest groups needed to press for the implementation of policy change.

As David once explained, "What we needed was a sales force that participated in political campaigns or town hall meetings, in rallies, to communicate to the public at large much of the information that these think tanks were creating."

In 1985, Fink and the Koch brothers formed Citizens for a Sound Economy. The group was inspired in part by the tactics of the Left, especially those of crusading consumer advocate Ralph Nader, who commanded a formidable activist army. Citizens for a

Sound Economy concentrated on doing, one former board member chuckled, "what Ralph Nader would do if he had any sense." It was in essence the bizarro-world version of Nader's Public Citizen. Where Nader fought to expand regulation, Citizens for a Sound Economy worked to eviscerate it. And where Nader battled corporate power, Citizens for a Sound Economy concentrated on harnessing it.

The group, fueled by donations from the Koch brothers, their company, and a variety of corporate backers, quickly developed political cachet within the Beltway. The Reagan administration appointed Fink to its Commission on Privatization, and he won a spot on the Federal Reserve's Consumer Advisory Council. Citizens for a Sound Economy's friends on Capitol Hill grew to include influential Republican congressmen John Boehner of Ohio and Dick Armey of Texas, the House majority leader, and it attracted high-profile conservatives to its board, such as Reagan administration budget director James Miller III and C. Boyden Gray, George H. W. Bush's White House counsel.

Its core mission consisted of promoting lower taxes and less government, for which it solicited large contributions from corporations with a direct financial interest in promoting or thwarting particular agendas. The issues Citizens for a Sound Economy advocated for or against, while consistent with its overarching philosophy, often appeared heavily influenced by its benefactors. Microsoft donated $380,000—Citizens for a Sound Economy lobbied Congress to cut the Justice Department's antitrust enforcement budget. Three sugar companies chipped in $700,000—the group mounted a campaign against an Army Corps of Engineers reclamation plan that would have encroached on cane-growing acreage in Florida's Everglades. The phone company US West ponied up $1 million; Citizens for a Sound Economy unleashed a telecommunications deregulation initiative.

One of the group's biggest backers was the tobacco industry.

Citizens for a Sound Economy repeatedly aligned with tobacco makers to repel tax increases on cigarettes and eradicate the long-standing federal tobacco program, which limited the amount of tobacco that could be sold and imposed price controls.

A consultant who worked with the group in the 1990s recalled once accompanying Citizens for a Sound Economy's leaders on a fund-raising expedition to the New York City headquarters of Philip Morris. There, executives from both groups plotted an antitax campaign orchestrated to appear like a grassroots uprising. "The concept was to find other like-minded potential donors, who would sign on to this front group concept, whether it was at the local level, or the state level, or the national level," the consultant explained. "In this particular case, what this discussion was about, was that CSE funding...would be co-mingled with Philip Morris funds, with the purpose of setting up these handful of front groups that would fight against excise taxes, or retail taxes....It was a very straight, bottom-line corporate interest." It was a corporate antitax effort packaged to appear as the will of the people.

"I'd never seen anything like it in the American political system," the consultant marveled, "and I thought I'd seen everything."

Not long after, Citizens for a Sound Economy and Philip Morris joined forces again to battle the Clinton administration's health care reform initiative. In 1994, as Hillary Clinton launched a national bus tour to promote the effort, Citizens for a Sound Economy rented a bus of its own. It was broken down and dilapidated; the group towed it from town to town as it shadowed the First Lady's route. When she arrived at a tour stop, waiting for her was Citizens for a Sound Economy's decrepit bus, "THIS IS CLINTON CARE" spray-painted on its side.

Citizens for a Sound Economy's activists came to the health care fight riding high from one of their most successful legislative coups: shooting down the Clinton administration's proposed

BTU tax. Clinton unveiled the measure during his first State of the Union address as part of a five-year deficit-cutting budget plan. He proposed taxing fuels based on their heat content, giving a leg up to sustainable energy sources such as wind and solar power.

Koch Industries considered killing the energy tax a matter of vital importance, and executives leaned heavily on members of Kansas's congressional delegation to repudiate the proposal. ("Our belief is that the tax, over time, may have destroyed our business," Fink later said.) According to the former consultant, Fink approached the American Petroleum Institute, the leading oil industry lobby and trade group, with a plan to eviscerate the BTU tax. "Rich walked into the American Petroleum Institute with a lump sum and said, 'Will you match it?'" he recalled. "API and the oil companies matched it, with a very specific targeted campaign aimed just at knocking out the BTU tax from that budget bill."

Pioneering the kind of tactics it would rely on time and again during the Clinton years, and which would reappear during the Obama administration, the group targeted key districts, organizing rallies and launching surgical strikes of print and radio ads. "With his budget vote, your congressman controls your cash and your job," one radio ad intoned ominously. "In next year's election, you'll control his job." Turning up the heat on lawmakers, Citizens for a Sound Economy set up a 1-800 number that patched callers through to the offices of their congressional representatives so they could express their displeasure directly.

The strategy, the consultant said, focused almost exclusively on swaying one critical Democratic senator—Oklahoma's David Boren, a member of the Senate Finance Committee. "It was all geared to making it profoundly uncomfortable for Boren," he said. Without his support, the tax was dead on arrival. When Boren eventually came out against it, the battle was over.

The victory gave the exuberant freedom fighters at Citizens for a Sound Economy their first real taste of political power and a model for future legislative skirmishes. "They thought, 'Wow, this is how it works, and it really works,'" said the consultant. "That sort of targeted money at a key senator or congressman, at a pivotal point in time....They took that initial victory and just made it a thing."

When the Obama administration took office, the populist slant of the country felt to Fink and the Koch brothers like déjà vu. Democrats controlled the executive and legislative branches, just like at the start of Bill Clinton's presidency. Obama, like Clinton, had ridden into office with ambitious plans to overhaul the health care system and touting energy policies the private sector found loathsome. They had been here before. Same fight, different decade.

Years earlier, during George W. Bush's first term, Citizens for a Sound Economy had imploded owing to an internal power struggle that pitted the Kochs and Fink against a group of employees and board members who thwarted their control of the organization. According to Dick Armey, who joined the advocacy group as its chairman following his eight-year reign as House majority leader, Charles and David had pressed for the firing of two employees. Armey and other board members balked. As tensions mounted, Armey said, a representative of the brothers threatened to sue the dissidents "into submission."

Eventually, the brothers walked, taking with them half of the Citizens for a Sound Economy organization. The group consisted of two entities—a 501(c)(4) organization through which the group conducted its advocacy and political activities and a 501(c)(3) foundation that focused on research and educational pursuits that wouldn't violate its tax status. 501(c)s, the colloquial terms for tax-exempt organizations, take their names from section 501 of the IRS code. 501(c)(3) nonprofits, to which contributions are tax deductible, are intended for educational or religious purposes.

501(c)(4)s can engage in political advocacy and lobbying, but donations to these groups are not deductible.

When the Koch faction split off, they decamped with about $5 million, Armey said, and maintained control of the foundation. The Kochs renamed it the Americans for Prosperity Foundation and created a sister political advocacy group, Americans for Prosperity. By the time Obama took office, Americans for Prosperity had formed chapters in nearly two-dozen states and claimed to command thousands of activists.

In the months leading up to Obama's inauguration on January 20, 2009, the country had descended into a period of tumult. The tinder was dry for an uprising. All it took was a spark—and after that, some vigorous fanning of the flames by Charles and David's advocacy group and other like-minded organizations.

The spark, one of them at least, came on the morning of February 19, 2009, on the floor of the Chicago Mercantile Exchange. During a live shot, CNBC's Rick Santelli launched into an on-air tirade, denouncing the administration's $75 billion plan to rescue struggling homeowners for "promoting bad behavior" and rewarding people who "drink the water" over those who "carry the water." Whoops and whistles rose up from the commodities traders around him.

"President Obama, are you listening!" the fired-up commentator said. "We're thinking of having a Chicago Tea Party!"

Santelli's diatribe went viral. It crystallized the shapeless anger over the government bailouts, which seemed to reinforce the irresponsible conduct of banks that had bought and sold time-bomb assets and of Americans who had borrowed far beyond their means.

Staffers at Americans for Prosperity—along with Freedom-Works, as the other half of Citizens for a Sound Economy, chaired by Dick Armey, had been renamed—quickly grasped that a watershed moment was unfolding and seized the moment to harness the public outrage. Hours after Santelli's rant, Phil Kerpen, an Americans for Prosperity executive, registered the domain name taxpayerteaparty.com. The advocacy group created a simple site, its homepage declaring: "Rick Santelli is dead right! Enough bailouts of everyone who acted recklessly! It's time to stand up for all the regular people who play by the rules! It is time for a taxpayer tea party!" The site was a clearinghouse for information on Tea Parties being organized around the country. ("Text 'TEATIME' to 74700 to join Americans for Prosperity and receive mobile updates on the tea parties!") And it provided a link to "Tea Party Talking Points": "Just as the citizens of a young republic came together in Boston in 1773 to reject excessive taxation by the Crown, so too do we come together now to reject oppressive taxation by our own government," the document read.

If Santelli's rant marked the moment of the Tea Party's conception, April 15, Tax Day, was its DOB: Hundreds of thousands of citizens rallied at more than 750 Tea Parties around the country. Organized by Americans for Prosperity and a host of other conservative groups, the events drew crowds ranging from a couple dozen to many thousands.

The nation's largest Tea Party took place in Atlanta, where as many as 15,000 people gathered in the streets around the gold-domed state capitol building. Americans for Prosperity had helped to organize the event, and the group's forty-four-year-old president, Tim Phillips, was on hand to rally the crowd. He wore a gray suit and a lavender tie and exuded the slippery persona of a car salesman or TV evangelist.

A veteran Republican operative from Virginia, Phillips considered himself a specialist in "grasstops" organizing—building a citizen movement atop a corporate-funded campaign. In the 1990s, he had formed a political consulting business, Century Strategies, with onetime Christian Coalition leader and influence peddler extraordinaire Ralph Reed. Their firm had close ties to

Jack Abramoff, the lobbyist who spent nearly four years in prison for defrauding Native American gaming interests of millions. Phillips (who was not accused of any wrongdoing) played a cameo role in the headline-grabbing corruption scandal, helping to establish a group called the Faith and Family Alliance, which served, on at least one occasion, as a pass-through for cash from Abramoff's gaming clients.

"You all know that we face the greatest challenge to our economic freedom in more than a generation," Phillips told the Tea Party crowd as he paced the stage with a yellow-tipped microphone in hand. "...And I'll tell you something, this Tea Party is not an ending it is a beginning. This is the beginning of taking our nation back, of protecting the freedoms that have made us great for so long, and we're going to do that and you're going to do that and it starts right here, right now!"

Across the country, mixed in with Gadsden flags, tricornered hats, and generic protest signs (GOT FREEDOM?), activists brandished placards that questioned the President's citizenship, called him the "new face of Hitler," depicted him slitting the throat of Uncle Sam, and accused him of plotting "white slavery."

Though not characteristic of the Tea Party as a whole, a strain of extremism thrived within the movement that seemed out of another era—Fred Koch's era. In the accusations of communism and socialism directed at the president, the paranoia about a United Nations power grab and one-world government, the undercurrent of racism, the claims that the country had come under the sway of an evil force, rang echoes of the John Birch Society in its heyday. Even some of the iconography was similar. In November 1963, ahead of John F. Kennedy's ill-fated visit to Dallas, "Wanted for Treason" leaflets with the president's picture, attributed to Birchers, blanketed the city. As the Tea Party gathered momentum, a similar "Wanted" poster bearing Obama's likeness was littered across the Internet.

"The modern-day Birchers are the Tea Party," David Welch, a former research director at the Republican National Committee (and no relation to the Birch Society's founder), would later argue in a *New York Times* op-ed. He lamented the absence of a William Buckley–esque figure to squelch the extremism of the Tea Party movement.

David and Charles had spent decades and tens of millions of dollars trying to foment an ideological awakening in the United States, to create a movement of Americans who cherished the same free-market ideals that they did. A movement of people who abhorred bailouts. Decried deficit spending. Believed that government-run entitlement programs were socialism lite. The brothers did not condone the uglier aspects of the Tea Party, but their movement had finally arrived.

Americans for Prosperity positioned itself at the vanguard of the anti-Obama rebellion. In late April, as House Democrats prepared to introduce cap and trade legislation to limit greenhouse gas emissions, the group launched a national "Hot Air" tour—replete with a red hot air balloon—warning of "global warming alarmism." It staged rallies targeting the union-friendly Employee Free Choice Act. And it stirred opposition to what Tim Phillips called "the clear and present threat" of the Obama administration's health care reform initiative, crisscrossing the country in a bus with the slogan HANDS OFF MY HEALTHCARE emblazoned on the side. Members of Congress returned to their districts during the typically sedate August recess in 2009 to raucous "recess rallies" organized by Americans for Prosperity and other groups, where apoplectic activists shouted down lawmakers during town hall meetings on the soon-to-be-unveiled health care legislation.

Conservative activists would later gripe that Americans for Prosperity often horned in on the organizing work of others and that Phillips tended to claim credit for campaigns in which his organization had only tangential involvement. "What they did was they ran to the head of the parade a lot," said a conservative strategist. "They attempted to buy the Tea Party as long as [the Tea Party] did what they wanted done."

But there was no denying that as the Tea Party took off, Americans for Prosperity seemed omnipresent. The group's role in organizing the unfolding mutiny begged the obvious question of who funded the organization. It didn't require much digging to discover the group had been created by two petrochemical billionaires who had been fighting to eviscerate taxes and government regulations since the 1970s.

As Charles and David surfaced as the moneymen behind the Tea Party–stoking Americans for Prosperity, Koch Industries tried to maintain the fiction that the group was just one "among the hundreds" of organizations the brothers supported. The advocacy group operated completely "independently" of Koch Industries, the company insisted. But even Americans for Prosperity's conservative allies roll their eyes at this notion. "AFP in many ways is a tool in the toolbox of a corporation to advance its corporate interests," said the leader of one conservative nonprofit who has worked with Americans for Prosperity in the past.

The brothers have a long history of unusually close involvement with the political groups and public policy shops they fund. "They are very active directors," said James Miller, an Americans for Prosperity board member and a long-serving chairman of its predecessor, Citizens for a Sound Economy. "They want to know what's going on and they give the organization directions— direction on how it's managed.... They are very focused on the organizations doing the most with the resources they have."

Americans for Prosperity is in some ways an appendage of Koch Industries and it has historically been staffed and managed by people who have long and deep loyalties to the Kochs. Americans for Prosperity's founding president was Nancy Pfotenhauer, who spent much of her professional life working for the Kochs, first as an executive at Citizens for a Sound Economy and later as the director of Koch Industries' DC lobbying operation. A former Koch lobbyist named Alan Cobb was the group's vice president of state operations. Meanwhile, Richard Fink served on the board of Americans for Prosperity's foundation arm alongside David, its chairman. According to a Republican strategist who has worked with the Kochs' political network, outside operatives in the brothers' employ had a hand in guiding some of Americans for Prosperity's activities, even playing a part in developing ads that ran under the group's name.

Accused of running a Koch Industries front group, Tim Phillips has pointed out that his organization has thousands of donors. Yet grassroots contributors of $25, $50, or even $100 did not keep the lights on at AFP's third-floor offices in Arlington, Virginia, let alone foot the bill for the pricey political ads saturating the airwaves. Americans for Prosperity's primary benefactors were the Kochs, major U.S. corporations (including, at one point, the State Farm insurance company), and crucially, an extensive network of wealthy conservative donors cultivated by fund-raisers employed by Koch Industries. This donor network alone would channel tens of millions of dollars into Americans for Prosperity's coffers in the years ahead.

David's name popped up more and more as the corporate Oz behind the curtain of the Tea Party, even more so than Charles, who did not have a formal role with Americans for Prosperity. Charles had been on a lifelong mission to promote economic freedom and transform society, but David, who considered medical research the main thrust of his philanthropy, became the figurehead of their political crusade.

David had played the role of face man in their relationship dating back to the late 1970s, when Charles urged David to run for vice president on the Libertarian Party's ticket. "I think he is the face on a lot of their politics stuff because Charles doesn't want to be," said one former Koch executive. "There is a bit of a character difference. Charles is a very reserved, shun the spotlight guy. David—and Bill, his twin brother—much more want to be in the public eye and are willing to do it."

James Miller said of Charles: "I think he has a great interest in the political process; I just think he doesn't want to do it himself. David is a little more willing to put himself out there."

David, however, did not relish the attention that accompanied the rise of the Tea Party; he preferred the pose-in-a-tux-at-Lincoln-Center variety. He seemed surprised to become the object of vitriol, surprised that anyone would even associate him with the protests unfolding around the country. "I've never been to a Tea-Party event," he told *New York* magazine in the summer of 2010. "No one representing the Tea Party has ever even approached me." Yet he funded and sat on the board of one of the groups leading the movement.

Being portrayed as the "tea party's wallet," as *New York* dubbed him, didn't play terribly well in liberal New York City, posing an unwelcome contrast to the Andrew Carnegie–esque image he preferred to project. But he couldn't have it both ways. In *New York* magazine (and New York City), David scoffed at the notion that he was a major Tea Party backer, but he displayed a different side among the Americans for Prosperity faithful.

David must have been aware that he was entering a hive of Tea Party organizing on the morning of October 3, 2009, when he strolled into the ballroom of Arlington, Virginia's Crystal Gateway Marriott. Americans for Prosperity had convened its annual Defending the American Dream conference and hundreds of Americans for Prosperity activists had gathered to revel in their muscular opposition to the Obama administration and its Democratic allies.

The ballroom that morning was bathed in red and blue light, as David stepped to the stage, wearing a dark pinstripe suit with a silver tie. Gripping the sides of the podium, he scanned the sea of activists before him.

It was a sight to behold.

"Five years ago," he began, "my brother Charles and I provided the funds to start the Americans for Prosperity and it's beyond my wildest dreams how AFP has grown into this enormous organization. Two thousand people here this weekend—this is a phenomenal success in my judgment. Eight hundred thousand activists from nothing five years ago—this is a remarkable achievement. And we're being effective in so many different ways."

"Days like today," he continued, "bring to reality the vision of our board of directors when we founded this organization....We envisioned a mass movement, a state-based one, but national in scope, of hundreds of thousands of American citizens from all walks of life standing up and fighting for the economic freedoms that have made our nation the most prosperous society in history." David concluded his speech by presenting the group's annual Washington award, given to a national leader who had distinguished himself as a defender of economic freedom, to that year's honoree—South Carolina's Jim DeMint, a Republican senator whose name would become synonymous with the Tea Party revolt that roiled Congress in the coming years.

Later that afternoon, David and Tim Phillips stood side by side on the stage while representatives from each of AFP's chapters took a turn at the microphone, addressing "Mr. Chairman" like soldiers sounding off to their general. They told of organizing "dozens of tea parties" and "relentlessly" hounding their congressional representatives to keep their "hands off our health care," spike cap and trade legislation, and jettison "the Employee No Choice Act." They spoke of doubling and tripling their memberships and of becoming a "political force" within their states.

A current of exuberance pulsed through the room. David—who would later scratch his head at being pegged as the Tea Party's mastermind—smiled down from the stage and brought his hands together heavily.

In mid-March 2010, an official-looking convoy of two forest green police cars and an ambulance painted the same shade pulled up in front of the National Museum of Natural History on the National Mall in Washington. The museum was debuting the new $20.7 million David H. Koch Hall of Human Origins. Human evolution had long been one of David's passions, and he had funded research on the subject for more than 30 years, including supporting the work of anthropologist Donald Johanson; with a pair of colleagues, the famed scientist had discovered "Lucy," the 3-million-year-old hominid skeleton that established a key evolutionary link between apes and man.

Young men and women piled out of the cars, wearing green jackets with CLIMATE CRIME UNIT stenciled on the back. The Greenpeace activists busied themselves cordoning off a "climate crime scene" and distributing "Wanted" leaflets containing pictures of David and his brother. "While David Koch's oil wealth may get his name on a museum exhibit, the Koch family legacy is one of environmental crimes," the group's wiry, goateed research director, Kert Davies, declared.

Richard Fink had warned the brothers that they would pay a price for stepping up their political involvement. The backlash had begun.

Davies had for more than a decade kept a folder on Koch Industries in the back of his filing cabinet, filling it periodically with newspaper clips and documents as they came across his desk. Starting in the fall of 2009, as the Tea Party gained steam, and as Americans for Prosperity became a primary foe of the climate change legislation that had narrowly passed the House but stalled in the Senate, Davies dusted off the file. He planned to drag the Koch brothers out of the shadows and onto the front pages.

Davies and his team of Greenpeace researchers had previously exposed Exxon's role in bankrolling think tanks and research studies that sowed doubt about climate change. They now began to scrutinize the giving of the Koch brothers and their company.

What they found astounded them. Foundations connected to the brothers had, in the three-year stretch between 2005 and 2008, directed nearly $25 million to dozens of conservative think tanks, policy institutes, and advocacy groups that had challenged the existence of global warming. Exxon, during that same period, had contributed about $9 million to similar outfits. Charles and David Koch had outspent a public company with one of the world's largest market caps by nearly 3 to 1.

The brothers controlled America's second largest private company. Koch Industries produced Dixie cups and Brawny paper towels. It swallowed the industrial giant Georgia-Pacific with barely a hiccup. But why, Davies and his colleagues wondered, had so few Americans heard of them? Why were so few people aware of the subterranean tentacles of their influence?

"We decided, why don't we expose them and make them a household name?" said Greenpeace researcher Aliya Haq. "The point was, let's bring these guys out into the spotlight. Who are they and why don't we know who they are?"

Greenpeace followed its Smithsonian stunt with the release of a report detailing the brothers' hefty contributions to dozens of "climate opposition groups"; it accused the brothers and their company of "secretly funding the climate denial machine."

The report was effective, if misleading. The brothers had for decades contributed to a wide constellation of conservative groups that amplified their free-market viewpoint. It was not exactly a secret. These same organizations—including the Cato Institute, the Heritage Foundation, the Mercatus Center, and many others—had indeed broadcast doubts about global warming and government-led efforts to address it. And the brothers themselves were certainly global warming skeptics. But it was a leap to suggest the millions the Kochs had donated to conservative think tanks and other outfits had been all or even mostly for the purpose of climate change denial. In reality, the Kochs' funding had gone to bankroll research and advocacy on a wide range of other issues—many of them, to be sure, loathsome to the political Left.

Though the report painted a distorted picture of the Kochs' giving, it entered the national conversation at a moment when political discourse had turned hyper-partisan. Around the time of its release, the long, acrimonious battle over health care reform had climaxed with a series of fractious "Kill the Bill" rallies held outside the Capitol in which the Koch brothers' Americans for Prosperity was front and center. The scene got so ugly that a protestor spat on Representative Emanuel Cleaver, a black Democrat from Missouri, as he made his way into the Capitol; an irate activist called out "faggot" as Representative Barney Frank, the openly gay congressman from Massachusetts, passed by. The Greenpeace report, coupled with news coverage linking Charles and David to the nasty health care brawl, set the stage for the Kochs to become cartoon villains.

On the Left, "the Koch brothers" became a political meme, a crude caricature of corporate fat cats subverting democracy and science as they secretly advanced their plutocratic agenda. The brothers were suddenly the Punch to Obama's Judy in the partisan puppet show. They were just the latest incarnation of a familiar American archetype that stretched from Thomas Nast's political cartoons through Lionel Barrymore's Mr. Potter in *It's a Wonderful Life*, and from the Duke brothers in *Trading Places* to *The Simpsons'* Montgomery Burns.

If Greenpeace had set out to make Charles and David Koch infamous, the plan worked even better than the activists had dreamed of. "It was almost like we let this balloon go," Davies recalled, "and then it just kept getting bigger and bigger."

*   *   *

At the White House, the Americans for Prosperity onslaught had become hard to ignore. During the health care reform fight that spring, the Koch brothers' advocacy group began targeting vulnerable congressional Democrats—including West Virginia's Alan Mollohan, Pennsylvania's Christopher Carney and Kathy Dahlkemper, Wisconsin's Steve Kagen, North Dakota's Earl Pomeroy, and New York's Michael Arcuri—with brutal attack ads. The spots, featuring a breast cancer survivor, suggested that these Democrats supported a government-run health care plan that could end up costing Americans their lives by denying mammograms to women under the age of fifty. These ads were rife with falsehoods—but they didn't have to be true to be effective.

"The issue was volume really more than anything else," remembered Bill Burton, who was then serving as the deputy White House press secretary. "Their ads are not well produced; but if you put enough money behind even a bad ad, you're going to get good results." He recalled that the topic of Americans for Prosperity and its billionaire backers began to arise as the president's top aides powwowed about the midterms and other political matters. "It would come up in communications and strategy meetings where we would talk about how to deal with it," Burton said. "It would come up in meetings where we discussed how to handle this from the podium…and the result was what you saw the President saying out there on the stump about the money that was pouring into these races." Obama's aides settled on a simple strategy: Show voters that Americans for Prosperity was not the grassroots group it claimed to be, but a vehicle for a shadowy corporate agenda.

President Obama road-tested this White House–crafted messaging on the afternoon of August 9, 2010, during a fund-raising swing through Texas. In the ballroom of the Four Seasons in Austin overlooking Lady Bird Lake, where Democratic donors noshed on watermelon salad with basil crème fraîche and a duo of crab cake and beef tenderloin, Obama declared:

> Right now all around this country there are groups with harmless-sounding names like Americans for Prosperity, who are running millions of dollars of ads against Democratic candidates all across the country. And they don't have to say who exactly the Americans for Prosperity are. You don't know if it's a foreign-controlled corporation. You don't know if it's a big oil company, or a big bank. You don't know if it's a [sic] insurance company that wants to see some of the provisions in health reform repealed because it's good for their bottom line, even if it's not good for the American people.

Obama stopped short of name-checking the Kochs or their company, but that would come from his lieutenants in the weeks leading up to the midterms.

One of the first shots came from David Axelrod, the president's chief political strategist. On September 23, in a *Washington Post* op-ed, Axelrod singled out the Koch brothers by name as he detailed the "audacious stealth campaign being mounted by powerful corporate special interests that are vying to put their Republican allies in control of Congress."

He wrote: "Yet another group, Americans for Prosperity, is funded by billionaire oil men, David and Charles Koch, to promote Republican candidates who support their right-wing agenda and corporate interests. The group has gone to great lengths to conceal information about its donors and their motives." Axelrod noted that a recent article by *The New Yorker*'s Jane Mayer had "revealed that this group has been quietly guiding the organizing efforts of the Tea Party—in other words, billionaire oilmen secretly underwriting what the public has been told is a grassroots movement for change in Washington."

No amount of forewarning prepared Charles for the experience of becoming a political punching bag. "I'm not sure it would ever cross Charles's mind that…a sitting president would single him out," said Charlie Chandler, the chairman and CEO of INTRUST Bank, whose board Charles has served on since the 1960s. "He thinks, 'I'm from Wichita, Kansas!'"

The attention to his political activities made him uncomfortable and he couldn't grasp why he was being portrayed as some greedy Republican overlord. He considered himself a member of neither political party and held politicians on both sides of the aisle in equal disdain. His cause was economic freedom—shoving the government out of the marketplace, so Americans could pursue their own economic interests and succeed or fail based on their own abilities—and he cared little whether there was a D or an R next to the name of the politician most likely to advocate for it. "He thinks he's John Galt," said a conservative strategist who knows Charles—and he must have felt like the persecuted hero of Ayn Rand's *Atlas Shrugged*, too, as he came into the Obama administration's crosshairs.

Richard Fink and the Koch brothers may have steeled themselves for things to get "ugly," but they failed to prepare the company for the increased scrutiny. Even though Fink had carefully modeled a range of scenarios that might play out if the brothers ratcheted up their political involvement, which he presented to Charles and David, key players including Melissa Cohlmia, Koch's communications director, and Mark Holden, the company's general counsel, were kept in the dark about their plans and the potential fallout. As the Koch brothers became the scourge of the Left, the company was initially caught off guard. And it showed.

At first, Koch Industries seemed unsure of how to handle the wave of attention, what to respond to and what to suffocate with silence. In 2010, for instance, as Tax Day loomed, Cohlmia preemptively e-mailed reporters and bloggers to remind them that neither the Koch brothers nor their company had provided funds "specifically to support the tea parties." The carefully worded statement seemed only to reinforce the notion that the Kochs were not being fully forthright about their political activities and had something to hide.

As Charles and David increasingly became leading characters in the political story line, the company shifted from a defensive crouch to a wartime posture, punching back aggressively at what it considered media distortions. "We were caught off guard, but I think we got prepared pretty quickly," said Cohlmia, a petite brunette of Lebanese extraction. Jane Mayer's *New Yorker* article on the Kochs, titled "Covert Operations," particularly infuriated David, who could not restrain himself from firing back in an interview with a reporter for the *Daily Beast*. "If what I and my brother believe in, and advocate for, is secret, it's the worst covert operation in history," he fumed.

Following the release of Mayer's article, Koch Industries vigorously attacked her credibility on its website. The *New York Post* later reported on an "apparently concerted campaign"—of unclear origins—"to smear" Mayer through the conservative press, including an abortive attempt by a reporter from Tucker Carlson's *Daily Caller* website to investigate the esteemed *New Yorker* journalist for plagiarism. When her story on the Kochs was nominated for a National Magazine Award, Mark Holden sent a lengthy missive to the executive director of the American Society of Magazine Editors slamming Mayer's reporting as "ideologically slanted and a prime example of a disturbing trend in journalism, where agenda-driven advocacy masquerades as objective reporting." Holden, meanwhile, had quietly launched an internal investigation into whether current or former Koch employees had provided information to Mayer.

By the end of the year, Koch Industries had set up a website, *KochFacts*, that was devoted to fighting back against the media onslaught. Along with acerbic rebuttals, it published e-mail correspondence with editors and reporters that displayed supposed evidence of media bias or dishonesty. Koch ran web ads targeting specific reporters and it created a ticker that cataloged each mention of Koch Industries that appeared in *The New York Times* in order to track the paper's "curious fixation" on the company. This was part of what one senior Koch executive described as "upping the transaction costs for the other side." By punching back, he said, "some of the mainstream media are more selective about what they report about us. They know if they step out of bounds or don't follow the rules or journalistic ethics and standards, we're going to hit back at them. That's what we do."

Charles told friends that he believed the onslaught of attention was coordinated and directed from the highest levels in Washington. "He thinks there are certain folks within the Democratic Party or even within the administration who decided to target them," said INTRUST's Charlie Chandler. Charles's company, in addition to jabbing back at journalists, complained that it had become the target of a "concerted smear campaign" and suggested this underhanded effort led all the way to 1600 Pennsylvania Avenue.

Charles and David had learned some important lessons from their decades of political and public policy involvement. One was that it takes a village—preferably one populated by outrageously wealthy people—to build a free-market army.

Starting during the Bush administration, Charles began holding biannual seminars that brought together deep-pocketed donors— from hedge fund billionaires to media moguls—who shared their political objectives. The purpose, at least at first, was to showcase conservative groups deemed worthy of their support. But over the years this network transformed into a central coordinating body for the purpose of strategically channeling resources into conservative, free-market causes—cash that flowed to groups including Americans for Prosperity to bankroll efforts to trounce Democrats in the upcoming midterms.

The brothers held their final conclave before the midterm elections on June 27 and 28, 2010, at the St. Regis Hotel in Aspen. The impressive roster of attendees hardly needed name tags, though they wore them anyway, in accordance with the security protocol they were reminded of before the start of every meeting. Mingling with Charles and David and their wives in the hotel's chandeliered Grand Ballroom was billionaire entrepreneur Phil Anschutz, owner of the Examiner newspapers and *The Weekly Standard*; leveraged buyout pioneer John Childs; megamillionaire investor Foster Friess; hedge fund manager Ken Griffin, founder and CEO of Citadel LLC; several members of the Marshall family, whose stake in Koch Industries was estimated at nearly $13 billion; and the Blackstone Group's CEO Stephen Schwarzman, one of David's neighbors at his New York residence at 740 Park Avenue. Charles's son, Chase, an executive at the family company, and his new wife, Annie, also attended, as did the CEO's daughter, Elizabeth, a Brooklyn-based writer.

The two-day conference featured back-to-back presentations and panel discussions on topics ranging from "Framing the Debate on Spending" to electing free-market allies in upcoming judicial elections, and from "Winning the Fight between Big Government and Free Enterprise" to "Mobilizing Citizens" for the November midterms (Americans for Prosperity's Tim Phillips was a presenter).

The *Wall Street Journal*'s Stephen Moore moderated a discussion on "Understanding the Persistent Threats We Face." A description of the session in the conference program noted: "The current administration swept into office with a promise to 'fundamentally transform America.' From the nationalization of healthcare to the rising power of unions, as well as a push for major new climate and energy regulations, financial regulation, and even more government spending, there is no lack of significant threats for us to understand and address."

The Aspen seminar's headliner was Glenn Beck, who Fox News would ease out the following year after his controversial diatribes provoked an advertiser boycott. Beck's Hayek-themed keynote was titled "Is America on the Road to Serfdom?"

There had been much talk during the conference about the upcoming midterm elections and knocking Nancy Pelosi and the House Democrats back into the congressional minority, but no sooner had the fleet of private jets cleared Aspen airspace than Charles turned his mind to an even bigger political fight—the 2012 presidential race.

As the midterms neared, Charles sent a letter to new members of the donor network, inviting them to the next conference, scheduled for late January 2011. " 'If not us, who? If not now, when?' " his letter began. "That question was posed by a member of our network of business and philanthropic leaders, who are dedicated to defending our free society. We cannot rely on politicians to do so, so it is up to us to combat what is now the greatest assault on American freedom and prosperity in our lifetimes."

He noted that the network's biannual meetings "have been critical in improving and expanding our efforts" to combat "the multitude of public policies that threaten to destroy America as we know it."

In Aspen, Charles wrote, "our group heard plans to activate citizens against the threat of government over-spending and to change the balance of power in Congress this November. In response, participants committed to an unprecedented level of support."

But they would not stop at the midterms.

"Everyone benefits from the prosperity that emerges from free societies," he wrote. "But that prosperity is under attack by the current Administration and many of our elected officials. Their policies threaten to erode our economic freedom and transfer vast sums of power to the state. We must stop—and reverse—this internal assault on our founding principles.

"Fighting back with incremental changes will only lead to a slower rate of decline. We must dedicate ourselves to making major advances in the direction of economic freedom."

Wearing a tweed overcoat and a tan scarf, David stepped out of the chill and into the gleaming, marble corridors of the U.S. Capitol. It was January 5, 2011, and the building teemed with lawmakers and their families, including the eighty-five Republican freshmen who had helped their party reclaim the House and were waiting to be sworn in that afternoon along with the rest of the new Congress.

Two months after the midterms, the pundit class was still guffawing over the Democrats' "shellacking" and attempting to wrap their minds around the ascendant Tea Party. The 2010 midterm elections had followed a similar script to 1994's "Republican Revolution." During both elections, one of the catalyzing issues had been health care. Each had likewise brought to power a Republican House majority with an ambitious agenda of drastically downsizing government and returning to core conservative principles.

The Koch brothers certainly deserved a share of the credit for the Democratic drubbing. In the lead-up to the midterms, their advocacy group carpet-bombed dozens of congressional swing districts with ads aimed at Democratic lawmakers. Americans for Prosperity rolled out an initiative dubbed "November Is Coming," featuring a petition drive commanding politicians to "oppose big government programs or any other freedom-killing policies or we will remember in November." The group mobilized thousands of activists to go door to door in their districts. It also provided them with a computerized phone-banking program that connected Americans for Prosperity volunteers to targeted voters, generating a script to read from. "I'm calling to encourage you to call Congressman John Salazar and tell him to stop his wasteful spending that is bankrupting America," read one script targeting the Colorado Democrat—and the brother of the Interior secretary—who ultimately went down to defeat. Also booted from Congress were Democrats including Representatives Alan Mollohan, Christopher Carney, Kathy Dahlkemper, Steve Kagen, Earl Pomeroy, and Michael Arcuri, the lawmakers Americans for Prosperity had targeted for early retirement with withering health-care-reform-related attack ads.

Americans for Prosperity formed just one prong of Charles and David's plan of attack for 2010. Their political operatives had parceled out their donor network's war chest to dozens of like-minded conservative groups, which hammered the Democrats from every conceivable angle. The brothers had together pledged at least $12 million toward the effort.

David had come to the Capitol that day for the gratifying experience of witnessing California's Nancy Pelosi pass the Speaker's gavel to Ohio's John Boehner, whose star had risen, fallen, and risen again during his two-decade congressional career. Their plan was working.

David was accompanied to the Capitol that day by Nancy Pfotenhauer, who after leaving Americans for Prosperity had become a policy advisor and spokeswoman for the 2008 presidential campaign of John McCain. When the media scrutiny of Charles and David had heated up, Koch Industries had retained Pfotenhauer—and other crisis communication specialists—as an outside PR consultant. Also by David's side was Pfotenhauer's Americans for Prosperity successor Tim Phillips, who had a meeting that day with Michigan's Fred Upton, the incoming chairman of the House Energy and Commerce Committee. Before the New Year, Phillips and Upton, a long-serving Republican lawmaker who had first come to Washington in the 1980s to work in Reagan's Office of

Management and Budget, had teamed up on a *Wall Street Journal* editorial calling the Environmental Protection Agency's efforts to regulate carbon emissions "an unconstitutional power grab that will kill millions of jobs."

After the swearing-in, David was hosting a welcome party for the new class of Republican lawmakers at the Capitol Hill Club, a private haunt for GOP powerbrokers where some of the real business of Washington gets done over single malts. A reporter for the liberal blog ThinkProgress approached him as he left the Capitol with Phillips that afternoon. Deaf in his left ear, David leaned down with his right.

"Are you proud of what Americans for Prosperity has achieved this year?" the reporter asked.

"You bet I am, man oh' man," David responded. "We're going to do more too in the next couple of years, you know."

Phillips, laughing nervously, tried to hurry David away. But the billionaire, who had flipped open a cell phone and put it to his ear, obliged the reporter with another question.

The journalist inquired about the Tea Party—was David proud of its accomplishments?

"Yeah," he responded. "There are some extremists there, but the rank and file are just normal people like us. And I admire them. It's probably the best grassroots uprising since 1776 in my opinion."

If this was the second coming of the American Revolution, then the midterms had been its Lexington and Concord. What came next was all-out war.

CHAPTER FOURTEEN

The Mother of All Wars

The chants wafted up from the street below.

Charles and David Koch:
Your corporate greed is making us broke!
Charles and David Koch:
Your corporate greed is making us broke!

It was January 30, 2011, the kickoff of Charles and David's next donor conclave, this one held in the Southern California resort city of Rancho Mirage, just outside Palm Springs. Among the conservative megadonors who jetted in to attend were Home Depot cofounder Ken Langone, Amway billionaire Richard DeVos, and Wisconsin building products mogul Diane Hendricks. The featured speakers were Eric Cantor and Paul Ryan, the incoming House majority leader and budget committee chairman, respectively.

For the first time in the eight years the Koch brothers had convened these strictly confidential gatherings, a copy of the invitation had leaked, giving away the location and allowing a collection of liberal advocacy groups and unions to mobilize. Watching from an upper balcony at the Rancho Las Palmas Resort and Spa, David and his wife, Julia, her head resting heavily in her left hand, grimaced at the clamorous scene below.

Hundreds of shouting, sign-waving protestors swarmed in front of the resort. Activists held up a yellow banner with biohazard symbols reading, QUARANTINE THE KOCHS. Another sign declared: KOCH KILLS. One protestor carried a cardboard placard splashed with fake blood and the slogan NEUTER FERAL FATCATS—the "s" doubling as a swastika.

It was the liberal analogue of a Tea Party. Instead of irate activists demanding the government keep its hands off their health care, these protestors were calling on the Kochs and their wealthy friends to keep their money out of the political system.

A line of police in riot gear guarded the driveway to the locked-down resort, while a contingent of Koch security guards, wearing gold "K" lapel pins, patrolled the grounds within the complex. Discovering *Politico* reporter Ken Vogel sleuthing on the premises, Koch's surly guards ejected the journalist under threat of a "night in the Riverside County jail."

Security wasn't just tight on the ground. The Federal Aviation Administration had taken the cautionary step of curbing access to the airspace above the resort. A couple of days earlier, Greenpeace had launched its 135-foot airship above Rancho Mirage. As guests began to arrive at the resort, they were greeted with the spectacle of the lime green, blimp-like craft circling overhead and displaying large banners with Charles and David's caricatures; sandwiched between their faces was the slogan KOCH BROTHERS: DIRTY MONEY.

The brothers were under the radar no more, their pictures used for left-wing propaganda and their family name a code word for corporate villainy. Experiencing the contempt firsthand was unnerving. And it materialized in some of the least expected places. A few weeks earlier, audience members had booed David at the opening of the *Nutcracker* at the Brooklyn Academy of Music, a holiday performance he had chipped in $2.5 million to sponsor. "He's an evil man," a voice in the audience whispered when he took the stage to say a few words about his contribution. It was an uncomfortable convergence of his life as a New York City philanthropist and his life as a billionaire bankroller of conservative causes.

Charles viewed the intensity of the onslaught as an omen of progress. "I believed that when we were considered effective we would be attacked," he told *The Weekly Standard*. Charles's father had made a nearly identical statement almost a half-century earlier, at the height of his infamy as a leader of the John Birch Society. "There are many who are attempting and will undoubtedly continue to smear us," Fred Koch griped to a reporter in 1960. "We've been called just about everything in the book but we consider that a sign of our effectiveness."

There was a big difference between Fred Koch's era and the present one, however. The Kochs were no longer fringe players on the political scene. The brothers had begun their political careers as idealists, third-party outsiders. Now the same establishmentarians that had kept Fred Koch's John Birch Society at bay and laughed off the Libertarian Party had started to embrace them. Even *National Review*, the arbiter of American conservatism that crusaded against both Birchism and Libertarianism, was defending the brothers from their liberal antagonists.

In the coming presidential election cycle, the Kochs would do battle on several fronts. On the surface, their objective was installing a Republican in the Oval Office and packing Congress with conservatives, but this fight was also about reshaping the Republican Party and crashing the gates of political power to claim a seat at the table. During the war ahead, the Kochs waged some of their most brutal combat not with ideological enemies, but with onetime allies from their early days in the political arena.

During breaks in the conference, curious attendees peeked outside to watch the protest, where police ultimately arrested twenty-five activists. If anything, the demonstration galvanized members of the Kochs' donor network. "It generated a lot of enthusiasm for what we are trying to do," a Koch official said at the time. Hanging out with the big, bad Koch brothers, the scourge of the Obama administration, had become a conservative status symbol.

That enthusiasm had been a long time in coming.

Since the 1970s, when Charles was the libertarian movement's primary benefactor, he had been intent on cultivating a group of like-minded business leaders to support the causes he held dear. "He wanted more guys like him who would put money into Cato and these different organizations," said Richard Wilcke, who ran the Koch-funded Council for a Competitive Economy. He was trying to "identify other Charles Kochs" and seeking to drum up "movement-type organizational support." A number of lonely years had passed before Charles began to find willing investors who shared his vision.

Through the biannual seminars, Charles hoped to build a deep network of business leaders and philanthropists that would grow and sustain a coterie of favored free-market think tanks, advocacy groups, and educational programs. The inaugural conference, held in Chicago in 2003, attracted just seventeen participants, many of them drawn from Charles's circle of friends. Back then, these invitation-only confabs, where presenters bored attendees senseless with marathon economics lectures, held little mystique. It was hard to read the long-winded name of these events—"Understanding and Addressing Threats to American Free Enterprise and Prosperity"— without stifling a yawn. The brothers didn't need a heavy security presence to keep people out—the problem was getting them in the door to start with.

"Their first few seminars were disasters. No one even came," said a Republican operative who has attended the donor summits.

Eventually Richard Fink and his staff began to spice up the tedious conferences with conservative celebrities and high-profile

Republican lawmakers. The events gradually drew a hundred, then two hundred attendees. Soon guests rubbed elbows with Rush Limbaugh, Charles Krauthammer, Senator Jim DeMint, Mississippi Governor Haley Barbour—even Supreme Court justices Antonin Scalia and Clarence Thomas. The more donors the events attracted, the more these gatherings became a magnet for politicians prowling for campaign contributions. "It became a libertarian Woodstock that you had to go to," a conservative strategist said.

By the 2008 election cycle, the Kochs' donor retreats began attracting the type of heavy hitters who wrote seven-figure checks without flinching. Kevin Gentry, Koch Industries' vice president for special projects and the brothers' chief fund-raiser, played an important role in transforming the donor summits into a well-oiled machine. An acolyte of conservative activist Morton Blackwell, Gentry served as a vice chairman of Virginia's Republican Party and he was an old pal of Tim Phillips, Americans for Prosperity's president; he had been a director of the Faith and Family Alliance, the Jack Abramoff–linked group that Phillips had helped to set up.

Gentry's entrée to the Koch universe came through George Mason University, where he was a fund-raiser for both the Mercatus Center and the Institute for Humane Studies. He was hired in 2003 by Charles's foundation and later went to work for Koch Industries directly, serving as a liaison between the Kochs and the organizations they funded.

Gentry employed a simple yet brutally effective fund-raising strategy at the donor retreats, which he organized and emceed. During lunch on the second day of the conference, after attendees had heard from a variety of speakers and been briefed on the Kochs' political strategy, Gentry often presided over a lively pledge-a-thon during which some of America's wealthiest men rose to their feet to one-up each other as they promised six- and seven-figure contributions to advance the cause of economic freedom.

"Literally, Kevin's at the front of the room with a microphone: 'Foster, what do you think you can pledge?' " said a political strategist who has attended these sessions. "They would get in this room and just feed off each other." Between ultracompetitive billionaires and business moguls, it almost became a contest over who could cut the bigger check. "Everybody gets so excited, and it's this human nature of 'my dick's longer than your dick.' They're tapping into basic human nature and they're raising tens of millions of dollars in the span of an hour."

Minnesota broadcasting billionaire Stanley Hubbard, a regular attendee of the Kochs' donor summits, said: "When people stand up and say, 'I'll give,' another guy will say, 'I'll give the same thing,' and another, 'I'll do the same thing.' And they raise a lot of money in a big hurry at lunch."

By the time the Rancho Mirage conference disbanded on Tuesday, February 1, Charles and David's political operation had banked $49 million toward the goal of completing the Republican takeover they had helped to set in motion in the midterms.

Several weeks later, at about 2:00 p.m. central time on February 22, Scott Walker, the newly elected Republican governor of Wisconsin, picked up the phone in his office. David Koch, he'd been told, wanted to speak with him. Koch Industries' political action committee had contributed $43,000 to Walker's campaign, making the company one of the governor's biggest financial backers. Koch's PAC had also directed more than $1 million to the Republican Governors Association, a political outfit focused on electing GOP chief executives across the nation; David had personally donated $1 million to the association, which had in turn sunk more than $3.4 million into Walker's race.

David was precisely the type of megadonor an ambitious politician like Walker wanted in his Rolodex. And if he called, you answered the phone.

"Hi, this is Scott Walker."

"Scott! David Koch. How are you?"

"Hey, David! I'm good. And yourself?"

"I'm very well. I'm a little disheartened by the situation there, but, uh, what's the latest?"

The situation was that thousands of people were protesting in the streets outside Walker's office in the state capitol in Madison. An angry throng of activists had made camp inside the building's three-story rotunda. Walker, the forty-four-year-old son of a Baptist minister, had stirred the outrage of tens of thousands of Wisconsinites when, less than a month into his new job, he "dropped the bomb," as he put it, on the public sector workers and unions of his state.

He had unveiled a piece of legislation intended to plug a $137 million hole in the state budget by, in part, slashing collective bargaining rights for public workers and forcing them to pay more for their health care and retirement benefits. The bill required an annual vote to keep a union functioning and, going a step further to weaken labor's power, curbed the ability of unions to collect money for political spending. Democratic members of the state Senate had fled Wisconsin to deny their Republican colleagues a quorum to vote on Walker's bill. The state was in turmoil.

Walker was not alone in his efforts to neuter organized labor at the state level. Other conservative governors, swept into power by riding the Tea Party wave of 2010, put forward their own bills targeting unions. Legislation similar to Walker's popped up in Iowa, Idaho, Alaska, and Ohio, sparking smaller protests in those states as well. The early months of 2011 saw a sustained assault on organized labor, of the kind that hadn't been seen since the right-to-work movement of the 1940s and 1950s, when Fred Koch and his right-wing ally Bob Love had successfully led the charge to make Kansas a right-to-work state.

As Walker came under fire, the Koch brothers' Americans for

Prosperity rallied to his aid. Wisconsin was home to one of the group's largest and most active state chapters, and in the past Walker had been a frequent speaker at Americans for Prosperity events. (Koch Industries also had a sizable presence in the state, where it employed some 3,000 employees, including at two Georgia-Pacific paper mills in the Green Bay area.) In an interview with *The New York Times*, Tim Phillips suggested that AFP leaders had encouraged Walker to battle the unions (though Phillips later denied saying this). And his group mobilized quickly to defend Walker from the pro-labor onslaught. It flooded the airwaves with issue ads urging citizens to "Stand with Walker," organized counterrallies, and launched a statewide bus tour in support of Walker's budget plan. (The advocacy group would later be pivotal in helping Walker keep his job, after his antiunion tactics culminated in a recall election.)

On the phone, Walker provided an insider's account of what was transpiring in Wisconsin and a preview of his plans. "The state Senate still has the 14 members missing," Walker said, "but what they're doing today is bringing up all sorts of other non-fiscal items, many of which are things that members in the Democratic side care about. And each day we're going to ratchet it up a little bit."

When the caller brought up the idea of "planting some troublemakers" among the crowd of protestors, Walker acknowledged that "we thought about that." And when he suggested the governor "bring a baseball bat" to a potential meeting with the fourteen Democratic senators who had left Wisconsin to bring the legislative session to a standstill, Walker responded, "I have one in my office; you'd be happy with that. I got a Slugger with my name on it."

"Well, I tell you what, Scott," the caller said as their conversation wound down, "once you crush these bastards I'll fly you out to Cali and really show you a good time." "All right, that would be outstanding," Walker replied. "Thanks for all the support in helping us to move the cause forward."

Walker rang off with three words that his critics would never let him forget: "Thanks a million."

David's secretary delivered the news that a gonzo journalist for a Buffalo alt-weekly had posed as him, holding a lengthy conversation with Wisconsin's embattled governor. And the cringe-inducing recording of the call was circulating online. The real David Koch's face flushed with anger. Protested, heckled, maligned—now someone had appropriated his identity.

The events in Wisconsin catapulted Walker onto the national stage. The battle also cemented the Koch brothers' image as the right-wing puppet masters orchestrating a national stealth campaign of self-interested conservative reforms.

The prank call doused gasoline on the Madison uprising. Walker's comments to the David Koch imposter fed into the tyrannical figure conjured up by the governor's enemies—the politician who refused to negotiate with Democrats and hadn't mentioned a word about his drastic budget proposal on the campaign trail, but who happily spent twenty minutes detailing his plans to a billionaire supporter. The call also reinforced the link between the governor and the Koch brothers in the minds of protestors, even though, as the recording confirmed, the men had never met nor spoken.

Post–prank call, the Kochs found their names plastered everywhere in Madison, and they became the targets of more public venom than they'd ever experienced in their lives. One popular theme declared Walker a KOCH WHORE. Another sign read, MR. WALKER, YOUR KOCH DEALER IS ON LINE 2...A third: SCOTT WALKER IS A KOCHLEAR IMPLANT. Meanwhile, boycott lists of Koch products were taped to the marble walls of the capitol. Brawny paper towels, Dixie cups, Quilted Northern toilet paper, Lycra, anything made by Georgia-Pacific: All of it was verboten.

Activists began to see nefarious signs of a Koch-Walker nexus everywhere. They pointed breathlessly to the fact that Koch Industries had recently opened a lobbying office in Madison, across the street from the state capitol. A provision in Walker's bill allowing Wisconsin to offload state-owned power plants in no-bid transactions spiraled into rumors that Walker planned to give Koch Industries a sweetheart deal. Within Koch Industries' public sector group—its public affairs, legal, and lobbying division—there was a debate about whether the company should respond to this conspiracy theory. Was the company really going to start issuing statements about deals it *wasn't* interested in, and would the tinfoil-hat-wearing activists spreading this rumor even believe the company? The company ultimately put out a statement denying any interest in the plants, which are "obsolete and do not in any way fit the Koch companies' current operations or their business plans moving forward." Sure enough, it seemed to do little good. "Are you reassured?" *The New York Times*'s Paul Krugman asked in a column.

After the company issued the denial, Mark Holden, Koch's lanky general counsel, left an angry voice mail for communications director Melissa Cohlmia. A former Akin Gump lawyer who hailed from Worcester, Massachusetts, Holden didn't blame Cohlmia per se. He was just furious at the situation. *Why did the company need to dignify this garbage with a response? Screw you, Paul Krugman!*

The brothers' opponents seemed to miss the forest for the trees as they strained to find evidence of the Kochs' hidden hand at work, a smoking gun that proved the governor of Wisconsin's marching orders came straight out of Wichita. The Kochs had indeed helped to influence the events playing out in Wisconsin and elsewhere in the country, where Republicans were trying to ram through proposals that curbed the clout of unions—but not as the Kochs' critics imagined. George Pearson, Charles's first political advisor, had once said that his boss "did not see politicians as setting the prevalent ideology but as reflecting it."

This explained the Kochs' political modus operandi. They had spent decades bankrolling the idea factories that had generated the policy recommendations and research underlying some of the same budget-cutting reforms that conservative governors like Scott Walker were now trying to implement. They had helped to elect politicians like Walker, who were inclined to enact these policies, and utilized groups like Americans for Prosperity to hold lawmakers' feet to the fire or mobilize reinforcements if they came under attack. Politicians were merely chess pieces advancing the agenda they'd been armed with.

Death threats ("The Koch brothers will DIE!!!!!") poured into Koch Industries in the months to come and hackers affiliated with the group Anonymous attempted to attack and infiltrate the company's computer networks. A vandal defaced Deerfield's Koch Center, the $68 million math and science building David had financed at his old boarding school, with statements including "money does not equal power." Activists projected a caricature of the industrialist on the side of the David H. Koch Theater at Lincoln Center with a thought bubble above it reading, "I bought this theater so I could hide my evil deeds."

Owing to security concerns, David and Julia began sending their children to school in a bulletproof car and his family received round-the-clock protection from ex–Navy SEALs. David told his three kids to think of the bodyguards as nannies. A security team protected Charles and Liz as well; Charles had hired the guards without bothering to inform his wife, who was livid. Cameras camouflaged in the trees of their Wichita compound, located at a busy intersection of chain restaurants and shopping plazas and ringed by a six-foot concrete wall, scanned the grounds for intruders. Even with these security measures in place, people close to the Kochs worried about "the Lee Harvey Oswalds of the world," as one family friend put it.

Jeff Jacobs, the CEO of the Boys & Girls Clubs of South Central

Kansas, recalled seeing helicopters hovering above the company's headquarters and assault-rifle-carrying guards posted on its roof following one bomb threat. One day, with the backlash against the company in full swing, Jacobs visited Charles in his office. The men had never met but Jacobs had requested an introduction, just to thank the CEO for the good works he and his employees had done in the community, especially their support of the local Boys & Girls Club. Jacobs had expected a brief meeting, but the men talked for more than a half hour.

"This has got to be such a burden," Jacobs said when he finally felt at ease enough with the billionaire to ask the question that had been on his mind. "I mean you could just run your business, make your money, go on vacation, and forget this policy stuff." So why didn't he?

"In America, we've kind of lost our way," Charles explained. The American dream had smiled on the Koch clan. He felt an obligation to get the country back on track.

"What do you think, Mr. Koch, are you making any headway with any of this?" Jacobs asked. "I mean, you're fighting a battle here."

"Well, I'll tell you, Preacher Man," Charles responded, referring to Jacobs's role as a local Catholic church deacon, "when you're preaching to the choir, they get it, but there are some people who just don't want to listen."

Richard Fink, whose own Northern Virginia home was posted with guards, considered Wisconsin "an escalation" in "an orchestrated campaign" by the Obama administration and its Democratic allies to target Koch Industries and its owners. "With the Left trying to intimidate the Koch brothers to back off of their support for freedom and signaling to others that this is what happens if you oppose the administration and its allies, we have no choice but to continue to fight," Fink said after the Walker prank call. "We will not step back at all."

The Koch brothers and their strategist had spent much of their lives planting the seeds of change that had started to bloom around the country. "This is a big part of our life's work," Fink said. "We are not going to stop."

In late June 2011, the Kochs assembled their network once again to plot an escalation of their own. The setting was Colorado's lush Vail Valley, where the Kochs and nearly three hundred guests had the run of the Ritz-Carlton nestled at the base of the Beaver Creek ski mountain. The same weekend that Charles and David were cajoling their friends to hand over millions to dump into the upcoming elections, their brother Bill dropped seven figures of his own nearby in Denver. The only known photograph of Billy the Kid was up for auction; Bill plunked down $2.3 million for the rare picture after a round of bidding so intense that spectators jumped to their feet in applause once the auction ended.

The evening of Sunday, June 26, was warm and clear, with a light wind blowing in from the west. At the end of a long day of panel discussions and strategy talks, conference attendees gathered in an outdoor pavilion for the opening reception. Guests received the customary warning that what was said that weekend was strictly confidential. To prevent outsiders from eavesdropping, the pavilion was encircled with outward-facing speakers droning sound-masking noise.

Before dinner, catered by Wolfgang Puck's Spago, Charles stepped to the microphone. "This is the mother of all wars we've got over the next 18 months, for the life or death of this country," he said, likening Saddam Hussein's description of the first Gulf War to the upcoming presidential election. "So, I'm not going to do this to put any pressure on anyone here, mind you. This is not pressure. But if this makes your heart feel glad and you want to be more forthcoming, then so be it. What I want to do is recognize not all of our great partners, but those partners who have given more than a billion—a mill…"

Laughter rippled through the crowd as Charles recovered from his flub. "Well, I was thinking of Obama and his billion-dollar campaign, so I thought we gotta do better than that." The CEO then read off the names of the more than two dozen donors who had chipped in a million dollars or more over the past year. "If you want to kick in a billion, believe me, we'll have a special seminar just for you."

Among the donors he recognized were investment guru Charles Schwab; Amway cofounders Richard and Helen DeVos; Foster Friess; Cintas CEO Dick Farmer; the Marshall clan; Variety Wholesalers scion Art Pope; and billionaire hedge fund manager Paul Singer.

"Ten more will remain anonymous, including David and me," Charles joked. "…The plan is the next seminar I'm going to read the names of the ten million."

David spoke briefly later that evening, introducing the keynote speaker, New Jersey's brash governor Chris Christie. Not yet two years into his term, Christie was already being floated as presidential timber. He was a hard-charging former U.S. Attorney, who, like Scott Walker, had entered into a fiscal showdown with his state's most powerful unions. Earlier that year, Christie had called on David at his Madison Avenue office, and they had spent close to two hours talking. David came away so impressed with Christie that he had invited the governor to headline June's donor conference.

In his introduction, David hailed Christie for his "courage and leadership," citing the recent passage of a bill in New Jersey downscaling the pension and health benefits of public employees and the governor's decision to pull out of a regional initiative to reduce greenhouse gas emissions. "We sincerely hope and trust that he will continue to be a strong voice for market-oriented policy," David said. "Who knows? With his enormous success in reforming

New Jersey, some day we might see him on a larger stage, where God knows, he is desperately needed."

Known for his combative style and high-octane speeches, Christie gave a typically energetic performance. During a Q&A session afterward, he deflected questions about his White House ambitions. "You're the first guy that I've seen who could beat Barack Obama," gushed one donor, who also happened to be a close friend of presidential candidate Tim Pawlenty.

Christie clearly left an impression. Within a couple weeks of the Vail meeting, David and other members of the donor network (including Ken Langone, Charles Schwab, and Paul Singer) began strongly urging the New Jersey governor to jump in the presidential race. They had surveyed the field—Herman Cain, Jon Huntsman, Michele Bachmann, Mitt Romney, Newt Gingrich, Rick Santorum, and Tim Pawlenty—and saw no clear superstar with the charisma to oust Obama. Of these candidates, David Koch was the closest to Romney, the former Massachusetts governor, whose 2008 presidential bid he had supported. But David wanted to win. Christie had a certain type of straight-talking magnetism and the kind of pugilistic temperament it took to survive a bruising primary campaign and general election.

Ken Langone led the Draft Christie effort. "Ken was the person who really pushed it really hard," remembered Christie's chief political strategist Mike DuHaime. And David, he noted, "was one of the people that Ken Langone brought forward in the recruitment process."

The month after the Vail seminar, Langone summoned Christie to the New York Health & Racquet Club in Manhattan. He wanted to show the governor precisely the kind of support he and his wealthy friends could deliver. Christie, joined by his wife and eldest son, Andrew, as well as DuHaime and another aide, had arrived expecting an intimate gathering. "I want you to come meet with me and a few friends," is how Langone had pitched the meeting to the governor. Dozens of influential people packed the room. Among the attendees was Rudy Giuliani's right-hand man Tony Carbonetti, hedge fund billionaire Stanley Druckenmiller, and even Henry Kissinger, the eighty-eight-year-old former secretary of state. At the front of the room was a row of chairs for Christie and his entourage, and nearby was a table with a speakerphone. Morgan Stanley's John Mack was on the line. So was David, who was traveling. "He spoke up and voiced his opinion that he would be with the governor if he decided to run," DuHaime recalled. "He said, 'If you run, I'll be with you.'"

To fund the Mother of All Wars, the Kochs and their advisors settled on a staggering budget of nearly $400 million. Arizona's John McCain had not even raised that amount during his entire presidential campaign in 2008. The Vail conference alone netted more than $70 million' worth of pledges. And Charles had vowed to his fellow donors to maximize the impact of their contributions. "I've pledged to all of you who've stepped forward and are partnering with us that we are absolutely going to do our utmost to invest this money wisely and get the best possible payoff for you in the future of the country," he said.

Disenchanted with traditional Republican Party organs, members of the Kochs' donor network had placed their faith in the Koch brothers. This was politics 2.0, a decentralization of party power caused by the gradual weakening of campaign finance laws and the rise of super-PACs and "dark money" nonprofits that allowed individuals and corporations to influence the political system as never before.

Characterizing donor sentiment, Charles's friend Nestor Weigand, a regular attendee of the conferences, said: "What it amounts to is I'm not putting my money in a hole again. I have more confidence in this than I do in the Republican Senatorial Trust Committee" and similar GOP institutions.

"They bring real credibility," said DuHaime, the Christie strategist and a former political director of the Republican National Committee. "I think other donors view them as smart donors. If the Kochs are behind something, then it has credibility. 'We should get behind it too.'"

"They're active, they're engaged, they're smart," he continued. "It's not just about television ads and things like that. They understand the evolution of data mining and all the different aspects that go into a long-term political operation. I'm hugely impressed with them."

The Kochs commanded a sophisticated operation that had evolved over the years into a kind of shadow party, occupying its own center of gravity within the GOP universe. They controlled an extensive fund-raising network with the ability to drum up as much cash as the Republican National Committee itself. Through Americans for Prosperity, they had ground operations in all the competitive electoral states and a readymade corps of volunteers for get-out-the-vote efforts—what David called "a citizen's army." A web of other political and advocacy outfits, meanwhile, were under varying degrees of Koch control. The brothers had even spearheaded an effort to build a comprehensive database for voter microtargeting—an area where President Obama's data-obsessed 2008 campaign had seriously outgunned the Republicans. Former Koch Industries executives ran the hush-hush operation, dubbed Themis after the Greek goddess of justice and divine order. It was a conscious effort to emulate the Democrats' Catalist, a clearinghouse for voter data that was cofounded by former Bill Clinton aide Harold Ickes.

Observers of the Kochs' political rise, from libertarian dilettantes to conservative powerbrokers, marvel at their ascent. "They were just gadflies; they had no political power," the consultant who worked for Citizens for a Sound Economy in the 1990s said.

"It is amazing to me how they've morphed and gone from spending money, hoping to have influence, to a point where they're perceived to have influence. It took them...years to get to that point."

Even prominent Democrats can't help admiring what the Koch brothers have achieved. "The Kochs—with the team of strategists and organizational leaders they've financed—have done something that no other Americans have ever accomplished," said Rob Stein, founder of the Democracy Alliance (the Democratic equivalent of the network controlled by the Kochs). "They began by building a distinct, durable wing—libertarianism—of a major political party that over the course of 35 years has become a dominant political force within Republicanism, and therefore within the country.

"They have accomplished this with deliberate strategic forethought, money, and superb organizing skills," he continued. "They have been opportunistic. They have seeded and built idea and people networks that control the politics of over thirty states and the U.S. House of Representatives. It's a brilliant, extraordinary accomplishment, and an unprecedented political phenomenon."

For all its growing influence within the Republican Party, the Koch faction nevertheless occupied a somewhat tenuous place in the GOP. The brothers had their own political agenda, which in some cases clashed with the party line. They often aligned with the Republicans on free-market issues and downsizing government, but they fell on the other side of the political spectrum when it came to the social issues that animated the party's powerful religious-conservative wing. Nor could Republicans count on the Kochs to fall in step on issues such as immigration, civil liberties, or defense, where they held more liberal views. The brothers and their company also opposed subsidies across the board, a position GOP members didn't always share. "The Republicans don't trust us," said one Koch political operative.

The brothers' government-spending zealotry also set them apart from the Republican mainstream. During the fight over raising the national debt ceiling that erupted in the summer of 2011, the Kochs' Americans for Prosperity (and other groups aligned with the insurgent Tea Party) leaned on Republican lawmakers to hold firm in their opposition to raising the debt limit, while more pragmatic GOP organizations, including those associated with strategist Karl Rove, supported efforts by House Speaker John Boehner to broker a debt deal.

Occasionally, the Kochs seemed to work at cross-purposes with presumed allies. Their microtargeting operation, for instance, competed directly with a similar effort underwritten by the Republican National Committee called Data Trust; the brothers' fund-raisers even canvassed some of the same donors Data Trust was soliciting, diluting the resources available for the party's official effort. And the Kochs angered Mitt Romney's campaign by holding one of their donor summits on the very same weekend when the candidate had scheduled a retreat for would-be campaign contributors.

In service of their larger goals, however, Charles and David's network forged an uneasy alliance with groups across the GOP spectrum, including Rove's American Crossroads super-PAC and its sister nonprofit, Crossroads GPS. In the lead-up to the midterms and again during the general election, emissaries of the Koch network attended meetings convened by Rove, where representatives of the GOP's major outside political groups strategized. This informal coalition was known as the Weaver Terrace Group, because Rove first convened these meetings at his Weaver Terrace home in the tony Palisades neighborhood of Northwest Washington DC.

One of the Koch network's liaisons to this ad hoc coordinating committee was a Phoenix-based political strategist named Sean Noble. A longtime congressional aide to Arizona Representative John Shadegg, Noble had flirted briefly with the idea of running for his boss's seat when the Republican lawmaker announced his retirement in 2008. Instead, he followed the path of many Hill alums, opening a political consulting shop, DC London. Randy Kendrick, wife of Arizona Diamondbacks owner, Ken Kendrick, brought Noble into the Koch network.

Before the midterms, Noble, who was hired as a consultant to manage the network's political spending, established a mysterious nonprofit called the Center to Protect Patient Rights. In documents filed with the Internal Revenue Service seeking tax-exempt status, Noble claimed the purpose of the organization was "building a coalition of like-minded organizations and individuals...to educate the public on issues related to health care with an emphasis on patients' rights."

In reality, the group acted as an ATM machine for dozens of conservative advocacy organizations. More than $200 million gushed into the nonprofit between late October 2009 (when Noble filed the paperwork to form it) and the fall of 2012; Noble dispensed this cash just as quickly as it arrived. The nonprofit formed one link in a daisy chain of trusts, LLCs, and nonprofits through which Koch network cash circulated en route to its final destination—one of any number of conservative political groups that included Americans for Prosperity, the Tea Party Patriots, the 60 Plus Association (a kind of right-wing counterpoint to the AARP), and many others. This elaborate system was designed to make it nearly impossible to trace contributions to their source. That's what Kevin Gentry, Charles and David's chief fund-raiser, had meant when he assured donors at the Vail meeting, "There is anonymity we can protect."

The Kochs' system for routing donor cash was more ingenious still. They created a 501(c)(6) nonprofit—typically used for business leagues and chambers of commerce—whose tax status could technically allow the Kochs and their donors to pour money into the political system and then write it off as a business expense.

Originally headed by an ex-Koch lobbyist named Wayne Gable, this operation routed more than a quarter-billion dollars to Noble's Center to Protect Patient Rights ($115 million), Americans for Prosperity ($32.3 million), and other groups in the year leading up to the 2012 election alone. The Kochs called their chamber of commerce the Association for American Innovation (it was later renamed Freedom Partners).

The Association for American Innovation was a cheeky moniker for a group bent on defeating the president, borrowing its name from an Obama administration economic policy called the "Strategy for American Innovation." The Association for American Innovation's founding documents, filed with the IRS, quoted the president and his strategy at length and suggested the group's mission centered on advancing key aspects of the president's policy. "This government policy and strategy is especially important today, when businesses, corporations, and even business innovation itself are under assault in the media and in the streets," its mission statement read.

What the group didn't say is that it planned to channel hundreds of millions of dollars into the 2012 elections in a bid to take down Obama and consolidate control of Congress. In fact, the Association for American Innovation told the IRS that it didn't expect to play in politics at all: "Though it does not presently intend to do so, AAI may, to an *insubstantial* extent, also conduct activities that might be viewed as supporting or opposing candidates for elective office."

The Koch faction's money, said the leader of one conservative nonprofit, always came with strings attached. "Nobody really works with them—they work for them, or they don't work with them at all," he said. "They are kind of creating a monopoly" and seeking to "make the conservative movement theirs."

The brothers' political advisors, including Kevin Gentry and Sean Noble, micromanaged the expenditure of donor funds, according to Republican operatives who have worked with them. "Sean Noble was down to editing direct mail copy," said a conservative strategist. Along with designing mailers, Koch operatives supplied political ads and approved messaging to recipients of Koch network cash. "If you want the money, here's what you're going to do with it," was the message from the brothers' political adjutants, said the leader of the conservative nonprofit. "These are the scripts you'll use." A GOP activist, who was employed by a group that received Koch donor cash, called contributions from the Koch network "directed grants."

Charles and David's top-down control, a Republican operative pointed out, conflicted with the decentralized, Market-Based Management practices of their company. "I joke with people that Obama, OFA [Obama for America], these guys operate from very much an entrepreneurial approach to politics, to advance more government, more of a state. Then you have these guys on the other side who are claiming they want to see less government, less spending, more diversified control, power, and they come from very much a command and control [perspective] to supposedly advance free-market entrepreneurism. It's ironic. It's centralized power to promote decentralized power."

The brothers closely monitored the groups they bankrolled. David, in particular, was known for asking probing questions of the leaders of these organizations. "You don't talk broad brush with David," said Nancy Pfotenhauer, the former Koch lobbyist who is a veteran of both Citizens for a Sound Economy and Americans for Prosperity. "You lose all credibility."

Americans for Prosperity board member James Miller said David "really raises questions, and if he doesn't get answers, he keeps boring in." Miller said the brothers have succeeded in their public policy philanthropy "because they've really gone about this in a businesslike manner" and because "they are hardheaded about making sure that the organizations are managed effectively."

But the brothers' "managerial approach to the movement," as Richard Wilcke, who headed the Koch-funded Council for a Competitive Economy, put it, has often caused friction. In the fall of 2011, Charles and David's effort to assert their authority over one of the cornerstones of their ideological empire ignited a civil war on the Right.

On October 26, 2011, seventy-eight-year-old William Niskanen, a former economic advisor to Ronald Reagan and the chairman emeritus of the Cato Institute, died after suffering a major stroke. His death brought a long-running (and secret) dispute between the Kochs and the leadership of the Cato Institute to an unavoidable head.

At issue was the unusual corporate structure of Cato, which had shareholders, unlike most nonprofits. (Before Charles excommunicated Murray Rothbard from the think tank in 1981, the libertarian economist had been one of them.)

Cato presently had four shareholders, including the Koch brothers and Ed Crane, Cato's cofounder and president. Niskanen was the fourth—and the question now was what would become of his stock. Would it pass to his widow, Kathryn Washburn, along with the rest of his estate? Or would it be handed back to Cato, leaving the Koch brothers in majority control? Ed Crane and Bob Levy, Cato's current board chairman, supported the former scenario. The Kochs and their advisors took the position that the shares were nontransferable, meaning the brothers controlled two-thirds of Cato and had the power to appoint the majority of the board.

When Cato was founded in 1977, Charles had pressed for this shareholder structure, believing it would provide an additional lever of control. Even as the composition of Cato's board changed over time, its shareholders could ensure that the institute never drifted from its founding mission of advancing libertarianism. Charles later organized the Council for a Competitive Economy

in the same way. "We want to make sure that we're not investing in something for ideological reasons that changes its focus,"
Richard Wilcke recalled Charles telling him of the shareholder
arrangement.

For close to two decades, Crane and other Cato officials had
tried to persuade Charles to reorganize the institute under a more
traditional scheme of nonprofit governance. Each time the subject
came up, Charles refused. But the issue could no longer be ignored.

Crane feared Charles would use Niskanen's death to make a
play for control of the think tank. Charles and David had become
politically toxic. The notion that they "owned" the think tank
would soil its independent reputation. "Who the hell is going
to take a think tank seriously that's controlled by billionaire oil
guys?" Crane wondered.

Relations between Ed Crane and Charles Koch had frayed
dramatically since Cato's founding. Before Richard Fink became
Charles's ideological soul mate, Crane had occupied this place in
the CEO's life. Crane called himself a "genetic libertarian." He and
Charles held nearly identical beliefs on personal liberties and free
markets. Crane didn't suck up to anyone—not politicians, not billionaires. Charles must have found this refreshing—at least at first.
In the early years, as Cato got off the ground, the pair consulted
by phone daily and they traveled together in the early 1980s to the
Soviet Union and China to see the depredations of communism up
close. But by 1991, their fifteen-year friendship had fallen apart.
Charles resigned from Cato's board and cut off his financial support. David, who joined the board in the 1980s, remained a director. The year Charles departed, he became a Cato shareholder.

Charles framed his split with Crane as a divergence of visions.
He told libertarian historian Brian Doherty: "I have strong ideas, I
want to see things go in a certain direction, and Crane has strong
ideas. I concluded, why argue with Ed? Rather than try to modify
his strategy, just go do my own thing and wish him well."

The sudden unraveling of their friendship perplexed Crane: "I'll go to my grave not knowing what happened."

One Cato scholar described their rift this way: "It's like a breakup. You kind of know what the reason was, but maybe you don't really understand why it ended."

Their friendship suffered a series of fractures before the final break. One came in the mid-1980s, when Charles was beginning to formalize his Market-Based Management theories and tried to implement them at Cato. At one point, Charles dispatched a team of Koch engineers to Washington to school Cato's staff in his management practices.

"We're all just looking at each other like, 'What the hell is this about?'" Crane recalled. "These guys were engineers, and you could tell that they didn't even understand what they were supposed to be teaching." Crane resisted the Market-Based Management regime, and Charles grudgingly let the matter drop.

In September 1990, during a second trip to the Soviet Union, Crane and Koch had another run-in. Cato was holding a landmark conference in Moscow at the Academy of Sciences' Uzkoe Hotel, where prominent Soviet scientists stayed during visits to the capital. The hotel was grim and worn, like a cut-rate college dormitory. Members of the Cato delegation were surprised to learn that the bedraggled building—which had three floors but whose elevator had buttons for ten—was less than two years old.

The signature event of the conference, dubbed "Transition to Freedom," was an open forum for Soviet citizens. At least 1,000 people attended, crowding into a room with a capacity of 700. The atmosphere was electric, charged with a sense of dawning freedom. In Crane's telling, the scene moved Charles so deeply that he approached Crane at the last minute to ask if he could speak at the event. Crane, who'd painstakingly choreographed the program, was brusque. "Charles, we have negotiated every 30 seconds here," Crane recalled telling him. "I can't do that."

Charles and Liz, who was traveling with her husband, departed Moscow the next day, cutting their trip short without explanation.

In Charles's version of this story, he never asked to speak, though he did pull Crane aside with concerns about the conference agenda—that it didn't delve deeply enough into the difficult transition from state-planned society to free-market economy. Crane, according to Charles, brushed these concerns aside.

Whatever took place, the conference formed a line of demarcation in their friendship. Political scientist Charles Murray, who presented there, recalled his surprise at Charles's sudden departure. Members of the Cato group had planned a sightseeing trip to Leningrad, where Murray hoped to introduce some Russian acquaintances to a real American billionaire. "They really wanted to see the billionaire," he recalled. Instead, he was forced to point out another wealthy member of their party: "That guy's worth about $600 million."

Murray remembered spending the evening before the citizens' forum locked in boisterous debate with Ed Crane and Charles Koch over Saddam Hussein's invasion of Kuwait the previous month. Crane and Koch, as usual, were simpatico: "I was being backed into a corner by both Charles and Ed because I was not as unequivocally anti-retaking Kuwait as they were." He added, "Charles and Ed were as I had always seen them, which was a very joking, very warm relationship.... They were completely as they had always been."

After Moscow, their relationship never recovered. By late 1990, the *Rothbard-Rockwell Report*, a libertarian newsletter authored by Murray Rothbard and former Ron Paul chief of staff Lew Rockwell, was gleefully reporting that Crane's star had sunk within the Kochtopus, while Richard Fink's had risen. "Richie, under Charles, now holds total power in Wichita," Rothbard's newsletter reported. It had to be true—Charles was no longer taking Crane's calls.

"What I learned is, never piss off a billionaire," Crane joked at a Cato gala years later, according to one think tank staffer, who said his boss occasionally made light of his bitter falling-out with Charles.

If only Crane had actually learned his lesson.

The bad blood between Crane and Koch was decades in the past, but a recent episode had reopened old wounds. *The New Yorker*'s Jane Mayer, in her August 2010 article about the Koch brothers, quoted a "top Cato official" disparaging Charles and Market-Based Management, a point of pride for the CEO who considered this philosophy the source of his company's success and the bed-rock of his legacy. Charles "thinks he's a genius," this official said. "He's the emperor, and he's convinced he's wearing clothes."

The remark infuriated Charles, and he and David were con-vinced they knew its source. The month after the story ran, David confronted Crane during a phone call. Was he Mayer's "top Cato official"? Crane eventually fessed up. "Charles is really upset," David told him during the call, according to Crane.

The brothers' next move wasn't subtle. That December, Charles called a Cato stockholders meeting, and the brothers invoked their shares for the first time anyone at the think tank could remem-ber to appoint two new board members—Nancy Pfotenhauer, the former Koch lobbyist, and Kevin Gentry, the brothers' chief fund-raiser and the organizer of their donor conferences. Both were Koch loyalists and neither was considered much of a libertarian (though Pfotenhauer, at least, had studied at George Mason Uni-versity, under libertarian economist Walter Williams). "Anybody who even suggests that they are libertarians has got their head somewhere where the sun isn't shining," Cato chairman Bob Levy fumed. Crane stewed over the board appointments.

Crane possessed a legendary temper, and his fury over the Kochs' power play finally erupted. In March 2011, during a board dinner held on the last Thursday of the month, Crane discussed Cato's ongoing capital fund-raising campaign. Pfotenhauer, a petite and telegenic blonde who started her career as a Republican National Committee economist, chimed in with a question. Crane had detailed plans for expanding Cato's physical facilities, but what was his vision for the think tank's policy team? she wondered.

Crane's short fuse turned to ash before everyone's eyes. "Let me say something about these two new Koch operatives who have been placed on this board," he snarled, crimson-faced, from his seat at the head of the table. He pointed to Kevin Gentry: "Kevin Gentry seated over there, has never once—never once!—invited me or any Cato scholar to speak at the donor conferences he organizes for Charles Koch."

He rounded on Pfotenhauer. "How would you ever know anything about Cato's policy priorities?"

Crane stomped off, as slack-jawed board members and Cato executives looked on.

"This was the accumulation of lots of things that were done by the Koch faction that Ed both thought were wrong as a management matter, and took personally," said Bob Levy, who was present. "You certainly could say that Ed was provoked over a period of time, and this really was sort of the straw that broke the camel's back."

Later that year, when William Niskanen died suddenly, tensions between Crane and the Kochs reached a boiling point.

The week after Niskanen's funeral, Levy flew from his home in Naples, Florida, to Dulles Airport, in the Virginia exurbs outside Washington DC. The seventy-year-old Cato chairman had requested an audience with David Koch. At the busy billionaire's request, they arranged to meet at the airport, in a bland conference room attached to the hangar where David's jet was parked.

Levy was a self-made millionaire who had started and subsequently sold a financial research firm, reinventing himself in his fifties as a lawyer and constitutional scholar. Levy hoped to avert a clash between the Crane and Koch camps over Niskanen's shares. He wanted to gauge where both sides stood and see if there was any common ground on which to build an agreement.

Richard Fink and Kevin Gentry accompanied David to the meeting. The mood was tense from the outset. Crane's belligerent treatment of Pfotenhauer and Gentry had angered David, who informed Levy bluntly that he and his brother wanted Crane gone within eight weeks, preferably sooner. Cato wouldn't get a penny of his money, David said, until he felt it was back on the right path and under responsible leadership.

The Kochs didn't just want a management change. The brothers and their advisors believed the think tank should do more to advance their political agenda in the upcoming election. The Republican Party, for all its flaws, offered the best hope for halting the country's slide to socialism, David told Levy. Cato, he said, needed to start translating "esoteric concepts into concrete deliverables."

What in the world did this even mean? Levy wondered.

"We would like you to provide intellectual ammunition that we can then use at Americans for Prosperity and our allied organizations," David explained, according to Levy.

Levy was puzzled. Cato produced plenty of intellectual ammo, if that's how you wanted to view the position papers and policy recommendations its scholars produced. Americans for Prosperity and any other outfit was free to use Cato's materials to blast away at Obama and the Democrats.

"What gives you the impression that we aren't providing intellectual ammunition?" Levy inquired. He never got a straight answer. After the meeting, Levy flew back home to Florida with a foreboding feeling.

*　　*　　*

The hostilities escalated throughout the winter of 2012, as both sides fruitlessly tried to reach a compromise. In return for eliminating the shareholder agreement, Levy offered to begin a search for Crane's successor and give the brothers veto power over his replacement—the Koch brothers rejected the proposal. The Kochs proposed entering nonbinding mediation and later floated a plan for a "standstill agreement" until after the presidential election—Crane and Levy declined both offers.

In March 2012, the internal struggle leapt into public view. Crane had scheduled a shareholders meeting on March 1, where he planned to recognize Niskanen's widow. Charles and David responded with a lawsuit to force Kathryn Washburn to relinquish her husband's shares. And they used their Cato stock to install four handpicked board members, including Charles himself, displacing four existing directors.

"They thought we would back down rather than risk additional criticism from them and others on top of the many attacks we already face from opponents of a free society," Charles said in a rare public statement. "They thought wrong."

On the afternoon of March 2, Crane convened about a dozen mostly senior Cato officials in a conference room on the seventh floor of the institute's headquarters, where its executives have their offices. One attendee described it as a "war meeting" that was led by Crane's fastidious number two, David Boaz, who'd worked for the think tank since the salad days on San Francisco's Montgomery Street. When Cato's strange corporate structure was explained, there was a moment of surprise among staffers, who assumed the institute had been set up like any other nonprofit. "A lot of us had no idea we had shareholders," the attendee recalled. But the meeting quickly turned pragmatic, he said, into "how do we stop this." They discussed the coming news onslaught, and later a multipage internal memo of talking points was distributed to participants. It read in part:

> Charles and David Koch have told Cato chairman Robert A. Levy that they intend to use their legal powers to remove Ed Crane, pack Cato's board of directors, and coordinate Cato's activities more closely with organizations that have political agendas. Predictably, their plans and motivations are not open and transparent. Charles Koch, David Koch and their representatives have publicly and privately declared their admiration for Ed Crane's achievements which they describe as "remarkable" and "incredibly effective over the years." Nevertheless David Koch told Bob Levy that the Koch family could only support Cato if Crane were removed as president. Koch offered no substantive reason for that demand. In a separate conversation Levy asked Charles Koch why he insisted on removing Crane after 35 years against the will of the board. Koch had no explanation other than that the two had a falling out some 20 years ago. The Kochs told Levy that they focused on defeating President Obama in 2012 and to that end they would like Cato to be the source of intellectual ammunition on key issues, advancing the efforts of Americans for Prosperity and allied groups by providing position papers, a media presence, and speakers on hot button issues.

Around Cato's Massachusetts Avenue offices, in a modernistic cube of a building with a glass façade, staffers expressed anger but also befuddlement. Many scholars owed their careers, at least in part, to Charles and David's philanthropy. They had done internships or fellowships sponsored by Charles's foundation, participated in seminars or summer programs held by the Koch-funded Institute for Humane Studies, worked their way up through any number of nonprofits that received backing from the brothers, or all of the above.

"You're talking about people at Cato who are big fans of Charles and David Koch," Levy said, "so it's inexplicable to them that the Kochs would do what they're doing."

The Kochs might as well have taken a bat to this hive of libertarian thought. Within days of the lawsuit, Catoites set up a "Save Cato" Facebook page and took to an assortment of blogs and news outlets to decry the alleged coup. "I don't think they expected the Institution itself would reject their move," said a Cato scholar. "When you take over an oil company, people might be scared they're going to be fired, but you're not going to have principled opposition. It's not a question of whether you have a business when you're done."

If the Kochs gained control, Cato scholars and executives privately discussed resorting to the "Taiwan option"—forming a new think tank with the backing of Cato donors who remained loyal to Crane.

The Kochs and Crane, meanwhile, traded barbs in the press and via terse public statements. Crane accused the Kochs of an effort to "turn the Cato Institute into some sort of auxiliary for the GOP." And he doubled down on his comments about Market-Based Management, calling Charles's *Science of Success*, in an interview with *Slate*, "one of the worst books ever written." David, resurrecting a charge once lobbed at Bill Koch during the brothers' legal entanglements, blasted Crane for pursuing a "rule or ruin" strategy.

The Kochs' reputation in libertarian and conservative circles for attempting to foist control over organizations they funded left them with scarce allies. *Breitbart*, the right-wing website founded by the late conservative firebrand Andrew Breitbart, emerged as one of their few defenders. It ran a series of unbylined articles that portrayed Ed Crane as a petulant, power-mad tyrant willing to burn the think tank to the ground if he could not run it. The eponymous website also floated thinly sourced allegations of sexual harassment by Crane, rumors amplified by websites associated with members of a libertarian faction loyal to the late Murray Rothbard.

Meanwhile, libertarian scholars and other allies on the Right closed ranks around their Cato comrades, pleading with the brothers publicly to back down, lest they do "irreparable harm to the credibility of Cato" and "undermine our community's intellectual defenses" at the worst possible time, as the leadership of FreedomWorks said in a statement. Liberals, usually only too glad to pillory Cato, joined in the anti-Koch pile-on. The enemy of their enemy was their friend.

The Kochs expected the wrath of the Left. Little did they imagine that as the 2012 presidential election loomed, they would take heavy fire from within the movement they had helped to create.

The Cato conflagration distracted from the main battle the Kochs were fighting against the Obama administration. When the president's reelection campaign unleashed its first ad of the general election in mid-January 2012, the spot didn't trifle with Mitt Romney, Newt Gingrich, or any of the other Republican contenders; they were doing a good enough job of eviscerating one another without outside help. Team Obama, rather, directed its fire at the Koch brothers, whom David Axelrod, the president's chief political strategist, had dubbed "contract killers in super-PAC land."

"Secretive oil billionaires attacking President Obama with ads fact checkers say are 'not tethered to the facts,'" the ad's narrator intoned. A still frame of an Americans for Prosperity issue ad, targeting Obama for his support of the bankrupt solar company Solyndra, flashed on the screen.

The president's political advisors devised the "secretive oil billionaires" ad as part of a carefully calibrated strategy to defang the Kochs and neutralize the impact of their attack ads. "Given the experience of 2010, at the outset of 2011 we were scared to death that between the Koch brothers and [Karl Rove's American] Crossroads that the campaign would be outspent by hundreds of millions of dollars," recalled Ben LaBolt, the Obama campaign's press secretary.

The fear of being outspent by the Kochs and their allies drove the Obama campaign, already known as pioneers in the use of microtargeting and voter analytics, to become that much more data-focused. "You can count the concern about the Koch brothers and the outside groups" in the dozens of staffers the campaign allocated to its analytics department, said Larry Grisolano, who oversaw the Obama campaign's advertising. Heading into the election, there remained only a small sliver of the electorate—perhaps 15 percent—who could be swayed left or right. Plans by the Kochs to dump hundreds of millions of dollars into the election motivated the Obama campaign to strive for ruthless efficiency in its own expenditures. The campaign developed a system called "the Optimizer," which mingled voter and TV viewer data and guided its hypertargeted ad strategy. The campaign couldn't play "the traditional advertising game of casting a really broad net and hoping that you get the fish," Grisolano said. "We wanted to basically have a very laser-like focus on where those targets were and have as little spillage into inefficient targets as possible. It was all because of our pre-occupation with spending by the Koch brothers and other outside groups."

The "secretive oil billionaires" ad was born of the Obama team's realization that it could not refute Americans for Prosperity ad for ad. When the campaign focus-grouped possible responses to Americans for Prosperity's attack ads, it found that viewers often disregarded the group's message once they became aware of AFP's connection to the billionaire Koch brothers. "If you just outlined who the Koch brothers were in that response ad," said LaBolt, "then people tended to discredit the argument. You could educate people about what AFP was, so that they would remember when they saw subsequent advertisements who was behind it."

The Obama campaign's debut ad reminded voters—as it would do over and over again throughout the election—that a pair of petrochemical billionaires lurked behind many of the political ads attacking the president. According to Grisolano, the campaign found that the name "Americans for Prosperity" itself made some voters suspicious. It sounded like a front group. "They kind of helped us in this idea of the secretive oil billionaires by the ambiguity of the name and what their aims were."

The Obama campaign's opening salvo touched a nerve. Former George W. Bush administration solicitor general Ted Olson, who represented Koch Industries, fired back in a *Wall Street Journal* op-ed that accused President Obama and his reelection team of engaging in Nixonian tactics against the Koch brothers in a "multiyear, carefully orchestrated campaign of vituperation."

The Obama campaign had no plans of retreating. In February, Obama's campaign manager Jim Messina invoked the brothers in a fund-raising appeal, noting that Mitt Romney, who was scheduled to appear at an Americans for Prosperity event, was courting men "whose business model is to make millions by jacking up prices at the pump" and "who bankrolled Tea Party extremism."

By March, as the Cato feud went public, the Obama team and Koch Industries were dueling in deliciously passive-aggressive open letters. "It is an abuse of the President's position and does a disservice to our nation for the President and his campaign to criticize private citizens simply for the act of engaging in their constitutional right of free speech about important matters of public policy," chided Philip Ellender, the president of Koch Industries' government and public affairs division.

Messina, who carefully tracked Americans for Prosperity's

spending on a whiteboard in his Chicago office, only too gladly replied: "It is a cynical stretch to describe the political activities of your employers as furthering democracy when they are courting huge checks from special interest donors to pay for negative ads, with no public disclosure of the identity of those donors." He challenged the Kochs to disclose Americans for Prosperity's contributors, who, the brothers' representatives insisted, disingenuously, were largely average citizens from "across the country and from all walks of life."

By May, the tit-for-tat graduated to web videos, each side responding acidly to the latest provocation.

"You may have heard of the Koch brothers," Obama's deputy campaign manager Stephanie Cutter said, speaking directly into the camera and betraying more than a tinge of annoyance. "...These guys are going to say whatever it takes to tear down the president. They will literally say anything....So we're going to call their BS when we see it."

Koch Industries' PR shop retorted with its own slickly produced video: "Yet again, low-minded invective aimed at job creators. The president and his campaign offer no solutions and no principled discussion."

While the bitter Republican primary campaign slogged on, it was as if President Obama were running against the Koch brothers.

While Charles and David fought for the political soul of the country and did battle over Cato, their brother Bill was busy waging wars of his own—against such evildoers as shady wine dealers and Oxbow employees he suspected of fraud. These fights, as usual, involved high-priced lawyers, shadowy investigators, and made-for-TV-movie-style intrigue.

By 2012, Bill was seven years into his latest legal crusade, one that had begun in 2005 when Boston's Museum of Fine Arts was preparing an exhibition of his eclectic collections of art and memorabilia called "Things I Love." He counted four bottles of eighteenth-century French wine, two Brane Mouton and two Lafite, engraved with the initials "Th.J," among the jewels of his collection. Bill had purchased the wine, said to have belonged to Thomas Jefferson, for $500,000 in 1988. But as his aides attempted to trace the provenance of the Jefferson bottles in preparation for the show, the story behind them grew murkier and murkier. It began to look like they were fakes.

If there was one thing that got Bill's blood boiling and drew out his most obsessive impulses, it was being cheated. "I've bought so much art, so many guns, so many other things, that if somebody's out to cheat me I want the son of a bitch to pay for it," he has said. Bill wanted the SOB who'd peddled the bogus Jefferson bottles to be locked up, and he turned to retired FBI agent Jim Elroy to spearhead the investigation. Elroy, whose cell phone ring tone was the theme for *The Good, the Bad, and the Ugly*, had a long history with Bill. They'd known each other since the late 1980s, when the veteran agent had worked on the Senate investigation that implicated Koch Industries in widespread oil theft from Native American lands. Since retiring from the FBI, Elroy had frequently performed investigative work for Bill, and he put together an international team of detectives that included a former Scotland Yard Inspector and an ex-MI6 agent to pursue the case.

The investigation led from Monticello, Thomas Jefferson's historic estate in Charlottesville, Virginia, to the Alps of southeastern France, where Elroy, toting two bulletproof suitcases that held the Jefferson bottles and two other suspected counterfeits, traveled to have them isotope-tested by a scientist who'd pioneered a novel method for dating wine. Though these tests proved inconclusive, Elroy also had the engravings on the Jefferson bottles analyzed. He discovered that only a power tool—perhaps a dental drill—could have made the markings.

The deeper Elroy looked, the deeper the fraud seemed to go. The problem went beyond a few phony bottles. Forgeries, shady dealers, and shadowy middlemen plagued the industry. Collectors who realized they'd been duped, meanwhile, often placed their counterfeit bottles back up for auction, offloading them on the next rube. Soon Bill's investigation expanded beyond the Jefferson bottles. He wanted to purge the industry of fake wine, one cheat at a time.

Bill and his inner circle thought about this quest—which at first had focused on a mysterious German wine aficionado named Hardy Rodenstock, the man who claimed to have discovered the Jefferson bottles—in cinematic terms. "This is *National Treasure*," his spokesman Brad Goldstein told Benjamin Wallace, author of *The Billionaire's Vinegar*, which recounts the gripping tale of the bogus Jefferson bottles. When it came to casting, Bill's aides joked that Michael Caine should play their boss in the movie version.

Before long, Bill presided over at least six civil lawsuits. He took on the wine auction house Zachys (eventually settling with the company) and sued Christie's (the case was ultimately thrown out). And he pursued alleged counterfeiters Hardy Rodenstock (who denied peddling phony wine and managed to elude Bill's legal dragnet, despite a default judgment entered against him) and Rudy Kurniawan (an Indonesian wine dealer who was arrested by the FBI in March 2012 and subsequently convicted of fraud).

One of Bill's recent targets was Silicon Valley entrepreneur Eric Greenberg, who Bill alleged had knowingly sold him two-dozen bottles of counterfeit Bordeaux—their vintages ranging from 1864 to 1950—for $355,000. Greenberg and his lawyer said that, upon learning the bottles were fakes, the tech tycoon repeatedly offered to reimburse Bill, but the billionaire rebuffed these entreaties. He wanted to make an example out of Greenberg—and eventually he did. In April 2013, Bill stood triumphantly outside a federal district courthouse in lower Manhattan clutching a bottle of bogus 1921 Château Pétrus, having won a jury award of nearly $380,000. (He was later awarded $12 million in punitive damages.) "I absolutely can't stand to be cheated," Bill told reporters. "Now we got one faker so we're marching down our hit list of fakers. This is just a start." Then he decamped to a pricey French restaurant on Manhattan's Upper East Side to savor his victory over a glass of fine wine.

Bill pursued crooked wine dealers like some litigious, latter-day Wyatt Earp, but he reserved a special brand of justice for employees of his energy company Oxbow who he believed had ripped him off.

In 2011, Bill had received a one-page anonymous letter. It accused three Oxbow employees—Larry Black, Kirby Martensen, and Charlie Zhan—of lining their pockets by secretly selling shipments of petroleum coke at preferential pricing to third-party buyers in China. Black, who oversaw the company's petroleum coke sales in Asia and was based in the Bay Area, had worked for Oxbow since 1984, rising to become the executive vice president of a subsidiary called Oxbow Carbon. He supervised Martensen, one of Oxbow's star salesmen in the Pacific Rim, who had recently relocated to Singapore at the company's request; and Zhan, a Chinese national who managed an Oxbow office in Tianjin, located in Northern China.

Though Bill had dabbled in alternative energy in the 1980s and 1990s, he ultimately built his business on more traditional energy sources. He owned coal mines in the western United States, and his company had become the world's largest distributor of petroleum coke ("petcoke," in industry shorthand), shipping 11 million metric tons of this coal-like fuel source annually. Asia—particularly Japan and Korea—was one of Oxbow's most lucrative markets.

After receiving the anonymous tip, Bill quietly launched an extensive internal investigation that included a forensic review of his employees' communications, including their e-mails and Skype records.

Bill grew convinced that there was indeed fraud afoot in his Asia operation, and by March 2012, he was finally ready to confront the culprits. He invited Black, Martensen, Zhan, and a few of their colleagues to attend a retreat at Bear Ranch, his 4,500-acre spread located a two-hour drive from Aspen. On this property, hemmed in by the Anthracite Range and the West Elk Mountains, Bill was constructing an elaborate replica of an Old West town. It featured dozens of buildings, including five saloons, a bank, a church, and even a faux brothel (which was being converted into guest quarters). The structures had come largely from a decommissioned MGM tourist attraction, which Bill bought for $3.1 million in 2010 and reassembled on his property. Showcasing his extensive collection of Western memorabilia, including a Springfield rifle that once belonged to General George Custer, the town served as a purely private playground for friends, family, and other guests. "It all gets back to trying to create a place where I can enjoy life and enjoy my family and friends without having to worry about my enemies," he once said. "And I'm doing it because I can."

Yet, in this instance, Bill had decided to lure his enemies to his refuge for a showdown. Black, who'd attended business meetings at Bear Ranch in the past, was told the purpose of the two-day retreat was to review his group's sales strategy and go over their 2011 results. The executive welcomed the opportunity. His division had just completed a record year, generating more than $200 million in profits.

On March 21, Black, Martensen, and Zhan flew from San Francisco to Aspen, where they had lunch with Bill at his home in the resort town, before lighting out together by car for his ranch. That evening, Bill wined and dined his guests at the main lodge on the property, where everyone spent the night. Cell phone service at the ranch was nonexistent, and the Oxbow employees were informed that the landline and Internet were down. This was no accident. The phone and Internet service had been deliberately cut off to prevent Bill's employees from communicating with the outside world.

After breakfast the following day, Black delivered a sales presentation. Then the visiting Oxbow employees drove out to the site of Bill's Western town, where the billionaire had organized a helicopter tour of the area. Lunch followed in the still-under-construction town, and afterward Bill announced unexpectedly that he wanted to hold employee reviews. Black, Martensen, and Zhan were split up and led into separate buildings.

Black and the others had started to get an eerie feeling—and not just from the Wild West décor and period weaponry on display. Something didn't feel right, but they had little choice but to go along with whatever their boss had planned. Bill conducted Black's review personally, asking the Oxbow executive vice president to assess the performance of Martensen, Zhan, and others. Black offered high praise for the members of his team.

Bill's genial demeanor quickly turned accusatory.

How would he feel about Zhan's performance if he knew that the Chinese national was stealing from Oxbow? Bill asked. And, he probed, "Would you feel the same way about Kirby if you thought he stole from the company?" Black was stunned. Bill walked out of the room and returned with a large stack of papers. One by one Bill showed Black documents, telling the executive that Zhan and Martensen had taken part in an elaborate conspiracy to defraud the company; it involved the purchase of Oxbow's petroleum coke at discounted rates by companies linked to Zhan, which went on to sell the product in China at high profit margins. A hidden camera rolled as Bill questioned Black, and in a nearby control room two Oxbow lawyers monitored the interview, along with the interrogations of Zhan and Martensen elsewhere in the town.

Oxbow chief operating officer Steven Fried and another employee grilled Martensen, a fifteen-year Oxbow veteran in his late forties. According to Martensen, they questioned him relentlessly for several hours, accusing him of accepting kickbacks from Zhan. At around 5:00 p.m., they escorted the shaken Oxbow salesman to a waiting SUV and told him to sit in the back. On the outskirts of Bill's town, the car stopped and a man handed a sheaf of documents to Martensen through an open window. These were his termination papers; he'd also been served with a lawsuit alleging that he, Black, and Zhan had defrauded Oxbow of millions.

Martensen was driven back to the main house on the ranch, which was now swarming with at least eight security guards. This contingent included current and former police officers with the Palm Beach and West Palm Beach police departments, who were moonlighting on Bill's security detail. Jim Elroy, Bill's loyal investigator, ran point on the operation and managed the security team.

One of the guards searched Martensen's bags and took away his company cell phone, replacing it with a cheap, prepaid mobile. Black experienced the same treatment. Neither of the men dared to use the cell phones, believing they might be tapped.

A member of Bill's security detail took Martensen to a cabin not far from the main lodge. A squad car from the Gunnison County Sheriff's Office sat outside. "A sheriff is here to make sure you don't wander off," the guard told him, according to Martensen. The fired executive spent the next several hours inside the cabin, panicking about the fate Bill Koch had in store for him. Was he going to be arrested? Martensen didn't know it at the time, but the cop posted outside his door was an off-duty sheriff's deputy who was being paid $50 an hour to be on the premises. (The department later placed the deputy on administrative leave and investigated him for misconduct, though no further action was taken.)

Martensen was finally told he'd be taken to the airport. He and Zhan were placed in an SUV, driven by two off-duty Palm Beach police officers. According to Martensen, he asked them to drive him to Aspen, where he was booked on a return flight to San Francisco the next morning. But the off-duty officers said other travel arrangements had been made. They instead drove three hours past Aspen to a small airport in Denver. When they arrived at 2:00 a.m., a private plane was waiting. On board, in addition to the pilot and copilot, was a former police officer who Martensen believed was armed. "For all intents and purposes," he would later recall, "especially after the policeman is parked outside the front door and I'm held in a room for three-and-a-half hours and then I'm told to get in the car and we're going to Denver, not the place I want to go. For all practical purposes, I'm under arrest."

The plane touched down in Oakland, California, at 4:00 a.m. Martensen's escort wanted to take him to a nearby Marriott hotel, but he refused. Martensen asked an airport employee to call him a cab and drove off into the darkness wondering what the hell had just happened to him.

Very little about the Bear Ranch episode made sense. Black, who'd been flown by private jet to Denver, before boarding a Southwest flight back to San Francisco, reconnected with Martensen and Zhan in the Bay Area on Friday, March 23. The men felt as if they'd just lived through the plot of a corporate thriller. Together, they read through the legal complaint against them, and Black learned that some of the accusations Bill had made against Martensen and Zhan were true. Zhan had indeed worked with a company called Nova Industries to resell Oxbow's petcoke in China. And Martensen had received payments of some $50,000 from Zhan. ("I gave this money to Kirby Martensen in exchange for his agreement to keep secret my improper involvement and arrangements with Nova," Zhan later said in a deposition. Bill eventually dropped Zhan and Black from the suit, but continued to pursue his case against Martensen.)

Martensen and Zhan had clearly committed fireable offenses—

but this begged the question: Why hadn't Bill simply fired them and filed suit? Why bring them out to Bear Ranch, give them a scenic helicopter tour, then drop the hammer? "I've known Bill for 28 years. He's the world's greatest planner," Black reflected later. "And he spends lots of money getting everything right....It was very well orchestrated. And this is the type of thing that Bill does."

The whole psychodrama seemed to fulfill little more than a primal desire for retribution. Bill, apparently unable to fathom that the questionable events at Bear Ranch could have any repercussions, was surprised and outraged when Kirby Martensen later retaliated with a lawsuit of his own. It accused the billionaire of kidnapping and false imprisonment. (The case is scheduled to go to trial in November 2014.)

Their legal fight also surfaced accusations that potentially had broader ramifications for Bill and his business empire. After filing suit against Bill, Martensen approached the Internal Revenue Service with allegations that Oxbow had engaged in a major tax evasion scheme.

Martensen divulged that, in 2010, Bill's company had created an entity called Oxbow International, located in the Bahamas. "The idea as explained to me in several conference calls was if Oxbow transferred its supply contracts (...with refineries that supplied petroleum coke to Oxbow) to OI and changed the point at which title was transferred to Oxbow's overseas customers from at ships rail at the load port, which is standard, to 'on the high seas, in international waters,' this would satisfy the basic requirements of the I.R.S.," Martensen told the agency in a whistleblower complaint (which is currently pending).

Meanwhile, according to Martensen, sales deals that Oxbow had previously completed in the United States the company now consummated in the Bahamas, where the tax rate was 15 percent; he estimated that during 2010 and 2011, Bill's company dodged paying $70 million in taxes. "It was clear no one wanted to explain to Bill that what we were asked to do may not be legal and certainly not ethical," he said. Martensen, Black, and other members of his division privately griped about the legality of this tax scheme via e-mail—missives, it turned out, that Bill and his investigators were closely monitoring. "It is strongly believed that our questioning of the tax avoidance scheme Oxbow had implemented... was a major contributor to our being fired," Martensen told the IRS.

Martensen's lawyers did not stop there: They also investigated possible anticompetitive practices by Oxbow at the Port of Long Beach, outside Los Angeles, where Bill's company controlled a significant amount of the shipping of petroleum coke and coal bound for the Asian market. Martensen's lawyers also pressed the Colorado Bureau of Investigation to launch a criminal probe into their client's false imprisonment charges. (The bureau declined to prosecute.)

If this onslaught hadn't targeted Bill, he would have had to admire the tactics of bringing all forms of pressure to bear on a legal adversary—a move right out of his own playbook.

Like their brother, Charles and David had underestimated their rivals. Their fight with the leadership of the Cato Institute triggered a severe backlash. Bad press was one thing, but the brothers also came under intense pressure from friends and members of their donor network. "People who had been around them their entire lives refused to speak to them," said a conservative activist.

Cato's chairman Bob Levy noted: "There's a lot of overlap between Cato donors and Koch donors.... And a lot of the folks who know both organizations were very upset by all of this, and I think made their views known, both to us and to David and Charles."

In the late spring of 2012, negotiations between the two warring sides quietly commenced. Both factions realized that if they maintained their current course, there might be nothing left to fight over—Cato would be reduced to rubble. Real estate investor Howard Rich, a longtime Cato board member who had worked with Charles in the past to promote libertarian causes, was among the Cato emissaries who traveled to Wichita to hammer out an accord with the CEO and his lawyers, according to Levy. Over two months, during a pair of meetings in Wichita and a series of conference calls, the outlines of an agreement took shape. Though a formal deal wouldn't be signed until late September, the cessation of the Cato-Koch feud was made official on the afternoon of June 25, when anxious Cato staffers piled into the think tank's Friedrich Hayek auditorium.

Levy outlined the agreement, announcing that Charles and David Koch had finally agreed to get rid of the shareholder agreement, ensuring Cato's lasting independence. In return, Ed Crane would have to step down. Libertarian philanthropist John A. Allison IV, a friend of Charles's and the former CEO of BB&T Bank, would replace him. Allison, who hailed from North Carolina, was known for handing out copies of Ayn Rand's *Atlas Shrugged* to new bank executives.

Under the deal, Cato's sixteen-member board would have four members, including David, selected by the Kochs. The think tank's directors in the future would choose their own successors. Along with stepping down as Cato's president, Crane was also forced to relinquish his seat on Cato's board. The sixty-eight-year-old, once described as "the lion king of button-down libertarianism," had poured more than half his life into Cato and its broader mission of advancing the libertarian worldview. Leaving it behind was agonizing.

"Basically, it was taken from him," said Levy. "He would not have stepped down when he did.... And it wouldn't have been under those circumstances. And it wouldn't have been to settle a disagreement with the Kochs, because I'm sure there's still difficulty between those parties." Levy added, "He definitely didn't like it. There's no question about that."

On his final day as a Cato employee later that year, Crane alluded only briefly to the "recent unpleasantness" in a short farewell e-mail to staff. "The essence of the American Experiment is a respect for the dignity of the individual," he wrote. "It is axiomatic that such dignity depends on liberty. That is what Cato is all about."

Crane signed off simply, "Aloha."

"In the end," said one friend of Crane's, "they paid him a fat sum. He left with a gag in his mouth and a non-compete clause that barely lets him get dressed in the morning."

In early July 2012, two weeks after the Cato settlement was announced, a small plane buzzed over the Atlantic, flying past David's $18 million Southampton estate. A large banner fluttered behind it: MITT ROMNEY HAS A KOCH PROBLEM. A cheer rose up through the throng of protestors who had gathered on the beach near the billionaire's home.

During David's bachelor days, the beachfront mansion had been the site of all-night parties that drew comparisons to Hugh Hefner's debauchery-filled soirees. On July 8, a more subdued crowd queued up on Meadow Lane in Range Rovers, Benzes, and Beamers awaiting entry to a $50,000-a-head fund-raiser ($75,000 per couple) benefiting the former Massachusetts governor.

Romney had clinched the Republican presidential nomination in late May, following a brutal primary fight in which the candidates had done Obama's work for him by savaging one another. Newt Gingrich, after all, had helped to cast Romney as a "vulture capitalist," whose tenure at private equity firm Bain Capital involved enriching himself while destroying jobs and businesses. The Obama campaign only too happily added to this portrait once Romney emerged as the de facto nominee. Thanks to the Tea Par-

tyized atmosphere, Romney—a historically moderate, Northeast-
ern Republican whose health-care reform effort in Massachusetts
formed the inspiration for Obama's—was running on a "severely
conservative" platform. Doing so forced him to engage in the kind
of political contortionism that made it seem like he was willing to
say anything to get elected.

David had supported Romney during his 2008 White House
bid. And in August 2010, before Romney officially announced his
second attempt on the presidency, he and Julia convened a Hamptons mixer for the politician attended by about 150 well-heeled
donors, including New York financier and former Port Authority
chairman Lew Eisenberg, private equity investor Donald Marron,
and real estate billionaire Stephen Ross. Despite this early signal
of support, David had changed horses by 2011 and pledged his
backing to Chris Christie, should the New Jersey governor decide
to enter the race.

In October 2011, after Christie publicly put an end to any presidential speculation, Romney quickly reached out to David seeking his endorsement, according to an internal Romney campaign
memo that described the Koch brother as "the financial engine of
the Tea Party." The following month, pursuing David's support,
Romney even skipped the famous Ronald Reagan Dinner in Des
Moines—where the other Republican hopefuls had gathered to
court Iowa voters ahead of the state's bellwether primary—to keynote an Americans for Prosperity conference in DC.

But David withheld his formal support until the candidate van-
quished his GOP rivals. "David very much admired Romney's
success in business and his values," said a close friend. "I know
that David and Romney and Romney's wife and Julia bonded. So
I think he was very much a Romney supporter." The friend added,
chuckling: "Charles loved the governor from New Mexico, Gary
Johnson," the Libertarian Party's presidential candidate.

David's twin brother, Bill, by contrast, did not play hard to get with his endorsement. His relationship with Romney stretched back to the 1980s, before Bill relocated from Massachusetts to Florida. Long before Romney clinched the nomination, Bill and companies he controlled began pouring money into Restore Our Future, the pro-Romney super-PAC. Over the course of the campaign, Bill steered at least $2 million to the group and hosted two Restore Our Future fund-raisers at his Palm Beach mansion. During one of them, held during the second half of 2012, the super-PAC's fund-raisers displayed a PowerPoint presentation outlining their strategy. One slide contained a picture of a Frederic Remington painting, depicting a Union cavalry officer galloping forward, gun drawn. The super-PAC, this image was meant to convey, was Romney's cavalry. Bill, according to an attendee, couldn't help pointing out that he owned the painting.

Bill also held multiple fund-raisers for the candidate himself, and he contributed more than just cash to Romney's candidacy. During a 2011 visit to Homeport, Bill's Cape Cod property, Romney recounted the story of how his parents read to him from Irving Stone's *Men to Match My Mountains* during childhood drives through national parks. Bill interrupted, saying, "You know, the title of that book comes from a poem." And he began to recite it.

Bring me men to match my mountains,
Bring me men to match my plains.
Men with empires in their purpose,
And new eras in their brains.

Romney committed Sam Walter Foss's 1894 poem "The Coming American" to memory and thereafter it became a fixture of his stump speech.

Before the July fund-raiser at the Kochs' Southampton compound, David and Julia huddled privately with the Romneys. Whatever was said during their half-hour tête-à-tête, the men emerged from an upstairs room with a confident glow about them, descending "like two world leaders with their first ladies," according to one guest. The Kochs served a simple dinner of tomato and mozzarella corn fritters and chicken and arugula salad to their guests. David was overheard that evening telling attendees soberly, "We can't afford these levels of debt.... We don't want to end up bankrupt like Greece."

The high-dollar fund-raiser—attended by donors including New York Jets owner Woody Johnson and Miami Marlins owner Jeffrey Loria—was one of a trio Romney attended in Southampton that day, which collectively netted $3 million for his campaign.

"I understand there is a plane out there saying Mitt Romney has 'a Koch problem,'" Romney remarked to attendees of David and Julia's fund-raiser. "I don't look at it as a problem; I look at it as an asset."

The following month, on August 30, Romney's asset awaited the candidate's grand entrance at the Republican National Convention in muggy Tampa. At the back of the Tampa Bay Times Forum, the black curtains parted and Romney emerged, holding a wide smile and wearing a navy suit as impeccable as his trademark gray-flecked coif. The band, competing with the crowd roar, launched into Kid Rock's "Born Free," the candidate's theme song. Romney worked his way slowly down the red-carpeted aisle, soaking up the adulation as he glided past the delegations from Tennessee, Indiana, and Idaho, then crossed the aisle to glad-hand supporters from Utah and Illinois.

When Romney reached New York's 95-member delegation, the candidate found David in the crowd and clasped his outstretched hand, on which David wore, as usual, his gold MIT class ring depicting the school's mascot, the industrious beaver. Romney clapped David on the back with his free hand and continued on toward the dais to formally accept the Republican presidential nomination.

The convention had attracted to Tampa all the disparate elements of the current Republican Party, along with the crew of megadonors who would help to make the 2012 presidential race the most expensive in American history. Wheelchair-bound casino mogul Sheldon Adelson (who alone pumped nearly $150 million into the 2012 race) took in the proceedings with Karl Rove from a fourth-floor skybox. Foster Friess ($2.5 million in publicly disclosed contributions, not counting his donations to the Koch network) leaned against a wall on the convention floor, proudly pulling out his cell phone to show a reporter a picture of the fourteen-foot crocodile he'd bagged on a recent hunting expedition in Tanzania.

But no one was more sought after than David, who had accepted the invitation of the chairman of New York's Republican Party, Ed Cox, to attend the convention as an alternate delegate. On the convention floor, where David often sat beside Cox, the son-in-law of the late Richard Nixon, delegates and journalists alike excitedly crept up to furtively snap pictures of the industrialist, who did his best to ignore the attention.

One evening, as Michele Bachmann sashayed up the aisle nearby wearing a flesh-colored knee-length dress, and twenty feet away Wisconsin's Scott Walker received a rock star's welcome from the Washington delegation, a pair of fresh-faced convention pages nervously sidled up to David. Getting his attention, the young men asked for career advice. "I'm the evil billionaire Koch brother," David replied, a grin spreading to his face. "You're not afraid of me?"

When roving journalists approached David on the convention floor, one of at least three PR representatives—among them, Nancy Pfotenhauer and Cristyne Nicholas, Rudy Giuliani's former communications director—intercepted them. Glued to his side throughout the four-day convention, the billionaire's handlers passed out a three-paragraph statement from David in lieu of interviews. "The 2012 election may be the most important of our lifetimes," it read in part. "Profoundly different political philosophies are competing for our hearts and minds—and our votes. I have made no secret about which philosophy I support—the one that provides the greatest economic and personal freedom possible."

Despite the force field surrounding him, David—considered a loose cannon within Koch's public affairs division—still managed to generate headlines when he espoused views that veered well to the left of Republican Party orthodoxy during an Americans for Prosperity reception held in his honor. "I believe in gay marriage," he told a *Politico* reporter. The Republicans, meanwhile, had just approved a party platform that supported a constitutional amendment banning it. David also confided that he backed reductions in defense spending and believed tax increases might be a necessary component of any deficit reduction strategy. (Congressional Republicans had fought bitterly to keep tax hikes off the table.) The brothers' political advisors cringed at his comments. It wasn't the time or place to break ranks with their GOP allies.

Romney's 37-minute convention speech drew tepid reviews from pundits and voters alike, but in the moment, with thousands of delegates and spectators on their feet and chanting his name, the convention crowd was electrified. Joined by his large family and his vice presidential running mate, Wisconsin's Paul Ryan, Romney beamed from the stage as thousands of red, white, and blue balloons floated down from the ceiling, blanketing the convention floor.

David stood in the aisle, clapping rhythmically and smiling up at the blizzard of confetti that swirled above. He high-fived a fellow delegate and swatted balloons as they rained down. A choir was singing "America the Beautiful" and David sang enthusiastically along with it. Moments later, one of his press handlers led him away through balloons and confetti and discarded MITT! signs. Slowly climbing a stairway out of the arena, he plaintively scanned the dissipating crowd and the clock in the corner of the arena that had been recording the dizzying amount of debt the United States had accrued since the convention started. He turned back, disappearing into the crowd.

Perhaps they could win this thing.

A little after 9:00 p.m. on November 6, the networks called Pennsylvania. Then Wisconsin, New Hampshire, and Iowa. As the battleground states fell into Obama's column, Romney's path to victory narrowed, then disappeared completely. "Four more years," the president tweeted at 11:16 p.m., after winning Ohio. On Fox News, Karl Rove refused to accept defeat, claiming that key Republican precincts had yet to report. But at 740 Park Avenue, reality was sinking in.

Late that evening David's home phone rang. He was monitoring the election results with disbelief. Obama had dispatched Romney easily. Meanwhile, Democrats had increased their ranks in the House and strengthened their Senate majority. He and his brother Charles had pulled out the stops to usher in a new conservative era, and they had almost nothing to show for their considerable efforts.

David answered the phone to the gravelly voice of his Deerfield friend John Damgard, who was calling to commiserate.

David "was pissed," Damgard recalled. The Republicans had a real opportunity to win the Senate, and heading into the election, it was hard to imagine a more vulnerable incumbent president than Obama, who was saddled with a major unemployment crisis. The stars had seemed aligned for the political transformation the Kochs and their allies had dreamt of. Then bone-headed candidates mired themselves in controversies over abortion and "legitimate rape." And Romney, playing to the Tea Party mood of the

GOP, alienated large swaths of the electorate—women, Hispanics, not to mention the 47 percent of Americans who "believe that they are entitled to health care, to food, to housing, to you name it," as the candidate inelegantly put it during a surreptitiously recorded fund-raiser. David believed the primary process, with its endless debates, had hobbled Romney from the start. He'd run so far to the Right that he could never course-correct back to the center.

"We've got to do better with primaries," David said, according to Damgard. "We've got to find ways to make sure our candidate is advantaged." And he complained about the crop of wild-eyed candidates who had derailed the GOP's chances of taking over Congress. "We've got to make sure better candidates surface."

David, still reeling from the loss, rang off. "Four more years of this guy," he groaned.

All the plotting and planning, the donor conclaves, the piles of money—it hardly seemed worth it. Charles and David had taken a high-profile stand, just as their political Svengali, Richard Fink, advised they should four years earlier. They had accepted the scorn and the death threats and the damage to their family legacy. But in the end they had paid the price without reaping the reward. They hadn't changed the country; they had only changed the way the country perceived them and their company, and not for the better.

Charles hated to lose at anything. He even golfed like he was competing in the Masters. ("You think that Michael Jordan is competitive—well, Charles is competitive," said one of his close friends.) And the political game had much higher stakes.

"We obviously miscalculated," the bitterly disappointed CEO confided to friends after the election. "We'll just have to work harder." According to his friend Nestor Weigand, Charles didn't point fingers. "He wasn't blaming Rich Fink. He wasn't blaming people. It's just that they perceived that there would be more people that would want a freer society and less governmental intervention and less people dependent upon the federal government. He thought…that people would see it, and they didn't." Charlie Chandler, another Wichita friend of Charles's and a member of the donor network, said the brothers were self-critical about the loss. "I never heard one word [of], 'so and so should have done this.' It was always, 'We failed. We didn't get where we wanted to be. End of story.'"

In the wake of Obama's reelection, though, there were still the donors to answer to—many who viewed politics through the businessman's lens of ROI (return on investment). The Kochs had pressed their wealthy friends and acquaintances to pony up a staggering amount of money, and they had delivered, pouring hundreds of millions of dollars into the Koch-led political effort. In the lead-up to the election, the level of confidence within the Kochs' political operation had bordered on euphoric. "They were pretty exuberant," said a conservative strategist. "They thought they had it." The Kochs and their overconfident political advisors, another political operative said, made big promises to their donors. "They…basically promised these donors that, 'if you continue to fund what we're doing, we will win this election through our efforts, through AFP and others.' There was quite a bit of overpromising."

After the election, some longtime contributors to the Koch network were understandably disappointed. Some blamed the electoral defeat on the quality of the Republican presidential candidate ("When you try and sell crap, you lose, right?" said Minnesota billionaire Stan Hubbard), but others wondered if the Koch brothers' vaunted political operation had lived up to its reputation, according to fund-raisers and strategists who know the conservative donor world well. "I've heard there are people who have pulled back and there are people asking, 'Where did my money go?'" said the conservative strategist. A Republican fund-raiser identified Wyoming investor Foster Friess—a major backer of the

Kochs' 2012 efforts—as one of the donors who'd grown deeply disillusioned with the brothers' political network. (Friess declined to comment.)

Charles had pledged to donors that his team would invest their contributions wisely to produce the maximum political dividends, but there was some question about whether their money had been well spent. Americans for Prosperity, a major recipient of donor funds, delivered an underwhelming performance. Its get-out-the-vote efforts fell flat and its political ads were poorly targeted. "In terms of the buying strategy, they were not particularly sophisticated," recalled Larry Grisolano, the Obama campaign's ad guru. The Obama team noticed early on that their real competition was Karl Rove's Crossroads groups, whose well-produced ads closely tracked their own buys. AFP's Tim Phillips, unveiling a $6.2 million ad campaign two months before the election, made a comment that seemed revealing in retrospect. "It's difficult to assess the kind of bang for buck, candidly," he told a reporter. "We just wanted to take a stand." This was the opposite of the hypertargeted, data-centric strategy employed by the Obama campaign (and Crossroads), which did not use its precious resources for symbolic purposes.

Themis, the voter microtargeting operation that the Kochs and their network funded to the tune of $18 million between 2010 and 2012, was also a disappointment. Activists who used Themis data said they found it rudimentary and ineffective. "I'm trying to figure out what the point is," said the leader of one conservative group. "Themis is nothing more than a massive database where they can find more donors and continue to build their empire."

Charles ruthlessly assessed performance within his company, measuring the contribution of each employee and jettisoning unprofitable business units without a second thought. Yet the scale of the post-2012 reckoning within the Kochs' political operation seemed muted, though a few heads did roll.

Most notably the brothers' main outside political strategist, Sean Noble, was "pushed aside," according to someone who knows him. "He's the fall guy for '12."

The instinct to keep Noble at arm's length was understandable. His political machinations had sparked a money-laundering investigation by California's political watchdog, the Fair Political Practices Commission, and the state's attorney general. The probe veered dangerously close to the Koch brothers.

In the run-up to the election, the commission had started looking into the mysterious source of an $11 million contribution to a local political action committee; this PAC, the Small Business Action Committee, had in turn poured the funds into two ballot measures. It backed one initiative curtailing the ability of unions to collect money for use in political campaigns and worked to defeat another raising the state's sales and income taxes. (The PAC failed on both counts.)

California authorities tracked the labyrinthine path, through three nonprofits, that the cash took before winding up in the Small Business Action Committee's bank account. Noble's Center to Protect Patient Rights, a conduit for the disbursement of Koch network money, formed one key link in the chain. Because of the seriousness of the allegations, Noble retained Malcolm Segal, one of California's top white-collar crime defense lawyers.

The California investigation slowly peeled back the layers of an elaborate financial shell game Noble and other political operatives had engaged in to obscure the source of contributions.

The main fund-raiser behind the California effort was a Sacramento-based strategist named Tony Russo. In 2011, inspired by Wisconsin Governor Scott Walker's triumph over his state's powerful public unions, Russo and his allies began crafting a plan of their own to take on organized labor in California. Russo believed the Kochs and their extensive political network might help in this fight, and he sat down with Noble in October 2011 to gauge his interest. "We had met with some other people from Koch, through some donors who are part of Koch," Russo recalled in a deposition. "...They have a network of c4's do issue advocacy. And so I ended up meeting with Sean because he's their outside consultant. And they had said that's who I should be meeting with."

Russo explained, "Conceptually, we talked about, would you guys be interested in engaging in this type of a fight in California?...It followed on the steps of Wisconsin." Noble signed on, and not long thereafter he footed the bill to hire Republican pollster Frank Luntz to conduct focus groups around the issues Russo and his allies were targeting; Noble also paid for the development and testing of ads. Russo initially envisioned conducting part of his campaign through a group called Americans for Job Security, but thanks to a quirk in California's campaign finance law, which strengthens disclosure requirements during the two months before an election, he had to abandon the plan. Fearing that donors who'd been promised anonymity could be outed, Russo turned to Noble.

"I have a big hiccup here in California," he told the Kochs' strategist during a phone call in early September 2012. "We have money raised...but I don't think we can spend it in California. Can we support some of your national efforts and, in turn, do you have groups that can help us in California?" Russo proposed donating the money he'd raised to the Kochs' political network, on the understanding that Noble would find a way to route it back into California through the web of national advocacy groups that received Koch donor funds. Noble agreed and told Russo to send his cash to the Center to Protect Patient Rights. In mid-October, as the election neared, Russo sent a text message to Noble requesting him to direct $11 million to the Small Business Action Committee. Barely had the check arrived—from an Arizona-based group Russo had never heard of called Americans for Responsible Leadership—when California's Fair Political Practices Commission began asking questions. They followed the money, and it led to Sean Noble.

The case resulted in a record $1 million fine for Noble's Center to Protect Patient Rights and Americans for Responsible Leadership. When a settlement was eventually announced, the commission's then-chair Ann Ravel said the case highlighted "the nationwide scourge of dark money nonprofit networks hiding the identities of their contributors." Ravel's commission directly implicated the "Koch brothers' dark money network," but Koch Industries responded in much the same way it had when Charles and David's names first surfaced as Tea Party financiers. *Who us?* "We were not involved in any of the activities at issue in California," said the company's spokeswoman Melissa Cohlmia.

On December 6, 2012, a month to the day after the election, an onward-and-upward e-mail from Charles arrived in the in-boxes of his fellow donors. "Despite November's disappointing election results, I am convinced that America's long-term decline is far from a foregone conclusion," he wrote. "Our goal of advancing a free and prosperous America is even more difficult than we envisioned, but it is essential that we continue, rather than abandon, this struggle."

Charles was writing to inform members of the donor network that he had decided to postpone the upcoming seminar, scheduled as usual for late January. "We are working hard to understand the election results and, based on that analysis, to re-examine our vision and the strategies and capabilities required for success."

When Charles and David finally convened their next donor retreat in late April 2013, the topics under discussion hinted at the strategic recalibration under way within the Kochtopus: "reaching the right people with the right message," "Hispanic, women and youth engagement," and "candidate recruitment and training." Koch fund-raiser Kevin Gentry told participants ahead of the conference that "a plan will be shared to help recruit more principled and effective advocates of free enterprise to run for office."

The caliber of the lawmakers who flocked to the event suggested that the Koch brothers' standing as conservative kingmakers hadn't declined. Attendees included South Carolina Gov. Nikki Haley, Ohio Gov. John Kasich, and Sens. Rand Paul of Kentucky and Ted Cruz of Texas, all of whom are considered possible presidential or vice presidential contenders in 2016.

The month after the conference, there were already signs that the Kochs were testing out new strategies. For decades, Charles and David had focused almost exclusively on free-market issues, but in May, as the immigration debate heated up on Capitol Hill, the Charles Koch Institute partnered with the website *BuzzFeed* to hold a "BuzzFeed Brews" forum on the topic, featuring a number of pro-reform panelists. It reflected an effort by the Kochs' political operation at youth engagement and an attempt to play a greater role in guiding the direction of the Republican Party away from some of the extreme positions that have turned off voters.

In June, a little more than a month after the Kochs unveiled their candidate recruitment plan to donors, Jeff Crank, the former chief operating officer of Americans for Prosperity, formed a political consultancy called Aegis Strategic to identify "electable advocates of the freedom and opportunity agenda." The firm, whose staff includes operatives with deep ties to the Kochs' political network, noted in its online marketing materials that it "takes on a limited number of candidates each election cycle and markets them to Aegis' exclusive fundraising network."

Charles and David, far from backing away from politics, are digging in for the electoral fights of the 2014 midterms and beyond, their friends say. "If you're going to play in this arena, you don't play only when it's lukewarm, you play when it gets hot, too, and it's gotten hot. They're still playing," said Charles's longtime friend Nestor Weigand.

And the brothers, observed a former Koch executive who knows them well, won't likely repeat the errors of 2012. "They were key in developing a strategy that at the end of the day didn't get them much," he said. "Did that make them less powerful? It may make them more powerful. They are smart people. They learn from their mistakes. They'll develop a better, more effective strategy next time. They're not the kind of people who will bury their heads in the sand and lick their wounds."

They had lost the battle, but the Mother of All Wars was far from done.

CHAPTER FIFTEEN

Legacy

Frederick Koch's Upper East Side town house sits on a quiet street off Fifth Avenue, near the Metropolitan Museum of Art. It is January 2013, and in a little over a week's time Frederick's hard-hat-wearing younger brother will dip a ceremonial shovel into a mound of dirt in front of the museum, officially breaking ground on the David H. Koch Plaza. Frederick has devoted his life to the arts, but it's David's name that's plastered on some of New York's most prestigious cultural real estate, including the former New York State Theater at Lincoln Center.

The world of the Upper East Side elite is a small one, and Frederick and David occasionally bump into each other at galas or charity functions. These short, awkward exchanges ("Oh, hi, Freddie") are pretty much the extent of their contact. Unlike David, who enjoys the status that comes with his high-profile philanthropy, Frederick conducts his life as if almost striving for obscurity. Thanks to Charles and David's recent political infamy, he is now thought of as one of the "other" Koch brothers.

Frederick is so private about his affairs that during the 1980s, after underwriting the $2.7 million construction of England's Swan Theatre in Stratford-upon-Avon (in the shell of a fire-ravaged Victorian playhouse), he kept quiet about his gift for several years as the British press tried to dig up the name of the angel donor. When Frederick's role was finally revealed, he told the BBC in a rare interview, "Never ask from where I came, nor what is my rank or name." He was quoting Lohengrin's warning to Elsa when the knight comes to her aid in Wagner's romantic opera. When Elsa later poses the forbidden question, her savior disappears in a boat pulled by a dove.

Built of white marble, Frederick's seven-story neoclassical town house is one of a trio commissioned in the early 1900s by dime-store magnate Frank Winfield Woolworth, and designed by Charles Pierrepont Henry Gilbert, one of several architects favored by New York's industrialists during the Gilded Age. Woolworth gave the town houses to each of his three daughters as wedding gifts. Six East 80th Street, the property Frederick now owns, belonged to the tycoon's youngest daughter, Jessie. Woolworth was said to have wept on the day he gave Jessie away to James Donahue, the Irish-American scion of a less prominent family who made its money in the fat-rendering business. Donahue was a man of vices—gambling, booze, and young men in particular—and Woolworth's doubts about the pairing proved well placed. In 1931, during a luncheon at the couple's home, Donahue excused himself from the table and locked himself in the bathroom. He staggered out a few minutes later exclaiming, "I've done it." Despondent over his finances and recently spurned by a young sailor, Donahue had gulped down seven mercury bichloride pills. He died within days.

Frederick acquired the property for $5 million in 1986, three years after cashing in his Koch Industries stock and in the throes of a frenetic buying spree of historic homes and artwork. Frederick's longtime architect Charles T. Young spent the next decade restoring the town house to its former splendor, and in many cases surpassing it. Frederick spared no expense. He continued a marble balustrade that ended after the first floor up the staircase and through the remaining five floors of the house. He replaced the crumbling plaster walls with carved limestone from the quarries of Caen in northwestern France, the kind that would be found in a Parisian town house of the French Régence period. In one case, Frederick made structural alterations just to create enough wall space to hang one of the masterpieces of his art collection, widening a pair of stone columns to fit William-Adolphe Bouguereau's *The Abduction of Psyche.*

"Sotheby's for years has been trying to take this away from me," Frederick tells a visitor. "And I keep telling them, 'I can't move it. It's part of the architecture of this room.'"

Frederick's office is located in what was James Donahue's bedroom. Ornate paneling that once adorned the Palace of Versailles lines the walls. A bookcase, as in some murder-mystery thriller, conceals a hidden passageway designed, Frederick explains, "so that the six servants in this house would not be aware of Mr. Donahue's comings and goings." It leads, past a row of stained-glass windows inlaid with the initials of the Donahue clan, to what was Jessie Donahue's bedroom and is now Frederick's.

Not that he actually sleeps there.

Frederick spent millions getting every hand-wrought, filigreed detail just right, but he doesn't actually live in the town house. When he's in New York—and he moves frequently between his collection of homes—he resides at 825 Fifth Avenue. He just entertains the occasional guest at the Woolworth mansion, his private museum.

Dressed in a navy blazer, striped shirt, and thin cobalt tie, Frederick moves through the rooms of his home like a curator, his arms folded behind him. "If you pull the carpet back you'll see a Versailles parquet," he says, touring the dining room. He pauses to point out paintings by Alexandre-Évariste Fragonard, Edward Burne-Jones, and Gilbert Stuart; Aubusson carpets; a set of ten mahogany dining room chairs that once belonged to financier J. P. Morgan.

In one bedroom, he shows off a canopied bed that he calls "the most important piece of furniture in the house." It belonged to Marie Antoinette, a wedding gift from the mayor of Paris when she married Louis XVI. "I'm amazed even to this day that I was able to get it out of France. I bought it in Monte Carlo, which may have been the reason."

He is at ease talking at length about every object in the house, and the intricacies of procuring or rehabilitating each of them. But when the topic turns briefly to his brothers, and whether they share his artistic sensibilities, Frederick tenses. "William does— David's twin brother," he replies. "He has a wonderful collection of all kinds of things." Then he changes the subject.

Frederick displays one of his most treasured pieces on the top floor, in a sun-drenched, glass-enclosed conservatory that was once Jessie Donahue's studio. On a pedestal beneath a circular skylight ringed with the signs of the zodiac sits a marble head wearing the headdress of an Egyptian pharaoh. The sculpture dates back to AD 130. "That is Antinous," Frederick explains, "who was the lover of Emperor Hadrian....Antinous accompanied Hadrian on a voyage down the Nile and at some point they stopped. Antinous went swimming and drowned in the Nile. The emperor was so grief stricken that he decided to immortalize Antinous and name him god of the Nile—and required people to worship him."

When the Roman Empire fell and Christians rose to power, they destroyed statues and icons depicting Hadrian's lover. "They very much resented having been ordered to worship the boyfriend of the emperor," Frederick says. The marble head of Antinous, severed from a larger statue, was discovered in the eighteenth century in a swamp on the grounds of what was Hadrian's estate in Tivoli.

What attracts Frederick to the objects he collects is not always their aesthetic value, but the hidden tales they tell, which he enjoys recounting with the flair of a raconteur. "Do you know the story of

Stanford White?" he inquires, gazing at a painting of the original Madison Square Garden, when it was located on Madison Avenue and 26th Street. White, the arena's architect, was gunned down in its rooftop restaurant in 1906 by Harry Thaw, the son of a Pittsburgh railroad magnate. Thaw was consumed with jealousy over White's past liaisons with Evelyn Nesbit, a former showgirl who had been the architect's mistress before marrying Thaw. "He was obsessed with Stanford White's previous relationship with Evelyn Nesbit," Frederick says. "After they married he tormented her by asking her to reveal all the sexual positions that she had enjoyed with Stanford White. All that did was fuel his rage."

Frederick thinks of himself as a writer, and though he never plied this trade professionally, his collection provides an outlet for his natural gift as a storyteller. There was a time, however, when Frederick had his own ambitions of literary and theatrical acclaim. After moving to New York City's West Village in his late twenties, Frederick had once approached John Mason Brown, an esteemed New York theater critic and author (as well as a fellow Harvard alum) for career advice. Frederick told Brown in a letter that he "hoped to be a playwright before too long—and a drama critic much sooner." But ultimately he never pursued these goals with much vigor, to the intense frustration of his industrious father.

But Frederick's mother took pride of her son's quiet, prolific arts patronage, especially his funding of the Swan Theatre, a name Frederick says he chose "in tribute to Shakespeare, who was sometimes called the Swan of Avon." In 1986, Mary Koch traveled to England to watch her son appear side by side with the Queen of England at the theater's opening.

During the 1980s, to house his growing collection of Victorian art, which was said to overrun warehouses on both sides of the Atlantic, Frederick envisioned creating a museum in London akin to New York's Frick Collection. "Frederick Koch had the eye of a true connoisseur," said London art dealer Julian Hartnoll, one of the agents Frederick enlisted to do his buying. "He did not follow the flash or the ostentatious preferring the academic, the intellectual, and the byways of art history, literature, and music."

Frederick proposed siting his gallery in historic St. John's Lodge, a neoclassical villa located in London's Regent's Park. But his plans to overhaul the interior led to a protracted standoff with British cultural authorities, during which Frederick threatened to return to America with his collection of nineteenth-century art, a move one local architectural historian dubbed "crude bluff and blackmail."

The fact that the Brits did not grasp his vision perplexed him. "The lodge is deteriorating rapidly now," Frederick fumed in the late 1980s. "If I don't take it on, it will probably go to some millionaire Arab." He wasn't far off the mark. St. John's Lodge now belongs to the Sultan of Brunei.

Fed up with bureaucratic wrangling and unwanted press attention, Frederick ultimately settled on a secondary location. Sutton Place was situated on more than 700 picturesque acres about a half-hour's drive from central London. A courtier to Henry VIII built the 50,000-square-foot Tudor mansion in the early sixteenth century, and it once belonged to the reclusive American oil billionaire John Paul Getty. Through a charitable foundation, Frederick purchased Sutton Place for £8 million from another reclusive American owner: Stanley Seeger, whose fortune, like Frederick's, derived from an industrial empire. Frederick embarked on an extensive £12 million restoration project. But even before completing it, he baffled the British art world when he began selling off the Victorian masterpieces he'd spent the previous decade amassing.

"It certainly smelled of a person who was over extended," said someone who knew him during the 1990s, adding, "It certainly appeared to me that it was going to pay the gardener." But which one? He owned three other estates that required exorbitant upkeep.

Finally, in 1999, Frederick put the newly restored home on the market for £25 million. Maintaining the large estate which had a staff of twenty cost a small fortune, and according to Frederick, he wanted to move on to other projects. "I found that you don't own the houses, the houses own you," he says. "They make so many demands on you." Sutton Place sat on the market until 2005, when a mysterious buyer purchased it through a middleman. Frederick later discovered the new owner was Russian oligarch Alisher Usmanov, number 34 on *Forbes*'s billionaire's list.

"I got my investment back," Frederick says with a trace of bitterness. Though he relinquished Sutton Place and, with it, his ambition of a museum dedicated to his art collection, his cultural legacy lives on in other venues. A trove of musical scores, manuscripts, historical documents, and artistic ephemera snatched up anonymously from the auction market during the 1980s reappeared in the Frederick R. Koch Collection, now housed in Yale's Beinecke Library.

The collection includes everything from the handwritten scores of Mozart, Schubert, and Stravinsky, to the letters of W. H. Auden, Charles Baudelaire, and Marcel Proust, and from the poems of Jean Cocteau and Victor Hugo to the manuscript drafts of Henry Miller and Oscar Wilde. "What struck me most was how he knew his collection in the most intricate detail," said Vincent Giroud, the Beinecke's former curator of modern books and manuscripts, who worked closely with Frederick to document the collection. "I've met many collectors who could be wonderful people and very generous, but are not very knowledgeable about what they have. That's not at all his case." He added, "He has the mind of a scholar himself in many ways."

Frederick lowers himself into an armchair in a second-floor sitting room. He has not spoken to the press in more than twenty-five years, since the British media descended on him like a pack of wolves. Even before that, he refused all interviews and stayed conspicuously quiet as his younger brothers savaged one another on the pages of national newspapers and magazines.

"Shall we delve into Koch world?" he asks.

But first a formality. He unclasps a clear plastic envelope and withdraws a crisp document. "If you would sign this, please." It's a contract requiring that "all writing pertaining to Frederick R. Koch, including personal subject matter revealed in research and interviews," be submitted "for his approval."

No journalist could agree to these terms, and when his visitor explains this, Frederick's genial demeanor ices over. "My brothers and I," he warns, "are practiced combatants in the field of public relations."

He shows his visitor out into the January chill. Nearby, excavators are gnawing through concrete, as preliminary construction for the Met's new David H. Koch Plaza gets under way.

As the Koch brothers reach their sunset years, each has left his mark in a vastly different way. If Frederick's imprint is the most understated, Bill's is as flamboyant as the Pucci silk that lines his suit jackets. Bill has lived on his own terms, played by his own rules—a maverick quality that led to some of his biggest triumphs, such as when he flipped the bird to the naysayers and claimed the America's Cup. But it also mired him in bizarre tabloid controversies and bruising lawsuits, such as the ongoing legal imbroglio over charges that he kidnapped and falsely imprisoned an employee.

Bill is a connoisseur of proverbs and aphorisms. One he has used often is, "Before you embark on a journey of revenge, dig two graves." But he seems to have difficulty discerning the sometimes thin line between justice and retribution. One could argue that Bill spent a lifetime digging graves.

Since boyhood, his search for the most basic tranquility often seemed only to create more turmoil. His pursuit of his rightful place within his family nearly destroyed it. The past tumult with his brothers has driven him to work doubly hard to forge the kind of togetherness among his own family—which includes five biological children and a stepson, whose ages range from eight to twenty-seven—that eluded him during his own upbringing.

He has done this, of course, in his own grandiose, Bill Koch way.

In recent years, he's created a series of extravagant family compounds, where one day he hopes his children and grandchildren will gather. The Western town—for which Bill bought a movie set's wardrobe so friends and family can dress in costume when they visit—is part of this plan. In late 2012, Bill seized what he called the "chance of several lifetimes" to buy two prized properties, one belonging to the Du Pont family and the other to Bunny Mellon, in the Cape Cod enclave of Osterville, where the billionaire has owned a home since the 1980s. Bill plans to join both plots, creating a Koch family version of the Kennedys' Hyannis Port.

These estates, he believes, will give his children "a reason, when they get older and they have their own families, for staying together." Bill will one day pass down a vast fortune to his descendants, but what he really hopes to leave to them—family equanimity—he can't draft into an estate plan.

Over the course of his life, in addition to building an enviable fortune, Bill has amassed an incredible collection of art, antiques, and historical artifacts, especially those of the old American West. He has given thought to whether he should divide the Picassos and Monets, the Homers and Remingtons, among his children or perhaps donate his treasures to museums. His own father's art collection had caused strife between Bill and his brothers. "I don't want to do that to my kids," he reflected. Nor did he want to foist his tastes on them. Bill saw in his collection his own life story of accomplishment and adversity, pleasure and pain, serenity and struggle. He wanted his children to experience "the thrill that I did doing my own thing; everybody has to find his or her own way in life," he said. "...I'm much more interested in having my children being my legacy than this art collection being my monument."

Charles also has an eye toward future generations. In the midst of the 2012 political campaign, and as Koch Industries posted record revenues of $115 billion, he became a grandfather. "My proudest accomplishment," he said of the baby boy, born to his son, Chase. The child's name is Charles.

The CEO has much to be proud of. The world will feel his impact long into the future. His company produces some of the most elemental ingredients of our modern society—energy, food, building and agricultural materials—and its products intersect every day with the lives of every American.

There is also the intangible, but no less pervasive, aspect of his influence. He has arguably done more than anyone else to promote free-market economics and the broader ideology surrounding it. By mainstreaming libertarianism, he helped to change the way people think. Absent his money and strategic vision, the country would be a different place. Few people can claim they changed the world, but this is undeniably true of Charles. And he's not done.

At seventy-eight, Charles has no plans to retire—"I'm going to ride my bicycle until I fall off," he has said. Koch Industries continues to grow and innovate under his leadership, always looking for new business opportunities, even if they take the company outside its comfort zone. In April 2013, word leaked that Koch Industries had commenced early talks to buy the Tribune newspaper chain—a prospect that stoked predictable outrage on the Left. The deal, involving turning around an ailing company and possible synergies with other Koch properties, such as papermaker Georgia-Pacific, seemed like a classic Koch transaction. But it also appeared to have an ideological component (though the company

denied this was the basis of its interest). "They always have a desire to better understand how the media works and how they can influence coverage really on economic issues," said one ex–Koch executive. "They would not have done this if it didn't make good business sense, but this wasn't just business." In the end, Koch passed on Tribune, and instead it paid $7.2 billion for electronics maker Molex, a major supplier of components to Apple.

For its enormous size, Koch Industries is a deeply personal creation that embodies the values, passions, personality, and philosophy of its CEO. Charles diffused Market-Based Management throughout every crevice of his empire so his philosophy would live on after his time.

His choice of successor is a secret Charles keeps even from his closest friends. He's often asked whether he's grooming his son, Chase, who works for Koch Industries' fertilizer division, to take over. "We have the best leaders and the most depth of leadership we've ever had," is his standard nonreply. But in 2013, thirty-six-year-old Chase joined Koch Industries' board of directors, a quiet sign that he's taking on a more prominent leadership role in the company. In December he was named president of Koch Fertilizer.

Chase's older sister, Elizabeth, another heir to the Koch kingdom, has taken little interest in the affairs of the family company. She's a thirty-eight-year-old writer who lives in Brooklyn and runs a small, boutique publishing house. "I remember declaring to my parents in about ninth grade that I was a bohemian who was never going to play sports or do anything related to math," she once told *Town & Country*. "My father is very big on creating value. I told him I may not make the world a better place—right away." Charles's literary daughter is deeply conflicted—haunted even— by her family's colossal wealth, and she has written unsparingly about her "disturbed and convoluted relationship with money."

"Even though I was born into an obscenely wealthy family, I

do not toss money around like garden fertilizer, especially not in places where anyone is likely to see me," she wrote in one essay. Elizabeth noted that she has "invested great amounts of creative energy into pretending" she does not come from money. "Gratitude is in me somewhere, but so buried in shame I have trouble finding it."

Both of Charles's children, family friends say, have their dad's humble bearing. Like his own father, Charles tried to ensure that his kids did not grow up with a silver-spoon mentality. "Elizabeth and Chase are down to earth, and they're just solid individuals," said Bob Buford, president of Wichita's Zenith Drilling. "That's not easy when you grow up in the atmosphere they've grown up in."

The way Charles's children came up contrasts sharply with the ostentatious upbringings of their cousins, said a close family friend. "There's no comparison to the way that David and Billy raised their children—no comparison."

David, like his older brother, owns 40 percent of Koch Industries, and one day his three children stand to inherit a major stake in the company. His eldest son, David Jr., is fifteen. He's a cerebral teen who's passionate about aviation and history. "Very intellectual, very smart," said his godfather, John Damgard. "He is a World War II history buff." His sister, Mary Julia, thirteen, is a talented ballerina. "Drop dead beautiful," Damgard said. "I don't know how David is going to deal with the first guy that wants to take her out on a date." John Mark, their youngest, is eight.

When the company eventually enters its third generation of family ownership, a new round of internal debate may well erupt over whether Koch Industries should remain private or go public. Their birthright, as Fred Koch warned their fathers, may be a blessing or a curse.

The Koch Industries of the future is likely to be a far less political place. Beyond donating to Republican candidates, Chase Koch

has had little involvement with his father's ideological projects. And according to one Koch veteran, many at the company wish Koch Industries would simply steer clear of politics. "A huge element of the company never understood why Koch got involved with politics to begin with," he said. "A good core leadership group there wants to run the business. They don't want to get into politics because there is no upside to the political game."

Charles and David hold like-minded political beliefs, but history will judge each differently. "David is a true philanthropist," the Koch veteran said. "David's [giving] is about making the world a better place. Charles's is about changing the world." It seems to matter little to Charles whether his name endures; he cares that his ideas live on. But David wants to be remembered for his benevolence, and any New Yorker can tell you that evidence of his good deeds is becoming harder and harder to miss.

On January 14, 2013, less than a week before Barack Obama was inaugurated to his second term, the Metropolitan Museum of Art celebrated David for his latest act of munificence—$65 million to finance new fountains and a facelift for the four-block stretch of Fifth Avenue between 80th and 84th Streets.

When the museum first announced his contribution the previous year, at the peak of his political vilification, the Met went out of its way to state that David's gift would not come with naming rights—a decision it later reversed. The Met's director, Thomas Campbell, would say only that the museum's board "reflected on the generosity and level of commitment that David's gift represents," and "thought it was the right thing to do." Donors weren't exactly standing in line to cut $65 million checks.

His contribution predictably made waves. "Boycott the Metropolitan Museum of Art," one New York art critic fulminated, "until it rejects the Koch cultural bribe."

At the groundbreaking ceremony, liberal New York politicians were placed in the awkward position of beatifying a man whose politics they repudiated. Seated to the right of the podium, then–Manhattan Borough President Scott Stringer maintained a straight face throughout the ceremony, fully aware of the irony of the spectacle he was witnessing. When the Democrat finally rose from his chair to take his turn lauding the Met's generous benefactor, he could not contain himself from saying what many others were thinking. "I never thought I'd see in my lifetime Manhattan liberals praising David Koch. Well, it's $65 million!"

Of the Koch brothers political duo, David emerged from the election with the most damage done to his legacy—part of this was inevitable as the wealthiest man in media-centric Manhattan. The taint of politics now intrudes on his reputation as one of America's most prolific philanthropists, the John D. Rockefeller of the modern era. In recent years, David has doled out eight- and nine-figure gifts with barely a second thought—$100 million for the David H. Koch Center, an ambulatory care facility at New York–Presbyterian Hospital; another $100 million for the David H. Koch Institute for Integrative Cancer Research at MIT, plus $20 million to build childcare facilities for its staff; $25 million for the David H. Koch Center for Applied Research of Genitourinary Cancers at the M. D. Anderson Cancer Center (where David receives treatment for his prostate cancer); and the list goes on. But his name has also become a homing beacon for left-wing activists. Protestors even occupied the American Museum of Natural History's David H. Koch Dinosaur Wing, which he paid $20 million to underwrite in 2006.

"While people may not agree with his politics, what he's doing has been extraordinarily helpful for the arts and in terms of medical research," said Rachel Moore, the CEO of the American Ballet Theatre, on whose board David has served for nearly thirty years. "It's too bad that people decided to cast aspersions on his philanthropy just because they don't like his politics, because they're very separate."

At least they used to be.

In October 2013, environmental activists picketed Boston's WGBH, where they delivered a petition, signed by 70,000 people, calling for the public television station to oust David from its board of trustees. A major financial backer of the station's popular science series NOVA, he had served on the board since the late 1990s without controversy, until his political activities began to attract notice. David's critics consider his role in bankrolling groups that sow doubt about the existence of climate change particularly objectionable. And they claim that his position may allow him to influence WGBH's programming agenda and perhaps NOVA's treatment of global warming.

There is no evidence to suggest David has ever attempted to sway coverage, though, as a major donor, he holds a certain indirect clout. This became clear after New York's WNET, where David also served as a trustee, aired a documentary called *Park Avenue: Money, Power and the American Dream*. The income equality–themed film, which debuted the week after the presidential election, focuses on 740 Park Avenue, the haven for New York's ultrarich where David and his family reside. David is one of the film's central characters, and it includes an interview with a former doorman who identified the billionaire as the 31-unit building's stingiest resident. "We would load up his trucks—two vans, usually—every weekend, for the Hamptons...multiple guys, in and out, in and out, heavy bags. We would never get a tip from Mr. Koch. We would never get a smile from Mr. Koch. Fifty-dollar check for Christmas, too—yeah, I mean, a check! At least you could give us cash."

The New Yorker's Jane Mayer reported that David was "apparently so offended" by the documentary that he decided against making a hefty contribution to WNET. Eventually, he resigned from the board outright. The fallout caused another Koch-related documentary in the PBS pipeline to get defunded. Called *Citizen*

Koch, it explores the increasing influence of money in politics, following the Supreme Court's *Citizens United* ruling, and it centers in part on Governor Scott Walker's battle with Wisconsin's public employee unions. "It's the very thing our film is about—public servants bowing to pressures, direct or indirect, from high-dollar donors," the filmmakers told Mayer.

When David donated $100 million to Lincoln Center in 2008 to underwrite the renovation of the New York State Theater (now the David H. Koch Theater) concerns about the political baggage of the Koch surname were of a different sort. One long-serving Lincoln Center board member said he worried that people would associate the theater with the former mayor of New York City, Ed Koch. "I said, 'Oh, Christ. People are going to call this the Koch' "—pronounced like scotch—" 'Theater.' "

"We were all aware of who he is and what he'd done and there were many who didn't agree with his politics," the board member noted, "but the fact of the matter is, he was very generous in his offer and, therefore, as a fiduciary, really, that was our sole consideration." He added, "I hate his politics, but there's no question of his genuine generosity in this area. It can't be doubted."

David's pledge for the New York State Theater coincided with a moment in Manhattan's philanthropic evolution when several major cultural institutions marketed branding opportunities as if they were sports franchises. David's friend and 740 Park Avenue neighbor Stephen Schwarzman set the financial bar, in early 2008, for the naming rights of a major cultural landmark with his $100 million donation to the New York Public Library. In recognition of his gift, the library etched his name onto the exterior of its iconic, flagship location at 42nd Street and Fifth Avenue. Schwarzman's contribution made Lincoln Center fund-raisers realize the true value of the status symbol they had to offer. Noticing David and his wife, Julia, making a conscious effort to raise their profile in New York, they zeroed in on the industrialist as their lead prospect.

"There are some people who carry around with them a certain sense of guilt over how much money they have, or a certain unease about it—he was not one of those people," said a former Lincoln Center official involved in the naming talks, who recalled the billionaire proudly showing off a model replica of his 25,000-square-foot Palm Beach villa during a meeting at his office. But he said that unlike other rich contributors, who give away money largely for reasons of self-aggrandizement, David wanted to ensure Lincoln Center remains a cultural mainstay for generations. The billionaire could have pressed for his name to remain on the theater in perpetuity—the deal granted to audio pioneer Avery Fisher, for whom another Lincoln Center venue is named—but he instead agreed to a term of fifty years (at which point his heirs will have the option to make another contribution to keep his name on the building). "In 50 years, you are going to need money again to fix this place up, and I don't want to stand in the way of that," David told Lincoln Center fund-raisers.

"That struck me as being incredibly enlightened and putting his own personal grandeur aside for the benefit of the public in New York City," the former official said.

Yet no one slaps his name on a Lincoln Center theater—or the Met, the Smithsonian, and any number of museums and medical research centers—without consideration for how future generations will remember him. It is an act of legacy burnishing as old as the industrial world itself, the cleansing of an unfathomable fortune amassed through the most brutish of industries. Despite David's motives, his philanthropy resembles the latest variation on Andrew Carnegie's "Gospel of Wealth," in which the tycoon who gives away his millions before he dies will find "no bar...at the gates of Paradise."

"Carnegie, Mellon—take any of these great philanthropists or these great industrialists of the late nineteenth or early twentieth century," the former Lincoln Center official said. "They are not remembered for the rape and pillage of our environment or the way they mistreated people. They are remembered for the contributions they've made financially as philanthropists. There is a long history of people who profit through other people's detriments and who also do a lot of good in different ways, and I think that's what will happen with the Kochs."

On October 30, 2013, New York's glitterati queued up in front of a headset-wearing event planner outside the David H. Koch Theater, located adjacent to two other Lincoln Center venues in a plaza featuring an elaborate fountain. She held a clipboard with a list of names, which she shouted over the rush-hour din as socialites took their turns mugging for the cameras in front of a Clinique "step and repeat" banner. When a bystander inquired about the glamorous, jewel-bedecked blonde who was presently posing for the paparazzi, a bearded photographer swiveled his head. "Don't know, don't care," he replied. "She's probably just married to some rich guy."

That evening the American Ballet Theatre was opening its fall season with the world premiere of *The Tempest*, the ballet company's adaptation of William Shakespeare's play, choreographed by Alexei Ratmansky, the former artistic director of Russia's famed Bolshoi Ballet. The performance, largely underwritten by David Koch, marked the American Ballet Theatre's return to this venue after nearly forty years. David played a behind-the-scenes role in making that happen. When he negotiated the naming rights of the theater, he expressed his desire—a wish, not a precondition—that the American Ballet Theatre might someday find a home in the newly rechristened David H. Koch Theater. "That was always his hope that we would perform there," said Rachel Moore. David later helped Moore's company negotiate a three-year contract to perform an annual two-week run at the Koch Theater.

As the 6:30 p.m. curtain approached, the celebrities began to trickle in. Down the red carpet sauntered Sigourney Weaver in a dark green sequined gown. Actress Bebe Neuwirth glided past wearing a red strapless dress, followed shortly by heiress Nicky Hilton in purple lace. Actor Alan Cumming wore a white cravat and Louboutin sneakers, stopping to flash a peace sign at the photographers before continuing on to the theater.

Finally, a six-foot blonde stepped in front of the cameras, wearing a turquoise floor-length gown. "Julia, look this way!" one of the paparazzi shouted. The photographers knew her by sight. The hostesses who had once thrown up speed bumps to Julia Koch's social ascent were now mere footnotes. Julia had started out fitting society ladies for events like these when she worked for Adolfo; now she was one of Manhattan's doyennes.

Julia arrived alone. Avoiding the red-carpet fanfare, her tuxedo-wearing husband, looking slim and tanned, joined her later in their balcony seats. Two short performances preceded *The Tempest*'s premiere, and as the orchestra played Tchaikovsky's Suite No. 3, David watched the ballerinas of the American Ballet Theatre dance en pointe in the George Balanchine–choreographed "Theme and Variations." He admired as usual the graceful athleticism of the dancers, one of the reasons that David, an old jock himself, enjoyed this form of theater over others.

Meanwhile, elsewhere in the Koch empire, far less graceful performances were playing out. At that moment in central Texas, cleanup crews worked to contain 17,000 gallons of oil that had spewed from a pipeline owned by a Koch Industries subsidiary. In the political wing of Koch world, Americans for Prosperity was unleashing attack ads against two Democratic senators whose 2014 races could decide control of the upper chamber of Congress.

Julia was cochairing the *Tempest*-themed gala that would follow the premiere. During intermission, the wait staff stood shoulder-to-shoulder on the theater's second-floor promenade, encircling the tables that had been set for the after party, which ballet benefactors had paid as much as $5,000 a person to attend. Event designer Bronson Van Wyck had transformed the space into a brooding seascape, which included a series of forty-foot pillars crafted to evoke tornadoes, a nod to the violent storm that opens the first act of Shakespeare's tale. A soundtrack rumbled with the low growl of approaching thunder, and smoke machines billowed a light fog that clung around David's feet as he clasped the hands of well-wishers and huddled in conversation with Peter Martins, the Danish dancer and choreographer who heads the New York City Ballet (the company that calls the Koch Theater home for the majority of the year). David may have been considered a conservative pariah in other parts of the country, but here he and Julia were royalty.

The curtain came up a short time later on Prospero, the sorcerer protagonist of Shakespeare's tale, preparing to exact revenge against the brother who usurped his throne by summoning a tempest. The story is one of power, betrayal, retribution, and redemption—themes that David understands better than most.

The maelstrom that consumed his family had lasted twenty years. At the eye of their storm was the love and legacy of a father who taught his sons to be tough and competitive, to stand their ground and land their punches, never realizing that his boys would one day turn these attributes to the destruction of one another.

After putting some distance on their feud, Bill reflected that one of the final sticking points that had prevented him from achieving peace with his brothers was an item that held nothing more than sentimental value. It was the portrait of their father, painted by a little-known Southwestern artist named Herman de Jori, which hung in the family home under the glow of a display light. Bill ultimately let it go. The contested painting remains in Wichita, where it hangs in Charles Koch's office to the right of his desk, the patriarch looking down on his son with his lips frozen in a tight smile.

Acknowledgments

Sons of Wichita is my first book, and when I began this project, in the fall of 2011, my editor John Brodie cautioned me that the process would feel a bit like summiting Everest. There's no question that there were times in the two years that followed when I wished someone would hand me an oxygen mask. Thankfully, John was with me every step of the way, spurring me on with advice, insight, and encouragement. This book is better in every way because of him, and he has my gratitude for seeing the promise in this project and in me. Thanks also to John's wonderful colleagues, in particular Grand Central Publishing's president and publisher, Jamie Raab; Hachette's senior vice president of legal and business affairs, Karen Andrews; production editor Yasmin Mathew; production associate Melissa Mathlin; plus the marketing and PR team including Brian McLendon, Amanda Pritzker, Amanda Brown, and Andrew Duncan, who were fantastic to work with from start to finish. Thanks, as well, to Liz McNamara.

Equally vital to this endeavor was my agent, Howard Yoon, who helped me transform a kernel of an idea into a biography and was key to shaping the vision for this book. Howard's partner, Gail Ross, was indispensable, and I feel extremely fortunate to have both of them in my corner. I'm also indebted to my friend Bruce Falconer, who read an early draft of the book and provided feedback that greatly improved the final product, sparing readers some terrible clichés.

A number of outstanding young journalists assisted me, and they have my sincere appreciation. Ryan Brown, now an author in her own right, contributed research and conducted a handful of interviews. Andy Kroll, my *Mother Jones* colleague, pitched in with some great reporting that appeared in "Out of the Shadows" and "The Mother of All Wars"; I hope our bull sessions about the Byzantine workings of Charles and David Koch's political network continue long into the future. Molly Redden tracked down hard-to-find court records—some stored in a literal salt mine—and arranged for me to view them. Noah Shannon helped with fact checking. Thanks, as well, to Matt Corley, Victoria Rossi, Perry Stein, and Chris Heller.

David Corn is *Mother Jones*'s Washington bureau chief, and I'm lucky to have him as a boss and to count him as a friend. David was the first person I consulted when I was considering writing a book, and he introduced me to my agent. Along with my thanks, I owe David an orca platter at the Old Ebbitt Grill. Monika Bauerlein and Clara Jeffery, the magazine's brilliant, indefatigable, and award-winning co-editors-in-chief, were incredibly supportive of this project from the outset and gave me the time to see it to fruition. Special thanks to Nick Baumann, who did double duty when I took book leave—and a shout-out to the rest of the MoJo family.

There were many fellow journalists who helped me at various stages of the reporting process. Among them is the phenomenal Leslie Wayne, formerly of *The New York Times*, who was one of the first reporters to pull back the curtain on the Koch clan. Her previous work was an incredible resource, and Leslie herself was a source of invaluable insight. She also generously shared with me her research materials, which this book benefited from greatly. Thanks to Carol Ann Whitmire, editor of the *Quanah-Tribune Chief*, for her hospitality when I visited Fred Koch's birthplace on an early reporting trip. At *The Wichita Eagle*, Sherry Chisenhall and Jean Hays provided me with access to the paper's "morgue";

the *Eagle* has done a tremendous job of covering Koch Industries and the Koch family over the years, and its archives were an important source of background material. The work of Bryan Burrough, who profiled Bill Koch for *Vanity Fair* in 1994, was another great resource, and I thank him for indulging my questions about obscure matters nearly two decades in the past. Last, a hat tip to Jeff Riggenbach, who patiently dug through old audiotapes and photos to unearth some gems from the early days of the Libertarian Party.

This book simply could not have been written without the participation of the scores of people I interviewed along the way. To anyone who returned my call; replied to my e-mail; agreed to meet for coffee or a drink; contributed insights and anecdotes; or pointed me in the right direction—you have my deepest appreciation. Thanks to each of you for being so generous with your time.

I also could not have done this without the support of my friends and family, who provided encouragement and inspiration throughout the process. My parents, Bernard and Linda Schulman, have been behind me at every step during my career, never more so than during the writing of this book. I owe them more than they know. My gratitude as well to the Schulman, Cooke, Silverman, and Zell families, as well as to my wonderful in-laws, Ray and Marilyn Pieczarka, and my sister- and brother-in-law, Kate and Greg Skouteris. Thanks, most of all, to my wife, Stacey, who was a beacon of confidence when I was overcome by doubt, who buoyed me with love and levity when I needed it most, and who gave me the strength to put one foot in front of the other and climb.

Notes

This book is the product of more than two years of research and reporting. It is based on hundreds of interviews with a wide range of sources: friends, relatives, classmates, and acquaintances; business associates and employees; political allies and adversaries; members of the philanthropic community; and many, many others who were gracious enough to share their perspectives on the Koch family and/or their companies. Unless specified in the source notes below, all quotations come from interviews conducted by me, or, in a handful of cases, by my research assistants Andy Kroll and Ryan Brown. Whenever possible, I strove to quote sources on the record, but in some cases interview subjects requested, and I granted, anonymity so they could speak candidly.

My research also benefited from a huge range of primary source documents, including thousands of pages of correspondence and other material, unearthed at more than a dozen archives. They include those located at the Chicago History Museum, Columbia University, Harvard University, the Hoover Institution, the Library of Congress, the Massachusetts Institute of Technology, Rice University, the Russian State Archive of Economics, the University of Michigan, the University of Oregon, the University of Southern California, Wichita State University, the Wisconsin Historical Society, and elsewhere. I relied as well on many thousands of pages of legal documents—transcripts, depositions, exhibits, motions, and more—produced through numerous lawsuits involving the Koch brothers, their father, and/or the family's various business entities. Any errors of omission or commission are mine and mine alone.

Prologue

Page 1, "Okay, boys": Interview with Jay Chapple.

Page 1, nineteen minutes younger: "Brother Versus Brother," *The New York Times*, April 28, 1998.

Page 1, shared a small room: Interview with John Damgard.

Page 2, a college boxer: "Knights of Padded MIT in First Meet Tomorrow," *The Tech*, March 5, 1920.

Page 2, "It would make 'Dallas' and 'Dynasty' look like a playpen": "Build Your Own Playpen," *New England Business*, September 1988.

Page 3, "10,000 orgasms": "Billionaire Bill Koch Wins $12 Million More From Wine Maven Who Sold Him Bogus Bordeaux," *New York Post*, April 13, 2013.

Page 3, Bill ranks 329th: "The World's Billionaires," *Forbes*, March 4, 2013.

Page 4, "the biggest company you've never heard of": "The Price of Immortality," *Portfolio*, October 15, 2008.

Page 4, former home to John D. Rockefeller Jr.: Michael Gross, *740 Park* (Broadway Books, 2005), p. 48.

Page 5, stage actors working off a script: Brian Doherty, *Radicals for Capitalism* (Public Affairs, 2007), p. 410.

Chapter 1. Sons of Wichita

Page 8, some of the earliest colonial settlers: Mary Judith Robinson, *Patriots and Loyalists: An American Family from Colonial Times* (2009).

Page 8, enjoyed visiting Fred's father: "Quanah Parker, Chief of the Comanches," *Kerrville Mountain Sun*, November 18, 1926.

Page 9, the Koch family's home phone number: "Fred Koch at Rice University," published by Rice University's Office of Public Affairs, November 2008.

Page 9, briefly captained the MIT team: "Matmen Campaign Proves Successful," *The Tech*, March 15, 1921.

Page 9, "The way up the ladder": "College Grad Seeks Job...And More," *Discovery*, July 2012.

Page 10, from plane manufacturing to gold mining: "C.F. De Ganahl, 69, Plane Maker, Dies: Manufacturer Also Had Been Gold Miner," *The New York Times*, May 15, 1939.

Page 10, **engineering challenges**: "Special Napthas with Pipe Still," F. C. Koch, *Oil and Gas Journal*, March 10, 1927.

Page 10, **"as brilliant a pair of brain lobes"**: Charles Francis de Ganahl, *The Life and Letters of Charles Francis de Ganahl Vol. II* (R. R. Smith, 1949), p. 379.

Page 10, **former Army sergeant**: *The National Cyclopædia of American Biography, Vol. 56* (J. T. White & Company, 1975), pp. 209-210.

Page 11, **Fred bought a one-third stake**: "Restructure, Inc."

Page 11, **lived in his office**: Ibid.

Page 11, **Mary's parents approved**: From an unpublished portion of an interview conducted with Mary Koch in 1986 by Leslie Wayne, then of *The New York Times*. At the time, she also interviewed Charles, Bill, and a handful of Koch Industries executives. Copies of the interview notes are in the possession of the author. (Hereafter, "Leslie Wayne interview notes.")

Page 11, **a month (and six dates)**: Ibid.

Page 11, **"a typical old country boy"**: "Family Feud at a Corporate Colossus," *Fortune*, July 26, 1982.

Page 11, **"Fred was a strong man"**: "A Visit with Mary Koch," *East Wichita News*, October 1988.

Page 12, **The inspiration for the elaborate trip**: *The Life and Letters of Charles F. de Ganahl.*

Page 12, **"But this is my trousseau!"**: "A Visit with Mary Koch."

Page 12, **After crisscrossing South America**: Details of their honeymoon come from films of their trip viewed by the author.

Page 13, **Fred felled a pair of leopards**: "Koch Family Matriarch Dies at 83," *The Wichita Eagle*, December 23, 1990.

Page 13, **Mary helped to exercise**: From a compilation of family films narrated by Mary Koch and viewed by the author.

Page 14, **the child's namesake telegrammed**: "Namesake and Mentor," *Discovery*, January 2010.

Page 14, **"The most glorious feeling"**: "A Letter's Legacy," *The Wichita Eagle*, March 15, 1998.

Page 14, **"He wanted to make sure"**: *Koch v. Koch Industries* (D. Kans., 1985), testimony of Charles Koch.

Page 14, **"country-club bums"**: "A Letter's Legacy," *The Wichita Eagle*, March 15, 1998.

Page 15, **"If we wanted to go to the movies"**: Ibid.

Page 15, **"He was like John Wayne"**: "David Koch Intends to Cure Cancer in His Lifetime and Remake American Politics," *Palm Beach Post*, February 18, 2012.

Page 15, **"The old man didn't put up with"**: "Captain America," *Sports Illustrated*, April 20, 1992.

Page 16, **"It used to be so hot there"**: "A Letter's Legacy," *The Wichita Eagle*, March 15, 1998.

Page 17, **"My father was quite a student of history"**: *Koch v. Koch Industries*, testimony of Charles Koch.

Page 17, **a cancerous tumor**: Details about Fred's palate condition come from Leslie Wayne's 1986 interview with Mary Koch and from: John Lincoln,

Rich Grass and Sweet Water: Ranch Life with the Koch Matador Cattle Company (Texas A&M University Press, 1989), pp. 5–6.

Page 18, **advertise their cattle brands**: "Early Day Newspapers in Quanah," *Quanah Tribune-Chief,* August 26, 1938.

Page 18, **10,000 acres**: Lincoln, *Rich Grass and Sweet Water,* p. 6.

Page 18, **Monet's *Field of Oats and Poppies***: George T. M. Shackelford and Elliot Bostwick Davis, *Things I Love: The Many Collections of William I. Koch* (MFA Publications, 2005), p. 24.

Page 18, **He sold a refinery**: Lincoln, *Rich Grass and Sweet Water,* p. 6.

Page 18, **"fat cattle and nutritious grass"**: Lincoln, *Rich Grass and Sweet Water,* p. 61.

Page 19, **driving there by a different route**: "A Letter's Legacy," *The Wichita Eagle,* March 15, 1998.

Page 19, **"It sure is clean here"**: "Koch and His Empire Grew Together," *The Wichita Eagle,* June 26, 1994.

Page 20, **"Freddie didn't want to learn"**: From a compilation of family film footage narrated by Mary Koch and viewed by the author.

Page 20, **"another world"**: Leslie Wayne interview notes.

Page 20, **Frederick had a nervous breakdown**: "The Curse on the Koch Brothers," *Fortune,* February 17, 1997.

Page 20, **"Father wanted to make all his boys"**: "Survival of the Richest," *Fame,* November 1989.

Page 21, **"Freddie sort of segregated himself"**: "Brothers at Odds," *The New York Times Magazine,* December 7, 1986.

Page 21, **"Freddie wanted no part"**: "Survival of the Richest."

Page 21, **"He and Mrs. Koch have three sons"**: "Responsible Leadership Through the John Birch Society," a pamphlet published by the public relations department of the John Birch Society.

Page 22, **tearfully pleading**: "Survival of the Richest."

Page 22, **"bad boy who turned good"**: "Brothers at Odds."

Page 23, **"I'm still alive"**: Leslie Wayne interview notes.

Page 23, **"Father put the fear of God in him"**: "The Curse on the Koch Brothers," *Fortune,* February 17, 1997.

Page 23, **"It was a miracle"**: "Charles Koch Remains Focused on Business," *The Wichita Eagle,* March 29, 1998.

Page 23, **In his baby book**: "Wild Bill Koch," *Vanity Fair,* June 1994.

Page 23, **desperate gambits for attention**: Ibid.

Page 23, **"He'd lash out"**: "Pulling the Wraps off Koch Industries," *The New York Times,* November 20, 1994.

Page 24, **"We had to get Charles away"**: "Brothers at Odds."

Page 24, **"to grow up amongst ourselves"**: "A Letter's Legacy," *The Wichita Eagle,* March 15, 1998.

Page 24, **"When you're one of four kids"**: "Wild Bill Koch," *Vanity Fair,* June 1994.

Page 24, **mischievous bully**: "Blood Feud," *Wall Street Journal,* August 9, 1989.

Page 25, **"For a long time"**: "Wild Bill Koch."

Page 26, **bashed his twin over the head with a polo mallet**: Ibid.

Page 26, **David still bears a scar**: Ibid.

Page 26, **"from an unsophisticated country boy"**: 2003 Deerfield Medal acceptance speech by David Koch.

Page 26, **had become unhinged**: Leslie Wayne interview notes.

Page 26, **"You've got to talk to a psychiatrist to analyze it"**: "Survival of the Richest."

Chapter 2. Stalin's Oil Man

Page 28, **2,500 cracking-related patents**: David McKnight Jr., *A Study of Patents on Petroleum Cracking* (University of Texas, 1938), p. 9.

Page 29, **sixteen contracts**: *Winkler-Koch v. Universal Oil Products* (S.D.N.Y., 1945), opinion, July 16, 1951.

Page 29, **"conducting a very aggressive, active campaign"**: *Universal Oil Products Co. v. Winkler-Koch Engineering and Globe Oil and Refining Co.* (D. Del., 1931), trial testimony of G. W. Miller.

Page 30, **they gathered their clients**: *Universal Oil Products v. Winkler-Koch Engineering Co. and Root Refining Co.* (D. Del., 1929), affidavit of Walter J. Blenko.

Page 30, **Koch and Winkler had incorporated a new company**: Charter of the Winkler-Koch Patent Company, February 20, 1929.

Page 30, **The plan initially called**: Details about the Winkler-Koch Patent Company and its legal defense fund come from documents and testimony in *Universal Oil Products v. Winkler-Koch Engineering Co. and Root Refining Co.*

Page 31, **Winkler had been Universal's chief engineer**: *The National Cyclopædia of American Biography, Vol. 56*, p. 209.

Page 31, **worked shoulder to shoulder with Carbon Dubbs**: Charles Remsberg and Hal Higdon, *Ideas for Rent: The UOP Story*, 1994 (UOP), p. 138.

Page 31, **declined to testify**: *Universal Oil Products v. Winkler-Koch Engineering Co., et al.* (D. Del., 1931), opinion, April 27, 1934.

Page 32, **"post graduates of Universal."**: Ibid.

Page 32, **"exclusively a patent holding company"**: *Universal Oil Products v. Winkler-Koch Engineering Co. and Root Refining Co.*, trial transcript.

Page 32, **"The differences that do exist are modifications"**: *Universal Oil Products v. Winkler-Koch Engineering Co., et al.*, opinion, April 27, 1934.

Page 32, **to proceed vigorously**: "Validity of Petroleum Cracking Patents Sustained," *Chemical Bulletin*, June 1934.

Page 32, **"We assume you will be interested"**: Hearings Before a Subcommittee of the Committee on Military Affairs, United States Senate, 78th Congress, "Monopoly and Cartel Practices: Universal Oil Products," November 3, 1943.

Page 33, **a federal grand jury indicted**: "Ex-Judge Davis Accused by Jury of Selling Favors," *The New York Times*, March 29, 1941.

Page 34, **$1.5 million from his foes**: Charles Koch, *The Science of Success* (Wiley, 2007), p. 7.

Page 34, **severed ties**: Ibid., p. 10.

Page 34, **"It was a living hell to him"**: *Koch v. Koch Industries*, trial testimony of David Koch.

Page 34, **Fred's advice to his sons**: Charles Koch, *The Science of Success* (Wiley, 2007), p. 7.

Page 35, **led the world in petroleum production**: Vagit Alekperov, *Oil of Russia* (East View Press, 2011), p. 80.

Page 36, **"a plan for a great world revolution"**: Hearings Before the Committee on Ways and Means, 71st Congress, "Prohibition of Importation of Goods Produced By Convict, Forced, or Indentured Labor," p. 153.

Page 37, **"its merit"**: "American Cracking for Soviet Refining," *Oil of Russia*, No. 4, 2012.

Page 37, **When Fred arrived in Moscow**: "Two Shores of Professor Sakhanov," *Oil of Russia*, No. 1, 2012.

Page 38, **"we will make you rotten to the core."**: Fred C. Koch, *A Business Man Looks at Communism* (1960), p. 8.

Page 38, **"Why did you save my life?"**: Ibid., p. 8.

Page 38, **"We are here just like slaves"**: Ibid., p. 38.

Page 39, **"I'll see you in the United States"**: Fred C. Koch to Howard E. Kershner, January 9, 1961, Howard E. Kershner Papers, Box 10, Special Collections and University Archives, University of Oregon Libraries.

Page 39, **"I was naïve enough to think"**: "John Birch Signer," *The Washington Post*, February 22, 1964.

Chapter 3. "The Dead Will Be the Lucky Ones"

Page 41, **"It's something I grew up with"**: Brian Doherty, *Radicals for Capitalism*, (Public Affairs, 2007), p. 407.

Page 42, **"the only sound countries in the world"**: Charles Francis de Ganahl, *The Life and Letters of Charles F. de Ganahl,Vol. II*, pp. 893–98.

Page 42, **"whether we are going to be free men or slaves"**: Fred C. Koch to Gen. Albert C. Wedemeyer, May 2, 1966, Albert C. Wedemeyer Papers, Box 45, Folder 30, Hoover Institution Archives.

Page 42, **returned to Moscow**: "Millionaires to Tell Russia 'It Isn't True,'" Associated Press, July 23, 1956.

Page 43, **"The meeting will be completely 'off the record' "**: Robert Welch to T. Coleman Andrews, October 27, 1958.

Page 43, **"Before tomorrow is over"**: A transcript of Welch's remarks in Indianapolis were published in *The Blue Book of the John Birch Society*.

Page 44, **gave him a job**: Koch, *A Business Man Looks at Communism* (1960), p. 7.

Page 44, **"He was always convinced that they pushed him out"**: "The Paranoid Style in Liberal Politics," *The Weekly Standard*, April 4, 2011.

Page 45, **"Here, Bob, we're in business"**: G. Edward Griffin, *The Life and Words of Robert Welch* (American Media, 1975), p. 274.

Page 46, **"the dead will be the lucky ones"**: Fred C. Koch to Rep. Al Ullman, May 11, 1961, Group Research Inc. Records, Box 190, Rare Book and Manuscript Library, Columbia University Library.

Page 46, **So many listeners called in**: Fred C. Koch to Howard E. Kershner, January 9, 1961, Howard E. Kershner Papers, Box 10, Special Collections and University Archives, University of Oregon Libraries.

Page 46, "It is not the Communists who are destroying America": Koch, *A Business Man Looks at Communism*, p. 5.

Page 47, "My father hated Picasso": "The Koch Collection: Sculptures, Paintings Chosen for Powerful Statements," *The Wichita Eagle*, September 6, 1992.

Page 47, Demand was so great: Fred C. Koch to Elizabeth Brown, November 9, 1961, Elizabeth Churchill Brown Papers, Box 2, Folder 19, Hoover Institution Archives.

Page 47, "a security risk": FBI file of Fred C. Koch.

Page 48, "The sad fact": "An Address Given on the Occasion of the Graduation Exercises at the Field House of the University of Wichita," June 5, 1960, Dr. John Rydjord Papers, Box 9, Folder 6, Special Collections and University Archives, Wichita State University Libraries.

Page 48, "you won't be very controversial lying in a ditch": "Bircher Warns America of Massive Conspiracy," Associated Press, August 16, 1961.

Page 49, "If many of the opinions": Koch, *A Business Man Looks at Communism*, p. 20.

Page 49, he and Fred had led the successful effort to curb the power of unions: J. Allen Broyles, *The John Birch Society: Anatomy of a Protest* (Beacon Press, 1966), p. 58; also, "Responsible Leadership Through the John Birch Society," a pamphlet published by the John Birch Society that included biographical sketches of its members.

Page 49, many of the same business leaders: Gene Grove, *Inside the John Birch Society* (Gold Medal, 1961), p. 96.

Page 49, "practically medieval": Broyles, *The John Birch Society: Anatomy of a Protest*, p. 56.

Page 50, McCarthyesque tactics: "Organizations: The Americanists," *Time*, March 10, 1961.

Pages 50–51, "They used my textbook on differential geometry": "In His Prime: Dirk Jan Struik Reflects on 103 Years of Mathematical and Political Activities," *Harvard Educational Review*, Vol. 69, No. 4, Winter 1999.

Page 51, "an MIT Alger Hiss": Fred C. Koch to Elizabeth Churchill Brown, February 9, 1962, Elizabeth Churchill Brown Papers, Box 2, Folder 19, Hoover Institution Archives.

Page 51, "down on Tech": Fred C. Koch to Robert M. Kimball, February 1, 1961, Massachusetts Institute of Technology, Office of the President, Records of Julius A. Stratton, AC 134, Box 124. Massachusetts Institute of Technology, Institute Archives and Special Collections.

Page 51, "said to have infiltrated Republican organizations": "Mutiny in the Birch Society," *Saturday Evening Post*, April 6, 1967.

Page 52, repealed by referendum a city fluoridation plan: "Fluoride Fight Has Long Rights, Passionate Advocates," *The Wichita Eagle*, October 27, 2012.

Page 52, "when the Communists...begin to light these racial fires": Fred C. Koch to Gen. Albert C. Wedemeyer, July 9, 1963, Albert C. Wedemeyer Papers, Box 45, Folder 30, Hoover Institution Archives.

Page 53, ordered 2,500 copies: Rick Perlstein, *Before the Storm: Barry Goldwater and the Unmaking of the American Consensus* (Hill & Wang, 2001), p. 62.

Page 53, "They are the kind we need in politics": "Goldwater Hits Birch Views," Associated Press, March 30, 1961.

Page 53, Buckley volunteered for the assignment: "Goldwater, the John Birch Society, and Me," *Commentary*, March 2008.

Page 53, "so far removed from common sense": Ibid.

Page 53, "a weapon of demagoguery": Jonathan Schoenwald, *A Time for Choosing: The Rise of Modern American Conservatism* (Oxford University Press, 2002), p. 63.

Page 53, "I wrote Buckley": Fred C. Koch to Elizabeth Churchill Brown, February 9, 1962, Elizabeth Churchill Brown Papers, Box 2, Folder 19, Hoover Institution Archives.

Page 54, ran twice, unsuccessfully, for Congress: "Civic, Business Leader, William Robinson, Dies," *The Wichita Eagle*, December 27, 1993.

Page 54, "Billy is a very compassionate guy": "Captain America," *Sports Illustrated*, April 20, 1992.

Page 54, "Father was paranoid about communism": "The Billionaire's Party," *New York*, July 25, 2010.

Page 55, "The U.S. government is trying to win votes": "U.S. Is Accused of Welfarism by a Speaker at KU," *Lawrence Daily Journal-World*, December 16, 1965.

Page 55, opened a John Birch Society bookstore: "Two Birch Society Members Open Bookstore," *The Wichita Eagle*, July 15, 1965.

Chapter 4. May Day at MIT

Page 57, dug an old ROTC uniform out of his closet: Interview with Kent Groninger.

Page 58, being pelted with bottles: "MIT, B.U. Riot Follows Hanging of Castro Effigy," *The Boston Globe*, May 2, 1961; and "700 Students in Riots," *The Tech*, May 3, 1961.

Page 58, "the Engineers prostrated themselves": "MIT Invades the Yard," *The Harvard Crimson*, May 2, 1961.

Pages 58–59, News of the anticommunist student uprising: Interview with Kent Groninger.

Page 59, a halfhearted MIT investigation: "Letters," *The Tech*, May 10, 1961.

Page 59, "Led by the brothers Koch": *MIT Technique*, 1962.

Page 59, "Great friends, wild parties": "MIT Class of 1962 25th Reunion," Institute Archives and Special Collections, MIT Libraries.

Page 61, A top rebounder: "Meet the Captains," *The Tech*, November 15, 1961.

Page 61, Bill was a second-stringer: "Interest High for Harvard Game Tomorrow," *The Tech*, December 9, 1960.

Page 61, MIT's basketball team had a dismal track record: "Hoopsters Have Losing Season; Win Only Three of Sixteen Games," *The Tech*, March 10, 1959.

Page 62, Recognizing their inexperience: "Barry Well Earns 'Coach of the Year' Title," *The Tech*, March 7, 1962.

Page 62, "He organized the team to compensate": "Captain America," *Sports Illustrated*, April 20, 1992.

Page 62, apologized to Barry: "Crimson Basketball Players Romp to Easy 84–34 Triumph at MIT," *The Harvard Crimson*, December 14, 1959.

Page 62, aggravated an old knee injury: "Cagers Beaten by Springfield, USCGS," *The Tech*, January 12, 1960.

Page 63, Averaging 24 points a game: "Area Coaches Pick Tech Star to All New England Team," *The Tech*, February 10, 1961.

Page 63, "The backbone of the team": "Tech Five Beats RPI in Finale," *The Tech*, March 10, 1961.

Page 63, "hustling, fighting, aggressive": "Meet the Captains," *The Tech*, November 15, 1961.

Page 64, "We didn't even have to attend class": "Succeeding Through the Foundations of Science," MIT speech, May 1, 1997.

Page 65, A heart attack had also claimed his older brother: Interview with Carol Margaret Allen.

Page 65, "remain in business until I died": Fred C. Koch to Robert Welch, August 19, 1966, Clarence E. Manion Papers, Chicago Historical Society, Box 74, Folder 4.

Page 66, left the faintest of impressions: Interviews with several Harvard classmates.

Page 66, "far more interesting work than what was required of me": Harvard College Class of 1955 Triennial Report, 1958.

Page 66, his master's thesis: Frederick R. Koch, "No Bed for Bacon: A Musical Comedy in 18 Scenes," Haas Family Arts Library, Special Collections, Yale University.

Page 67, "familiar with a booklet or pamphlet": Frederick R. Koch to ONE Institute, July 15, 1959, Box 29, ONE Incorporated records, ONE National Gay & Lesbian Archives, Los Angeles, California.

Page 68, "My father was quite concerned": *Koch v. Koch Industries*, testimony of Frederick Koch.

Page 68, "inferiority complex": Leslie Wayne interview notes.

Page 68, "Freddie never composed anything himself": "Survival of the Richest," *Fame*, November 1989.

Page 69, "He told me either you come back here": "Koch vs. Koch," *The Wichita Eagle*, March 8, 1998.

Page 69, "I hope your first deal is a loser": Charles Koch, *The Science of Success* (Wiley, 2007), p. 10.

Page 69, "I have tried to discourage him": Fred C. Koch to Elizabeth Brown, January 22, 1962, Elizabeth Churchill Brown Papers, Box 2, Folder 19, Hoover Institution Archives.

Page 70, "I think we are going to pour the money down the drain": Fred Chase Koch to Elizabeth Brown, February 9, 1962, Elizabeth Churchill Brown Papers, Box 2, Folder 19, Hoover Institution Archives.

Page 70, "the junk": "Family Feud at a Corporate Colossus," *Fortune*, August 26, 1982.

Page 70, **"Who?"**: John Lincoln, *Rich Grass and Sweet Water: Ranch Life with the Koch Matador Cattle Company* (Texas A&M University Press, 1989), p. 14.

Page 71, **"He really taught me a lot about the importance of people"**: "Koch and His Empire Grew Together," *The Wichita Eagle*, June 26, 1994.

Page 71, **"my father was initially furious"**: Koch, *The Science of Success*, p. 10.

Page 72, **He suffered a major heart attack**: "Industrialist Fred Koch Dies on Hunting Trip," *The Wichita Eagle*, November 19, 1967.

Page 72, **"Boy, that was a magnificent shot"**: "The Billionaire's Party," *New York*, July 25, 2010.

Chapter 5. Successor

Page 73, **"His death threw responsibility"**: "Industrialist Fred Koch Dies on Hunting Trip," *The Wichita Eagle*, November 19, 1967.

Page 73, **"he was never impressed with flattery"**: Pastor Rang W. Morgan's eulogy, Clarence E. Manion Papers, Chicago Historical Society, Box 74, Folder 4.

Page 74, **boarded a small plane**: "Wild Bill Koch," *Vanity Fair*, June 1994.

Page 74, **"It may be either a blessing or a curse"**: text of the letter provided by Koch Industries.

Page 75, **Their father removed Frederick from his will**: *In the Matter of the Estate of Mary R. Koch* (18th Kan., 1991), testimony of Charles Koch.

Page 75, **unaware of Frederick's removal**: Leslie Wayne interview notes.

Page 75, **"said that she would never favor"**: *In the Matter of the Estate of Mary R. Koch*, testimony of Frederick Koch.

Page 75, **"I have never forgotten your saying"**: *In the Matter of the Estate of Mary R. Koch,* trial transcript.

Page 76, **Mary resisted Frederick's efforts**: Ibid.

Page 76, **Fred left**: Last Will and Testament of Fred C. Koch, 1966.

Page 76, **counseled Charles to sell his father's corporate assets**: *Koch v. Koch Industries*, trial testimony of Sterling Varner.

Page 77, **"I was scared"**: *Koch v. Koch Industries*, trial testimony of Charles Koch.

Page 77, **"We don't typically want to broadcast"**: "High Profit, Low Profile," *Forbes*, July 15, 1974.

Page 77, **"Our change of corporate identity"**: "Koch Industries Reveals Plans, Changes Name," *The Wichita Eagle*, June 27, 1968.

Page 78, **"Charles had all of his father's ability"**: J. Howard Marshall II, *Done in Oil* (Texas A&M University Press, 1994), p. 253.

Page 78, **"I generally do not like partners"**: Ibid., p. 254.

Page 78, **"Charles had been pressing"**: *Koch v. Koch Industries*, trial testimony of Sterling Varner.

Page 79, **"we were handling around a fifth"**: Ibid.

Page 79, **"We were willing to build"**: Charles Koch, *The Science of Success* (Wiley, 2007), p. 12.

Pages 79–80, **"I have wanted one of those big tractors"**: John Lincoln, *Rich Grass and Sweet Water: Ranch Life with the Koch Matador Cattle Company* (Texas A&M University Press, 1989), p. 14.

Page 80, "he always priced them way above the market": Ibid., p. 14.

Page 80, nearly $500 million: "Family Feud at a Corporate Colossus," *Fortune*, July 26, 1982.

Page 81, He grew so accustomed to fielding middle-of-the-night calls: Interview with Nancy Pfotenhauer.

Page 81, "get the most exercise": "High Profit, Low Profile," *Forbes*, July 15, 1974.

Page 81, convened a meeting on a Sunday afternoon: "Koch and His Empire Grew Together," *The Wichita Eagle*, June 26, 1994.

Page 81, 650 employees: *Koch v. Koch Industries*, trial testimony of Charles Koch.

Page 82, "Frederick and I had quite different interests": Ibid.

Page 82, "I had accepted my father's analysis of Freddie": *In the Matter of the Estate of Mary R. Koch*, testimony of Charles Koch.

Page 83, "I thought it was presumptuous": *Koch v. Koch Industries*, testimony of Frederick Koch.

Page 83, $16,000 a year: *Koch v. Koch Industries*, testimony of David Koch.

Page 84, developing cigarette filters: *Koch v. Koch Industries*, deposition of David Koch, October 3, 1991.

Page 84, "Kitzbuhl's where the swingers are": "Social Roulette a la Harvard," *The Boston Globe*, February 15, 1967.

Page 85, "very technical, but also sales oriented": *Koch v. Koch Industries*, trial testimony of Sterling Varner.

Page 85, "I took great pride": *Koch v. Koch Industries*, trial testimony of Bill Koch.

Page 86, "He almost killed us": *Koch v. Koch Industries*, trial testimony of Sterling Varner.

Page 86, The Buzzis owned a chain of department stores: "Former President of Hinkel's Dies," *The Wichita Eagle*, June 18, 1999.

Page 86, Charles delivered his marriage proposal: "Koch and His Empire Grew Together," *The Wichita Eagle*, June 26, 1994.

Page 87, "I am so goal-oriented": "Koch and His Empire Grew Together," *The Wichita Eagle*, June 26, 1994.

Page 87, discourses on economics: "Charles Koch Relentless in Pursuing His Goals," *The Wichita Eagle*, October 11, 2012.

Chapter 6. Rise of the Kochtopus

Page 89, Nestled into this pastoral tableau: Robert LeFevre, *A Way to Be Free, Volume II* (Pulpless, 1999), pp. 274–75.

Page 90, "with the power of thunder": "Conservatives at Freedom School to Prepare a New Federal Constitution," *The New York Times*, June 13, 1965.

Page 90, He also spoke of having an out-of-body experience: George Thayer, *The Farther Shores of Politics* (Simon & Schuster, 1967), p. 268.

Page 91, His experiences dealing with city bureaucrats: "Conservatives at Freedom School to Prepare a New Federal Constitution," *The New York Times*, June 13, 1965.

Page 91, "Voting is the method for obtaining legal power": "Abstain from Beans," Voluntaryist.com.

Page 91, "slavery is rationalized": LeFevre, *A Way to Be Free*, p. 319.

Page 91, LeFevre was so puritanical: Brian Doherty, *Radicals for Capitalism* (Public Affairs, 2007), p. 316.

Page 92, roped David into enrolling: Doherty, *Radicals for Capitalism*, p. 407.

Page 92, Charles often sequestered himself: "The Front Lines: Charles Koch Teaches Staff to Run a Firm Like a Free Nation," *Wall Street Journal,* April 18, 1997.

Page 93, credited two works: Charles Koch, *The Science of Success* (Wiley, 2007), p. ix.

Page 93, "economics is not about goods and services": Ludwig von Mises, *Human Action* (Ludwig von Mises Institute, 1998), p. 491.

Page 93, "a society that chooses between capitalism and socialism": Ibid., p. 676.

Page 93, "increased output per hour of work": F. A. Harper, *Why Wages Rise* (Foundation for Economic Education, Inc., 1957), p. 19.

Page 93, "greatest opportunity...for a quick increase in wages": Ibid., p. 72.

Page 93, "compulsory employment devices": Ibid., p. 94.

Page 93, "I've never looked back": Remarks by Charles Koch to the Association of Private Enterprise Education, April 3, 2005.

Page 94, "societal well being was only possible": Speech by Charles Koch to the Philanthropy Roundtable, October 28, 2011.

Page 94, "Every time I hear of an entrepreneur": "U.S. Is Accused of Welfarism by a Speaker at KU," *Lawrence Daily Journal-World,* December 16, 1965.

Page 94, "sturdy shoes": Freedom School 1963 Prospectus, Group Research Inc. Records, Box 144, Rare Book and Manuscript Library, Columbia University.

Page 95, "they would be excluded from class discussions": Ibid.

Page 95, his school had yet to admit a black person: "Conservatives at Freedom School to Prepare a New Federal Constitution," *The New York Times,* June 13, 1965.

Page 95, Charles became one of six officers at the school: Freedom Schools, Inc. Form 990, 1964, Group Research Inc. Records, Box 144, Rare Book and Manuscript Library, Columbia University.

Page 95, donated nearly $7,000: Ibid.

Page 95, disapproved of LeFevre's offbeat teachings and his approach: Craig Miner, *Grede of Milwaukee* (Watermark Press, 1989), p. 245.

Page 96, "Let's Get Out of Vietnam Now": Ibid., p. 234.

Page 96, "You belong with us in this fight": Robert Welch to Charles Koch, November 4, 1968, William J. Grede Papers, Wisconsin Historical Society.

Page 96, describing them as "devotees": "Covert Operations," *The New Yorker,* August 30, 2010.

Page 96, "they were never 'devotees' ": "The New Yorker's Koch Story Is Not Credible Journalism," KochFacts.com, September 29, 2010.

Page 97, "a defining moment in my life": "Hans F. Sennholz, 1922–2007," *The Freeman,* October 1, 2007.

Page 97, "converted" his wife "to anarchy in about 30 minutes.": Walter Block, Ed., *I Chose Liberty: Autobiographies of Contemporary Libertarians* (Ludwig von Mises Institute, 2010), p. 377.

Page 97, "I was looking for ways to develop, apply, and spread": Remarks by Charles Koch to the Association of Private Enterprise Education, April 3, 2005.

Page 97, "no one was familiar with these ideas": "The Paranoid Style in Liberal Politics," *The Weekly Standard*, April 4, 2011.

Page 99, "We did not see politicians as setting the prevalent ideology": "Comments Made at Meeting of Foundation Directors Sponsored by the Hegeler Institute," Benjamin A. Rogge Papers, 1945–2005, Box 24, Hoover Institution Archives.

Page 100, "He taught us about liberty": F. A. Harper, *The Writings of F.A. Harper, Volume One: The Major Works* (Institute for Humane Studies, 1978), p. 1.

Page 101, Their plan called for the formation of a Libertarian Society: Justin Raimondo, *An Enemy of the State: The Life of Murray N. Rothbard,* (Prometheus Books, 2000), p. 216.

Page 101, "Now, we have quite a few scholars in the libertarian movement": Ibid., p. 217.

Page 102, "He was more hard-core than I was": "The Battle for the Cato Institute," *Washingtonian*, May 30, 2012.

Page 103, "It would be nice to have a libertarian think tank": Ibid.

Page 103, Portraits of what the Catoites called the "dead libertarians": Interview with Jeff Riggenbach.

Page 104, the distinctly shabbier offices: Interview with Milton Mueller.

Page 104, Childs had first struck up a correspondence: Roy Childs to George Pearson, June 14, 1969, Roy A. Childs Papers, Box 5, Hoover Institution Archives.

Page 105, In one case, Charles grew angry: Roy Childs to Charles Koch, November 26, 1969, Roy A. Childs Papers, Box 5, Hoover Institution Archives.

Page 105, spotted at the greasy spoon down the street: Interview with Justin Raimondo.

Page 105, raised his fists in the boxing stance: Interview with Walter Block.

Page 106, "It is to serve as a night watchman": "Wichita Millionaire Blasts Government Intervention," United Press International, June 13, 1979.

Page 106, "How discrediting it is for us": "The Business Community: Resisting Regulation," *Libertarian Review*, May 1978.

Page 107, "Who is against liberty?": "Libertarians & Conservatives," *National Review*, June 8, 1979.

Page 107, A separate article focused on Cato: "Cato Institute & the Invisible Finger," *National Review*, June 9, 1979.

Page 108, "buy the major Libertarian institutions": Samuel Edward Konkin III, *New Libertarian Manifesto* (Komen Publishing, 1983), p. 7.

Page 109, he cajoled Bill and David: Leslie Wayne interview notes.

Page 109, "Here was a great guy": "How Those Libertarians Pay the Bills," *New York*, November 3, 1980.

Page 110, David circulated a letter: "Libertarians in Convention," *Libertarian Review*, November 1979.

Page 110, "I was disturbed by it": "Seducing the Left," *Mother Jones*, May 1980.

Page 111, "We are no longer at the stage where the movement can be 'bought' ": "Libertarians in Convention," *Libertarian Review*, November 1979.

Page 111, "short but very valuable": Audio recording of David Koch's speech to the Libertarian Party convention in possession of the author.

Page 112, "**Before you can teach**": "Libertarian Candidate Says Campaign Symbolic," *Fort Worth Star-Telegram*, November 19, 1979.

Page 112, "**The real threat to the [Libertarian Party]**": "Reason Profile," *Reason*, December 1974.

Page 112, "**Our greatest strength**": "Reminiscences & Prognostications," *Reason*, May 1978.

Page 113, "**pushing the party into a stance**": David Nolan to Ed Clark, March 13, 1980, Ed Clark Papers, Box 8, Hoover Institution Archives.

Page 113, "**a paradigm shift in all parts of the 'Kochtopus' **": Doherty, *Radicals for Capitalism*, p. 416.

Page 113, "**low-tax liberalism**": Ibid., p. 415.

Page 114, **more than $2 million**: Ibid., p. 414.

Page 114, **David reflected on the campaign as a personal triumph**: "MIT Class of 1962 25th Reunion," Institute Archives and Special Collections, MIT Libraries.

Page 114, "**The Clark/Koch campaign was a fourfold disaster**": "The Clark Campaign: Never Again," *Libertarian Forum*, September–December 1980.

Page 114, "SMASH THE CRANE MACHINE": "Free Radical; Libertarian—and Contrarian—Ed Crane Has Run the Cato Institute for 25 Years. His Way," *The Washington Post*, May 9, 2002.

Page 115, "**we believe it would be difficult, if not impossible**": "It Usually Ends with Ed Crane," *Libertarian Forum*, January–April 1981.

Page 115, "**This action is illegal**": Ibid.

Page 115, **had angered its benefactor**: Interview with Justin Raimondo.

Page 116, "**The massive shift of the Kochtopus to D.C.**": "The State of the Movement: The Implosion," *Libertarian Forum*, September–December 1984.

Chapter 7. The Divorce

Page 117, **Christmas Day 1979**: This account is drawn from a variety of sources, including Charles Koch's trial testimony in *Koch v. Koch Industries* and *In the Matter of the Estate of Mary R. Koch*; Leslie Wayne's 1986 interview with Mary Koch; and "Brothers at Odds," *The New York Times*, December 7, 1986. Asked about this episode during the *Koch v. Koch Industries* trial, Bill responded, "I don't remember that."

Page 117, **perceived Mary as cool and distant**: "Wild Bill Koch," *Vanity Fair*, June 1994.

Page 118, **pressed her on the disposition of the family's art collection**: *In the Matter of the Estate of Mary R. Koch*, trial testimony of Charles Koch.

Page 118, "**just leave her alone**": "Testimony Discloses Emotional Cost of Koch Family Split," *The Wichita Eagle*, December 6, 1991.

Page 118, **Bill laid into Charles**: Leslie Wayne interview notes.

Page 118, **a company lawyer had presented Bill with a draft estate plan**: *Koch v. Koch Industries*, trial testimony of Bill Koch.

Page 118, **Sobbing**: "Brothers at Odds," *The New York Times Magazine*, December 7, 1986.

Page 119, "**He had a country-club attitude**": "Wild Bill Koch."

Page 119, **bleeding $90,000**: "The Curse on the Koch Brothers," *Fortune*, February 17, 1997.

Page 119, "**Bill couldn't get to work on time**": Ibid.

Page 119, **The deal netted Koch $5 million**: *Koch v. Koch Industries*, testimony of Bill Koch.

Page 120, **Koch executives felt he could waffle**: Leslie Wayne interview notes.

Page 120, **Koch Carbon did not fare well**: "The Curse on the Koch Brothers."

Page 120, "**Bill was never happy running a division**": *Koch v. Koch Industries*, trial testimony of Sterling Varner.

Page 120, "**It was important for Bill to be important**": "The Curse on the Koch Brothers."

Page 120, "**He wanted unilateral authority**": *Koch v. Koch Industries*, trial testimony of David Koch.

Page 121, **a surefire morale killer**: *Koch v. Koch Industries*, trial testimony of Charles Koch.

Page 121, "**We don't want to go out and acquire the world**": *Koch v. Koch Industries*, trial testimony of Bill Koch.

Page 121, "**He was very upset**": *Koch v. Koch Industries*, trial testimony of David Koch.

Page 121, "**My emotions carried me away**": Ibid.

Page 122, "**Prince Charles**": Ibid.

Page 122, **Bill trashed Charles**: Ibid.

Page 122, "**What is the purpose of these attacks on me?**": *Koch v. Koch Industries*, trial transcript.

Page 123, **returned criminal indictments**: "Koch Industries Inc., Unit Officers Indicted on Conspiracy Charge," *Wall Street Journal*, June 19, 1980.

Page 123, **more than $1 billion**: *Koch v. Koch Industries*, trial testimony of Bill Koch; also, "Former Koch Employee Testifies," *Topeka Capital-Journal*, April 19, 1998.

Page 123, **overcharging on sales of propane**: "FEA Hits Koch Gas Prices," *The Wichita Eagle*, April 11, 1975.

Page 123, "**libertarian revolution causes**": *Koch v. Koch Industries*, trial testimony of Bill Koch.

Page 123, "**the political philosophy of one man**": *Koch v. Koch Industries* (D. Kans., 1982), deposition of Bill Koch, December 20, 1982.

Page 124, **about 6 percent**: *Koch v. Koch Industries*, trial testimony of David Koch.

Page 124, "**That was our religion**": *Koch v. Koch Industries*, trial testimony of Sterling Varner.

Page 124, "**insatiable**": *Koch v. Koch Industries*, trial testimony of David Koch.

Page 124, **nearly $4 million**: Ibid.

Page 125, "**literally over my dead body**": "Mr. Big," *Forbes*, March 3, 2006.

Page 125, "**the officers and directors would be in jail**": *Koch v. Koch Industries*, trial testimony of Bill Koch. Cordes said: "I testified fully to all of those facts some 16 years ago in a jury case and the jury found in our favor, so I really don't remember any of the details. Billy made a lot of allegations that the jury rejected, so that's all I can say."

Page 125, **had known about the illegal activities**: Ibid.

Page 125, **an eleven-page single-spaced letter**: *Koch v. Koch Industries*, trial transcripts.

Page 126, "W.I.K. Has Leveled Serious Charges": Ibid.

Page 127, "Charles Koch is the boss": Ibid.

Page 127, "I don't believe I have misread Bill's intention": Ibid.

Page 128, "I said I would live up to the rules of the corporation": *Koch v. Koch Industries*, trial testimony of Bill Koch.

Page 128, "progress had been made in clearing up these harsh feelings": *Koch v. Koch Industries*, trial testimony of David Koch.

Page 128, He was as uneasy as ever: *Koch v. Koch Industries*, trial testimony of Bill Koch.

Page 128, "If you have irrevocably decided that you cannot tolerate me": Ibid.

Page 129, "Corporate democracy": Ibid.

Page 129, Bill's consortium: The share breakdown comes from *Koch v. Koch Industries*, trial transcripts and related documents filed in the case.

Page 129, The extent of his involvement: *Koch v. Koch Industries*, trial testimony of Frederick Koch.

Page 130, a homosexual blackmail attempt: "The Curse on the Koch Brothers."

Page 131, "My primary effort": *Koch v. Koch Industries*, trial transcripts.

Page 131, he told the banker a parable: *Koch v. Koch Industries* (1982), deposition of Bill Koch, December 21, 1982.

Page 132, Bill stepped into Charles's office: The account of their meeting comes from *Koch v. Koch Industries*, trial testimony of Charles and Bill Koch.

Page 133, "One piece of advice": "Secretive Koch Reveals Power Struggle," *The Wichita Eagle*, July 10, 1982.

Page 133, He wanted to gauge where Frederick stood: *Koch v. Koch Industries*, trial testimony of David Koch.

Page 133, "Fred listened attentively": Ibid.

Page 134, "I got this notice, Freddie, what's going on?": Ibid.

Page 134, the goal was not to remove Charles as CEO: *In the Matter of the Estate of Mary R. Koch*, trial testimony of Frederick Koch.

Page 135, "either the smartest or the luckiest thing I ever did": J. Howard Marshall II, *Done in Oil* (Texas A&M University Press, 1994), p. 254.

Page 135, Marshall had reassured Koch's worried CEO: *Koch v. Koch Industries*, trial testimony of Charles Koch.

Page 135, "What do we do now?": Marshall, *Done in Oil*, p. 256.

Page 135, "there's one thing that Howard III understands": *Koch v. Koch Industries*, trial testimony of Charles Koch.

Page 136, he offered to double it: Ibid.

Page 136, brought the old man to tears: Ibid.

Page 136, stored in a safety-deposit box: Ibid.

Page 137, $140 a share: *Koch v. Koch Industries*, trial testimony of David Koch.

Page 137, their safety could not be guaranteed: *Koch v. Koch Industries*, trial testimony of James Linn. Don Cordes would later deny making a threat, saying, "This story developed a life of its own." In addition to Linn, two members of the Simmons family remember this episode.

Page 137, He sent the presents back: *Koch v. Koch Industries*, trial testimony of Bill Koch.

Page 137, **Charles told his mother:** *In the Matter of the Estate of Mary R. Koch*, trial testimony of Charles and David Koch.

Page 138, **"He was almost paralyzed":** "Wild Bill Koch," *Vanity Fair*, June 1994.

Page 138, **urged him to visit a Boston psychiatrist:** *Koch v. Koch Industries*, Simmons plaintiffs' statement, March 31, 1998.

Page 138, **"I asked a number of questions":** Ibid.

Page 139, **"Bill was a very demanding client":** *Koch v. Koch Industries*, deposition of Alfred Eckert, October 21, 1992.

Page 140, **Another pressure point was publicity:** *Koch v. Koch Industries*, deposition of Bill Koch, March 5, 1993.

Page 140, **the corporate discord spilled into the press:** "Family Feud at a Corporate Colossus," *Fortune*, July 26, 1982.

Page 140, **later turned out to be Bill:** *Koch v. Koch Industries*, trial testimony of Bill Koch.

Page 141, **Charles and David retaliated with a $400 million countersuit:** "Court Filing Continues in Koch Feud," *The Wichita Eagle*, January 11, 1983.

Page 141, **"We came into this fight together":** *Koch v. Koch Industries*, deposition of Bill Koch, April 6, 1993.

Page 142, **"horse trading to around $220":** Ibid.

Page 142, **"I'm not going to go with their draft":** Ibid.

Page 142, **"We've got our business affairs separated":** "Witness Recalls Charles Koch Snub," *Topeka Capital-Journal*, April 10, 1998.

Page 143, **a symbolic resolution:** Koch Industries board resolution, 1984.

Chapter 8. Mighty Mary

Page 144, **She felt his absence most acutely:** Mary expressed her feelings about the feud between her sons in correspondence introduced in a lawsuit over her will (*In the Matter of the Estate of Mary R. Koch*); Mary Koch to Bill Koch and Joan Granlund, October 26, 1984.

Page 144, **she lay awake nights:** Mary Koch to Bill Koch, undated.

Page 144, **"made of stubborn Dutch stock":** Ibid.

Page 145, **act of "character assassination":** Mary Koch to Bill Koch and Joan Granlund, July 14, 1982.

Page 145, **"You have judged Charles":** Mary Koch to William and Joan Koch, October 19, 1982.

Page 146, **"help me to mend bridges not destroy them":** Mary Koch to Frederick Koch, undated.

Page 146, **"This conflict is tearing me down":** Mary Koch to Bill Koch, undated.

Page 146, **"Please listen to me before I die!":** Mary Koch to Bill Koch and Joan Granlund, October 19, 1982.

Page 146, **"I never was so relieved":** Mary Koch to Frederick Koch, June 16, 1983.

Page 146, **"I trust & pray that you can find some business":** Mary Koch to Bill Koch, July 10, 1983.

Page 146, **"emotionally wrenching":** Leslie Wayne interview notes.

Page 147, **"Howard, I want you to do something for me":** *In the Matter of the Estate of Mary R. Koch*, testimony of Robert Howard.

Page 147, "**My heart aches**": Mary Koch to Bill Koch, July 10, 1983.

Page 147, "**The buying goes on relentlessly**": "The Great Victorian Hoard," *Daily Telegraph*, October 30, 1986.

Page 149, "**like a kid let out of reform school**": "The Curse on the Koch Brothers," *Fortune*, February 17, 1997.

Page 149, "**After eating so many gourmet meals**": "Build Your Own Playpen," *New England Business*, September 1988.

Page 150, "**The best thing that ever could have happened to me**": Ibid.

Page 150, **more than $800 million**: "Pulling the Wraps off Koch Industries," *The New York Times*, November 20, 1994.

Page 150, "**How could they have so much cash?**": "The Curse on the Koch Brothers."

Page 151, **The suit alleged**: *Koch v. Koch Industries*, second amended complaint.

Page 151, "**I don't think the lawsuit has anything to do with money**": "Brothers at Odds," *The New York Times*, December 7, 1986.

Page 151, "**Now, that's sibling rivalry**": "Forbes 400," *Forbes*, October 28, 1985.

Page 152, **Mary had sought companionship**: Interview with Michael Oliver.

Page 153, "**My mother was afraid of my father**": "Wild Bill Koch," *Vanity Fair*, June 1994.

Page 154, "**a woman of all seasons**": "Koch Family Matriarch Dies at 83," *The Wichita Eagle*, December 23, 1990.

Page 154, **deadly marksmanship**: Ibid.

Page 155, "**Charles was running the Foundation for his own benefit**": *William I. Koch and Frederick R. Koch v. Charles G. Koch, et al.* (18th Kan., 1988), deposition of Bill Koch, November 16, 1988.

Page 155, "**I was dissatisfied**": *William I. Koch and Frederick R. Koch v. Charles G. Koch, et al.*, deposition of Frederick Koch, December 6, 1988.

Page 156, **tried to keep the peace**: Mary Koch to Frederick Koch, May 13, 1985.

Page 156, **dredged up Murray Rothbard**: *William I. Koch and Frederick R. Koch v. Charles G. Koch, et al.*, "Murray N. Rothbard—Summary of Anticipated Deposition Testimony," April 3, 1989.

Page 157, "**cannot tolerate dissent**": Ibid.

Page 157, **A surreal courtroom scene**: *William I. Koch and Frederick R. Koch v. Charles G. Koch, et al.*, trial transcript.

Page 158, "**Have you seen this?**": *In the Matter of the Estate of Mary R. Koch*, trial testimony of Robert Howard.

Page 158, "**To hear William Koch tell it**": "Blood Feud," *Wall Street Journal*, August 9, 1989.

Page 158, "**In light of what they're saying**": *In the Matter of the Estate of Mary R. Koch*, trial testimony of Robert Howard.

Page 159, **a new clause to her will**: The Last Will and Testament of Mary R. Koch, 1989.

Page 159, "**killing Charles**": *In the Matter of the Estate of Mary R. Koch*, trial testimony of Robert Howard.

Page 159, **Mary's health deteriorated**: Interview with Michael Oliver.

Page 159, **belonged to the Hemlock Society**: "For Close Relatives, a Suicide Can Bring Relief or More Suffering," *People*, June 25, 1990.

Page 159, **invited Mary to join them in a suicide pact:** Interview with Michael Oliver.

Page 160, **"All I want to do is see my children one more time":** Ibid.

Page 160, **had to seek Liz's permission:** Ibid.

Page 161, **"Mary doesn't need you now, but I do":** Ibid.

Page 161, **Liz called back the following day:** Ibid.

Page 162, **"These are my personal papers":** Ibid.

Chapter 9. "My God, I'm Going to Die!"

Page 163, **His shoes were off:** "Recollections of My Survival of an Airplane Crash," letter sent by David Koch to friends, February 13, 1991.

Page 163, **David had a date:** Interview with John Damgard.

Page 164, **"Stay down, stay down, stay down!":** "Recollections of My Survival of an Airplane Crash."

Page 164, **scoured the floor for his loafers:** Ibid.

Page 164, **"I'm going to die!":** "The Price of Immortality," *Portfolio*, October 15, 2008.

Page 165, **"Oh, what the hell!":** "Recollections of My Survival of an Airplane Crash."

Page 166, **58 messages:** Ibid.

Page 166, **crushing sense of guilt:** "Cleared for Disaster," *Air Disasters*, Smithsonian Channel.

Page 166, **"This may sound odd":** "The Billionaire's Party," *New York*, July 25, 2010.

Page 168, **"liked having a lot of women around":** "David Koch's Ex: 'I Was Just One of Many Girls'," *New York Observer*, March 30, 2012.

Page 168, **"Marla's a babe":** "Ivana's New Life," *New York*, October 15, 1990.

Page 168, **"a third of which were beautiful, wild, single women":** "A Personal Stake in Giving," *The Chronicle of Philanthropy*, April 3, 2008.

Page 168, **he served guests two meals:** "Dave Koch Lives It Up," *Newsday*, August 10, 1993.

Page 169, **"gun-shy":** "Survival of the Richest," *Fame*, November 1989.

Page 169, **assistant to the fashion designer Adolfo:** "Woman Ascending a Marble Staircase," *The New York Times*, January 11, 1998.

Page 169, **"It was the sort of place":** Donald Trump, *Trump: The Art of the Deal* (Ballantine, 1987), p. 95.

Page 169, **"forward with my humor":** "The Billionaire's Party," *New York*, July 25, 2010.

Page 169, **"Afterward we shook hands":** "Woman Ascending a Marble Staircase."

Page 170, **"David, we went out together":** Ibid.

Page 170, **"Julia gave me two choices":** "Woman Ascending a Marble Staircase."

Page 170, **triple emerald cut diamond ring:** "Birth Pangs for Patty, Mac," *New York Daily News*, January 3, 1996.

Page 171, **"many thought she'd be his trophy wife":** "Damp with an Occasional Spritz," NewYorkSocialDiary.com, August 26, 2010.

Page 171, "the construction of Julia Koch": "Woman Ascending a Marble Staircase."

Page 172, chronicled Julia's supposed high-society faux pas: "How New York Rejected Its Leading Socialite," *New York Post*, February 23, 1999.

Page 172, "Julia's fingerprints were all over it": Ibid.

Page 173, "I DON'T THINK WE'RE IN KANSAS ANYMORE": "String Game: The Kochs Host a Joshua Bell Recital," *Women's Wear Daily*, January 6, 2012.

Page 173, "That puts the fear of God in you!": "The Team Builder," *Philanthropy*, Summer 2012.

Page 173, champagne-fueled Southampton soiree: "One Cheer for the Pony Express," *Rocky Mountain News*, August 17, 1993.

Page 174, "The side effects": "Donald Trump Doesn't Have Support of Billionaire David Koch—Money-wise—as Presidential Candidate," *New York Daily News*, May 3, 2011.

Page 174, "I'm a chemical engineer": Hearing before the Government Activities and Transportation Subcommittee of the Committee on Government Operations, House of Representatives, 102nd Congress, "Aircraft Cabin Safety and Fire Survivability," April 11, 1991.

Page 174, "Discovering that I had cancer": "The Team Builder."

Page 175, place a bet on the winner: "The Science of Giving," *Quest*, October 2011.

Chapter 10. The Art of War

Page 176, "Is that what you're thinking?": Paul C. Larsen, *To the Third Power* (Tilsbury House, 1995), pp. 26–27.

Page 177, "replaces the family harmony": "On an Outside Tack," *The Boston Globe Magazine*, April 19, 1992.

Page 177, "$30,000-a-month": "Captain America," *Sports Illustrated*, April 20, 1992.

Page 177, handed day-to-day control: Larsen, *To the Third Power*, p. 255.

Page 178, 200 people: Ibid., p. 195.

Page 178, glimpsing a virtual ocean: "Scientific Sailing Bill Koch Uses High Tech in Pursuit of America's Cup," *Sun Sentinel*, May 5, 1991.

Page 178, "the Gerald Ford of sailing": "Koch, He's the Real Thing," *Sports Illustrated*, May 25, 1992.

Page 179, he spotted the Cup: Larsen, *To the Third Power*, p. 193.

Page 179, "I learned a lot about myself": Ibid., p. 202.

Page 179, "The real issue is why did he want the Cup": "Wild Bill Koch," *Vanity Fair*, June 1994.

Page 179, "I can't bet against my brother": "Captain America," *Sports Illustrated*, April 20, 1992.

Page 180, pledged $500,000: "Koch Spurs Plans for Downtown Boathouse," *The Wichita Eagle*, August 29, 1992.

Page 180, "I'm a celebrity in Kansas": "Pulling the Wraps off Koch Industries," *The New York Times*, November 20, 1994.

Page 180, admiral of the Kansas Navy: "Koch in Command of Kansas' Proud But Land-Locked Navy," *The Wichita Eagle*, December 11, 1994.

Page 181, "She took my brothers' side": "Koch Names Yacht After His Mother," *The Wichita Eagle*, March 3, 1995.

Page 181, "the best coverage money can buy": "Ethics Questions Arise as Koch Courts Media," *Kansas Business Report*, October 1, 1994.

Page 182, "listening to the suitors": "Koch May Set Sail in Race Against Brownback," *Lawrence Journal-World*, December 27, 1997.

Page 182, "Billy wouldn't even have a rowboat": "Pulling the Wraps off Koch Industries."

Page 183, rejected a $50,000 contribution: "Rival Koch Brothers Sporting Controversy," *Topeka Capital-Journal*, November 23, 1997.

Page 183, "I've had a lot of bad PR": Ibid.

Page 184, barreled through the intersection: "Loss of 12-Year-Old Zac Pains Family, Classmates," *The Wichita Eagle*, September 21, 1993.

Page 184, "every eye in that church was on them": "Koch and His Empire Grew Together," *The Wichita Eagle*, June 26, 1994.

Page 184, 100 hours of community service: "Teenager Gets Service Work, Probation," *The Wichita Eagle*, January 12, 1994.

Page 185, "our whole strategy was that no one needed to know anything": "Pulling the Wraps off Koch Industries."

Page 185, "You won't even see his smoke": "Koch's Hidden Message: Houston Expansion Is About More Than Business," *The Wichita Eagle*, March 23, 1997.

Page 185, "We're up against a very secretive company": "Journalists, or Detectives? Depends on Who's Asking," *The New York Times*, July 28, 1999.

Page 186, "has wiretapped their discussions": *Michael P. Aquilina v. William I. Koch, et al.* (C.D. Cal., 1988), declaration of Michael P. Aquilina, July 18, 1988.

Page 186, "I didn't authorize using it, and never will": "Wild Bill Koch."

Page 186, "The recording wasn't worth shit": Ibid.

Page 186, resulted in a temporary restraining order: *Koch v. Koch Industries*, Memorandum and Order, March 20, 1998.

Page 186, "a man whose closet is free of skeletons": "Wild Bill Koch."

Page 187, "Santa Barbara surfing girl": "Koch: Mistress Wanted $5 Million," *Boston Herald*, November 21, 1995.

Page 188, "She started kissing me quite passionately": "Housing Court Hears Billionaire Tell of Love Affair Gone Bad," *The Boston Globe*, November 15, 1995.

Page 188, "Hot Love From Your X-rated Protestant Princess": "Eviction Style of Very Rich Titillates Boston," *The Philadelphia Inquirer*, November 23, 1995.

Page 188, "My poor nerve endings are already hungry": Facing Up to the Fax, *The Boston Globe*, November 22, 1995.

Page 188, "It is beyond calculation": "Court Hears Lurid Faxes of Ex-Model, Millionaire." Associated Press, November 28, 1995.

Page 189, "There were moles and spies all over": "Wild Bill Koch."

Page 189, drafted a bogus memo: *Koch v. Koch Industries*, Plaintiffs' Reply Brief in Support of Plaintiffs' Motions in Limine, March 25, 1998.

Page 189, "he changed completely": "Wild Bill Koch."

Page 189, "This is war": "On an Outside Tack," *The Boston Globe Magazine*, April 19, 1992.

Page 190, "Keep the King": Larsen, *To The Third Power*, pp. 105–6.

Page 190, "I wasn't alone": "Cup Costs, Spying Irk Koch," *Palm Beach Post*, May 16, 1992.

Page 190, hired Italian speakers: "Wild Bill Koch."

Page 190, "how many times we go to the bathroom": "Bold Espionage Tactics Stir Up Cup Emotions," *Los Angeles Times*, May 9, 1992.

Page 190, spent more than $2 million: "Old Fashioned Spying Aids America," *Boston Herald*, May 16, 1992.

Page 190, "the Bill Koch rule": "Wild Bill Koch."

Page 193, $300 per interview: *Koch v. Koch Industries*, Plaintiffs' Reply Brief in Support of Motion to Re-Open Discovery, December 29, 1995.

Page 193, "I would gain from 3 to 4 barrels of oil": *Koch v. Koch Industries*, Plaintiffs' Reply Brief in Support of Motion to Re-Open Discovery, affidavit of Robert Gould, July 22, 1988.

Page 194, "Always help Charlie out": *USA v. Koch Industries* (S.D. Tex., 1995), deposition of David F. Toliver, October 17, 1995.

Page 194, "Keep Old Charlie Happy": Interview with Bob Buford.

Page 195, "Top management-directed theft": Hearings Before the Special Committee on Investigations of the Select Committee on Indian Affairs, US Senate, 101st Congress, "Natural Resources on Indian Lands," May 9, 1989.

Page 195, Bill's "vendetta.": "U.S. Attorney Handling Oil Theft Probe," Associated Press, June 25, 1989.

Page 195, "political skullduggery": "Bob Dole's Oil Patch Pals," *Business-Week*, March 31, 1996.

Page 195, hired a group of high-powered Democratic lobbyists: "The Kochs Can Play Washington's Power Game," *The National Journal*, May 16, 1992.

Page 195, "systematic theft": A Report of the Special Committee on investigations of the Select Committee on Indian Affairs, US Senate, 101st Congress, "A New Federalism for American Indians," November 20, 1989.

Page 196, stolen at least $31 million worth of oil: Ibid.

Page 196, "the pattern of oil theft is so pervasive": Frederick Koch to Mary Koch, November 23, 1989; letter in possession of the author.

Page 196, "come back in a body bag": "D(oil)e," *The Nation*, August 26, 1996.

Page 197, "U.S. government to brand you as a racketeer": "Blood Feud," *Wall Street Journal*, August 9, 1989.

Page 197, "I was cold-blooded and Machiavellian": "The Curse on the Koch Brothers," *Fortune*, February 17, 1997.

Page 197, "I almost wish": "Blood Feud," *Wall Street Journal*, August 9, 1989.

Page 197, "the stage for the unraveling of a family": "Survival of the Richest," *Fame*, November 1989.

Page 198, "a man consumed by hatred": *Koch v. Koch Industries*, Defendants' Brief in Opposition to Plaintiffs' Eight Motions in Limine, February 20, 1998.

Page 199, "a childhood tussle on the school playground": *Koch v. Koch Industries*, Memorandum and Order, March 23, 1998.

Page 199, The seating had even been arranged: "Attorneys Focus on Koch Brawls," Associated Press, April 13, 1998.

Page 200, "surpassed $200,000 per week": "Zero Is the Verdict in $2 Billion Koch Family Feud," *The New York Times*, June 20, 1998.

Page 200, "There's no poor people": "All Four Brothers Attend Trial Opening," *The Wichita Eagle*, April 7, 1998.

Page 200, "Business is war": "The Billionaires' Brawl," *USA Today*, April 8, 1998.

Page 200, "a truly fascinating Kansas family": *Koch v. Koch Industries*, trial transcript.

Page 201, "peace that has never come to Kansas": Ibid.

Page 202, "This is tough to talk about": Ibid.

Page 204, "largely involved in charitable activities": Ibid.

Page 204, Bartlit launched his examination: Ibid.

Page 206, "Work for Koch Industries": Ibid.

Page 207, "distracted and preoccupied": "Kochs' Friends Prepare for More Legal Action," *The Wichita Eagle*, June 20, 1998.

Page 207, hundreds of layoffs: "Layoffs Follow Koch Setbacks," *The Wichita Eagle*, April 11, 1999.

Page 208, "The only thing that people like this recognize": *Koch v. Koch Industries*, trial transcript.

Page 209, for research purposes: "Koch Trial Inspires Man to Study Law," *The Wichita Eagle*, July 22, 2000.

Page 209, "They're guilty of misrepresentation": "Koch Inc. Prevails," *The Wichita Eagle*, June 20, 1998.

Page 210, "the jury unanimously ruled": "Kochs' Friends Prepare for More Legal Action," *The Wichita Eagle*, June 20, 1998.

Page 210, Charles delivered the news: "Koch Inc. Prevails," *The Wichita Eagle*, June 20, 1998.

Page 210, "breath or money": "Blood Feud," *Wall Street Journal*, August 9, 1989.

Page 210, "15-round championship fight": "Zero Is the Verdict in $2 Billion Koch Family Feud," *The New York Times*, June 20, 1998.

Chapter 11. There Will Be Blood

Page 211, plans for her farewell party: "Two Teens Mourned in Kaufman County Blast," *Dallas Morning News*, August 26, 1996.

Page 211, buy him a new Harley: *Smalley v. Koch Industries* (86th Tex., 1997), testimony of Danny Smalley.

Page 211, The smell had gotten worse: "Blast That Killed 2 Teens Exposed Koch's History of Harmful Mistakes," *Austin American-Statesman*, July 23, 2001.

Page 212, "like it was strafed by Napalm": *Smalley v. Koch Industries*, testimony of George York.

Page 212, "You're no God!": Ibid.

Page 213, The pressure in the Sterling I pipeline: *Smalley v. Koch Industries*, testimony of Danny Mills.

Page 213, Unknown to Danny Smalley: "Blast That Killed 2 Teens."

Page 214, "Good God": *Smalley v. Koch Industries*, trial transcript.

Page 214, All he saw was her burnt corpse: *Smalley v. Koch Industries*, testimony of Danny Smalley.

Page 214, became suicidal: Interview with Ted Lyon.

Page 214, offering $10 million: Interview with Marquette Wolf.

Page 215, the decrepit state: "Oil Spills Bring 2nd Koch Probe," *Minnesota Star Tribune*, May 3, 1998.

Page 216, just 420 gallons of oil had spilled: Ibid.

Page 216, Koch officials pleaded the Fifth Amendment: *P.D. Hamilton v. Koch Industries* (E.D. Tex., 2001), affidavit of Linda Eads.

Page 216, "Many of Koch's spills": *USA v. Koch Industries* (S.D. Tex., 1995), affidavit of Philip Dubose.

Page 217, hired a security firm to sweep for listening devices: Interview with Ted Lyon.

Page 218, the company was having Danny Smalley tailed: Ibid.

Page 219, The supervisor's callous response: *Smalley v. Koch Industries*, deposition of Kenoth Whitstine.

Page 219, "Given the time-value of money": *P.D. Hamilton v. Koch Industries*, affidavit of Linda Eads.

Page 219, it could reap an additional $8 million: "Blast That Killed 2 Teens."

Page 220, evidence of corrosion in 583 locations: Ibid.

Page 220, "Koch Industries is definitely responsible": *Smalley v. Koch Industries*, deposition of Billy Ray Caffey, April 14, 1999.

Pages 220–221, "Money to them is blood": *Smalley v. Koch Industries*, testimony of Danny Smalley.

Page 221, "There is no more horrible death": *Smalley v. Koch Industries*, trial transcript.

Page 221, failed to corroborate the charges: "Grand Jury Clears Koch Oil No Charges Planned in Indian Lands Case," *The Daily Oklahoman*, April 3, 1992.

Page 222, "Bill Koch has been attacking Charles": "Bill Says He Wants to Reconcile with Charles," *The Wichita Eagle*, September 26, 1999.

Page 222, plunged into darkness: "Koch Courtroom Is a Multimedia Spectacular, *The Wichita Eagle*, October 24, 1999.

Page 223, Bell displayed a pyramid of photographs: "Sides Trade Shots as Latest Koch Trial Starts," *The Wichita Eagle*, October 5, 1999.

Page 223, sent copies of the tape: Interviews with Marquette Wolf and Ted Lyon.

Page 223, Seated at the cramped counsel's table: "Former Employees Across Midwest Testify," Associated Press, October 7, 1999.

Page 223, "I felt that it was stealing oil": "Former Koch Industries Workers Describe 'Bringing in the Barrel,'" Associated Press, October 8, 1999.

Page 223, "It was enough to bother my conscience": "Ex-Koch Gaugers Tell of Underreporting," *Tulsa World*, October 9, 1999.

Page 223, "I feel like I'm up here telling the whole world": "Former Koch Manager Says Oil Adjustments Discussed at Meetings," Associated Press, October 15, 1999.

Page 224, "I had to do what they said to do": "Former Koch Workers Testify About Oil Collection," *The Wichita Eagle*, October 7, 1999.

Page 224, "I made what I felt were necessary and fair adjustments": "Koch Oil Rebuts Allegations of Gauge Cheating," *Tulsa World*, November 10, 1999.

Page 224, "explained to me the nature of the crude oil measuring business": "Oil Firm's Chief Executive Defends Company at Tulsa, Okla., Trial," *Tulsa World*, December 10, 1999.

Page 224, **"accepted on both sides"**: "Oil Company Owner Gives His Side of the Story," Associated Press, December 10, 1999.

Page 224, **"they're going to take volume away from you"**: "Tulsa, Okla., Jury Hears Last Day of Testimony in Oil-Theft Trial," *Tulsa World*, December 11, 1999.

Page 224, **found Koch guilty of nearly 25,000 false claims**: "Jury Finds Koch Underreported Oil Purchases," Associated Press, December 24, 1999.

Page 225, **"Billy has stalked his brothers"**: "Koch Industries, Oil Industry Disappointed by Verdict," Koch Industries, December 23, 1999.

Page 225, **"a company that practiced organized, white-collar crime"**: "Jury Finds Koch Cheated," *Tulsa World*, December 24, 1999.

Page 226, **"There were times when...yeah, we lied"**: "State Took Koch at Its Word in False Records Case," *Minnesota Star-Tribune*, July 19, 1998.

Page 227, **Woodlief asked his distracted boss for a word**: Interview with Tony Woodlief.

Page 228, **"egregious violations"**: "Koch Industries to Pay Record Fine for Oil Spills in Six States," Department of Justice, January 13, 2000.

Page 228, **"We should *not* cave in"**: "The Business Community: Resisting Regulation," *Libertarian Review*, August 1978.

Page 229, **"While business was becoming increasingly regulated"**: Charles Koch, *The Science of Success* (Wiley, 2007), pp. 44–45.

Page 231, **"It was something he could not get over"**: "How Angela Outslicked Oilman Ex," *New York Post*, February 20, 2001.

Page 231, **"He was not fun to be around"**: Ibid.

Page 231, **threatened "to beat his whole family to death with his belt"**: "Yachtsman Bill Koch Charged with Domestic Abuse," Associated Press, July 20, 2000.

Page 231, **Angela was granted a restraining order**: "Palm Beacher Bill Koch Under Restraining Order," *Palm Beach Post*, July 21, 2000.

Page 232, **"It was frightening, and embarrassing"**: "How Angela Outslicked Oilman Ex," *New York Post*, February 20, 2001.

Page 232, **"I'll litigate you into the ground"**: Ibid.

Page 232, **she dropped a civil suit against Bill**: "Domestic Violence Charges Against Koch Are Dropped," *The Boston Globe*, December 6, 2000.

Page 232, **"I liked looking at it when I was happily married"**: "Koch's Delight," *Palm Beach Daily News*, December 31, 2000.

Page 233, **eventually settled for $25 million**: "Koch Brothers End 21-Year Feud," *The Wichita Eagle*, May 26, 2001.

Page 233, **initiated a cautious rapprochement**: "Koch Brothers Settle Suit," *Palm Beach Post*, May 27, 2001.

Page 233, **"During the settlement discussions"**: George T. M. Shackelford and Elliot Bostwick Davis, *Things I Love: The Many Collections of William I. Koch* (MFA Publications, 2005), p. 37.

Page 233, **"We ended up in a heated argument"**: "Why Does Bill Koch Collect So Much Stuff? 'I Collect What Makes Me Feel Good,'" *Palm Beach Post*, September 18, 2005.

Page 233, **"organized crime"**: "Blood & Oil," *60 Minutes II*, November 28, 2000.

Page 235, **"There's nothing more explosive"**: "Koch Brothers Finally Bury the Hatchet After 20 Years," Cox News Service, May 29, 2001.

Page 235, **Out of all the other children at the preschool**: "The Price of Immortality," *Portfolio*, October 15, 2008.

Page 235, **Bill and Bridget invited David and Julia**: "Koch Birthday Bash a Studio 54 Redux," *Palm Beach Daily News*, May 5, 2002.

Page 236, **"Welcome to El Sarmiento"**: "Don't Look for Sympathy on Royally Insulted Island," *Palm Beach Daily News*, December 7, 2003.

Page 236, **"Who would have thought 10 years ago"**: "28-Story Mast to Be Visible For Miles," *Palm Beach Post*, February 20, 2005.

Page 237, **"Come to the Emerald City"**: "Billionaire David Koch had a *Wizard of Oz*-Themed Birthday Party," *New York*, May 18, 2010.

Page 238, **"the brother of the twin"**: "Inside the Koch Empire: How the Brothers Plan to Reshape America," *Forbes*, December 5, 2012.

Page 239, **"peaceful coexistence"**: "Bill Koch's Wild West Adventure," *5280*, February 2013.

Chapter 12. Planet Koch

Page 242, **"I just bought Georgia-Pacific"**: Interview with John Damgard.

Page 243, **"We thought we were in the oil business"**: "Market-Based Management at Koch Industries: Discovery, Dissemination, and Integration of Knowledge," *Competitive Intelligence Review*, Vol. 6, No. 4, 1995.

Page 243, **asbestos-related lawsuits**: "Georgia-Pacific Choked by Asbestos Lawsuits," *Atlanta Business Chronicle*, January 29, 2001.

Page 244, **reliance on untested theories**: Brian Doherty, *Radicals for Capitalism*, (Public Affairs, 2007), p. 409.

Page 245, **It deemphasized job titles**: "Profitable Theory—Market Based Management Drives Koch Industries," *The Wichita Eagle*, December 3, 2005.

Page 246, **"Everybody's after everybody else's throat"**: "A Company Tries to Manage the Future," *The Wichita Eagle*, June 27, 1994.

Page 247, **"generally hiring one type of 'clone' "**: *Gary Gorman v. Koch Industries* (D. Kan., 1997), complaint.

Page 247, **"The concepts became little more than buzzwords"**: Charles Koch, *The Science of Success* (Wiley, 2007), p. 42.

Page 249, **"Koch has a pattern of delaying"**: *P. D. Hamilton vs. Koch Industries*, affidavit of Linda Eads.

Page 249, **"If I get a concept in my head"**: "Mr. Big," *Forbes*, March 13, 2006.

Page 250, **ignited an acrimonious uprising at the school**: "Collegiate Parents in Uproar over Resignation," *The Wichita Eagle*, March 5, 1993.

Page 250, **hung in effigy around campus**: "Interim Chief at Collegiate Is Seeking Solution," *The Wichita Eagle*, March 7, 1993.

Page 251, **"the Shadow falling on Rivendell"**: "Shadow of the Kochtopus," Aaeblog.com, May 5, 2008.

Page 251, **"stamped on the time cards of factory workers"**: "Big Brothers," *The Nation*, April 21, 2011.

Page 252, **recruiting talent from elite universities**: Interview with Tony Woodlief.

Page 252, **"discredited science"**: "Perspective," *Discovery*, April 2008.

Page 253, **"the greatest loss of liberty"**: "Perspective," *Discovery*, January 2008.

Page 253, **"Imagine what our world could be like"**: "Perspective," *Discovery*, October 2008.

Page 253, **"the George Orwell book, *1984*"**: Glassdoor.com.

Page 254, **"in a fifty-fifty deal"**: "The Curse on the Koch Brothers," *Fortune*, February 17, 1997.

Page 254, **"I am Charles Koch"**: "The Front Lines: Charles Koch Teaches Staff to Run a Firm Like a Free Society," *Wall Street Journal*, April 18, 1997.

Chapter 13. Out of the Shadows

Page 258, **"dedicated egalitarian"**: "The Paranoid Style in Liberal Politics," *The Weekly Standard*, April 4, 2011.

Page 258, **"hard core economic socialist"**: Ibid.

Page 258, **"If we are going to do this"**: "The Kochs' Quest to Save America," *The Wichita Eagle*, October 11, 2012.

Page 259, **accused the library of whitewashing history**: Interview with John Damgard.

Page 260, **"If we do it right"**: "The Kochs' Quest to Save America," *The Wichita Eagle*, October 11, 2012.

Page 260, **invited Fink to Wichita**: "The Paranoid Style in Liberal Politics."

Page 261, **he came through with $150,000**: "The Center for Market Processes," University of Virginia Darden School Foundation, 1983.

Page 261, **"I like polyester"**: "The Kochs' Quest to Save America."

Page 261, **"There are a lot of people who have ideas"**: "The Paranoid Style in Liberal Politics."

Page 262, **14 of the 23 federal rules**: "Rule Breaker: In Washington, Tiny Think Tank Wields Big Stick on Regulation," *Wall Street Journal*, July 16, 2004.

Page 263, **$10,000 bequest**: Last Will and Testament of Mary Koch, 1989.

Page 264, **"a third-rate political hack"**: "Koch Versus Cato: Unraveling the Riddle," CharlesRowley.com, March 5, 2012.

Page 264, **"When we apply this model"**: "From Ideas to Action: The Role of Universities, Think Tanks, and Activist Groups," *Philanthropy*, Winter 1996.

Page 265, **totaled nearly $31 million**: "Koch Millions Spread Influence Through Nonprofits," InvestigativeReportingWorkshop.org, July 1, 2013.

Page 265, **veto power over job candidates**: "Billionaire's Role in Hiring Decisions at Florida State University Raises Questions," *Tampa Bay Times*, May 9, 2011.

Page 266, **"What we needed was a sales force"**: "The Paranoid Style in Liberal Politics."

Page 267, **friends on Capitol Hill grew**: "Grass-Roots Goliath," *National Journal*, July 13, 1996.

Page 267, **Microsoft donated $380,000**: "Think Tanks: Corporations' Quiet Weapon," *The Washington Post*, January 29, 2000.

Page 268, **"THIS IS CLINTON CARE"**: "When CSE Brings Its Big Guns to Bear," *National Journal*, July 13, 1996.

Page 269, **"Our belief is that the tax"**: "Politics That Can't Be Pigeonholed," *The Wichita Eagle*, June 26, 1994.

Page 270, **"into submission"**: Interview with Dick Armey.

Page 272, **registered the domain name taxpayerteaparty.com**: "'Tea Party' Label Invites Discord," *USA Today*, February 6, 2010.

Page 272, **"reject excessive taxation by the Crown"**: "Tea Party Talking Points," Americans for Prosperity, April 2009.

Page 273, **played a cameo role**: "Consultants for Va. Candidate Linked to Indicted Lobbyist," *The Washington Post*, November 3, 2005.

Page 274, **"The modern-day Birchers"**: "Where Have You Gone, Bill Buckley," *The New York Times*, December 3, 2012.

Page 277, **"I've never been to a Tea-Party event"**: "The Billionaire's Party," *New York*, July 25, 2010.

Page 280, **directed nearly $25 million**: "Koch Industries: Secretly Funding the Climate Denial Machine," Greenpeace, March 2010.

Page 283, **"audacious stealth campaign"**: "The Election Campaigns We Can't See," *The Washington Post*, September 23, 2010.

Page 285, **"it's the worst covert operation in history"**: "'Tea Party Billionaire' Fires Back," TheDailyBeast.com, September 10, 2010.

Page 285, **"apparently concerted campaign"**: "Smear Disappears," *New York Post*, January 5, 2011.

Page 285, **"a disturbing trend in journalism"**: Mark Holden to Sid Holt, April 25, 2011.

Page 288, **"If not us, who?"**: Letter to members of the Koch donor network, September 24, 2010.

Page 290, **pledged at least $12 million**: "Koch Conference Under Scrutiny," *Politico*, January 27, 2011.

Page 291, **"an unconstitutional power grab"**: "How Congress Can Stop the EPA's Power Grab," *Wall Street Journal*, December 28, 2010.

Page 291, **"You bet I am"**: "Exclusive: Polluter Billionaire David Koch Says Tea Party 'Rank And File Are Just Normal People Like Us,'" ThinkProgress.com, January 6, 2011.

Chapter 14. The Mother of All Wars

Page 293, **ejected the journalist**: "The Kochs Fight Back," *Politico*, February 2, 2011.

Page 293, **"He's an evil man"**: "Koch Ventures into the Brooklyn Lion's Den," FT.com, December 24, 2010.

Page 294, **"we would be attacked"**: "The Paranoid Style in Liberal Politics," *The Weekly Standard*, April 4, 2011.

Page 294, **"We've been called just about everything"**: "Birch Society Leader Warns of Red Danger," *The Wichita Eagle*, October 10, 1960.

Page 295, **"It generated a lot of enthusiasm"**: "Inside Today's Koch Brothers 'Billionaire's Caucus,'" Forbes.com, January 31, 2011.

Page 299, **encouraged Walker to battle the unions**: "Billionaire Brothers' Money Plays Role in Wisconsin Dispute," *The New York Times*, February 21, 2011.

Page 300, **David's secretary delivered the news**: "The Paranoid Style in Liberal Politics."

Page 301, **"Are you reassured?"**: "Shock Doctrine, U.S.A.," *The New York Times*, February 24, 2011.

Page 301, **left an angry voice mail**: Interview with Mark Holden.

Page 302, **"The Koch brothers will DIE!!!!!"**: "Charles Koch, Employees Reveal E-mailed Threats from Past Year," *The Wichita Eagle*, February 17, 2012.

Page 302, **round-the-clock protection**: Interview with John Damgard.

Page 304, **"We are not going to stop"**: "Koch Executives Speak Out on Wisconsin," *National Review*, February 24, 2011.

Page 304, **"This is the mother of all wars"**: "Inside the Koch Brothers' Secret Seminar," MotherJones.com, September 6, 2011.

Page 307, **$70 million' worth of pledges**: "Karl Rove vs. the Koch Brothers," *Politico*, October 10, 2011.

Page 310, **angered Mitt Romney's campaign**: Jonathan Alter, *The Center Holds: Obama and His Enemies* (Simon & Schuster, 2013), p. 223.

Page 311, **"building a coalition of like-minded organizations"**: Center to Protect Patient Rights, Form 1024, October 8, 2009.

Page 312, **"This government policy and strategy"**: Association for American Innovation, Form 1024, November 4, 2011.

Page 315, **"Who the hell"**: "Who the Hell Is Going to Take a Think Tank Seriously If It's Controlled by Billionaire Oil Guys?" Slate.com, March 22, 2012.

Page 315, **"genetic libertarian"**: "Free Radical; Libertarian—and Contrarian—Ed Crane Has Run the Cato Institute for 25 Years. His Way," *The Washington Post*, May 9, 2002.

Page 316, **"I'll go to my grave"**: Brian Doherty, *Radicals for Capitalism* (Public Affairs, 2007), pp. 603–4.

Page 316, **" 'What the hell is this about?' "**: "The Battle for the Cato Institute," *Washingtonian*, May 30, 2012.

Page 316, **the bedraggled building**: David Boaz, *The Politics of Freedom* (Cato Institute, 2008), p. 244.

Page 316, **Crane recalled telling him. "I can't do that."**: "The Battle for the Cato Institute."

Page 317, **Crane's star had sunk**: "The Ear," *The Rothbard-Rockwell Report*, August 1991.

Page 317, **no longer taking Crane's calls**: "The Battle for the Cato Institute."

Page 318, **"He's the emperor"**: "Covert Operations," *The New Yorker*, August 30, 2010.

Page 318, **"Charles is really upset"**: "The Battle for the Cato Institute."

Page 319, **"Kevin Gentry seated over there"**: "The Crane Chronicles Part 2: The Care and Feeding of Board Members," Breitbart.com, April 4, 2012.

Page 320, **"esoteric concepts"**: Statement by David H. Koch, March 22, 2012.

Page 320, **"providing intellectual ammunition"**: "Cato Goes to War," Slate.com, March 5, 2012.

Page 321, **"They thought wrong"**: Statement by Charles G. Koch, March 8, 2012.

Page 323, **"some sort of auxiliary for the GOP"**: "Cato Institute Is Caught in a Rift Over Its Direction," *The New York Times*, March 6, 2012.

Page 323, **"rule or ruin" strategy**: Statement by David H. Koch, March 22, 2012.

Page 324, **"undermine our community's intellectual defenses"**: FreedomWorks Statement Regarding Koch-Cato Lawsuit, April 12, 2012.

Page 324, "contract killers in super-PAC land": "Obama Campaign to Go After 'Contract-Killer' Super Pac Ads," *Roll Call*, May 7, 2012.

Page 326, "carefully orchestrated campaign of vituperation": "Obama's Enemies List," *Wall Street Journal*, February 1, 2012.

Page 328, "if somebody's out to cheat me": "The Jefferson Bottles," *The New Yorker*, September 3, 2007.

Page 328, cell phone ring tone: Ibid.

Page 328, perhaps a dental drill: Benjamin Wallace, *The Billionaire's Vinegar* (Crown, 2008), p. 250.

Page 329, "This is *National Treasure*": Ibid., p. 254.

Page 330, "I absolutely can't stand to be cheated": "Billionaire William Koch Wins Trial over Fake French Wine," Bloomberg.com, April 12, 2013.

Page 330, over a glass of fine wine: "Billionaire Wins Wine Fight; Jury Awards Him $380,000," Associated Press, April 11, 2013.

Pages 330–331, a forensic review of his employees' communications: *Oxbow Carbon v. Kirby Martensen* (15th Fla., 2012), complaint.

Page 331, "I'm doing it because I can": "Bill Koch's Wild West Adventure," *5280*, February 2013.

Page 332, The phone and Internet service: Colorado Bureau of Investigation, "Gunnison County Sheriff's Office Official Misconduct Report," November 5, 2012.

Page 332, "Would you feel the same way about Kirby": *Kirby Martensen v. William Koch* (N.D. Cal., 2012), deposition of Lawrence Black, June 25, 2013.

Page 332, A hidden camera rolled: Colorado Bureau of Investigation, "Investigative Supplement Report," June 28, 2013.

Page 333, at least eight security guards: Ibid.

Page 333, current and former police officers: *Kirby Martensen v. William Koch*, Opposition to William Koch's Motion for Partial Reconsideration.

Page 333, "A sheriff is here": *Kirby Martensen v. William Koch*, complaint.

Page 333, placed the deputy on administrative leave: Colorado Bureau of Investigation, "Gunnison County Sheriff's Office Official Misconduct Report," November 5, 2012.

Pages 333–334, off-duty Palm Beach police officers: *Kirby Martensen v. William Koch*, Opposition to William Koch's Motion for Partial Reconsideration.

Page 334, "For all intents and purposes": *Kirby Martensen v. William Koch*, deposition of Kirby Martensen, May 16, 2013.

Page 334, "I gave this money to Kirby Martensen": *Kirby Martensen v. William Koch*, deposition of Charlie Zhan, January 9, 2013.

Page 335, "this is the type of thing that Bill does": *Kirby Martensen v. William Koch* (N.D. Cal., 2012), deposition of Lawrence Black, June 25, 2013.

Page 335, "The idea as explained to me": Martensen whistleblower complaint, May 13, 2013.

Page 337, "the lion king of button-down libertarianism": "Free Radical; Libertarian—and Contrarian—Ed Crane."

Page 339, convened a Hamptons mixer: "Romney in the Hamptons with David Koch," *Politico*, August 16, 2010.

Page 339, "the financial engine of the Tea Party": "Internal Memo: Romney Courting Kochs, Tea Party," *Washington Examiner*, November 2, 2011.

Page 340, **"the title of that book comes from a poem"**: "Mitt Romney Reveals a Literary Connection with a Koch Brother," *The Washington Post*, August 22, 2012.

Page 341, **"like two world leaders with their first ladies"**: "Mitt: What Koch Problem?" *New York Post*, July 10, 2012.

Page 341, **"I look at it as an asset"**: Ibid.

Page 343, **"I believe in gay marriage"**: "David Koch Breaks from the GOP on Gay Marriage, Taxes, Defense Cuts," *Politico*, August 30, 2012.

Page 345, **"We've got to do better with primaries"**: Interview with John Damgard.

Page 347, **"difficult to assess the kind of bang for buck"**: "Americans for Prosperity Chief: We Don't Know if $27 Million in Anti-Obama Ads Has Any Effect," MotherJones.com, September 3, 2012.

Page 349, **"We had met with some other people from Koch"**: Deposition of Anthony Russo, July 17, 2013.

Page 350, **"We were not involved"**: "The Koch Brothers in California," New Yorker.com, October 25, 2013.

Page 350, **"Despite November's disappointing election results"**: "Kochs Postpone Post-Election Meeting," *National Review*, December 11, 2012.

Page 350, **"reaching the right people with the right message"**: "Exclusive: Read the Koch Brothers' Plans for Their Upcoming Donor Retreat," MotherJones.com, April 23, 2013.

Chapter 15. Legacy

Page 353, **"Oh, hi, Freddie"**: Interview with John Damgard.

Page 354, **"Never ask from where I came"**: "Call Me Frederick," *The Daily Telegraph*, November 14, 1986.

Page 354, **Donahue was a man of vices**: Christopher Wilson, *Dancing with the Devil: The Windsors and Jimmy Donahue* (St. Martin's Press, 2000), pp. 32–35.

Page 354, **"I've done it"**: "James Donahue, Social Leader, Kills Himself," Associated Press, April 23, 1931.

Page 357, **"hoped to be a playwright"**: Frederick R. Koch to John Mason Brown, July 19, 1961, John Mason Brown Papers, Houghton Library, Harvard University.

Page 358, **"crude bluff and blackmail"**: "Wrangle over Dreams for Mansion," *The Times of London*, May 7, 1986.

Page 358, **"The lodge is deteriorating"**: "Pass My Plans or Treasures Leave Britain, Says Billionaire," *Daily Mail*, May 6, 1986.

Page 358, **baffled the British art world**: "Philanthropist Stays Silent on Art Museum," *The Times of London*, May 11, 1993.

Page 360, **"dig two graves"**: "Captain America," *Sports Illustrated*, April 20, 1992.

Page 361, **"chance of several lifetimes"**: "Osterville House Sells for $19 Million," *Cape Cod Times*, January 11, 2013.

Page 361, **"for staying together"**: "Bill Koch's Wild West Adventure," *5280*, February 2013.

Page 361, **"I don't want to do that to my kids"**: George T. M. Shackelford and Elliot Bostwick Davis, *Things I Love: The Many Collections of William I. Koch* (MFA Publications, 2005), p. 37.

Page 362, **"My proudest accomplishment"**: "Inside the Koch Empire: How the Brothers Plan to Reshape America," *Forbes*, December 24, 2012.

Page 362, **"I'm going to ride my bicycle until I fall off"**: "The Private Empire of Koch Industries," *Financial Times*, January 30, 2004.

Page 363, **"We have the best leaders"**: "Inside the Koch Empire," *Forbes*.

Page 363, **Chase joined Koch Industries' board of directors**: Interview with Nestor Weigand.

Page 363, **"I was a bohemian"**: "Adventures in Publishing," *Town & Country*, May 2012.

Page 363, **"disturbed and convoluted relationship with money"**: "The World Compatibility Test: Back in Tokyo, Part 1," Smithmag.net, March 30, 2007.

Page 365, **"thought it was the right thing to do"**: "Ground Is Officially Broken on Met's 'David H. Koch Plaza,'" *The New York Times*, January 14, 2013.

Page 365, **"Boycott the Metropolitan Museum of Art"**: "The Two Kochs," Artnet.com, February 8, 2012.

Page 366, **"Well, it's $65 million!"**: "$65-Million Naming Opportunity: Groundbreaking for Metropolitan Museum's 'David H. Koch Plaza,'" ArtsJournal.com, January 16, 2013.

Page 367, **"apparently so offended"**: "A Word from Our Sponsors," *The New Yorker*, May 27, 2013.

Page 372, **the portrait of their father**: Shackelford and Bostwick Davis, *Things I Love: The Many Collections of William I. Koch*, p. 37.

Index